EASTERN PHILOSOPHY

WORLD CLASSICS LIBRARY

EASTERN PHILOSOPHY

The Art of War ✤ Tao Te Ching

The Analects of Confucius

The Way of the Samurai

The Works of Mencius

ARCTURUS

ARCTURUS

This edition published in 2020 by Arcturus Publishing Limited
26/27 Bickels Yard, 151–153 Bermondsey Street,
London SE1 3HA

ISBN: 978-1-78950-987-8
AD007835UK

Printed in China

CONTENTS

CONTENTS

INTRODUCTION

The great works of Eastern philosophy have had a significant impact upon the world both far and near. These texts were devoutly followed within their countries of origin for centuries before globalization saw them translated into a number of languages and their influence spread across the globe. In this collection you will find five of the most important and widely read works: *The Art of War*, the *Tao Te Ching*, *The Analects*, *The Way of the Samurai* and *The Works of Mencius*.

Sun Tzu's *The Art of War* is one of the earliest discourses on military strategy and tactics and almost certainly one of the most influential. The work is traditionally dated to the 5th century BCE a period of Chinese history known as the Warring States. This was a time characterized by warfare that eventually paved the way for the unification of China. Authorship is attributed to the Chinese general Sun Tzu, where Tzu is an honorific title which means 'Master'. Though there has been scepticism as to the existence of such a man due to anachronisms within the historical record, there is no doubting the significance of the text. *The Art of War* is still considered one of the great pillars of classical literature within China.

Since its first appearance, the text has been seen as vital for Chinese military leaders. Its authority later spread throughout the east, particularly in Japan, where it was first translated in the 8th century CE. It was first brought to the West by the French

Jesuit missionary Jean Joseph Marie Amiot who translated the book in 1772, Napoleon is believed to have been one of its earliest followers. It was first translated into English in 1910 by Lionel Giles, and it is this translation you will find in this volume.

Lionel Giles was a sinologist, writer and philosopher, and the son of the British diplomat Herbert Giles, who is well known for his part in the romanization of Mandarin through his modification of a system developed by Thomas Francis Wade. The system became known as the Wade-Giles system and was used throughout the English-speaking world for most of the 20th century CE. This was the system employed by Lionel when following in the footsteps of his father as a translator of Eastern philosophy.

Though originally revered for its military strategy, *The Art of War* has more recently been applied to fields as varied as politics, sports, and business. The work has even gained prominence in popular culture, as the 1987 film *Wall Street* brought it into the spotlight and later *The Sopranos* television series led to a resurgence in its popularity.

According to tradition, the *Tao Te Ching* was written in the 6th century BCE by Taoist sage Lao Tzu, though as with many ancient texts, the date and indeed the existence of a single person called Lao Tzu is now debated. Tradition states that when Lao Tzu tired of the world, he rode a water buffalo towards the West – 'the West' here referring to the location of the afterlife in Chinese mythology. Upon reaching the western edge of the kingdom, he was recognized as a sage and asked to write down his wisdom. It took him only one night to do so. After warning that the teachings within were only of worth if put into practice, he mounted his water buffalo and continued west, never to be seen again.

The book is one of the fundamental texts of both religious and philosophical Taoism, and it is renowned for its wisdom and guidance on living well – a value affirmed by the English translation of its title, *The Classic Book of the Way and its Power (or Virtue)*.

Translation of the text has proved notoriously difficult due to the ancient nature of the text, the differences between Eastern and Western thought, and the ambiguity and multiple possible definitions that could be applied to the original Chinese characters. This version was translated by John H. McDonald, who consulted many editions in order to produce a definitive version.

The Analects of Confucius, by tradition a contemporary of Lao Tzu, is a collection of sayings and ideas attributed to Confucius that were believed to have been collected and recorded by his followers. The sayings concern themselves with the cultivation of a virtuous or moral character ensuring both good government and self-development.

Confucius was born in 551 BCE. The sudden death of his father led to a childhood of poverty, but he set his mind on attaining wisdom early in his life. Though the details of his later life are lost, he is believed to have travelled widely, spreading his wisdom and acting as a minister and teacher to a variety of nobles.

The Analects were first translated into a Western language in 1582, when the Jesuit Matteo Ricci translated the work into Italian, shortly after he began proselytizing in China. He would remain in the country until his death in 1610, and Ricci played an important role in bridging the gap between East and West. He is also believed to have given the Chinese philosopher K'ung Ch'iu his Latin name 'Confucius'. Confucius said 'to devote oneself earnestly to one's duty to humanity', it is easy to see why the writings remain relevant 2,500 years after their first recording.

This edition was translated by William Edward Soothill in 1910. Soothill was a Methodist missionary who went on to become Professor of Chinese at University College, Oxford. For his services in association with the Chinese Labour Corps, he was awarded the Chinese military award the Order of Wen-Hu (third class) in 1921.

Inazo Nitobe (1862–1933) was a Japanese agricultural economist, writer, diplomat, educator and politician. His most famous work was the pioneering *Bushido: The Soul of Japan*, now more commonly known as *The Way of the Samurai*. Nitobe's own samurai heritage can be traced to the 12th century CE, when his ancestor Tsunehide Chiba was awarded a fiefdom for services in battle. Chiba subsequently moved his family to a new part of his domain, Nitobe, and five generations later his family would take Nitobe as their name.

First published in English for a Western audience, this pioneering account of the traditions of the samurai and the prominent role their ideals had upon Japanese culture provided great insight into the culture of a country which Westerners found so alien to their own.

The Bushido code, which was first formulated in the 8th century CE and continued to develop over the following centuries, governed the conduct of the samurai. This class of aristocratic or noble military officers is known for their ideals of chivalry and strict honour code, and they have often been likened to the European knight. One such ideal was that of benevolence, samurai were encouraged to develop compassion and help their fellow men at every opportunity – and even to seek out such an opportunity if one did not arise. The publication of the text was the first insight into the formerly 'closed doors' of feudal Japan, and it is this that has led to the text's enduring popularity.

The Works of Mencius were likely written down sometime in the 4th century BCE by followers of the Confucian thinker Mencius. It is considered one of the most important texts of early Confucianism and was seen to build on *The Analects* and its ideas of good government. Witnessing the devastation of the Warring States period, he believed that the solution to the despair and anarchy of war was a benevolent leader stating that 'He who has no pleasure in killing men can so unite it'. The writings, however, were not considered a classic of the Chinese canon until almost 1,000 years later.

Mencius was born around 372 BCE and his teachings were formed around the belief that humans were innately good, though this goodness may need cultivating. He was purportedly taught by the grandson of Confucius himself, Zisi, and much like Confucius, he was also said to have travelled the kingdom imparting his wisdom.

This version was translated in 1875 by the Scottish missionary James Legge who was the first Professor of Chinese at Oxford University. He is most well-known for preparing, along with Max Müller, the colossal 50 volume *Sacred Books of the East* series.

These five texts provide an essential foundation for understanding Eastern cultures, philosophies and belief systems.

THE ART
OF WAR

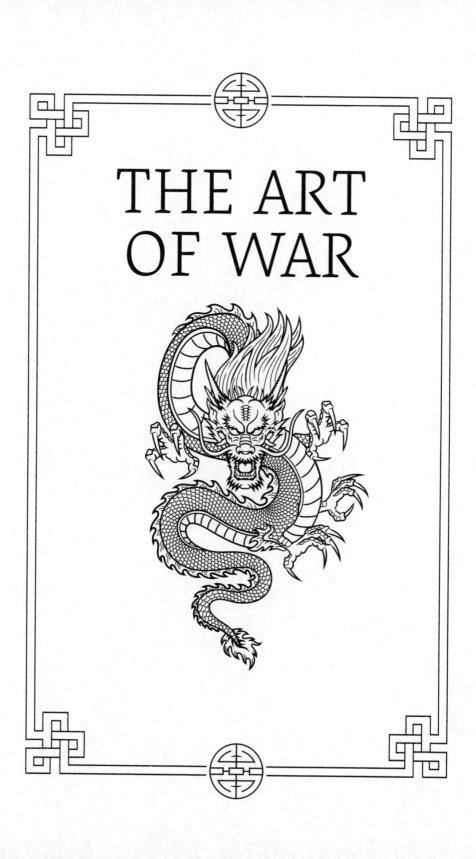

CONTENTS

CONTENTS

CHAPTER ONE

LAYING PLANS

1   Sun Tzu said: The art of war is of vital importance to the State.

2   It is a matter of life and death, a road either to safety or to ruin. Hence it is a subject of inquiry which can on no account be neglected.

3   The art of war, then, is governed by five constant factors, to be taken into account in one's deliberations, when seeking to determine the conditions obtaining in the field.

4   These are:
  (1) The Moral Law;
  (2) Heaven;
  (3) Earth;
  (4) The Commander;
  (5) Method and Discipline.

5
&
6   The Moral Law causes the people to be in complete accord with their ruler, so that they will follow him regardless of their lives, undismayed by any danger.

7   Heaven signifies night and day, cold and heat, times and seasons.

8   Earth comprises distances, great and small; danger and security; open ground and narrow passes; the chances of life and death.

9   The Commander stands for the virtues of wisdom, sincerity, benevolence, courage and strictness.

10   By Method and Discipline are to be understood the marshalling of the army in its proper subdivisions, the graduations of rank among the officers, the maintenance of roads by which supplies may reach the army, and the control of military expenditure.

11   These five heads should be familiar to every general: he who knows them will be victorious; he who knows them not will fail.

12   Therefore, in your deliberations, when seeking to determine the military conditions, let them be made the basis of a comparison, in this wise:—

13   (1) Which of the two sovereigns is imbued with the Moral Law?
(2) Which of the two generals has most ability?
(3) With whom lie the advantages derived from Heaven and Earth?
(4) On which side is Discipline most rigorously enforced?
(5) Which army is stronger?
(6) On which side are officers and men more highly trained?
(7) In which army is there the greater constancy both in reward and punishment?

14 By means of these seven considerations I can forecast victory or defeat.

15 The general that hearkens to my counsel and acts upon it, will conquer: let such a one be retained in command! The general that hearkens not to my counsel nor acts upon it, will suffer defeat:— let such a one be dismissed!

16 While heeding the profit of my counsel, avail yourself also of any helpful circumstances over and beyond the ordinary rules.

17 According as circumstances are favourable, one should modify one's plans.

18 All warfare is based on deception.

19 Hence, when able to attack, we must seem unable; when using our forces, we must seem inactive; when we are near, we must make the enemy believe we are far away; when far away, we must make him believe we are near.

20 Hold out baits to entice the enemy. Feign disorder, and crush him.

21 If he is secure at all points, be prepared for him. If he is in superior strength, evade him.

22 If your opponent is of choleric temper, seek to irritate him. Pretend to be weak, that he may grow arrogant.

23 If he is taking his ease, give him no rest. If his forces are united, separate them.

24 Attack him where he is unprepared, appear where you are not expected.

25 These military devices, leading to victory, must not be divulged beforehand.

26 Now the general who wins a battle makes many calculations in his temple ere the battle is fought. The general who loses a battle makes but few calculations beforehand. Thus do many calculations lead to victory, and few calculations to defeat: how much more no calculation at all! It is by attention to this point that I can foresee who is likely to win or lose.

CHAPTER TWO

WAGING WAR

1   Sun Tzu said: In the operations of war, where there are in the field a thousand swift chariots, as many heavy chariots, and a hundred thousand mail-clad soldiers, with provisions enough to carry them a thousand *li**, the expenditure at home and at the front, including entertainment of guests, small items such as glue and paint, and sums spent on chariots and armour, will reach the total of a thousand ounces of silver per day. Such is the cost of raising an army of 100,000 men.

2   When you engage in actual fighting, if victory is long in coming, then men's weapons will grow dull and their ardour will be damped. If you lay siege to a town, you will exhaust your strength.

3   Again, if the campaign is protracted, the resources of the State will not be equal to the strain.

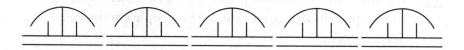

* One *li* is equal to half a kilometre.

4   Now, when your weapons are dulled, your ardour damped, your strength exhausted and your treasure spent, other chieftains will spring up to take advantage of your extremity. Then no man, however wise, will be able to avert the consequences that must ensue.

5   Thus, though we have heard of stupid haste in war, cleverness has never been seen associated with long delays.

6   There is no instance of a country having benefited from prolonged warfare.

7   It is only one who is thoroughly acquainted with the evils of war that can thoroughly understand the profitable way of carrying it on.

8   The skilful soldier does not raise a second levy, neither are his supply-wagons loaded more than twice.

9   Bring war material with you from home, but forage on the enemy. Thus the army will have food enough for its needs.

10   Poverty of the State Exchequer causes an army to be maintained by contributions from a distance. Contributing to maintain an army at a distance causes the people to be impoverished.

11   On the other hand, the proximity of an army causes prices to go up; and high prices cause the people's substance to be drained away.

12 When their substance is drained away, the peasantry will be afflicted by heavy exactions.

13 & 14 With this loss of substance and exhaustion of strength, the homes of the people will be stripped bare, and three-tenths of their income will be dissipated; while government expenses for broken chariots, worn-out horses, breast-plates and helmets, bows and arrows, spears and shields, protective mantles, draught-oxen and heavy wagons, will amount to four-tenths of its total revenue.

15 Hence a wise general makes a point of foraging on the enemy. One cartload of the enemy's provisions is equivalent to twenty of one's own, and likewise a single *picul** of his provender is equivalent to twenty from one's own store.

16 Now in order to kill the enemy, our men must be roused to anger; that there may be advantage from defeating the enemy, they must have their rewards.

17 Therefore in chariot fighting, when ten or more chariots have been taken, those should be rewarded who took the first. Our own flags should be substituted for those of the enemy, and the chariots mingled and used in conjunction with ours. The captured soldiers should be kindly treated and kept.

18 This is called using the conquered foe to augment one's own strength.

---

* One *picul* weighs approximately 133 lbs.

19 In war, then, let your great object be victory, not lengthy campaigns.

20 Thus it may be known that the leader of armies is the arbiter of the people's fate, the man on whom it depends whether the nation shall be in peace or in peril.

CHAPTER THREE

ATTACK BY STRATAGEM

1   Sun Tzu said: In the practical art of war, the best thing of all is to take the enemy's country whole and intact; to shatter and destroy it is not so good. So, too, it is better to recapture an army entire than to destroy it, to capture a regiment, a detachment or a company entire than to destroy them.

2   Hence to fight and conquer in all your battles is not supreme excellence; supreme excellence consists in breaking the enemy's resistance without fighting.

3   Thus the highest form of generalship is to balk the enemy's plans; the next best is to prevent the junction of the enemy's forces; the next in order is to attack the enemy's army in the field; and the worst policy of all is to besiege walled cities.

4   The rule is, not to besiege walled cities if it can possibly be avoided. The preparation of mantlets, movable shelters, and various implements of war, will take up three whole months; and the piling up of mounds against the walls will take three months more.

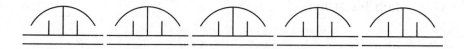

5   The general, unable to control his irritation, will launch his men to the assault like swarming ants, with the result that one-third of his men are slain, while the town still remains untaken. Such are the disastrous effects of a siege.

6   Therefore the skilful leader subdues the enemy's troops without any fighting; he captures their cities without laying siege to them; he overthrows their kingdom without lengthy operations in the field.

7   With his forces intact he will dispute the mastery of the Empire, and thus, without losing a man, his triumph will be complete. This is the method of attacking by stratagem.

8   It is the rule in war, if our forces are ten to the enemy's one, to surround him; if five to one, to attack him; if twice as numerous, to divide our army into two.

9   If equally matched, we can offer battle; if slightly inferior in numbers, we can avoid the enemy; if quite unequal in every way, we can flee from him.

10   Hence, though an obstinate fight may be made by a small force, in the end it must be captured by the larger force.

11   Now the general is the bulwark of the State; if the bulwark is complete at all points, the State will be strong; if the bulwark is defective, the State will be weak.

12   There are three ways in which a ruler can bring misfortune upon his army:—

13 (1) By commanding the army to advance or to retreat, being ignorant of the fact that it cannot obey. This is called hobbling the army.

14 (2) By attempting to govern an army in the same way as he administers a kingdom, being ignorant of the conditions which obtain in an army. This causes restlessness in the soldier's minds.

15 (3) By employing the officers of his army without discrimination, through ignorance of the military principle of adaptation to circumstances. This shakes the confidence of the soldiers.

16 But when the army is restless and distrustful, trouble is sure to come from the other feudal princes. This is simply bringing anarchy into the army, and flinging victory away.

17 Thus we may know that there are five essentials for victory:
> (1) He will win who knows when to fight and when not to fight.
> (2) He will win who knows how to handle both superior and inferior forces.
> (3) He will win whose army is animated by the same spirit throughout all its ranks.
> (4) He will win who, prepared himself, waits to take the enemy unprepared.
> (5) He will win who has military capacity and is not interfered with by the sovereign.

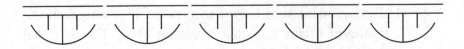

18 Hence the saying: If you know the enemy and know your-self, you need not fear the result of a hundred battles. If you know yourself but not the enemy, for every victory gained you will also suffer a defeat. If you know neither the enemy nor yourself, you will succumb in every battle.

CHAPTER FOUR

TACTICAL DISPOSITIONS

1   Sun Tzu said: The good fighters of old first put themselves beyond the possibility of defeat, and then waited for an opportunity of defeating the enemy.

2   To secure ourselves against defeat lies in our own hands, but the opportunity of defeating the enemy is provided by the enemy himself.

3   Thus the good fighter is able to secure himself against defeat, but cannot make certain of defeating the enemy.

4   Hence the saying: One may know how to conquer without being able to do it.

5   Security against defeat implies defensive tactics; ability to defeat the enemy means taking the offensive.

6   Standing on the defensive indicates insufficient strength; attacking, a superabundance of strength.

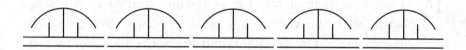

7   The general who is skilled in defence hides in the most secret recesses of the earth; he who is skilled in attack flashes forth from the topmost heights of heaven. Thus on the one hand we have the ability to protect ourselves; on the other, a victory that is complete.

8   To see victory only when it is within the ken of the common herd is not the acme of excellence.

9   Neither is it the acme of excellence if you fight and conquer and the whole Empire says: 'Well done!'

10   To lift an autumn leaf is no sign of great strength; to see the sun and moon is no sign of sharp sight; to hear the noise of thunder is no sign of a quick ear.

11   What the ancients called a clever fighter is one who not only wins, but excels in winning with ease.

12   Hence his victories bring him neither reputation for wisdom nor credit for courage.

13   He wins his battles by making no mistakes. Making no mistakes is what establishes the certainty of victory, for it means conquering an enemy that is already defeated.

14   Hence the skilful fighter puts himself into a position which makes defeat impossible, and does not miss the moment for defeating the enemy.

15   Thus it is that in war the victorious strategist only seeks battle after the victory has been won, whereas he who is destined to defeat first fights and afterwards looks for victory.

16 The consummate leader cultivates the Moral Law, and strictly adheres to method and discipline; thus it is in his power to control success.

17 In respect of military method, we have, firstly, Measurement; secondly, Estimation of quantity; thirdly, Calculation; fourthly, Balancing of chances; fifthly, Victory.

18 Measurement owes its existence to Earth; Estimation of quantity to Measurement; Calculation to Estimation of quantity; Balancing of chances to Calculation; and Victory to Balancing of chances.

19 A victorious army opposed to a routed one, is as a pound's weight placed in the scale against a single grain.

20 The onrush of a conquering force is like the bursting of pent-up waters into a chasm a thousand fathoms deep.

CHAPTER FIVE

ENERGY

1   Sun Tzu said: The control of a large force is the same principle as the control of a few men: it is merely a question of dividing up their numbers.

2   Fighting with a large army under your command is nowise different from fighting with a small one: it is merely a question of instituting signs and signals.

3   To ensure that your whole host may withstand the brunt of the enemy's attack and remain unshaken – this is effected by manoeuvres direct and indirect.

4   That the impact of your army may be like a grindstone dashed against an egg – this is effected by the science of weak points and strong.

5   In all fighting, the direct method may be used for joining battle, but indirect methods will be needed in order to secure victory.

6   Indirect tactics, efficiently applied, are inexhaustible as Heaven and Earth, unending as the flow of rivers and streams; like the sun and moon, they end but to begin anew; like the four seasons, they pass away to return once more.

7   There are not more than five musical notes, yet the combinations of these five give rise to more melodies than can ever be heard.

8   There are not more than five primary colours (blue, yellow, red, white and black), yet in combination they produce more hues than can ever be seen.

9   There are not more than five cardinal tastes (sour, acrid, salt, sweet and bitter), yet combinations of them yield more flavours than can ever be tasted.

10   In battle, there are not more than two methods of attack – the direct and the indirect; yet these two in combination give rise to an endless series of manoeuvres.

11   The direct and the indirect lead on to each other in turn. It is like moving in a circle – you never come to an end. Who can exhaust the possibilities of their combination?

12   The onset of troops is like the rush of a torrent which will even roll stones along in its course.

13   The quality of decision is like the well-timed swoop of a falcon which enables it to strike and destroy its victim.

14   Therefore the good fighter will be terrible in his onset, and prompt in his decision.

15   Energy may be likened to the bending of a crossbow; decision, to the releasing of a trigger.

16 Amid the turmoil and tumult of battle, there may be seeming disorder and yet no real disorder at all; amid confusion and chaos, your array may be without head or tail, yet it will be proof against defeat.

17 Simulated disorder postulates perfect discipline, simulated fear postulates courage; simulated weakness postulates strength.

18 Hiding order beneath the cloak of disorder is simply a question of subdivision; concealing courage under a show of timidity presupposes a fund of latent energy; masking strength with weakness is to be effected by tactical dispositions.

19 Thus one who is skilful at keeping the enemy on the move maintains deceitful appearances, according to which the enemy will act. He sacrifices something, that the enemy may snatch at it.

20 By holding out baits, he keeps him on the march; then with a body of picked men he lies in wait for him.

21 The clever combatant looks to the effect of combined energy, and does not require too much from individuals. Hence his ability to pick out the right men and utilize combined energy.

22 When he utilizes combined energy, his fighting men become as it were like unto rolling logs or stones. For it is the nature of a log or stone to remain motionless on level ground, and to move when on a slope; if four-cornered, to come to a standstill, but if round-shaped, to go rolling down.

23 Thus the energy developed by good fighting men is as the momentum of a round stone rolled down a mountain thousands of feet in height. So much on the subject of energy.

CHAPTER SIX

WEAK POINTS AND STRONG

1   Sun Tzu said: Whoever is first in the field and awaits the coming of the enemy, will be fresh for the fight; whoever is second in the field and has to hasten to battle will arrive exhausted.

2   Therefore the clever combatant imposes his will on the enemy, but does not allow the enemy's will to be imposed on him.

3   By holding out advantages to him, he can cause the enemy to approach of his own accord; or, by inflicting damage, he can make it impossible for the enemy to draw near.

4   If the enemy is taking his ease, he can harass him; if well supplied with food, he can starve him out; if quietly encamped, he can force him to move.

5   Appear at points which the enemy must hasten to defend; march swiftly to places where you are not expected.

6   An army may march great distances without distress, if it marches through country where the enemy is not.

7 You can be sure of succeeding in your attacks if you only attack places which are undefended. You can ensure the safety of your defence if you only hold positions that cannot be attacked.

8 Hence that general is skilful in attack whose opponent does not know what to defend; and he is skilful in defence whose opponent does not know what to attack.

9 O divine art of subtlety and secrecy! Through you we learn to be invisible, through you inaudible; and hence we can hold the enemy's fate in our hands.

10 You may advance and be absolutely irresistible, if you make for the enemy's weak points; you may retire and be safe from pursuit if your movements are more rapid than those of the enemy.

11 If we wish to fight, the enemy can be forced to an engagement even though he be sheltered behind a high rampart and a deep ditch. All we need do is attack some other place that he will be obliged to relieve.

12 If we do not wish to fight, we can prevent the enemy from engaging us even though the lines of our encampment be merely traced out on the ground. All we need do is to throw something odd and unaccountable in his way.

13 By discovering the enemy's dispositions and remaining invisible ourselves, we can keep our forces concentrated, while the enemy's must be divided.

14 We can form a single united body, while the enemy must split up into fractions. Hence there will be a whole pitted against separate parts of a whole, which means that we shall be many to the enemy's few.

15 And if we are able thus to attack an inferior force with a superior one, our opponents will be in dire straits.

16 The spot where we intend to fight must not be made known; for then the enemy will have to prepare against a possible attack at several different points; and his forces being thus distributed in many directions, the numbers we shall have to face at any given point will be proportionately few.

17 For should the enemy strengthen his van, he will weaken his rear; should he strengthen his rear, he will weaken his van; should he strengthen his left, he will weaken his right; should he strengthen his right, he will weaken his left. If he sends reinforcements everywhere, he will everywhere be weak.

18 Numerical weakness comes from having to prepare against possible attacks; numerical strength, from compelling our adversary to make these preparations against us.

19 Knowing the place and the time of the coming battle, we may concentrate from the greatest distances in order to fight.

20 But if neither time nor place be known, then the left wing will be impotent to succour the right, the right equally impotent to succour the left, the van unable to relieve the rear, or the rear to support the van. How much more so if the furthest portions of the army are anything under a hundred *li* apart, and even the nearest are separated by several *li*!

21 Though according to my estimate the soldiers of Yueh exceed our own in number, that shall advantage them nothing in the matter of victory. I say then that victory can be achieved.

22 Though the enemy be stronger in numbers, we may prevent him from fighting. Scheme so as to discover his plans and the likelihood of their success.

23 Rouse him, and learn the principle of his activity or inactivity. Force him to reveal himself, so as to find out his vulnerable spots.

24 Carefully compare the opposing army with your own, so that you may know where strength is superabundant and where it is deficient.

25 In making tactical dispositions, the highest pitch you can attain is to conceal them; conceal your dispositions, and you will be safe from the prying of the subtlest spies, from the machinations of the wisest brains.

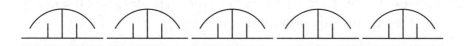

26 How victory may be produced for them out of the enemy's own tactics – that is what the multitude cannot comprehend.

27 All men can see the tactics whereby I conquer, but what none can see is the strategy out of which victory is evolved.

28 Do not repeat the tactics which have gained you one victory, but let your methods be regulated by the infinite variety of circumstances.

29 Military tactics are like unto water; for water in its natural course runs away from high places and hastens downwards.

30 So in war, the way is to avoid what is strong and to strike at what is weak.

31 Water shapes its course according to the nature of the ground over which it flows; the soldier works out his victory in relation to the foe whom he is facing.

32 Therefore, just as water retains no constant shape, so in warfare there are no constant conditions.

33 He who can modify his tactics in relation to his opponent and thereby succeed in winning, may be called a heaven-born captain.

34 The five elements (water, fire, wood, metal, earth) are not always equally predominant; the four seasons make way for each other in turn. There are short days and long; the moon has its periods of waning and waxing.

CHAPTER SEVEN

MANOEUVRING

1   Sun Tzu said: In war, the general receives his commands from the sovereign.

2   Having collected an army and concentrated his forces, he must blend and harmonize the different elements thereof before pitching his camp.

3   After that, comes tactical manoeuvring, than which there is nothing more difficult. The difficulty of tactical manoeuvring consists in turning the devious into the direct, and misfortune into gain.

4   Thus, to take a long and circuitous route, after enticing the enemy out of the way, and though starting after him, to contrive to reach the goal before him, shows knowledge of the artifice of deviation.

5   Manoeuvring with an army is advantageous; with an undisciplined multitude, most dangerous.

6   If you set a fully equipped army in march in order to snatch an advantage, the chances are that you will be too late. On the other hand, to detach a flying column for the purpose involves the sacrifice of its baggage and stores.

7   Thus, if you order your men to roll up their buff-coats, and make forced marches without halting day or night, covering double the usual distance at a stretch, doing a hundred *li* in order to wrest an advantage, the leaders of all your three divisions will fall into the hands of the enemy.

8   The stronger men will be in front, the jaded ones will fall behind, and on this plan only one-tenth of your army will reach its destination.

9   If you march fifty *li* in order to outmanoeuvre the enemy, you will lose the leader of your first division, and only half your force will reach the goal.

10 If you march thirty *li* with the same object, two-thirds of your army will arrive.

11 We may take it then that an army without its baggage-train is lost; without provisions it is lost; without bases of supply it is lost.

12 We cannot enter into alliances until we are acquainted with the designs of our neighbours.

13 We are not fit to lead an army on the march unless we are familiar with the face of the country – its mountains and forests, its pitfalls and precipices, its marshes and swamps.

14 We shall be unable to turn natural advantage to account unless we make use of local guides.

15 In war, practise dissimulation, and you will succeed.

16 Whether to concentrate or to divide your troops must be decided by circumstances.

17 Let your rapidity be that of the wind, your compactness be that of the forest.

18 In raiding and plundering be like fire, in immovability like a mountain.

19 Let your plans be dark and impenetrable as night, and when you move, fall like a thunderbolt.

20 When you plunder a countryside, let the spoil be divided amongst your men; when you capture new territory, cut it up into allotments for the benefit of the soldiery.

21 Ponder and deliberate before you make a move.

22 He will conquer who has learnt the artifice of deviation. Such is the art of manoeuvring.

23 The Book of Army Management says: On the field of battle, the spoken word does not carry far enough: hence the institution of gongs and drums. Nor can ordinary objects be seen clearly enough: hence the institution of banners and flags.

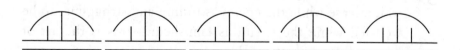

24   Gongs and drums, banners and flags, are means whereby the ears and eyes of the host may be focused on one particular point.

25   The host thus forming a single united body, it is impossible either for the brave to advance alone, or for the cowardly to retreat alone. This is the art of handling large masses of men.

26   In night-fighting, then, make much use of signal-fires and drums, and in fighting by day, of flags and banners, as a means of influencing the ears and eyes of your army.

27   A whole army may be robbed of its spirit; a commander-in-chief may be robbed of his presence of mind.

28   Now a soldier's spirit is keenest in the morning; by noonday it has begun to flag; and in the evening, his mind is bent only on returning to camp.

29   A clever general, therefore, avoids an army when its spirit is keen, but attacks it when it is sluggish and inclined to return. This is the art of studying moods.

30   Disciplined and calm, to await the appearance of disorder and hubbub amongst the enemy: – this is the art of retaining self-possession.

31   To be near the goal while the enemy is still far from it, to wait at ease while the enemy is toiling and struggling, to be well-fed while the enemy is famished: – this is the art of husbanding one's strength.

32 To refrain from intercepting an enemy whose banners are in perfect order, to refrain from attacking an army drawn up in calm and confident array: – this is the art of studying circumstances.

33 It is a military axiom not to advance uphill against the enemy, nor to oppose him when he comes downhill.

34 Do not pursue an enemy who simulates flight; do not attack soldiers whose temper is keen.

35 Do not swallow bait offered by the enemy. Do not interfere with an army that is returning home.

36 When you surround an army, leave an outlet free. Do not press a desperate foe too hard.

37 Such is the art of warfare.

CHAPTER EIGHT

VARIATION IN TACTICS

1   Sun Tzu said: In war, the general receives his commands from the sovereign, collects his army and concentrates his forces.

2   When in difficult country, do not encamp. In country where high roads intersect, join hands with your allies. Do not linger in dangerously isolated positions. In hemmed-in situations, you must resort to stratagem. In desperate positions, you must fight.

3   There are roads which must not be followed, armies which must not be attacked, towns which must not be besieged, positions which must not be contested, commands of the sovereign which must not be obeyed.

4   The general who thoroughly understands the advantages that accompany variation of tactics knows how to handle his troops.

5   The general who does not understand these, may be well acquainted with the configuration of the country, yet he will not be able to turn his knowledge to practical account.

6 So, the student of war who is unversed in the art of war of varying his plans, even though he be acquainted with the Five Advantages, will fail to make the best use of his men.

7 Hence in the wise leader's plans, considerations of advantage and of disadvantage will be blended together.

8 If our expectation of advantage be tempered in this way, we may succeed in accomplishing the essential part of our schemes.

9 If, on the other hand, in the midst of difficulties we are always ready to seize an advantage, we may extricate ourselves from misfortune.

10 Reduce the hostile chiefs by inflicting damage on them; and make trouble for them, and keep them constantly engaged; hold out specious allurements, and make them rush to any given point.

11 The art of war teaches us to rely not on the likelihood of the enemy's not coming, but on our own readiness to receive him; not on the chance of his not attacking, but rather on the fact that we have made our position unassailable.

12 There are five dangerous faults which may affect a general:
   (1) Recklessness, which leads to destruction;
   (2) cowardice, which leads to capture;
   (3) a hasty temper, which can be provoked by insults;
   (4) a delicacy of honour which is sensitive to shame;
   (5) over-solicitude for his men, which exposes him to worry and trouble.

13 These are the five besetting sins of a general, ruinous to the conduct of war.

14 When an army is overthrown and its leader slain, the cause will surely be found among these five dangerous faults. Let them be a subject of meditation.

CHAPTER NINE

THE ARMY ON THE MARCH

1. Sun Tzu said: We come now to the question of encamping the army, and observing signs of the enemy. Pass quickly over mountains, and keep in the neighbourhood of valleys.

2. Camp in high places, facing the sun. Do not climb heights in order to fight. So much for mountain warfare.

3. After crossing a river, you should get far away from it.

4. When an invading force crosses a river in its onward march, do not advance to meet it in mid-stream. It will be best to let half the army get across, and then deliver your attack.

5. If you are anxious to fight, you should not go to meet the invader near a river which he has to cross.

6. Moor your craft higher up than the enemy, and facing the sun. Do not move up-stream to meet the enemy. So much for river warfare.

7. In crossing salt-marshes, your sole concern should be to get over them quickly, without any delay.

8 If forced to fight in a salt-marsh, you should have water and grass near you, and get your back to a clump of trees. So much for operations in salt-marshes.

9 In dry, level country, take up an easily accessible position with rising ground to your right and on your rear, so that the danger may be in front, and safety lie behind. So much for campaigning in flat country.

10 These are the four useful branches of military knowledge which enabled the Yellow Emperor to vanquish four other sovereigns.

11 All armies prefer high ground to low and sunny places to dark.

12 If you are careful of your men, and camp on hard ground, the army will be free from disease of every kind, and this will spell victory.

13 When you come to a hill or a bank, occupy the sunny side, with the slope on your right rear. Thus you will at once act for the benefit of your soldiers and utilize the natural advantages of the ground.

14 When, in consequence of heavy rains up-country, a river which you wish to ford is swollen and flecked with foam, you must wait until it subsides.

15 Country in which there are precipitous cliffs with torrents running between, deep natural hollows, confined places, tangled thickets, quagmires and crevasses, should be left with all possible speed and not approached.

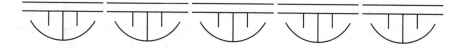

16 While we keep away from such places, we should get the enemy to approach them; while we face them, we should let the enemy have them on his rear.

17 If in the neighbourhood of your camp there should be any hilly country, ponds surrounded by aquatic grass, hollow basins filled with reeds, or woods with thick undergrowth, they must be carefully routed out and searched; for these are places where men in ambush or insidious spies are likely to be lurking.

18 When the enemy is close at hand and remains quiet, he is relying on the natural strength of his position.

19 When he keeps aloof and tries to provoke a battle, he is anxious for the other side to advance.

20 If his place of encampment is easy of access, he is tendering a bait.

21 Movement amongst the trees of a forest shows that the enemy is advancing. The appearance of a number of screens in the midst of thick grass means that the enemy wants to make us suspicious.

22 The rising of birds in their flight is the sign of an ambuscade. Startled beasts indicate that a sudden attack is coming.

23 When there is dust rising in a high column, it is the sign of chariots advancing; when the dust is low, but spread over a wide area, it betokens the approach of infantry. When it branches out in different directions, it shows that parties have been sent to collect firewood. A few clouds of dust moving to and fro signify that the army is encamping.

24 Humble words and increased preparations are signs that the enemy is about to advance. Violent language and driving forward as if to the attack are signs that he will retreat.

25 When the light chariots come out first and take up a position on the wings, it is a sign that the enemy is forming for battle.

26 Peace proposals unaccompanied by a sworn covenant indicate a plot.

27 When there is much running about and the soldiers fall into rank, it means that the critical moment has come.

28 When some are seen advancing and some retreating, it is a lure.

29 When the soldiers stand leaning on their spears, they are faint from want of food.

30 If those who are sent to draw water begin by drinking themselves, the army is suffering from thirst.

31 If the enemy sees an advantage to be gained and makes no effort to secure it, the soldiers are exhausted.

32 If birds gather on any spot, it is unoccupied. Clamour by night betokens nervousness.

33 If there is disturbance in the camp, the general's authority is weak. If the banners and flags are shifted about, sedition is afoot. If the officers are angry, it means that the men are weary.

34 When an army feeds its horses with grain and kills its cattle for food, and when the men do not hang their cooking-pots over the camp-fires, showing that they will not return to their tents, you may know that they are determined to fight to the death.

35 The sight of men whispering together in small knots or speaking in subdued tones points to disaffection amongst the rank and file.

36 Too frequent rewards signify that the enemy is at the end of his resources; too many punishments betray a condition of dire distress.

37 To begin by bluster, but afterwards to take fright at the enemy's numbers, shows a supreme lack of intelligence.

38 When envoys are sent with compliments in their mouths, it is a sign that the enemy wishes for a truce.

39 If the enemy's troops march up angrily and remain facing ours for a long time without either joining battle or taking themselves off again, the situation is one that demands great vigilance and circumspection.

40 If our troops are no more in number than the enemy, that is amply sufficient; it only means that no direct attack can be made. What we can do is simply to concentrate all our available strength, keep a close watch on the enemy, and obtain reinforcements.

41 He who exercises no forethought but makes light of his opponents is sure to be captured by them.

42 If soldiers are punished before they have grown attached to you, they will not prove submissive; and, unless submissive, they will be practically useless. If, when the soldiers have become attached to you, punishments are not enforced, they will still be useless.

43 Therefore soldiers must be treated in the first instance with humanity, but kept under control by means of iron discipline. This is a certain road to victory.

44 If in training soldiers commands are habitually enforced, the army will be well-disciplined; if not, its discipline will be bad.

45 If a general shows confidence in his men but always insists on his orders being obeyed, the gain will be mutual.

CHAPTER TEN

TERRAIN

1   Sun Tzu said: We may distinguish six kinds of terrain, to wit:
- (1) Accessible ground;
- (2) entangling ground;
- (3) temporizing ground;
- (4) narrow passes;
- (5) precipitous heights;
- (6) positions at a great distance from the enemy.

2   Ground which can be freely traversed by both sides is called accessible.

3   With regard to ground of this nature, be before the enemy in occupying the raised and sunny spots, and carefully guard your line of supplies. Then you will be able to fight with advantage.

4   Ground which can be abandoned but is hard to re-occupy is called entangling.

5   From a position of this sort, if the enemy is unprepared, you may sally forth and defeat him. But if the enemy is prepared for your coming, and you fail to defeat him, then, return being impossible, disaster will ensue.

6 When the position is such that neither side will gain by making the first move, it is called temporizing ground.

7 In a position of this sort, even though the enemy should offer us an attractive bait, it will be advisable not to stir forth, but rather to retreat, thus enticing the enemy in his turn; then, when part of his army has come out, we may deliver our attack with advantage.

8 With regard to narrow passes, if you can occupy them first, let them be strongly garrisoned and await the advent of the enemy.

9 Should the army forestall you in occupying a pass, do not go after him if the pass is fully garrisoned, but only if it is weakly garrisoned.

10 With regard to precipitous heights, if you are beforehand with your adversary, you should occupy the raised and sunny spots, and there wait for him to come up.

11 If the enemy has occupied them before you, do not follow him, but retreat and try to entice him away.

12 If you are situated at a great distance from the enemy, and the strength of the two armies is equal, it is not easy to provoke a battle, and fighting will be to your disadvantage.

13 These six are the principles connected with Earth. The general who has attained a responsible post must be careful to study them.

14 Now an army is exposed to six calamities, not arising from natural causes, but from faults for which the general is responsible. These are:
  (1) Flight;
  (2) insubordination;
  (3) collapse;
  (4) ruin;
  (5) disorganization;
  (6) rout.

15 Other conditions being equal, if one force is hurled against another ten times its size, the result will be the flight of the former.

16 When the common soldiers are too strong and their officers too weak, the result is insubordination. When the officers are too strong and the common soldiers too weak, the result is collapse.

17 When the higher officers are angry and insubordinate, and on meeting the enemy give battle on their own account from a feeling of resentment, before the commander-in-chief can tell whether or not he is in a position to fight, the result is ruin.

18 When the general is weak and without authority; when his orders are not clear and distinct; when there are no fixed duties assigned to officers and men, and the ranks are formed in a slovenly haphazard manner, the result is utter disorganization.

19 When a general, unable to estimate the enemy's strength, allows an inferior force to engage a larger one, or hurls a weak detachment against a powerful one, and neglects to place picked soldiers in the front rank, the result must be a rout.

20 These are six ways of courting defeat, which must be carefully noted by the general who has attained a responsible post.

21 The natural formation of the country is the soldier's best ally; but a power of estimating the adversary, of controlling the forces of victory, and of shrewdly calculating difficulties, dangers and distances, constitutes the test of a great general.

22 He who knows these things, and in fighting puts his knowledge into practice, will win his battles. He who knows them not, nor practises them, will surely be defeated.

23 If fighting is sure to result in victory, then you must fight, even though the ruler forbid it; if fighting will not result in victory, then you must not fight even at the ruler's bidding.

24 The general who advances without coveting fame and retreats without fearing disgrace, whose only thought is to protect his country and do good service for his sovereign, is the jewel of the kingdom.

25 Regard your soldiers as your children, and they will follow you into the deepest valleys; look upon them as your own beloved sons, and they will stand by you even unto death.

26 If, however, you are indulgent, but unable to make your authority felt; kind-hearted, but unable to enforce your commands; and incapable, moreover, of quelling disorder: then your soldiers must be likened to spoilt children; they are useless for any practical purpose.

27 If we know that our own men are in a condition to attack, but are unaware that the enemy is not open to attack, we have gone only halfway towards victory.

28 If we know that the enemy is open to attack, but are unaware that our own men are not in a condition to attack, we have gone only halfway towards victory.

29 If we know that the enemy is open to attack, and also know our men are in a condition to attack, but are unaware that the nature of the ground makes fighting impracticable, we have still gone only halfway towards victory.

30 Hence the experienced soldier, once in motion, is never bewildered; once he has broken camp, he is never at a loss.

31 Hence the saying: If you know the enemy and know yourself, your victory will not stand in doubt; if you know Heaven and know Earth, you may make your victory complete.

CHAPTER ELEVEN

THE NINE SITUATIONS

1   Sun Tzu said: The art of war recognizes nine varieties of ground:

         (1) Dispersive ground;

         (2) facile ground;

         (3) contentious ground;

         (4) open ground;

         (5) ground of intersecting highways;

         (6) serious ground;

         (7) difficult ground;

         (8) hemmed-in ground;

         (9) desperate ground.

2   When a chieftain is fighting in his own territory, it is dispersive ground.

3   When he has penetrated into hostile territory, but to no great distance, it is facile ground.

4   Ground the possession of which imports great advantage to either side, is contentious ground.

5   Ground on which each side has liberty of movement is open ground.

6 Ground which forms the key to three contiguous states, so that he who occupies it first has most of the Empire at his command, is a ground of intersecting highways.

7 When an army has penetrated into the heart of a hostile country, leaving a number of fortified cities in its rear, it is serious ground.

8 Mountain forests, rugged steeps, marshes and fens – all country that is hard to traverse: this is difficult ground.

9 Ground which is reached through narrow gorges, and from which we can only retire by tortuous paths, so that a small number of the enemy would suffice to crush a large body of our men: this is hemmed-in ground.

10 Ground on which we can only be saved from destruction by fighting without delay, is desperate ground.

11 On dispersive ground, therefore, fight not. On facile ground, halt not. On contentious ground, attack not.

12 On open ground, do not try to block the enemy's way. On the ground of intersecting highways, join hands with your allies.

13 On serious ground, gather in plunder. In difficult ground, keep steadily on the march.

14 On hemmed-in ground, resort to stratagem. On desperate ground, fight.

15 Those who were called skilful leaders of old knew how to drive a wedge between the enemy's front and rear; to prevent co-operation between his large and small divisions; to hinder the good troops from rescuing the bad, the officers from rallying their men.

16 When the enemy's men were united, they managed to keep them in disorder.

17 When it was to their advantage, they made a forward move; when otherwise, they stopped still.

18 If asked how to cope with a great host of the enemy in orderly array and on the point of marching to the attack, I should say: 'Begin by seizing something which your opponent holds dear; then he will be amenable to your will.'

19 Rapidity is the essence of war: take advantage of the enemy's unreadiness, make your way by unexpected routes, and attack unguarded spots.

20 The following are the principles to be observed by an invading force: The further you penetrate into a country, the greater will be the solidarity of your troops, and thus the defenders will not prevail against you.

21 Make forays in fertile country in order to supply your army with food.

22 Carefully study the well-being of your men, and do not overtax them. Concentrate your energy and hoard your strength. Keep your army continually on the move, and devise unfathomable plans.

23 Throw your soldiers into positions whence there is no escape, and they will prefer death to flight. If they will face death, there is nothing they may not achieve. Officers and men alike will put forth their uttermost strength.

24 Soldiers when in desperate straits lose the sense of fear. If there is no place of refuge, they will stand firm. If they are in hostile country, they will show a stubborn front. If there is no help for it, they will fight hard.

25 Thus, without waiting to be marshalled, the soldiers will be constantly on the *qui vive*; without waiting to be asked, they will do your will; without restrictions, they will be faithful; without giving orders, they can be trusted.

26 Prohibit the taking of omens, and do away with superstitious doubts. Then, until death itself comes, no calamity need be feared.

27 If our soldiers are not overburdened with money, it is not because they have a distaste for riches; if their lives are not unduly long, it is not because they are disinclined to longevity.

28   On the day they are ordered out to battle, your soldiers may weep, those sitting up bedewing their garments, and those lying down letting the tears run down their cheeks. But let them once be brought to bay, and they will display the courage of a Chu or a Kuei.

29   The skilful tactician may be likened to the shuai-jan. Now the shuai-jan is a snake that is found in the Ch'ang mountains. Strike at its head, and you will be attacked by its tail; strike at its tail, and you will be attacked by its head; strike at its middle, and you will be attacked by head and tail both.

30   Asked if an army can be made to imitate the shuai-jan, I should answer, 'Yes'. For the men of Wu and the men of Yueh are enemies; yet if they are crossing a river in the same boat and are caught by a storm, they will come to each other's assistance just as the left hand helps the right.

31   Hence it is not enough to put one's trust in the tethering of horses, and the burying of chariot wheels in the ground.

32   The principle on which to manage an army is to set up one standard of courage which all must reach.

33   How to make the best of both strong and weak, that is a question involving the proper use of ground.

34   Thus the skilful general conducts his army just as though he were leading a single man, willy-nilly, by the hand.

35   It is the business of a general to be quiet and thus ensure secrecy; upright and just, and thus maintain order.

36 He must be able to mystify his officers and men by false reports and appearances, and thus keep them in total ignorance.

37 By altering his arrangements and changing his plans, he keeps the enemy without definite knowledge. By shifting his camp and taking circuitous routes, he prevents the enemy from anticipating his purpose.

38 At the critical moment, the leader of an army acts like one who has climbed up a height and then kicks away the ladder behind him. He carries his men deep into hostile territory before he shows his hand.

39 He burns his boats and breaks his cooking-pots; like a shepherd driving a flock of sheep, he drives his men this way and that, and nothing knows whither he is going.

40 To muster his host and bring it into danger: – this may be termed the business of the general.

41 The different measures suited to the nine varieties of ground; the expediency of aggressive or defensive tactics; and the fundamental laws of human nature: these are things that must most certainly be studied.

42 When invading hostile territory, the general principle is that penetrating deeply brings cohesion; penetrating but a short way means dispersion.

43 When you leave your own country behind, and take your army across neighbourhood territory, you find yourself on critical ground. When there are means of communication on all four sides, the ground is one of intersecting highways.

44 When you penetrate deeply into a country, it is serious ground. When you penetrate but a little way, it is facile ground.

45 When you have the enemy's strongholds in your rear, and narrow passes in front, it is hemmed-in ground. When there is no place of refuge at all, it is desperate ground.

46 Therefore, on dispersive ground, I would inspire my men with unity of purpose. On facile ground, I would see that there is close connection between all parts of my army.

47 On contentious ground, I would hurry up my rear.

48 On open ground, I would keep a vigilant eye on my defences. On ground of intersecting highways, I would consolidate my alliances.

49 On serious ground, I would try to ensure a continuous stream of supplies. On difficult ground, I would keep pushing on along the road.

50 On hemmed-in ground, I would block any way of retreat. On desperate ground, I would proclaim to my soldiers the hopelessness of saving their lives.

51 For it is the soldier's disposition to offer an obstinate resistance when surrounded, to fight hard when he cannot help himself, and to obey promptly when he has fallen into danger.

52 We cannot enter into alliance with neighbouring princes until we are acquainted with their designs. We are not fit to lead an army on the march unless we are familiar with the face of the country – its mountains and forests, its pitfalls and precipices, its marshes and swamps. We shall be unable to turn natural advantages to account unless we make use of local guides.

53 To be ignorant of any one of the following four or five principles does not befit a warlike prince.

54 When a warlike prince attacks a powerful state, his generalship shows itself in preventing the concentration of the enemy's forces. He overawes his opponents, and their allies are prevented from joining against him.

55 Hence he does not strive to ally himself with all and sundry, nor does he foster the power of other states. He carries out his own secret designs, keeping his antagonists in awe. Thus he is able to capture their cities and overthrow their kingdoms.

56 Bestow rewards without regard to rule, issue orders without regard to previous arrangements; and you will be able to handle a whole army as though you had to do with but a single man.

57 Confront your soldiers with the deed itself; never let them know your design. When the outlook is bright, bring it before their eyes; but tell them nothing when the situation is gloomy.

58 Place your army in deadly peril, and it will survive; plunge it into desperate straits, and it will come off in safety.

59 For it is precisely when a force has fallen into harm's way that it is capable of striking a blow for victory.

60 Success in warfare is gained by carefully accommodating ourselves to the enemy's purpose.

61 By persistently hanging on the enemy's flank, we shall succeed in the long run in killing the commander-in-chief.

62 This is called the ability to accomplish a thing by sheer cunning.

63 On the day that you take up your command, block the frontier passes, destroy the official tallies, and stop the passage of all emissaries.

64 Be stern in the council-chamber, so that you may control the situation.

65 If the enemy leaves a door open, you must rush in.

66 Forestall your opponent by seizing what he holds dear, and subtly contrive to time his arrival on the ground.

67 Walk in the path defined by rule, and accommodate yourself to the enemy until you can fight a decisive battle.

68 At first, then, exhibit the coyness of a maiden, until the enemy gives you an opening; afterwards emulate the rapidity of a running hare, and it will be too late for the enemy to oppose you.

CHAPTER TWELVE

ATTACK BY FIRE

1   Sun Tzu said: There are five ways of attacking with fire. The first is to burn soldiers in their camp; the second is to burn stores; the third is to burn baggage trains; the fourth is to burn arsenals and magazines; the fifth is to hurl dropping fire amongst the enemy.

2   In order to carry out an attack, we must have means available. The material for raising fire should always be kept in readiness.

3   There is a proper season for making attacks with fire, and special days for starting a conflagration.

4   The proper season is when the weather is very dry; the special days are those when the moon is in the constellations of the Sieve, the Wall, the Wing or the Cross-bar; for these four are all days of rising wind.

5   In attacking with fire, one should be prepared to meet five possible developments:

6   (1) When fire breaks out inside the enemy's camp, respond at once with an attack from without.

7   (2) If there is an outbreak of fire, but the enemy's soldiers remain quiet, bide your time and do not attack.

8   (3) When the force of the flames has reached its height, follow it up with an attack, if that is practicable; if not, stay where you are.

9   (4) If it is possible to make an assault with fire from without, do not wait for it to break out within, but deliver your attack at a favourable moment.

10   (5) When you start a fire, be to windward of it. Do not attack from the leeward.

11   A wind that rises in the daytime lasts long, but a night breeze soon falls.

12   In every army, the five developments connected with fire must be known, the movements of the stars calculated, and a watch kept for the proper days.

13   Hence those who use fire as an aid to the attack show intelligence; those who use water as an aid to the attack gain an accession of strength.

14   By means of water, an enemy may be intercepted, but not robbed of all his belongings.

15   Unhappy is the fate of one who tries to win his battles and succeed in his attacks without cultivating the spirit of enterprise; for the result is waste of time and general stagnation.

16 Hence the saying: The enlightened ruler lays his plans well ahead; the good general cultivates his resources.

17 Move not unless you see an advantage; use not your troops unless there is something to be gained; fight not unless the position is critical.

18 No ruler should put troops into the field merely to gratify his own spleen; no general should fight a battle simply out of pique.

19 If it is to your advantage, make a forward move; if not, stay where you are.

20 Anger may in time change to gladness; vexation may be succeeded by content.

21 But a kingdom that has once been destroyed can never come again into being; nor can the dead ever be brought back to life.

22 Hence the enlightened ruler is heedful, and the good general full of caution. This is the way to keep a country at peace and an army intact.

CHAPTER THIRTEEN

THE USE OF SPIES

1   Sun Tzu said: Raising a host of a hundred thousand men and marching them great distances entails heavy loss on the people and a drain on the resources of the State. The daily expenditure will amount to a thousand ounces of silver. There will be commotion at home and abroad, and men will drop down exhausted on the highways. As many as seven hundred thousand families will be impeded in their labour.

2   Hostile armies may face each other for years, striving for the victory which is decided in a single day. This being so, to remain in ignorance of the enemy's condition simply because one grudges the outlay of a hundred ounces of silver in honours and emoluments, is the height of inhumanity.

3   One who acts thus is no leader of men, no present help to his sovereign, no master of victory.

4   Thus, what enables the wise sovereign and the good general to strike and conquer, and achieve things beyond the reach of ordinary men, is foreknowledge.

5   Now this foreknowledge cannot be elicited from spirits; it cannot be obtained inductively from experience, nor by any deductive calculation.

6 Knowledge of the enemy's dispositions can only be obtained from other men.

7 Hence the use of spies, of whom there are five classes:
(1) Local spies;
(2) inward spies;
(3) converted spies;
(4) doomed spies;
(5) surviving spies.

8 When these five kinds of spy are all at work, none can discover the secret system. This is called 'divine manipulation of the threads'. It is the sovereign's most precious faculty.

9 Having local spies means employing the services of the inhabitants of a district.

10 Having inward spies, means making use of officials of the enemy.

11 Having converted spies, means getting hold of the enemy's spies and using them for our own purposes.

12 Having doomed spies, doing certain things openly for purposes of deception, and allowing our spies to know of them and report them to the enemy.

13 Surviving spies, finally, are those who bring back news from the enemy's camp.

14 Hence it is that with none in the whole army are more intimate relations to be maintained than with spies. None should be more liberally rewarded. In no other business should greater secrecy be preserved.

15 Spies cannot be usefully employed without a certain intuitive sagacity.

16 They cannot be properly managed without benevolence and straightforwardness.

17 Without subtle ingenuity of mind, one cannot make certain of the truth of their reports.

18 Be subtle! be subtle! and use your spies for every kind of business.

19 If a secret piece of news is divulged by a spy before the time is ripe, he must be put to death together with the man to whom the secret was told.

20 Whether the object be to crush an army, to storm a city, or to assassinate an individual, it is always necessary to begin by finding out the names of the attendants, the aides-de-camp, and door-keepers and sentries of the general in command. Our spies must be commissioned to ascertain these.

21 The enemy's spies who have come to spy on us must be sought out, tempted with bribes, led away and comfortably housed. Thus they will become converted spies and available for our service.

22 It is through the information brought by the converted spy that we are able to acquire and employ local and inward spies.

23 It is owing to his information, again, that we can cause the doomed spy to carry false tidings to the enemy.

24 Lastly, it is by his information that the surviving spy can be used on appointed occasions.

25 The end and aim of spying in all its five varieties is knowledge of the enemy; and this knowledge can only be derived, in the first instance, from the converted spy. Hence it is essential that the converted spy be treated with the utmost liberality.

26 Of old, the rise of the Yin dynasty was due to I Chih who had served under the Hsia. Likewise, the rise of the Chou dynasty was due to Lu Ya who had served under the Yin.

27 Hence it is only the enlightened ruler and the wise general who will use the highest intelligence of the army for purposes of spying and thereby they achieve great results. Spies are a most important element in warfare, because on them depends an army's ability to move.

TAO TE CHING

1

The tao that can be described
is not the eternal Tao.
The name that can be spoken
is not the eternal Name.

The nameless is the boundary of Heaven and Earth.
The named is the mother of creation.

Freed from desire, you can see the hidden mystery.
By having desire, you can only see what is visibly real.

Yet mystery and reality
emerge from the same source.
This source is called darkness.

Darkness born from darkness.
The beginning of all understanding.

2

When people see things as beautiful,
ugliness is created.
When people see things as good,
evil is created.

Being and non-being produce each other.
Difficult and easy complement each other.
Long and short define each other.
High and low oppose each other.
Fore and aft follow each other.
Therefore the Master
can act without doing anything
and teach without saying a word.
Things come her way and she does not stop them;
things leave and she lets them go.
She has without possessing,
and acts without any expectations.
When her work is done, she takes no credit.
That is why it will last forever.

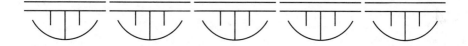

3

If you overesteem talented individuals,
people will become overly competitive.
If you overvalue possessions,
people will begin to steal.

Do not display your treasures
or people will become envious.

The Master leads by
emptying people's minds,
filling their bellies,
weakening their ambitions,
and making them become strong.
Preferring simplicity and freedom from desires,
avoiding the pitfalls of knowledge and wrong action.

For those who practise not-doing,
everything will fall into place.

4

The Tao is like an empty container:
it can never be emptied and can never be filled.
Infinitely deep, it is the source of all things.
It dulls the sharp, unties the knotted, shades the lighted, and
    unites all of creation with dust.
It is hidden but always present.
I don't know who gave birth to it.
It is older than the concept of God.

5

Heaven and Earth are impartial;
they treat all of creation as straw dogs.
The Master doesn't take sides;
she treats everyone like a straw dog.

The space between Heaven and Earth is like a bellows;
it is empty, yet has not lost its power.
The more it is used, the more it produces;
the more you talk of it, the less you comprehend.

It is better not to speak of things you do not understand.

6

The spirit of emptiness is immortal.
It is called the Great Mother
because it gives birth to Heaven and Earth.

It is like a vapour,
barely seen but always present.
Use it effortlessly.

7

The Tao of Heaven is eternal,
and the earth is long enduring.
Why are they long enduring?
They do not live for themselves;
thus they are present for all beings.

The Master puts herself last;
and finds herself in the place of authority.
She detaches herself from all things;
therefore she is united with all things.
She gives no thought to self.
She is perfectly fulfilled.

8

The supreme good is like water,
which benefits all of creation
without trying to compete with it.
It gathers in unpopular places.
Thus it is like the Tao.

The location makes the dwelling good.
Depth of understanding makes the mind good.
A kind heart makes the giving good.
Integrity makes the government good.
Accomplishment makes your labours good.
Proper timing makes a decision good.

Only when there is no competition
will we all live in peace.

9

It is easier to carry an empty cup
than one that is filled to the brim.

The sharper the knife,
the easier it is to dull.
The more wealth you possess,
the harder it is to protect.
Pride brings its own trouble.

When you have accomplished your goal,
simply walk away.
This is the pathway to Heaven.

10

Nurture the darkness of your soul
until you become whole.
Can you do this and not fail?
Can you focus your life-breath until you become
supple as a newborn child?
While you cleanse your inner vision
will you be found without fault?
Can you love people and lead them
without forcing your will on them?
When Heaven gives and takes away,
can you be content with the outcome?
When you understand all things,
can you step back from your own understanding?

Giving birth and nourishing,
making without possessing,
expecting nothing in return.
To grow, yet not to control:
This is the mysterious virtue.

11

Thirty spokes are joined together in a wheel,
but it is the centre hole
that allows the wheel to function.

We mould clay into a pot,
but it is the emptiness inside
that makes the vessel useful.

We fashion wood for a house,
but it is the emptiness inside
that makes it liveable.

We work with the substantial,
but the emptiness is what we use.

12

Five colours blind the eye.
Five notes deafen the ear.
Five flavours make the palate go stale.
Too much activity deranges the mind.
Too much wealth causes crime.
The Master acts on what she feels and not what she sees.
She shuns the latter, and prefers to seek the former.

13

Success is as dangerous as failure,
and we are often our own worst enemy.

What does it mean that success is as dangerous as failure?
He who is superior is also someone's subordinate.
Receiving favour and losing it both cause alarm.
That is what is meant by success is as dangerous as failure.
What does it mean that we are often our own worst enemy?
The reason I have an enemy is because I have 'self'.
If I no longer had a 'self', I would no longer have an enemy.

Love the whole world as if it were your self;
then you will truly care for all things.

14

Look for it, and it can't be seen.
Listen for it, and it can't be heard.
Grasp for it, and it can't be caught.
These three cannot be further described,
so we treat them as The One.

Its highest is not bright.
Its depths are not dark.
Unending, unnameable, it returns to nothingness.
Formless forms, and imageless images,
subtle, beyond all understanding.

Approach it and you will not see a beginning;
follow it and there will be no end.
When we grasp the Tao of the ancient ones,
we can use it to direct our life today.
To know the ancient origin of Tao:
this is the beginning of wisdom.

15

The Sages of old were profound
and knew the ways of subtlety and discernment.
Their wisdom is beyond our comprehension.
Because their knowledge was so far superior
I can only give a poor description.

They were careful
as someone crossing a frozen stream in winter.
Alert as if surrounded on all sides by the enemy.
Courteous as a guest.
Fluid as melting ice.
Whole as an uncarved block of wood.
Receptive as a valley.
Turbid as muddied water.

Who can be still
until their mud settles
and the water is cleared by itself?
Can you remain tranquil until right action occurs by itself?

The Master doesn't seek fulfilment.
For only those who are not full are able to be used,
which brings the feeling of completeness.

16

If you can empty your mind of all thoughts
your heart will embrace the tranquillity of peace.
Watch the workings of all of creation,
but contemplate their return to the source.

All creatures in the universe
return to the point where they began.
Returning to the source is tranquillity
because we submit to Heaven's mandate.

Returning to Heaven's mandate is called being constant.
Knowing the constant is called 'enlightenment'.
Not knowing the constant is the source of evil deeds
because we have no roots.
By knowing the constant we can accept things as they are.
By accepting things as they are, we become impartial.
By being impartial, we become one with Heaven.
By being one with Heaven, we become one with Tao.
Being one with Tao, we are no longer concerned about losing
    our life because we know the Tao is constant and we are
    one with Tao.

17

The best leaders are those the people hardly know exist.
The next best is a leader who is loved and praised.
Next comes the one who is feared.
The worst one is the leader who is despised.

If you don't trust the people,
they will become untrustworthy.

The best leaders value their words, and use them sparingly.
When the Master has accomplished her task,
the people say, 'Amazing:
we did it, all by ourselves!'

18

When the great Tao is abandoned,
charity and righteousness appear.
When intellectualism arises,
hypocrisy is close behind.

When there is strife in the family unit,
people talk about 'brotherly love'.

When the country falls into chaos,
politicians talk about 'patriotism'.

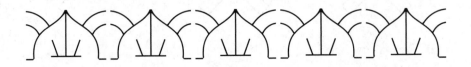

19

Forget about knowledge and wisdom,
and people will be a hundred times better off.
Throw away charity and righteousness,
and people will return to brotherly love.
Throw away profit and greed,
and there won't be any thieves.

These three are superficial and aren't enough
to keep us at the centre of the circle, so we must also:

Embrace simplicity.
Put others first.
Desire little.

20

Renounce knowledge and your problems will end.
What is the difference between yes and no?
What is the difference between good and evil?
Must you fear what others fear?
Nonsense, look how far you have missed the mark!

Other people are joyous,
as though they were at a spring festival.
I alone am unconcerned and expressionless,
like an infant before it has learned to smile.
Other people have more than they need;
I alone seem to possess nothing.
I am lost and drift about with no place to go.
I am like a fool, my mind is in chaos.

Ordinary people are bright;
I alone am dark.
Ordinary people are clever;
I alone am dull.
Ordinary people seem discriminating;
I alone am muddled and confused.
I drift on the waves on the ocean,
blown at the mercy of the wind.
Other people have their goals,
I alone am dull and uncouth.

I am different from ordinary people.
I nurse from the Great Mother's breasts.

21

The greatest virtue you can have
comes from following only the Tao;
which takes a form that is intangible and evasive.

Even though the Tao is intangible and evasive,
we are able to know it exists.
Intangible and evasive, yet it has a manifestation.
Secluded and dark, yet there is a vitality within it.
Its vitality is very genuine.
Within it we can find order.

Since the beginning of time, the Tao has always existed.
It is beyond existing and not existing.
How do I know where creation comes from?
I look inside myself and see it.

22

If you want to become whole,
first let yourself become broken.
If you want to become straight,
first let yourself become twisted.
If you want to become full,
first let yourself become empty.
If you want to become new,
first let yourself become old.
Those whose desires are few get them,
those whose desires are great go astray.

For this reason the Master embraces the Tao,
as an example for the world to follow.
Because she isn't self-centred,
people can see the light in her.
Because she does not boast of herself,
she becomes a shining example.
Because she does not glorify herself,
she becomes a person of merit.
Because she wants nothing from the world,
the world cannot overcome her.
When the ancient Masters said,
'If you want to become whole,
then first let yourself be broken,'
they weren't using empty words.
All who do this will be made complete.

23

Nature uses few words:
when the gale blows, it will not last long;
when it rains hard, it lasts but a little while;
What causes these to happen? Heaven and Earth.

Why do we humans go on endlessly about little
when nature does much in a little time?
If you open yourself to the Tao,
you and Tao become one.
If you open yourself to Virtue,
then you can become virtuous.
If you open yourself to loss,
then you will become lost.

If you open yourself to the Tao,
the Tao will eagerly welcome you.
If you open yourself to virtue,
virtue will become a part of you.
If you open yourself to loss,
the lost are glad to see you.

When you do not trust people,
people will become untrustworthy.

24

Those who stand on tiptoes
do not stand firmly.
Those who rush ahead
don't get very far.
Those who try to outshine others
dim their own light.
Those who call themselves righteous
can't know how wrong they are.
Those who boast of their accomplishments
diminish the things they have done.

Compared to the Tao, these actions are unworthy.
If we are to follow the Tao, we must not do these things.

25

Before the universe was born
there was something in the chaos of the heavens.
It stands alone and empty,
solitary and unchanging.
It is ever present and secure.
It may be regarded as the Mother of the universe.
Because I do not know its name,
I call it the Tao.
If forced to give it a name,
I would call it 'Great'.

Because it is Great means it is everywhere.
Being everywhere means it is eternal.
Being eternal means everything returns to it.

Tao is great.
Heaven is great.
Earth is great.
Humanity is great.
Within the universe, these are the four great things.

Humanity follows the earth.
Earth follows Heaven.
Heaven follows the Tao.
The Tao follows only itself.

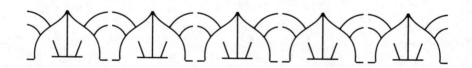

26

Heaviness is the basis of lightness.
Stillness is the standard of activity.

Thus the Master travels all day
without ever leaving her wagon.
Even though she has much to see,
she is at peace in her indifference.

Why should the lord of a thousand chariots
be amused at the foolishness of the world?
If you abandon yourself to foolishness,
you lose touch with your beginnings.
If you let yourself become distracted,
you will lose the basis of your power.

27

A good traveller leaves no tracks,
and a skilful speaker is well rehearsed.
A good bookkeeper has an excellent memory,
and a well-made door is easy to open and needs no locks.
A good knot needs no rope and it can not come undone.

Thus the Master is willing to help everyone,
and doesn't know the meaning of rejection.
She is there to help all of creation,
and doesn't abandon even the smallest creature.
This is called embracing the light.

What is a good person but a bad person's teacher?
What is a bad person but raw material for his teacher?
If you fail to honour your teacher or fail to enjoy your student,
you will become deluded no matter how smart you are.
It is the secret of prime importance.

28

Know the masculine,
but keep to the feminine:
and become a watershed to the world.
If you embrace the world,
the Tao will never leave you
and you become as a little child.

Know the white,
yet keep to the black:
be a model for the world.
If you are a model for the world,
the Tao inside you will strengthen
and you will return whole to your eternal beginning.

Know the honourable,
but do not shun the disgraced:
embracing the world as it is.
If you embrace the world with compassion,
then your virtue will return you to the
Uncarved Block.

The block of wood is carved into utensils
by carving void into the wood.
The Master uses the utensils, yet prefers to keep to the block
because of its limitless possibilities.
Great works do not involve discarding substance.

29

Do you want to rule the world and control it?
I don't think it can ever be done.

The world is a sacred vessel
and it can not be controlled.
You will only make it worse if you try.
It may slip through your fingers and disappear.

Some are meant to lead,
and others are meant to follow;
Some must always strain,
and others have an easy time;
Some are naturally big and strong,
and others will always be small;
Some will be protected and nurtured,
and others will meet with destruction.

The Master accepts things as they are,
and out of compassion avoids extravagance,
excess and the extremes.

30

Those who lead people by following the Tao
don't use weapons to enforce their will.
Using force always leads to unseen troubles.

In the places where armies march,
thorns and briars bloom and grow.
After armies take to war,
bad years must always follow.
The skilful commander
strikes a decisive blow, then stops.
When victory is won over the enemy through war
it is not a thing of great pride.
When the battle is over,
arrogance is the new enemy.
War can result when no other alternative is given,
so the one who overcomes an enemy should not dominate
    them.
The strong are always weakened with time.

This is not the way of the Tao.
That which is not of the Tao will soon end.

31

Weapons are the bearers of bad news;
all people should detest them.

The wise man values the left side,
and in time of war he values the right.
Weapons are meant for destruction,
and thus are avoided by the wise.
Only as a last resort
will a wise person use a deadly weapon.
If peace is her true objective
how can she rejoice in the victory of war?
Those who rejoice in victory
delight in the slaughter of humanity.
Those who resort to violence
will never bring peace to the world.
The left side is a place of honour on happy occasions.
The right side is reserved for mourning at a funeral.
When the lieutenants take the left side to prepare for war,
the general should be on the right side,
because he knows the outcome will be death.
The death of many should be greeted with great sorrow,
and the victory celebration should honour those who have died.

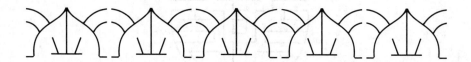

32

The Tao is nameless and unchanging.
Although it appears insignificant,
nothing in the world can contain it.

If a ruler abides by its principles,
then her people will willingly follow.
Heaven would then reign on earth,
like sweet rain falling on paradise.
People would have no need for laws,
because the law would be written on their hearts.

Naming is a necessity for order,
but naming can not order all things.
Naming often makes things impersonal,
so we should know when naming should end.
Knowing when to stop naming,
you can avoid the pitfall it brings.

All things end in the Tao
just as the small streams and the largest rivers
flow through valleys to the sea.

33

Those who know others are intelligent;
those who know themselves are truly wise.
Those who master others are strong;
those who master themselves have true power.

Those who know they have enough are truly wealthy.

Those who persist will reach their goal.

Those who keep their course have a strong will.
Those who embrace death will not perish,
but have life everlasting.

34

The great Tao flows unobstructed in every direction.
All things rely on it to conceive and be born,
and it does not deny even the smallest of creation.
When it has accomplished great wonders,
it does not claim them for itself.
It nourishes infinite worlds,
yet it doesn't seek to master the smallest creature.
Since it is without wants and desires,
it can be considered humble.
All of creation seeks it for refuge
yet it does not seek to master or control.
Because it does not seek greatness,
it is able to accomplish truly great things.

35

She who follows the way of the Tao
will draw the world to her steps.
She can go without fear of being injured,
because she has found peace and tranquillity in her heart.

Where there is music and good food,
people will stop to enjoy it.
But words spoken of the Tao
seem to them boring and stale.
When looked at, there is nothing for them to see.
When listened for, there is nothing for them to hear.
Yet if they put it to use, it would never be exhausted.

36

If you want something to return to the source,
you must first allow it to spread out.
If you want something to weaken,
you must first allow it to become strong.
If you want something to be removed,
you must first allow it to flourish.
If you want to possess something,
you must first give it away.

This is called the subtle understanding
of how things are meant to be.

The soft and pliable overcomes the hard and inflexible.

Just as fish remain hidden in deep waters,
it is best to keep weapons out of sight.

37

The Tao never acts with force,
yet there is nothing that it cannot do.

If rulers could follow the way of the Tao,
then all of creation would willingly follow their example.
If selfish desires were to arise after their transformation,
I would erase them with the power of the Uncarved Block.

By the power of the Uncarved Block,
future generations would lose their selfish desires.
By losing their selfish desires,
the world would naturally settle into peace.

38

The highest good is not to seek to do good,
but to allow yourself to become it.
The ordinary person seeks to do good things,
and finds that they can not do them continually.

The Master does not force virtue on others,
thus she is able to accomplish her task.
The ordinary person who uses force,
will find that they accomplish nothing.

The kind person acts from the heart,
and accomplishes a multitude of things.
The righteous person acts out of pity,
yet leaves many things undone.
The moral person will act out of duty,
and when no one responds
will roll up his sleeves and use force.

When the Tao is forgotten, there is righteousness.
When righteousness is forgotten, there is morality.
When morality is forgotten, there is the law.
The law is the husk of faith,
and trust is the beginning of chaos.

Our basic understandings are not from the Tao
because they come from the depths of our misunderstanding.
The master abides in the fruit and not in the husk.
She dwells in the Tao,
and not with the things that hide it.
This is how she increases in wisdom.

39

The masters of old attained unity with the Tao.
Heaven attained unity and became pure.
The earth attained unity and found peace.
The spirits attained unity so they could minister.
The valleys attained unity that they might be full.
Humanity attained unity that they might flourish.
Their leaders attained unity that they might set the example.
This is the power of unity.

Without unity, the sky becomes filthy.
Without unity, the earth becomes unstable.
Without unity, the spirits become unresponsive and disappear.
Without unity, the valleys become dry as a desert.
Without unity, humankind can't reproduce and becomes extinct.
Without unity, our leaders become corrupt and fall.

The great view the small as their source,
and the high take the low as their foundation.
Their greatest asset becomes their humility.
They speak of themselves as orphans and widows,
thus they truly seek humility.
Do not shine like the precious gem,
but be as dull as a common stone.

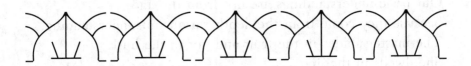

40

All movement returns to the Tao.
Weakness is how the Tao works.

All of creation is born from substance.
Substance is born of nothing-ness.

41

When a superior person hears of the Tao,
she diligently puts it into practice.
When an average person hears of the Tao,
he believes half of it, and doubts the other half.
When a foolish person hears of the Tao,
he laughs out loud at the very idea.
If he didn't laugh,
it wouldn't be the Tao.

Thus it is said:
The brightness of the Tao seems like darkness,
the advancement of the Tao seems like retreat,
the level path seems rough,
the superior path seems empty,
the pure seems to be tarnished,
and true virtue doesn't seem to be enough.
The virtue of caution seems like cowardice,
the pure seems to be polluted,
the true square seems to have no corners,
the best vessels take the most time to finish,
the greatest sounds cannot be heard,
and the greatest image has no form.

The Tao hides in the unnamed,
Yet it alone nourishes and completes all things.

42

The Tao gave birth to One.
The One gave birth to Two.
The Two gave birth to Three.
The Three gave birth to all of creation.

All things carry Yin
yet embrace Yang.
They blend their life breaths
in order to produce harmony.

People despise being orphaned, widowed and poor.
But the noble ones take these as their titles.
In losing, much is gained,
and, in gaining, much is lost.

What others teach I too will teach:
'The strong and violent will not die a natural death.'

43

That which offers no resistance,
overcomes the hardest substances.
That which offers no resistance
can enter where there is no space.

Few in the world can comprehend
the teaching without words,
or understand the value of non-action.

44

Which is more important, your honour or your life?
Which is more valuable, your possessions or your person?
Which is more destructive, success or failure?

Great love extracts a great cost
and true wealth requires greater loss.

Knowing when you have enough avoids dishonour,
and knowing when to stop will keep you from danger
and bring you a long, happy life.

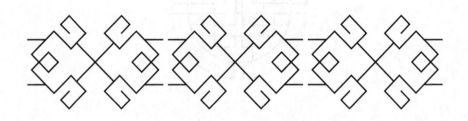

45

The greatest accomplishments seem imperfect,
yet their usefulness is not diminished.
The greatest fullness seems empty,
yet it will be inexhaustible.

The greatest straightness seems crooked.
The most valued skill seems like clumsiness.
The greatest speech seems full of stammers.

Movement overcomes the cold,
and stillness overcomes the heat.
That which is pure and still is the universal ideal.

46

When the world follows the Tao,
horses run free to fertilize the fields.
When the world does not follow the Tao,
war horses are bred outside the cities.

There is no greater transgression
than condoning people's selfish desires,
no greater disaster than being discontent,
and no greater retribution than for greed.

Whoever knows contentment will be at peace forever.

47

Without opening your door,
you can know the whole world.
Without looking out of your window,
you can understand the way of the Tao.

The more knowledge you seek,
the less you will understand.

The Master understands without leaving,
sees clearly without looking,
accomplishes much without doing anything.

48

One who seeks knowledge learns something new every day.
One who seeks the Tao unlearns something new every day.
Less and less remains until you arrive at non-action.
When you arrive at non-action,
nothing will be left undone.

Mastery of the world is achieved
by letting things take their natural course.
You can not master the world by changing the natural way.

49

The Master has no mind of her own.
She understands the mind of the people.

Those who are good she treats as good.
Those who aren't good she also treats as good.
This is how she attains true goodness.

She trusts people who are trustworthy.
She also trusts people who aren't trustworthy.
This is how she gains true trust.

The Master's mind is shut off from the world.
Only for the sake of the people does she muddle her mind.
They look to her in anticipation. Yet she treats them all as her
    children.

50

Those who leave the womb at birth
and those who enter their source at death;
of these, three out of ten celebrate life,
three out of ten celebrate death,
and three out of ten simply go from life to death.
What is the reason for this?
Because they are afraid of dying,
therefore they cannot live.

I have heard that those who celebrate life
walk safely among the wild animals.
When they go into battle, they remain unharmed.
The animals find no place to attack them
and the weapons are unable to harm them.
Why? Because they can find no place for death in them.

51

The Tao gives birth to all of creation.
The virtue of Tao in nature nurtures them,
and their family gives them their form.
Their environment then shapes them into completion.
That is why every creature honours the Tao and its virtue.

No one tells them to honour the Tao and its virtue,
it happens all by itself.
So the Tao gives them birth,
and its virtue cultivates them,
cares for them,
nurtures them,
gives them a place of refuge and peace,
helps them to grow and shelters them.

It gives them life without wanting to possess them,
and cares for them expecting nothing in return.
It is their master, but it does not seek to dominate them.
This is called the dark and mysterious virtue.

52

The world had a beginning
which we call the Great Mother.
Once we have found the Mother,
we begin to know what Her children should be.

When we know we are the Mother's child,
we begin to guard the qualities of the Mother in us.
She will protect us from all danger
even if we lose our life.

Keep your mouth closed
and embrace a simple life,
and you will live carefree until the end of your days.
If you try to talk your way into a better life,
there will be no end to your trouble.

To understand the small is called clarity.
Knowing how to yield is called strength.
To use your inner light for understanding
regardless of the danger
is called depending on the Constant.

53

If I understood only one thing,
I would want to use it to follow the Tao.
My only fear would be one of pride.
The Tao goes in the level places,
but people prefer to take the short cuts.

If too much time is spent cleaning the house
the land will become neglected and full of weeds,
and the granaries will soon become empty
because there is no one out working the fields.
To wear fancy clothes and ornaments,
to have your fill of food and drink
and to waste all of your money buying possessions
is called the crime of excess.
Oh, how these things go against the way of the Tao!

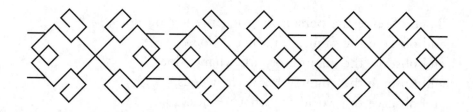

54

That which is well built
will never be torn down.
That which is well latched
can not slip away.
Those who do things well
will be honoured from generation to generation.

If this idea is cultivated in the individual,
then his virtue will become genuine.
If this idea is cultivated in your family,
then virtue in your family will be great.
If this idea is cultivated in your community,
then virtue will go a long way.
If this idea is cultivated in your country,
then virtue will be in many places.
If this idea is cultivated in the world,
then virtue will be with everyone.

Then observe the person for what the person does,
and observe the family for what it does,
and observe the community for what it does,
and observe the country for what it does,
and observe the world for what it does.
How do I know this saying is true?
I observe these things and see.

55

One who is filled with the Tao
is like a newborn child.
The infant is protected from
the stinging insects, wild beasts and birds of prey.
Its bones are soft, its muscles are weak,
but its grip is firm and strong.
It doesn't know about the union
of male and female,
yet his penis can stand erect
because of the power of life within him.
It can cry all day and never become hoarse.
This is perfect harmony.

To understand harmony is to understand the Constant.
To know the Constant is to be called 'enlightened'.
To unnaturally try to extend life is not appropriate.
To try and alter the life-breath is unnatural.
The master understands that when something reaches its prime
it will soon begin to decline.
Changing the natural is against the way of the Tao.
Those who do it will come to an early end.

56

Those who know do not talk.
Those who talk do not know.

Stop talking,
meditate in silence,
blunt your sharpness,
release your worries,
harmonize your inner light,
and become one with the dust.
Doing this is called the dark and mysterious identity.

Those who have achieved the mysterious identity
can not be approached, and they can not be alienated.
They can not be benefited nor harmed.
They can not be made noble nor to suffer disgrace.
This makes them the most noble of all under the heavens.

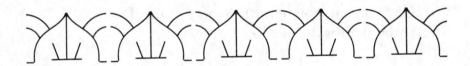

57

Govern your country with integrity,
weapons of war can be used with great cunning,
but loyalty is only won by not-doing.
How do I know the way things are?
By these:

The more prohibitions you make,
the poorer people will be.
The more weapons you possess,
the greater the chaos in your country.
The more knowledge that is acquired,
the stranger the world will become.
The more laws that you make,
the greater the number of criminals.

Therefore the Master says:
I do nothing,
and people become good by themselves.
I seek peace,
and people take care of their own problems.
I do not meddle in their personal lives,
and the people become prosperous.
I let go of all my desires,
and the people return to the Uncarved Block.

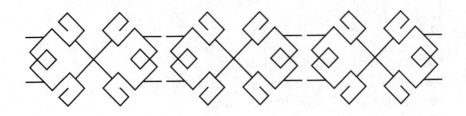

58

If a government is unobtrusive,
the people become whole.
If a government is repressive,
the people become treacherous.

Good fortune has its roots in disaster,
and disaster lurks with good fortune.
Who knows why these things happen,
or when this cycle will end?
Good things seem to change into bad,
and bad things often turn out for good.
These things have always been hard to comprehend.

Thus the Master makes things change
without interfering.
She is probing yet causes no harm.
Straightforward, yet does not impose her will.
Radiant, and easy on the eye.

59

There is nothing better than moderation
for teaching people or serving Heaven.
Those who use moderation
are already on the path to the Tao.

Those who follow the Tao early
will have an abundance of virtue.
When there is an abundance of virtue,
there is nothing that cannot be done.
Where there is limitless ability,
then the kingdom is within your grasp.
When you know the Mother of the kingdom,
then you will be long enduring.

This is spoken of as the deep root and the firm trunk,
the Way to a long life and great spiritual vision.

60

Governing a large country
is like frying small fish.
Too much poking spoils the meat.

When the Tao is used to govern the world
then evil will lose its power to harm the people.
Not that evil will no longer exist,
but only because it has lost its power.
Just as evil can lose its ability to harm,
the Master shuns the use of violence.

If you give evil nothing to oppose,
then virtue will return by itself.

61

A large country should take the low place like a great
    watershed,
which from its low position assumes the female role.
The female overcomes the male by the power of her position.
Her tranquillity gives rise to her humility.

If a large country takes the low position,
it will be able to influence smaller countries.
If smaller countries take the lower position,
then they can allow themselves to be influenced.
So both seek to take the lower position
in order to influence the other, or be influenced.

Large countries should desire to protect and help the people,
and small countries should desire to serve others.
Both large and small countries benefit greatly from humility.

62

The Tao is the tabernacle of creation,
it is a treasure for those who are good,
and a place of refuge for those who are not.

How can those who are not good be abandoned?
Words that are beautiful are worth much,
but good behaviour can only be learned by example.

When a new leader takes office,
don't give him gifts and offerings.
These things are not as valuable
as teaching him about the Tao.

Why was the Tao esteemed by the ancient Masters?
Is it not said: 'With it we find without looking.
With it we find forgiveness for our transgressions'?
That is why the world cannot understand it.

63

Act by not acting;
do by not doing.
Enjoy the plain and simple.
Find that greatness in the small.
Take care of difficult problems
while they are still easy;
Do easy things before they become too hard.

Difficult problems are best solved while they are easy.
Great projects are best started while they are small.
The Master never takes on more than she can handle,
which means that she leaves nothing undone.

When an affirmation is given too lightly,
keep your eyes open for trouble ahead.
When something seems too easy,
difficulty is hiding in the details.
The Master expects great difficulty,
so the task is always easier than planned.

64

Things are easier to control while they are quiet.
Things are easier to plan far in advance.
Things break easier while they are still brittle.
Things are easier hid while they are still small.

Prevent problems before they arise.
Take action before things get out of hand.
The tallest tree
begins as a tiny sprout.
The tallest building
starts with one shovel of dirt.
A journey of a thousand miles
starts with a single footstep.

If you rush into action, you will fail.
If you hold on too tight, you will lose your grip.

Therefore the Master lets things take their course
and thus never fails.
She doesn't hold on to things
and never loses them.
By pursuing your goals too relentlessly,
you let them slip away.

If you are as concerned about the outcome
as you are about the beginning,
then it is hard to do things wrong.
The Master seeks no possessions.
She learns by unlearning,
thus she is able to understand all things.
This gives her the ability to help all of creation.

65

The ancient Masters
who understood the way of the Tao,
did not educate people, but made them forget.

Smart people are difficult to guide,
because they think they are too clever.
To use cleverness to rule a country,
is to lead the country to ruin.
To avoid cleverness in ruling a country,
is to lead the country to prosperity.

Knowing the two alternatives is a pattern.
Remaining aware of the pattern is a virtue.
This dark and mysterious virtue is profound.
It is opposite our natural inclination,
but leads to harmony with the heavens.

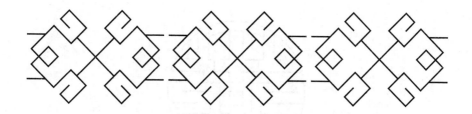

66

Rivers and seas are rulers
of the streams of hundreds of valleys
because of the power of their low position.

If you want to be the ruler of people,
you must speak to them like you are their servant.
If you want to lead other people,
you must put their interests ahead of your own.

The people will not feel burdened,
if a wise person is in a position of power.
The people will not feel like they are being manipulated,
if a wise person is in front as their leader.
The whole world will ask for her guidance,
and will never get tired of her.
Because she does not like to compete,
no one can compete with the things she accomplishes.

67

The world talks about honouring the Tao,
but you can't tell it from their actions.
Because it is thought of as great,
the world makes light of it.
It seems too easy for anyone to use.

There are three jewels that I cherish:
compassion, moderation, and humility.
With compassion, you will be able to be brave,
With moderation, you will be able to give to others,
With humility, you will be able to become a great leader.
To abandon compassion while seeking to be brave,
or abandoning moderation while being benevolent,
or abandoning humility while seeking to lead
will only lead to greater trouble.
The compassionate warrior will be the winner,
and if compassion is your defence you will be secure.
Compassion is the protector of Heaven's salvation.

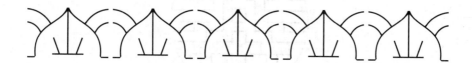

68

The best warriors
do not use violence.
The best generals
do not destroy indiscriminately.
The best tacticians
try to avoid confrontation.
The best leaders
become servants of their people.

This is called the virtue of non-competition.
This is called the power to manage others.
This is called attaining harmony with the heavens.

69

There is an old saying:
'It is better to become passive
in order to see what will happen.
It is better to retreat a foot
than to advance only an inch.'

This is called
being flexible while advancing,
pushing back without using force,
and destroying the enemy without engaging him.

There is no greater disaster
than underestimating your enemy.
Underestimating your enemy
means losing your greatest assets.
When equal forces meet in battle,
victory will go to the one
that enters with the greatest sorrow.

70

My words are easy to understand
and easier to put into practice.
Yet no one in the world seems to understand them,
nor are they able to apply what I teach.

My teachings come from the ancients,
the things I do are done for a reason.

Because you do not know me,
you are not able to understand my teachings.
Because those who know me are few,
my teachings become even more precious.

71

Knowing you don't know is wholeness.
Thinking you know is a disease.
Only by recognizing that you have an illness
can you move to seek a cure.

The Master is whole because
she sees her illnesses and treats them,
and thus is able to remain whole.

72

When people become overly bold,
then disaster will soon arrive.

Do not meddle with people's livelihood;
by respecting them they will in turn respect you.

Therefore, the Master knows herself but is not arrogant.
She loves herself but also loves others.
This is how she is able to make appropriate choices.

73

Being overbold and confident is deadly.
The wise use of caution will keep you alive.

One is the way to death,
and the other is the way to preserve your life.
Who can understand the workings of Heaven?

The Tao of the universe
does not compete, yet wins;
does not speak, yet responds;
does not command, yet is obeyed;
and does not act, but is good at directing.

The nets of Heaven are wide,
but nothing escapes its grasp.

74

If you do not fear death,
then how can it intimidate you?
If you aren't afraid of dying,
there is nothing you cannot do.

Those who harm others
are like inexperienced boys
trying to take the place
of a great lumberjack.
Trying to fill his shoes
will only get them seriously hurt.

75

When people go hungry,
the government's taxes are too high.
When people become rebellious,
the government has become too intrusive.

When people begin to view death lightly,
wealthy people have too much,
which causes others to starve.

Only those who do not cling to their life can save it.

76

The living are soft and yielding;
the dead are rigid and stiff.
Living plants are flexible and tender;
the dead are brittle and dry.

Those who are stiff and rigid
are the disciples of death.
Those who are soft and yielding
are the disciples of life.

The rigid and stiff will be broken.
The soft and yielding will overcome.

77

The Tao of Heaven works in the world
like the drawing of a bow.
The top is bent downward;
the bottom is bent up.
The excess is taken from,
and the deficient is given to.

The Tao works to use the excess,
and gives to that which is depleted.
The way of people is to take from the depleted,
and give to those who already have an excess.

Who is able to give to the needy from their excess?
Only someone who is following the way of the Tao.

This is why the Master gives,
expecting nothing in return.
She does not dwell on her past accomplishments,
and does not glory in any praise.

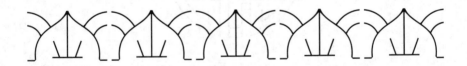

78

Water is the softest and most yielding substance.
Yet nothing is better than water,
for overcoming the hard and rigid,
because nothing can compete with it.

Everyone knows that the soft and yielding
overcomes the rigid and hard,
but few can put this knowledge into practice.

Therefore the Master says:
'Only he who is the lowest servant of the kingdom,
is worthy of becoming its ruler.
He who is willing to tackle the most unpleasant tasks,
is the best ruler in the world.'

True sayings seem contradictory.

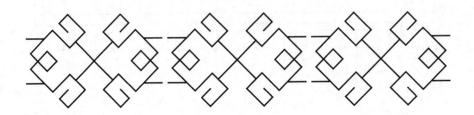

79

Difficulties remain, even after solving a problem.
How, then, can we consider that as good?

Therefore the Master
does what she knows is right,
and makes no demands of others.
A virtuous person will do the right thing,
and persons with no virtue will take advantage of others.

The Tao does not choose sides,
the good person receives from the Tao
because she is on its side.

80

Small countries with few people are best.
Give them all of the things they want,
and they will see that they do not need them.
Teach them that death is a serious thing,
and to be content to never leave their homes.
Even though they have plenty
of horses, wagons and boats,
they won't feel that they need to use them.
Even if they have weapons and shields,
they will keep them out of sight.
Let people enjoy the simple technologies,
let them enjoy their food,
let them make their own clothes,
let them be content with their own homes,
and delight in the customs that they cherish.
Although the next country is close enough
that they can hear their roosters crowing and dogs barking,
they are content never to visit each other
all of the days of their life.

81

True words do not sound beautiful;
beautiful sounding words are not true.
Wise men don't need to debate;
men who need to debate are not wise.

Wise men are not scholars,
and scholars are not wise.
The Master desires no possessions.
Since the things she does are for the people,
she has more than she needs.
The more she gives to others,
the more she has for herself.

The Tao of Heaven nourishes by not forcing.
The Tao of the Wise Person acts by not competing.

THE
ANALECTS

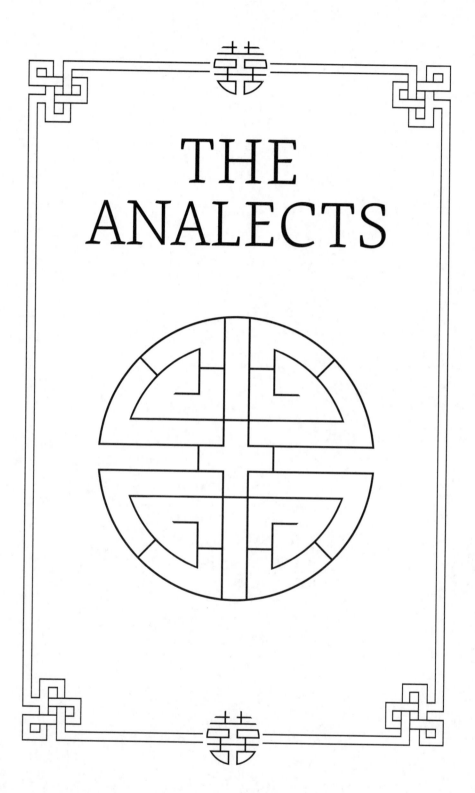

CONTENTS

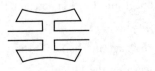

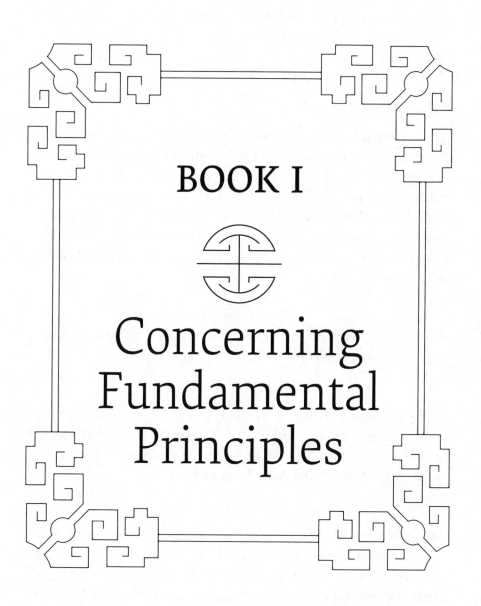

BOOK I

Concerning Fundamental Principles

The Master said: 'Is it not indeed a pleasure to acquire knowledge and constantly to exercise oneself therein? And is it not delightful to have men of kindred spirit come to one from afar? But is not he a true philosopher who, though he be unrecognized of men, cherishes no resentment?'

The philosopher Yu[1] said: 'He who lives a filial life, respecting the elders, who yet is wishful to give offence to those above him, is rare; and there has never been any one unwishful to offend those above him, who has yet been fond of creating disorder. The true philosopher devotes himself to the fundamentals, for when those have been established right courses naturally evolve; and are not filial devotion and respect for elders the very foundations of an unselfish life?'

The Master said: 'Artful speech and an ingratiating demeanour rarely accompany virtue.'

The philosopher Tseng[1] said: 'I daily examine myself on three points – In planning for others have I failed in conscientiousness? In intercourse with friends have I been insincere? And have I failed to practise what I have been taught?'

The Master said: 'To conduct the government of a State of a thousand chariots there must be religious attention to business and good faith, economy in expenditure and love of the people, and their employment on public works at the proper seasons.'

The Master said: 'When a youth is at home let him be filial, when abroad respectful to his elders; let him be circumspect and truthful and, while exhibiting a comprehensive love for all men, let him ally himself with the good. Having so acted, if he have energy to spare, let him employ it in polite studies.'

Tzu Hsia[1] said: 'He who transfers his mind from feminine allurement to excelling in moral excellence; who in serving his parents is ready to do so to the utmost of his ability; who in the service of his prince is prepared to lay down his life; and who in intercourse with his friends is sincere in what he says – though others may speak of him as uneducated, I should certainly call him educated.'

The Master said: 'A scholar who is not grave will not inspire respect, and his learning will therefore lack stability. His chief principles should be conscientiousness and sincerity. Let him have no friends unequal to himself. And when in the wrong let him not hesitate to amend.'

The philosopher Tseng said: 'Solicitude on the decease of parents, and the pursuit of this for long after, would cause an abundant restoration of the people's morals.'

Tzu Ch'in[1] inquired of Tzu Kung[1] saying: 'When the Master arrives at any State he always hears about its administration. Does he ask for this information, or, is it tendered to him?' 'The Master,' said Tzu Kung, 'is benign, frank, courteous, temperate, deferential and thus obtains it. The Master's way of asking – how different it is from that of others!'

The philosopher Yu said: 'In the usages of decorum it is naturalness that is of value. In the regulations of the ancient kings this was the admirable feature, both small and great deriving therefrom. But there is a naturalness that is not permissible; for to know to be natural, and yet to be so beyond the restraints of decorum is also not permissible.'

The philosopher Yu said: 'When you make a promise consistent with what is right, you can keep your word. When you show respect consistent with good taste, you keep shame and disgrace at a distance. When he in whom you confide is one who does not fail his friends, you may trust him fully.'

The Master said: 'The scholar who in his food does not seek the gratification of his appetite, nor in his dwelling is solicitous of comfort, who is diligent in his work, and guarded in his speech, who associates with the high-principled, and thereby directs himself aright – such a one may really be said to love learning.'

'What do you think,' asked Tzu Kung, 'of the man who is poor yet not servile, or who is rich yet not proud?'
'He will do,' replied the Master, 'but he is not equal to the

man who is poor and yet happy, or rich and yet loves courtesy.'
Tzu Kung remarked:

> 'The Ode says this is
> Like cutting, then filing;
> Like chiselling, then grinding.
> That is the meaning of your remark, is it not?'

'Tz'u!' said the Master. 'Now indeed I can begin to talk with him
about the Odes, for when I tell him the premise he knows the
conclusion.'

The Master said: 'I will not grieve that men do not know me; I
will grieve that I do not know men.'

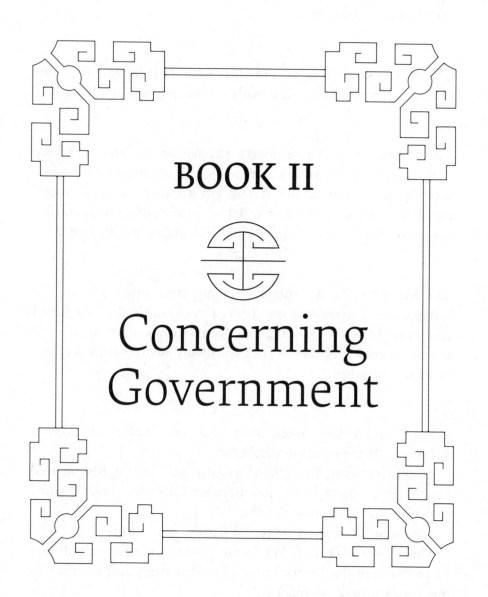

BOOK II

Concerning Government

The Master said: 'He who governs by his moral excellence may be compared to the pole-star, which abides in its place, while all the stars bow towards it.'

The Master said: 'Though the Odes number three hundred, one phrase can cover them all, namely, "With purpose undiverted".'[2]

The Master said: 'If you govern the people by laws, and keep them in order by penalties, they will avoid the penalties, yet lose their sense of shame. But if you govern them by your moral excellence, and keep them in order by your dutiful conduct, they will retain their sense of shame, and also live up to this standard.'

The Master said: 'At fifteen I set my mind upon wisdom. At thirty I stood firm. At forty I was free from doubts. At fifty I understood the laws of Heaven. At sixty my ear was docile. At seventy I could follow the desires of my heart without transgressing the right.'

When Meng I Tzu[3] asked what filial duty meant, the Master answered: 'It is not being disobedient.'

Afterwards when Fan Ch'ih[4] was driving him the Master told him, saying: 'Meng Sun asked me what filial piety meant, and I replied: "Not being disobedient."'

Fan Ch'ih thereupon asked, 'What did you mean?'

The Master answered: 'While parents live serve them rightfully; when they are dead bury them with filial rites, and sacrifice to them with proper ordinances.'

When Meng Wu Po[3] asked what filial duty meant the Master answered: 'Parents should only have anxiety when their children are ill.'

When Tzu Yu[4] asked the meaning of filial piety the Master said: 'The filial piety of the present day merely means to feed one's parents; but even one's dogs and horses receive their food; without reverence wherein lies the difference?'

The Master said: 'I could talk to Hui[4] for a whole day and, as if he were stupid, he never raised an objection; but when he withdrew and I examined into his conduct when not with me, I nevertheless found him fully competent to demonstrate what I had taught him. Hui! he was not stupid.'

The Master said: 'Observe what he does; look into his motives; find out in what he is at peace. Can a man hide himself? Can a man hide himself?'

The Master said: 'He who keeps on reviewing his old and acquiring new knowledge may become a teacher of others.'

The Master said: 'The higher type of man is not a machine.'

On Tzu Kung asking about the nobler type of man the Master said: 'He first practises what he preaches and afterwards preaches according to his practice.'

The Master said: 'The nobler type of man is broad-minded and not prejudiced. The inferior man is prejudiced and not broad-minded.'

The Master said: 'Learning without thinking is useless. Thinking without learning is dangerous.'

The Master said: 'To devote oneself to irregular speculations is decidedly harmful.'

The Master said: 'Yu! Shall I teach you the meaning of knowledge? When you know a thing to recognize that you know it; and when you do not, to know that you do not know – that is knowledge.'

Tzu Chang[4] was studying with a view to preferment. The Master said to him: 'Hear much, be reserved in what causes you doubt, and speak guardedly of the rest; you will then suffer little criticism. See much, be reserved in what seems imprudent, and act guardedly as to the rest; you will then have few regrets. With little for criticism in your speech, and little to regret in your conduct – herein you will find preferment.'

Duke Ai[5] inquired saying: 'What should I do to insure the contentment of the people?' 'If you promote the upright and dismiss the
ill-doer,' replied Confucius, 'the people will be contented; but if
you promote the ill-doer and dismiss the upright, the people will
be discontented.'

When Chi K'ang Tzu[6] asked how to inspire the people with
respect and loyalty, so that they might be mutually emulous (for
the welfare of the state), the Master said: 'Lead them with dignity
and they will also be dutiful; be filial and kind and they will be
loyal; promote those who excel and teach the incompetent, and
they will encourage each other.'

The Master said: 'A man who is without good faith – I do not
know how he is to manage! How can a waggon without its yoke-bar
for the ox, or a carriage without its collar-bar for the horses, be
made to move?'

The Master said: 'To sacrifice to a spirit of an ancestor not one's
own is sycophancy. To see the right and not do it is cowardice.'

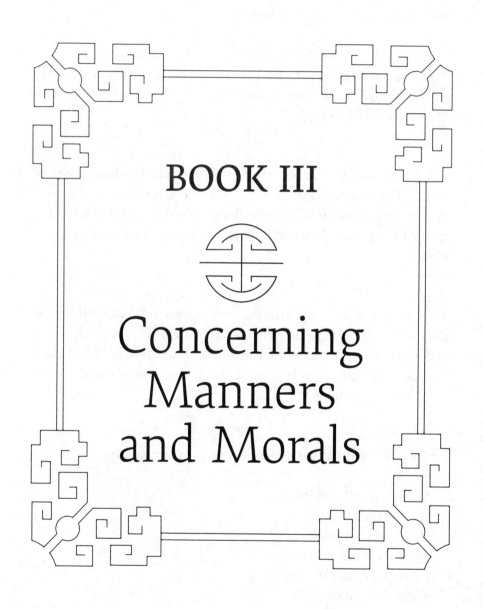

BOOK III

Concerning
Manners
and Morals

Confucius said of the head of the House of Chi, who had eight rows of dancers performing in his Temple: 'If he can bear to do this, what can he not bear to do?'[7]

The Master said: 'A man who is not virtuous, what has he to do with worship? A man who is not virtuous, what has he to do with the music of the temple?'

Lin Fang[8] asked what was the chief principle in observances of ritual. The Master answered: 'A great question indeed! In ceremonies in general, it is better to be simple than lavish: and in the rites of mourning, heart-felt distress is better than observance of detail.'

The Master said: 'A gentleman never contends in anything he does – except perhaps in archery. Even then, he bows to his rival and yields him the way as they ascend the pavilion; in like manner he descends and offers him the penalty cup – in his contentions he is still a gentleman.'

Tzu Hsia asked: 'What is the meaning of the passage –

"As she artfully smiles
What dimples appear!
Her bewitching eyes
Show their colours so clear.
Ground spotless and candid
For tracery splendid!"?'

'The painting comes after the ground-work,' answered the Master. 'Then manners are secondary?' said Tzu Hsia.

"'Tis Shang [Tzu Hsia] who unfolds my meaning,' replied the Master. 'Now indeed, I can begin to discuss the poets with him.'

He sacrificed to his forefathers as if they were present; he sacrificed to the gods as if the gods were present. The Master said: 'For me not to be present at a sacrifice is as if I did not sacrifice.'

The Master said: 'Chou had the advantage of surveying the two preceding dynasties. How full was its culture! I follow Chou dynasty ideas.'⁹

When the Master first entered the Grand Temple he asked about everything, whereupon some one remarked: 'Who says the son of the man of Tsou knows the correct forms? On entering the Grand Temple he asks about everything.' The Master hearing of it remarked: 'This too is correct form.'

The Master said: 'In archery piercing the target is not the essential, for men are not of equal strength. Such was the rule of yore.'

Tzu Kung wished to dispense with the live sheep presented in the Ducal Temple at the announcement of the new moon. The Master said: 'T'zu! You care for the sheep. I care for the ritual.'

The Master said: 'If one were to serve one's prince with perfect homage, people today would deem it sycophancy.'

When Duke Ting[10] asked how a prince should employ his ministers, and how ministers should serve their prince, Confucius replied saying: 'A prince should employ his ministers with courtesy. A minister should serve his prince with loyalty.'

When Duke Ai asked Tsai Wo[11] concerning the altars to the tutelary deities of the land, Tsai Wo responded: 'The sovereign of Hsia adopted the pine, the men of Yin the cypress, but the men of Chou the chestnut, intimating that the people should stand in dread.'

On the Master hearing of this he said: 'When a deed is done it is useless to discuss it, when a thing has taken its course it is useless to remonstrate, what is past and gone it is useless to blame.'

The Master spoke of the Shao music as perfectly beautiful in form and perfectly good in its influence. He spoke of the Wu music as perfectly beautiful in form but not perfectly good in its influence.[12]

The Master said: 'High station filled without magnanimity, religious observances performed without reverence, and "mourning" conducted without grief – from what standpoint shall I view such ways?'

BOOK IV

Concerning Virtue

The Master said: 'It is the moral character of a neighbourhood that constitutes its excellence, and how can he be considered wise who does not elect to dwell in moral surroundings?'

The Master said: 'A man without virtue cannot long abide in adversity, nor can he long abide in happiness; but the virtuous man is at rest in virtue, and the wise man covets it.'

The Master said: 'Only the virtuous are competent to love or to hate men.'

The Master said: 'He who has really set his mind on virtue will do no evil.'

The Master said: 'Wealth and rank are what men desire, but unless they be obtained in the right way they may not be possessed. Poverty and obscurity are what men detest; but unless prosperity be brought about in the right way, they are not to be abandoned. If a man of honour forsakes virtue how is he to fulfil the obligations of his name? A man of honour never disregards virtue, even for the space of a single meal. In moments of haste he cleaves to it; in seasons of peril he cleaves to it.'

The Master said: 'I have never seen one who loved virtue, nor one who hated what was not virtuous. He who loved virtue would esteem nothing above it; and he who hated what is not virtuous would himself be so virtuous that he would allow nothing evil to adhere to him. Is there any one able for a single day to devote his strength to virtue? I have never seen such a one whose ability would be sufficient. If perchance there be such I have never seen him.'

The Master said: 'A man's faults all conform to his type of mind. Observe his faults and you may know his virtues.'

The Master said: 'He who heard the truth in the morning might die content in the evening.'

The Master said: 'The student who aims at wisdom, and yet who is ashamed of shabby clothes and poor food, is not yet worthy to be discoursed with.'

The Master said: 'The wise man in his attitude towards the world has neither predilections nor prejudices. He is on the side of what is right.'

The Master said: 'The man of honour thinks of his character, the inferior man of his position. The man of honour desires justice, the inferior man favour.'

The Master said: 'He who works for his own interests will arouse much animosity.'

The Master said: 'Is a prince able to rule his country with courtesy and deference – then what difficulty will he have? And if he cannot rule his country with courtesy and deference, what use are the forms of courtesy to him?'

The Master said: 'One should not be concerned at lack of position, but should be concerned about what will fit him to occupy it. One should not be concerned at being unknown, but should seek to be worthy of being known.'

The Master said: 'Shen! My teaching contains one all-pervading principle.' 'Yes,' replied Tseng Tzu. When the Master had left the room the disciples asked, 'What did he mean?' Tseng Tzu replied, 'Our Master's teaching is simply this: Conscientiousness within and consideration for others.'

The Master said: 'The wise man is informed in what is right. The inferior man is informed in what will pay.'

The Master said: 'When you see a man of worth, think how to rise to his level. When you see an unworthy man, then look within and examine yourself.'

The Master said: 'In his duty to his parents a son may gently remonstrate with them. If he sees that they are not inclined to yield, he should be increasingly respectful but not desist, and though they deal hardly with him he must not complain.'

The Master said: 'The age of one's parents should ever be kept in mind, as an occasion at once for joy and for fear.'

The Master said: 'The men of old were reserved in speech out of shame lest they should come short in deed.'

The Master said: 'The self-restrained seldom err.'

The Master said: 'The wise man desires to be slow to speak but quick to act.'

The Master said: 'Virtue never dwells alone; it always has neighbours.'

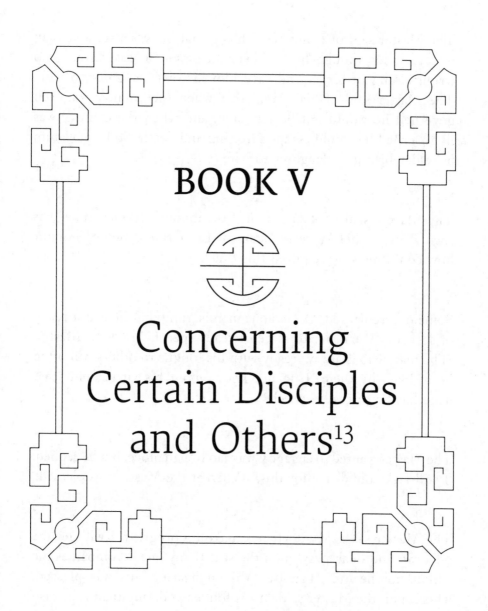

BOOK V

Concerning Certain Disciples and Others[13]

The Master said of Kung Yeh Ch'ang that he was a suitable man to marry, for though he had been in prison it was through no wrong-doing of his. So he gave him his own daughter to wife. The Master said of Nan Yung that when the country was well governed he would not be set aside, and when the country was ill governed he would escape suffering and death. So he gave him his elder brother's daughter to wife.

The Master said of Tzu Chien: 'An honourable man indeed is such a one as he! Were the state of Lu without men of honour how could he have acquired this excellence?'

Some one remarked: 'A virtuous man is Yung, but he is not ready of speech.' 'What need has he of ready speech?' said the Master. 'The man who is always ready with his tongue to others will often be disliked by them. I do not know about his virtue, but what need has he of ready speech?'

The Master wanted to engage Ch'i-tiao K'ai in office, but he replied: 'I still lack confidence for this.' Whereat the Master was pleased.

The Master said: 'My doctrines make no progress. I will get me on a raft and float away upon the sea! If any one accompanies me will it not be Yu?' Tzu Lu [Yu] on hearing this was pleased; whereupon the Master said: 'Yu is fonder of daring than I; he also exercises no discretion.'

The Master addressing Tzu Kung said: 'Which is the superior, you or Hui?' 'How dare I look at Hui?' he answered; 'Hui hears one point and from it apprehends the whole ten. I hear one point and apprehend a second therefrom.' The Master said: 'You are not equal to him, I grant you, you are not equal to him.'

Tsai Yü spending the daytime in sleep, the Master said: 'Rotten wood is unfit for carving, and a wall of dirt unfit for plastering. As to Yü – what is the use of reproving him!' 'Formerly,' he continued, 'my attitude towards others was to hear what they said and give them credit for their deeds. Now my attitude towards others is to listen to what they say and note what they do. It is through Yü that I have made this change.'

The Master said: 'I have never seen a man of strong character.'
  Some one remarked, 'There is Shen Ch'eng.'
  'Ch'eng!' said the Master. 'He is under the influence of his passions, and how can he be possessed of strength of character?'

Tzu Kung said: 'What I do not wish others to do to me, that also I wish not to do to them.'
  'Tzu!' observed the Master, 'that is a point to which you have not attained.'

Tzu Kung said: 'Our Master's culture and refinement all may hear; but our Master's discourse on the nature of man and the laws of heaven it is not given to all to hear.'

When Tzu Lu heard any precept and had not yet been able to put it into practice, he was only afraid lest he should hear some other.

Tzu Kung asked: 'On what ground has K'ung Tzu[14] received his posthumous title of Wen?'

'He was clever and fond of learning,' replied the Master, 'and he was not ashamed to seek knowledge from his inferiors – that is why he has been styled "Cultured".'

The Master remarked of Tzu Ch'an[15] that he had four of the Ideal Man's characteristics – in his personal conduct he was serious, in his duty to his superior he was deferential, in providing for the people he was beneficent, and in directing them he was just.

The Master said: 'Yen P'ing Chung was gifted in the art of friendship. Whatever the lapse of time, he maintained towards his friends the same consideration.'

The Master said: 'Tsang Wen Chung kept a large tortoise in an edifice, on whose pillar-tops were representations of hills, and on its king-posts of water plants – of what sort was his wisdom?'

Chi Wen Tzu used to think thrice before acting. The Master hearing of it said: 'Twice would do.'

The Master said: 'While good order prevailed in his state, Ning Wu Tzu was a wise man. When the state fell into disorder, he was a fool. His wisdom may be equalled, his folly cannot be equalled.'

Once when Yen Yüan and Tzu Lu were standing by him the Master said: 'Suppose each of you tells his wishes?'
'I should like,' said Tzu Lu, 'to have carriages and horses and light furs to wear, so as to share them with my friends, nor would I feel any annoyance if they spoilt them.' 'I should like,' said Yen Yüan, 'never to make a display of my good qualities, nor a parade of my merits.' 'May we hear the Master's wishes?' asked Tzu Lu. 'They would be,' said the Master, 'to comfort the aged, be faithful to my friends, and cherish the young.'

The Master said: 'It is all in vain! I have never yet seen a man who could perceive his own faults and bring the charge home against himself.'

The Master said: 'Even in a hamlet of ten houses there must be men as conscientious and sincere as myself, but none as fond of learning as I am.'

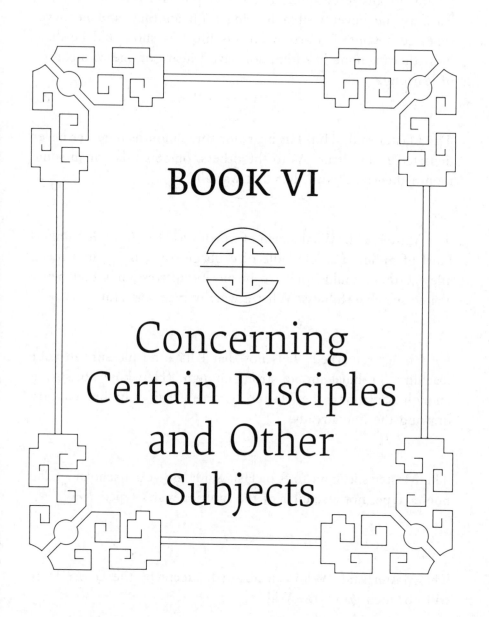

BOOK VI

Concerning Certain Disciples and Other Subjects

Duke Ai asked which of the disciples was fond of learning. Confucius answered him: 'There was Yen Hui – he was fond of learning; he never visited his anger on another, and he never repeated a fault. Unfortunately his life was short and he died. Now there is none like him, nor have I heard of one who is fond of learning.'

The Master said, 'Hui! His heart for three months together never departed from virtue. As to the others, on some day or in some month they reached it, but that was all.'

The Master said: 'What a man of worth was Hui! A single bamboo bowl of millet; a single ladle of cabbage soup; living in a mean alley! Others could not have borne his distress, but Hui never abated his cheerfulness. What a worthy man was Hui!'

Jan Ch'iu[16] remarked: 'It is not that I have no pleasure in your teaching, Sir, but I am not strong enough.' 'He who is not strong enough,' answered the Master, 'gives up half way, but you are drawing the line already.'

The Master speaking to Tzu Hsia said: 'Be you a scholar of the nobler type, not a scholar of the inferior man's type.'

The Master said: 'Who can go forth except by the Door? Why will not men go by the Way?'

The Master said: 'When nature exceeds training, you have the rustic. When training exceeds nature, you have the clerk. It is only when nature and training are proportionately blended that you have the higher type of man.'

The Master said: 'Man is born for uprightness. Without it he is lucky to escape with his life!'

The Master said: 'He who knows the truth is not equal to him who loves it, and he who loves it is not equal to him who delights in it.'

The Master said: 'To men above the average one may discourse on higher things; but to those who are below the average one may not discourse on higher things.'

When Fan Ch'ih asked what constituted wisdom the Master replied: 'To devote oneself earnestly to one's duty to humanity and, while respecting the spirits of the departed, to avoid them, may be called wisdom.'

On his asking about virtue, the Master replied: 'The man of virtue puts duty first, however difficult, and makes what he will gain thereby an after consideration – and this may be called virtue.'

The Master said: 'The clever delight in water, the virtuous in the hills; the clever are restless, the virtuous calm; the clever enjoy life, the virtuous prolong life.'

Tsai Wo asked, saying: 'An altruist, even if some one said to him, "There is a man in the well," would, I suppose, go in after him?'

'Why should he act like that?' answered the Master. 'The higher type of man might hasten to the well, but not precipitate himself into it; he might be imposed upon, but not utterly hoodwinked.'

Tzu Kung said: 'Suppose there was one who conferred benefits far and wide upon the people, and who was able to succour the multitude, what might one say of him? Could he be called a philanthropist?'

'What has he to do with philanthropy?' said the Master. 'Must he not be a sage? Even Yao and Shun[17] felt their deficiency herein. For the philanthropist is one who desiring to maintain himself sustains others, and desiring to develop himself develops others. To be able from one's own self to draw a parallel for the treatment of others – that may be called the rule of philanthropy.'

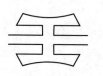

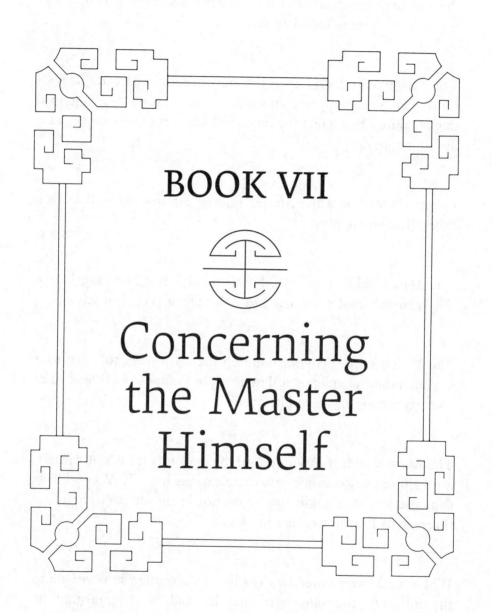

BOOK VII

Concerning
the Master
Himself

The Master said: 'The meditative treasuring up of knowledge, the unwearying pursuit of wisdom, the tireless instruction of others – which of these is found in me?'

The Master said: 'Neglect in the cultivation of character, lack of thoroughness in study, incompetency to move towards recognized duty, inability to correct my imperfections – these are what cause me solicitude.'

In his leisure hours the Master relaxed his manner and wore a cheerful countenance.

The Master said: 'How utterly fallen off I am! For long I have not dreamed as of yore that I saw the Duke [Wen] of Chou.'

The Master said: 'Fix your mind on the right way; hold fast to it in your moral character; follow it up in kindness to others; take your recreation in the polite arts.'

The Master said: 'I expound nothing to him who is not earnest, nor help out any one not anxious to express himself. When I have demonstrated one angle and he cannot bring me back the other three, then I do not repeat my lesson.'

When the Master dined by the side of a mourner he never ate to the full. On the same day that he had been mourning he never sang.

The Master addressing Yen Yüan said: 'To accept office when required, and to dwell in retirement when set aside – only you and I have this spirit.'

'But suppose,' said Tzu Lu, 'that the Master had the conduct of the armies of a great state, whom would he associate with him?'

'The man,' replied the Master, 'who bare-armed would beard a tiger, or rush a river, dying without regret – him I would not have with me. If I must have a colleague, he should be one who on the verge of an encounter would be apprehensive, and who loved strategy and its successful issue.'

The Master said: 'If wealth were a thing one could count on finding, even though it meant my becoming a whip-holding groom, I would do it. As one cannot count on finding it, I will follow the quests that I love better.'

The subjects which the Master treated with great solicitude were – fasting, war, and disease.

When the Master was in Ch'i he heard the Shao music and for three months was unconscious of the taste of meat. 'I did not imagine,' said he, 'that music had reached such perfection as this.'

The Master said: 'With coarse food to eat, water for drink, and a bent arm for a pillow – even in such a state I could be happy, for wealth and honour obtained unworthily are to me as a fleeting cloud.'

The Master said: 'Given a few more years of life to finish my study of the *Book of Changes*,[18] and I may be free from great errors.'

The subjects on which the Master most frequently discoursed were – the Odes, the History, and the observances of the Rites – on all these he constantly dwelt.

The Duke of She asked Tzu Lu what he thought about Confucius, but Tzu Lu returned him no answer. 'Why did you not say,' said the Master, 'he is simply a man so eager for improvement that he forgets his food, so happy therein that he forgets his sorrows, and so does not observe that old age is at hand?'

The Master said: 'I am not one who has innate knowledge, but one who, loving antiquity, is diligent in seeking it therein.'

The Master would not discuss prodigies, prowess, lawlessness, or the supernatural.

The Master said: 'When walking in a party of three, my teachers are always present. I can select the good qualities of the one and copy them, and the unsatisfactory qualities of the other and correct them in myself.'

The Master took four subjects for his teaching – culture, conduct, conscientiousness, and good faith.

The Master said: 'It is not mine to see an inspired man. Could I behold a noble man, I would be content.'

The Master said: 'It is not mine to see a really good man. Could I see a man of constant purpose, I would be content. Affecting to have when they have not, empty yet affecting to be full, in straits yet affecting to be prosperous – how hard it is for such men to have constancy of purpose!'

The Master fished with a line, but not with a net; when shooting he did not aim at a resting bird.

The Master said: 'There are men, probably, who do things correctly without knowing the reason why, but I am not like that: I hear much, select the good and follow it; I see much and treasure it up. This is the next best thing to philosophical knowledge.'

The Master said: 'Is virtue indeed afar off? I crave for virtue and lo! virtue is at hand.'

The Master said: 'In literature perhaps I may compare with others, but as to my living the noble life, to that I have not yet attained.'

The Master said: 'As to being a sage, or a man of virtue, how dare I presume to such a claim? But as to striving thereafter unwearyingly, and teaching others therein without flagging – that can be said of me, and that is all.'

'And that,' said Kung-hsi Hua,[19] 'is just what we disciples cannot learn.'

The Master said: 'Men, if prodigal, are uncontrolled; if frugal then narrow: but better be narrow than uncontrolled.'

The Master said: 'The noble man is calm and serene, the inferior man is continually worried and anxious.'

The Master was affable yet dignified, commanding yet not overbearing, courteous yet easy.

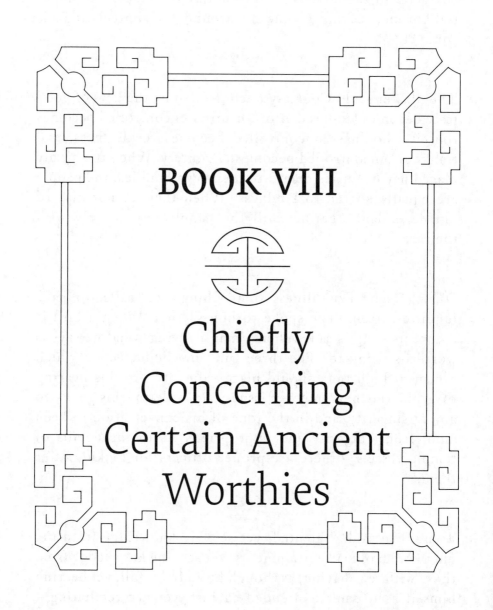

BOOK VIII

Chiefly Concerning Certain Ancient Worthies

The Master said: 'T'ai Po may be described as possessing a character of the noblest. He resolutely renounced the imperial throne, leaving people no ground for appreciating his conduct.'

The Master said: 'Courtesy uncontrolled by the laws of good taste becomes laboured effort, caution uncontrolled becomes timidity, boldness uncontrolled becomes recklessness, and frankness uncontrolled becomes effrontery. When the highly placed pay generous regard to their own families, the people are equally stirred to kindness. When they do not discard old dependants, neither will the people deal meanly with theirs.'

During Tseng Tzu's illness Meng Ching Tzu[20] called to make inquiries. Tseng Tzu spoke to him saying: 'When a bird is dying, its song is sad. When a man is dying, what he says is worth listening to. The three rules of conduct upon which a man of high rank should place value are – in his bearing to avoid rudeness and remissness, in ordering his looks to aim at sincerity, and in the tone of his conversation to keep aloof from vulgarity and impropriety. As to the details of temple vessels – there are proper officers for looking after them.'

Tseng Tzu said: 'Talented, yet seeking knowledge from the untalented; of many attainments, yet seeking knowledge from those with few; having, as though he had not; full, yet bearing himself as if empty; offended against, yet not retaliating – once upon a time I had a friend who lived after this manner.'

Tseng Tzu said: 'The scholar must not be without capacity and fortitude, for his load is heavy and the road is long. He takes virtue for his load, and is not that heavy? Only with death does his course end, and is not that long?'

The Master said: 'Let the character be formed by the poets; established by the laws of right behaviour; and perfected by music.'

The Master said: 'The people may be made to follow a course but not to understand the reason why.'

The Master said: 'Love of daring and resentment of poverty drive men to desperate deeds; and men who lack moral character, if resentment of them be carried too far, will be driven to similar deeds.'

The Master said: 'If a man has gifts as admirable as those of Duke Chou [King Wen], yet be vain and mean, his other gifts are unworthy of notice.'

The Master said: 'It is not easy to find a man who has studied for three years without aiming at pay.'

The Master said: 'The man of unwavering sincerity and love of moral discipline will keep to the death his excellent principles.

He will not enter a tottering state nor dwell in a rebellious one. When law and order prevail in the empire, he is in evidence. When it is without law and order, he withdraws. When law and order prevail in his state, he is ashamed to be needy and of no account. When law and order fail, he is ashamed to be in affluence and honour.'

The Master said: 'He who does not occupy the office does not discuss its policy.'

The Master said: 'With the impulsive yet evasive, the simple yet dishonest, the stupid yet untruthful, I hold no acquaintance.'

The Master said: 'Learn as if you were not reaching your goal, and as though you were afraid of missing it.'

The Master said: 'How sublime the way Shun and Yü[21] undertook the empire, and yet as if it were nothing to them!'

The Master said: 'In Yü I can find no room for criticism. Simple in his own food and drink, he was unsparing in his filial offerings to the spirits. Shabby in his workaday clothes he was most scrupulous as to the elegance of his kneeling-apron and sacrificial crown. Humble as to the character of his palace, he spent his strength in the draining and ditching of the country. In Yü I find no room for criticism.'

BOOK IX

Chiefly Personal

The Master seldom spoke on profit, on the orderings of Providence, and on perfection.

The Master was entirely free from four things: he had no preconceptions, no predeterminations, no obduracy, and no egoism.

When the Master was in jeopardy in K'uang, he said, 'Since King Wen is no longer alive, does not the mantle of enlightenment (*wen*) rest here on me? If heaven were going to destroy this enlightenment, a mortal like me would not have obtained such a connexion with it. Since heaven is not ready to destroy this enlightenment, what can the men of K'uang do to me?'[22]

A great minister inquired of Tzu Kung saying, 'Your Master – he is surely inspired? What varied acquirements he has!' Tzu Kung answered, 'Of a truth Heaven has lavishly endowed him, to the point of inspiration, and his acquirements are also many.'

When the Master heard of it, he said: 'Does the minister really know me? In my youth I was in humble circumstances, and for that reason gained a variety of acquirements – in common matters: but does nobleness of character depend on variety? It does not depend on variety.'

Lao[23] said, 'The Master used to say, "I have not been occupied in official life, and so have had time to become acquainted with the arts!"'

The Master said: 'Am I indeed a man with innate knowledge? I have no such knowledge; but when an uncultivated person, in all simplicity, comes to me with a question, I thrash out its pros and cons until I fathom it.'

Yen Yüan heaved a deep sigh and said: 'The more I look up at It, the higher It rises. The more I probe It, the more impenetrable It becomes. I catch a glimpse of It in front, and It is instantly behind. But our Master step by step skilfully lures men on. He has broadened me by culture, and restrained me by reverence. If I wished to stop I could not, and when at times I have exhausted all my powers, something seems to stand majestically before me; yet though I seek to pursue my path towards It, I find never a way.'

Tzu Kung asked: 'If I had a lovely jewel here, should I shut it up in a casket and keep it, or seek a good price and sell it?' 'By all means sell it! Sell it!' answered the Master – 'But I myself would wait for a good offer.'[24]

The Master proposed to go and dwell among the nine uncivilized tribes of the east; whereupon some one remarked: 'But they are so uncivilized, how can you do that?' The Master responded, 'Were a man of noble character to dwell among them, what lack of civilization would there be?'

The Master said: 'It was only after my return from Wei to Lu that music was revised, and that the secular and sacred pieces were properly differentiated.'

The Master said: 'In public life to do my duty to my prince or minister; in private life to do my duty to my fathers and brethren;

in my duties to the departed never daring to be otherwise than diligent; and never to be overcome with wine – in which of these am I successful?'

Once when the Master was standing by a stream he observed: 'All is transient, like this! Unceasing day and night!'

The Master said: 'I have never yet seen a man whose love of virtue equalled his love of woman.'

The Master said: 'Suppose I am raising a mound, and, while it is still unfinished by a basketful, I stop short, it is I that stops short. Or, suppose I begin on the level ground – although I throw down but one basketful, and continue to do so, then it is I that makes progress.'

The Master said: 'Ah! Hui was the one to whom I could tell things and who never failed to attend to them.'

The Master, referring to Yen Yüan [Hui], said: 'Alas! I ever saw him make progress, and never saw him stand still.'

The Master said: 'There are blades that spring up and never flower, and there are others that flower but never fruit.'

The Master said: 'Can any one refuse assent to words of just admonition? But it is amendment that is of value. Can any one be otherwise than pleased with advice persuasively offered? But it is the application that is of value. Mere interest without application, mere assent without amendment – I can do nothing whatever with men of such calibre.'

The Master said: 'Make conscientiousness and sincerity your leading principles. Have no friends inferior to yourself. And when in the wrong, do not hesitate to amend.'

The Master said: 'You may rob a three corps army of its commander-in-chief, but you cannot rob even a common man of his will.'

The Master said: 'Wearing a shabby, hemp-quilted robe, and standing by others dressed in fox and badger, yet in no way abashed – Yu [Tzu Lu] would be the one for that, eh? Unfriendly to none, and courting none, what does he that is not excellent?'

As Tzu Lu afterwards was perpetually intoning this, the Master observed: 'But how can those two points alone be sufficient for excellence?'

The Master said: 'Only when the year grows cold do we realize that the pine and the cypress are the last to fade.'

The Master said: 'The enlightened are free from doubt, the virtuous from anxiety, and the brave from fear.'

The Master said: 'There are some with whom one can associate in study, but who are not yet able to make common advance towards the truth: there are others who can make common advance towards the truth, but who are not yet able to take with you a like firm stand; and there are others with whom you can take such a firm stand, but with whom you cannot associate in judgement.'

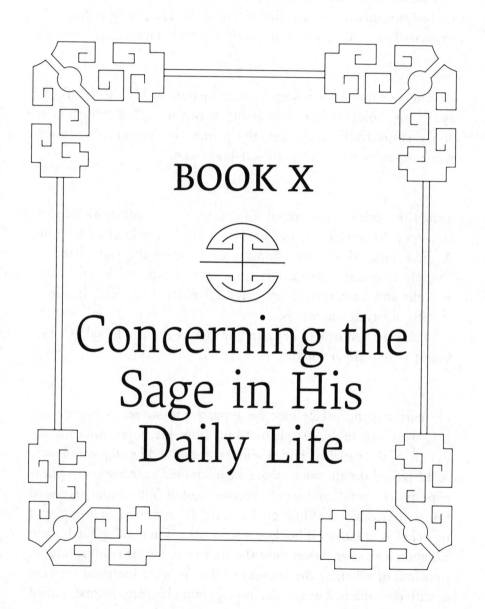

BOOK X

Concerning the Sage in His Daily Life

Confucius in his native village bore himself with simplicity, as if he had no gifts of speech. But when in the temple or at court, he expressed himself readily and clearly, yet with a measure of reserve.

At court, when conversing with ministers of his own rank, he spoke out boldly; when conversing with the higher ministers he spoke respectfully; but when the prince was present, his movements were nervous, though self-possessed.

When the prince summoned him to receive a visitor, his expression seemed to change, and his knees as it were bent under him. As he saluted those who stood with him, on the right hand or the left as occasion required, his robe in front and behind hung straight and undisturbed; and, as he hastened forward, it was as if with outstretched wings.

When the visitor had departed he always reported, saying, 'The Guest is no longer looking back at us.'

On entering the palace gate he appeared to stoop, as though the gate were not high enough to admit him. He never stood in the middle of the gateway, nor in going through did he step on the sill. As he passed the throne he wore a constrained expression, his knees appeared to bend, and words seemed to fail him. As he ascended the audience hall, holding up his skirt, he appeared to stoop, and he held his breath as if he dare not breathe. On coming forth from his audience, after descending the first step, his expression relaxed into one of relief; at the bottom of the steps he hastened forward as with outstretched wings, and on regaining his place he maintained an attitude of nervous respect.

He carried the ducal mace with bent back, as if unequal to its weight, neither higher than when making a bow, nor lower than when offering a gift: his expression, too, was perturbed and anxious, and he dragged his feet as if something were trailing behind.

While offering the presents with which he was commissioned he wore an easy look; and at the subsequent private audience he bore himself with amiability.

He did not wear facings of purple or mauve, nor even in undress did he use red or crimson. In the hot weather he wore an unlined gown of fine or loose woven material, but always outside and over another. With a black robe he wore black lambskin, with a light robe fawn, and with a yellow robe fox. His undress fur gown was long, with the right sleeve cut short. He always had his sleeping-garment made half as long again as his body. He had thick fox or badger for home wear. When out of mourning he omitted none of the usual ornaments. His skirts, all save his court skirt, he always shaped towards the waist. He did not pay visits of condolence in dark lamb's fur or a dark hat. At the new moon he always put on his court robes and presented himself at court.

When fasting he always wore a spotless suit of linen cloth. When fasting, too, he always altered his diet, and in his dwelling always changed his seat.

He had no objection to his rice being of the finest, nor to having his meat finely minced. Rice affected by the weather, or turned, he would not eat, nor fish that was unsound, nor flesh that was tainted.

Neither would he eat anything discoloured, nor that smelt, nor that was under- or over-cooked, or not in season. He would not eat anything improperly cut, nor anything served without its proper seasoning. However much meat there might be, he did not allow what he took to exceed the flavour of the rice; only in wine he had no set limit, short of mental confusion. Bought wine or dried meat from the market he would not eat. He was never without ginger at his meals; but he was not a great eater. After the sacrifices in the ducal temple he never kept his share of the flesh overnight, nor the flesh of his ancestral sacrifices more than three days, lest after three days it might not be eaten. He did not converse while eating, nor talk when in bed. Though his food were only coarse rice and vegetable broth, he invariably offered a little in sacrifice, and always with solemnity.

He would not sit on his mat unless it were straight.

When his fellow villagers had a feast he only left after the elders had departed. When his fellow villagers held a procession to expel the pestilential influences, he put on his court robes and stood on the eastern steps.

When sending complimentary inquiries to any one in another state, he bowed twice as he escorted his messenger forth. On K'ang Tzu[25] sending him a present of medicine he bowed and accepted it, but said: 'As I am not well acquainted with it, I do not dare to taste it.'

When the prince sent him a present of food, he always adjusted his mat and first tasted it himself; but if the prince's present were fresh meat, he always had it cooked, and set it before his ancestors. Were the prince's present living, he always kept it alive. When in attendance on the prince at a state dinner, while the prince sacrificed he acted the subordinate part of first tasting the dishes. When he was ill and the prince came to see him, he had his head laid to the east, and his court robes thrown over him, with his sash drawn across. When his prince commanded his presence, he did not wait while his carriage was being yoked, but started on foot.

On entering the imperial Ancestral Temple, he asked about every detail.

When a friend died, with no one to see to the rites, he would say, 'I will see to his funeral.' On receiving a present from a friend, unless it were sacrificial flesh, he never made obeisance, not even if it were a carriage and horses.

In bed he did not lie like a corpse. At home he wore no formal air. Whenever he saw any one in mourning, even though it were an intimate acquaintance, his expression always changed, and when he saw any one in a cap of state, or a blind man, even though not in public, he always showed respect. On meeting any one in deep mourning, he would bow to the crossbar of his carriage, as he did also to any one carrying the census boards. When entertained at a rich repast, he always expressed his appreciation with an altered look and by standing up. On a sudden clap of thunder, or a violent storm of wind, his countenance always changed.

When mounting his carriage he always stood correctly, holding the mounting-cord in his hand. In the carriage he did not look behind, nor speak hastily, nor point with his hands.

BOOK XI

Chiefly Concerning the Disciples

The Master observed: 'In the arts of civilization our forerunners are esteemed uncultivated, while in those arts, their successors are looked upon as cultured gentlemen. But when I have need of those arts, I follow our forerunners.'

The Master said: 'Of all who were with me in Ch'en and Ch'ai, not one now comes to my door.'[26]

Noted for moral character there were Yen Yüan, Min Tzu Ch'ien, Jan Niu and Chung Kung; for gifts of speech Tsai Wo and Tzu Kung; for administrative ability Jan Yu and Chi Lu [Tzu Lu]; and for literature and learning Tzu Yu and Tzu Hsia.

The Master said: 'Hui was not one who gave me any assistance. He was invariably satisfied with whatever I said.'

The Master said: 'What a filial son Min Tzu Ch'ien has been! No one takes exception to what his parents and brothers have said of him!'

When Yen Yüan died the Master said: 'Alas! Heaven has bereft me; Heaven has bereft me.'

When Yen Yüan died the Master bewailed him with exceeding grief, whereupon his followers said to him, 'Sir! You are carrying your grief to excess.'

'Have I gone to excess?' asked he. 'But if I may not grieve exceedingly over this man, for whom shall I grieve?'

When Yen Hui [Yen Yüan] died the other disciples proposed to give him an imposing funeral, to which the Master said: 'It will not do.' Nevertheless they buried him with pomp.

'Hui!' said the Master, 'You regarded me as a father, while I am not permitted to regard you as my son. But it is not I who do this. It is these disciples.'

When Chi Lu asked about his duty to the spirits the Master replied: 'While still unable to do your duty to the living, how can you do your duty to the dead?'

When he ventured to ask about death, Confucius answered: 'Not yet understanding life, how can you understand death?'

Once when Min Tzu was standing by the Master's side he looked so self-reliant, Tzu Lu so full of energy, and Jan Yu and Tzu Kung so frank and fearless that the Master was highly gratified.

'But,' said he, 'a man like Yu will not come to a natural death.'[27]

When the men of Lu were for rebuilding the Long Treasury, Min Tzu Ch'ien observed, 'How would it do to restore it as before? Why need it be reconstructed?' The Master said: 'This man seldom speaks, but when he does he is sure to hit the mark.'

Tzu Kung asked which was the better, Shih or Shang?[28] The Master replied: 'Shih exceeds, Shang comes short.'

'So then,' queried he, 'Shih surpasses Shang, eh?'

'To go beyond the mark,' replied the Master, 'is as bad as to come short of it.'

Ch'ai was simple-minded; Shen dull; Shih shallow; Yu unrefined.[29]

The Master said: 'Hui! he was almost perfect, yet he was often in want. T'zu[30] was not content with his lot, and yet his goods increased abundantly; nevertheless in his judgements he often hit the mark.'

When Tzu Chang asked what characterized the way of the man of natural goodness, the Master replied: 'He does not tread the beaten track, nor yet does he enter into the inner sanctum of philosophy.'

The Master said: 'That a man's address may be solid and reliable, this one may grant; but does it follow that he is a man of the higher type, or is his seriousness only in appearance?'

When Tzu Lu asked whether he should put what he heard into immediate practice, the Master answered, 'You have parents and elders still living, why should you at once put all you hear into practice?'

When Jan Yu asked whether he should put what he heard into immediate practice, the Master answered, 'Put what you hear at once into practice.'

Kung-hsi Hua asked: 'When Yu asked if he should put the precepts he heard into immediate practice, you, Sir, replied, "You have parents and elders alive"; but when Ch'iu asked if he should put the precepts he heard into immediate practice, you, Sir, replied, "Put what you hear at once into practice." As I am perplexed about your meaning I venture to ask a solution.'

'Ch'iu,' answered the Master, 'lags behind, so I urged him forward; but Yu has energy for two men, so I held him back.'

When the Master was put in peril in K'uang, Yen Hui fell behind. On the Master saying to him, 'I thought you were dead,' he replied, 'While you, Sir, live, how should I dare to die?'

When Chi Tzu-jan[31] asked if Chung Yu and Jan Ch'iu could be called great ministers, the Master replied, 'I thought, Sir, you were going to ask about something extraordinary, and it is only a question about Yu and Ch'iu. He who may be called a great minister is one who serves his prince according to the right, and when that cannot be, resigns. Now, as for Yu and Ch'iu, they may be styled ordinary ministers.'

'So, then,' said Tzu Jan, 'they would follow their chief, eh?'

'A parricide or regicide,' answered the Master, 'they would assuredly not follow, however.'

When Tzu Lu obtained the appointment of Tzu Kao as governor of Pi, the Master said, 'You are doing an ill turn to another man's son.'

'He will have his people and officers,' replied Tzu Lu, 'he will also have the altars of the land and the grain, why must he read books before he is considered educated?'

'It is because of this kind of talk,' said the Master, 'that I hate glib people.'

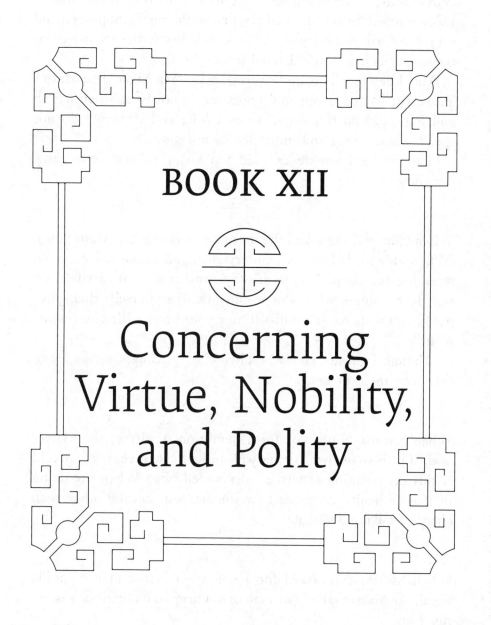

BOOK XII

Concerning Virtue, Nobility, and Polity

When Yen Yüan asked the meaning of virtue, the Master replied: 'Virtue is the denial of self and response to what is right and proper. Deny yourself for one day and respond to the right and proper, and everybody will accord you virtuous. For has virtue its source in oneself, or is it forsooth derived from others?'

'May I beg for the main features?' asked Yen Yüan. The Master answered: 'When wrong and improper do not look, when wrong and improper do not listen, when wrong and improper do not speak, when wrong and improper do not move.'

'Though I am not clever,' said Yen Yüan, 'permit me to carry out these precepts.'

When Chung Kung asked the meaning of virtue, the Master said: 'When abroad, behave as if interviewing an honoured guest; in directing the people, act as if officiating at a great sacrifice; do not do to others what you would not like yourself; then your public life will arouse no ill-will nor your private life any resentment.'

'Though I am not clever,' replied Chung Kung, 'permit me to carry out these precepts.'

When Ssu-ma Niu asked for a definition of virtue, the Master said: 'The man of virtue is chary of speech.' 'He is chary of speech! Is this the meaning of virtue?' demanded Niu. 'When the doing of it is difficult,' responded Confucius, 'can one be other than chary of talking about it?'

When Ssu-ma Niu asked for a definition of the man of noble mind, the Master said: 'The man of noble mind has neither anxiety nor fear.'

'Neither anxiety nor fear!' he rejoined. 'Is this the definition of a noble man?'

'On searching within,' replied the Master, 'he finds no chronic ill, so why should he be anxious or why should he be afraid?'

Once when Ssu-ma Niu sorrowfully remarked, 'Other men all have their brothers, I alone am without,'[32] Tzu Hsia responded: 'I have heard it said, "Death and life are divine dispensations, and wealth and honours are with Heaven. When the man of noble mind unfailingly conducts himself with self-respect, and is courteous and well-behaved with others, then all within the four seas are his brothers. How, then, can a fine man grieve that he is without a brother?"'

When Tzu Chang asked what was meant by insight, the Master replied: 'He who is unmoved by the insidious soaking in of slander, or by urgent representations of direct personal injury, may truly be called a man of insight. Indeed, he who is unmoved by the insidious soaking in of slander or by urgent representations of direct personal injury, may also indeed be called far-sighted.'

When Tzu Kung asked what were the essentials of government, the Master replied: 'Sufficient food, sufficient forces, and the confidence of the people.'

'Suppose,' rejoined Tzu Kung, 'I were compelled to dispense with one, which of these three should I forgo first?'

'Forgo the forces,' was the reply.

'Suppose,' said Tzu Kung, 'I were compelled to eliminate another, which of the other two should I forgo?'

'The food,' was the reply; 'for from of old death has been the lot of all men, but a people without faith cannot stand.'

Chi Tzu-Ch'eng[33] remarked: 'For a man of high character to be natural is quite sufficient; what need is there of art to make him such?'

'Alas!' said Tzu Kung, 'Your Excellency's words are those of a noble man, but a team of four horses cannot overtake the tongue. Art, as it were, is nature; as nature, so to speak, is art. The hairless hide of a tiger or a leopard is about the same as the hide of a dog or a sheep.'

When Tzu Chang asked the best way to improve his character and to discriminate in what was irrational, the Master said: 'Take conscientiousness and sincerity as your ruling principles, submit also your mind to right conditions, and your character will improve. When you love a man you want him to live, when you hate him you wish he were dead; but you have already wanted him to live and yet again you wish he were dead. This is an instance of the irrational.

"Not indeed because of wealth,
But solely because talented."'

When Duke Ching of Ch'i inquired of Confucius the principles of government, Confucius answered saying: 'Let the prince be prince, the minister minister, the father father, and the son son.'

'Excellent!' said the Duke. 'Truly, if the prince be not prince, the minister not minister, the father not father, and the son not son, however much grain I may have, shall I be allowed to eat it?'

The Master said: 'Yu was a fellow! He could decide a dispute with half a word.' Tzu Lu [Yu] never slept over a promise.

The Master said: 'I can try a lawsuit as well as other men, but surely the great thing is to bring about that there be no going to law.'

When Tzu Chang asked about the art of government, the Master replied: 'Ponder untiringly over your plans, and then conscientiously carry them into execution.'

The Master said: 'The man of noble mind seeks to achieve the good in others and not their evil. The little-minded man is the reverse of this.'

When Chi K'ang Tzu asked Confucius for a definition of government, Confucius replied: 'To govern means to guide aright. If you, Sir, will lead the way aright, who will dare to deviate from the right?'

Chi K'ang Tzu, being plagued with robbers, consulted Confucius, who answered him saying: 'If you, Sir, be free from the love of wealth, although you pay people, they will not steal.'

Chi K'ang Tzu asked the opinion of Confucius on government and said: 'How would it do to execute the lawless for the good of the law-abiding?'

'What need, Sir, is there of capital punishment in your administration?' responded Confucius. 'If your aspirations are for good, Sir, the people will be good. The moral character of those in high position is the breeze, the character of those below is the grass. When the grass has the breeze upon it, it assuredly bends.'

Tzu Chang asked what a man must be like in order to gain general estimation.

'What is it that you mean by general estimation?' inquired the Master.

'To ensure popularity abroad and to ensure it at home,' replied Tzu Chang.

'That,' said the Master, 'is popularity, not esteem. As for the man who meets with general esteem, he is natural, upright, and a lover of justice; he weighs what men say and observes their expression, and his anxiety is to be more lowly than others; and so he ensures esteem abroad, as he ensures it also at home. As to the seeker of popularity, he assumes an air of magnanimity which his actions belie, while his self-assurance knows never a misgiving, and so he ensures popularity abroad, as he also ensures it at home.'

Once when Fan Ch'ih was rambling along with the Master under the trees at the Rain Altars, he remarked: 'May I venture to ask how one may improve one's character, correct one's personal faults, and discriminate in what is irrational?'

'An excellent question,' rejoined the Master. 'If a man put duty first and success after, will not that improve his character? If he attacks his own failings instead of those of others, will he not remedy his personal faults? For a morning's anger to forget his own safety and involve that of his relatives, is not this irrational?'

Once when Fan Ch'ih asked the meaning of virtue, the Master replied, 'Love your fellow men.'

On his asking the meaning of knowledge, the Master said: 'Know your fellow men.'

Fan Ch'ih not having comprehended, the Master added: 'By promoting the straight and degrading the crooked you can make even the crooked straight.'

Fan Ch'ih withdrew and afterwards meeting Tzu Hsia said to him: 'A little while ago, when I had an interview with the Master, and asked for a definition of knowledge, he replied, "By promoting the straight and degrading the crooked you can make even the crooked straight" – what can he have meant?'

'What a rich maxim that is!' replied Tzu Hsia. 'When Shun had the empire, he chose from amongst the multitude and promoted Kao Yao, whereupon all who were devoid of virtue disappeared. And when T'ang had the empire, he too chose from amongst the multitude and promoted I Yin, whereupon all who were devoid of virtue disappeared.'

On Tzu Kung inquiring the duties to a friend, the Master replied: 'Advise him conscientiously and guide him discreetly. If he be unwilling, then cease; do not court humiliation.'

The philosopher Tseng said: 'The wise man by his culture gathers his friends, and by his friends develops his goodness of character.'

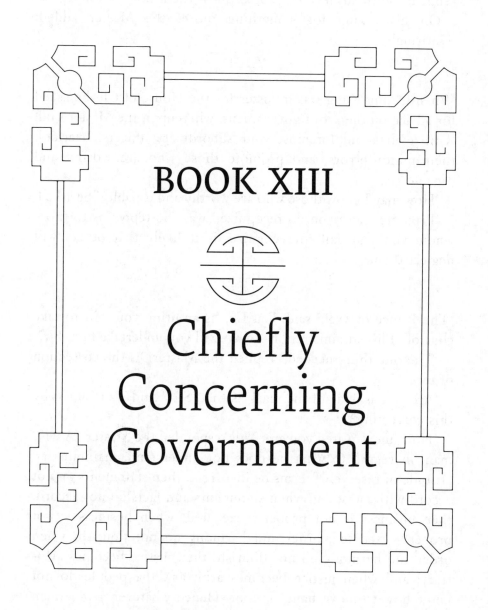

BOOK XIII

Chiefly Concerning Government

When Tzu Lu asked about the art of government the Master replied: 'Be in advance of people; show them how to work.'

On his asking for something more, the Master added: 'Untiringly.'

When Chung Kung was minister for the House of Chi he asked for advice on the art of government, whereupon the Master said: 'Utilize first and foremost your subordinate officers, overlook their minor errors, and promote those who are worthy and capable.'

'How may I know those who are worthy and capable?' he asked.

'Promote those you do recognize;' was the reply; 'as to those whom you may fail to recognize, is it likely that others will neglect them?'

'The Prince of Wei,' said Tzu Lu, 'is awaiting you, Sir, to take control of his administration – what will you undertake first, Sir?'

'The one thing needed,' replied the Master, 'is the correction of terms.'

'Are you as wide of the mark as that, Sir?' said Tzu Lu. 'Why this correcting?'

'How uncultivated you are, Yu!' responded the Master. 'A wise man, in regard to what he does not understand, maintains an attitude of reserve. If terms be incorrect, then statements do not accord with facts; and when statements and facts do not accord, then business is not properly executed; when business is not properly executed, order and harmony do not flourish; when order and harmony do not flourish, then justice becomes arbitrary; and when justice becomes arbitrary, the people do not know how to move hand or foot. Hence whatever a wise man states he can always define, and what he so defines, he can always carry into practice; for the wise man will on no account have anything remiss in his definitions.'

On Fan Ch'ih requesting to be taught agriculture, the Master replied, 'I am not as good as an old farmer for that.' When he asked to be taught gardening the Master answered, 'I am not as good as an old gardener for that.' On Fan Ch'ih withdrawing, the Master said: 'What a little-minded man is Fan Hsü! When a ruler loves good manners, his people will not let themselves be disrespectful; when a ruler loves justice, his people will not let themselves be unsubmissive; when a ruler loves good faith, his people will not venture to be insincere; and if he be like this, then people will come from every quarter carrying their children strapped on their backs – what does he want with learning agriculture?'

On Fan Ch'ih withdrawing, the Master said: 'A man may be able to recite the three hundred Odes, but if, when given a post in the administration, he proves to be without practical ability, or when sent anywhere on a mission, he is unable of himself to answer a question, although his knowledge is extensive, of what use is it?'

The Master said: 'If a ruler is himself upright, his people will do their duty without orders; but if he himself be not upright, although he may order they will not obey.'

The Master said of [Prince] Ching, a scion of the ducal House of Wei, that he dwelt well content in his house. When first he began to possess property, he called it 'a passable accumulation';

when he had prospered somewhat, he called it 'passably complete'; and when he had amassed plenty, he called it 'passably fine'.

When the Master was travelling to Wei, Jan Yu drove him. 'What a numerous population!' remarked the Master.

'The people having grown so numerous, what next should be done for them?' asked Jan Yu. 'Enrich them,' was the reply.

'And when you have enriched them, what next should be done?' he asked. 'Educate them,' was the answer.

The Master said: 'Were any prince to employ me, in a twelvemonth something could have been done, but in three years the work could be completed.'

The Master remarked: 'How true is the saying: "If good men ruled the country for a hundred years, they could even tame the brutal and abolish capital punishment!"'

The Master said: 'If a kingly ruler were to arise, it would take a generation before virtue prevailed, however.'

The Master said: 'If a man put himself aright, what difficulty will he have in the public service; but if he cannot put himself aright, how is he going to put others right?'

Duke Ting [of Lu] inquired whether there were any one phrase by the adoption of which a country could be made prosperous.

'No phrase can be expected to have such force as that,' replied Confucius. 'But there is the popular saying, "It is hard to be a prince, and not easy to be a minister." If a prince perceive the difficulty of being a prince, may he not expect through that one phrase to prosper his country?'

'Is there any one phrase,' he asked, 'through which a country may be ruined?'

'No phrase can be expected to have such force as that,' replied Confucius. 'But there is the popular saying, "I should have no gratification in being a prince, unless none opposed my commands." If those are good, and no one opposes them, that surely is well. But if they are not good, and no one opposes them, may he not expect in that one phrase to ruin his country?'

When the Duke of She[34] asked the meaning of good government, the Master answered: 'The near are happy and the distant attracted.'

When Tzu Hsia was magistrate of Chü-fu,[35] he asked what should be his policy, whereupon the Master said: 'Do not be in a hurry; do not be intent on minor advantages. When one is in a hurry, nothing is thorough; and when one is intent on minor advantages, nothing great is accomplished.'

Once when Fan Ch'ih asked about virtue, the Master said: 'In private life be courteous, in handling public business be serious, with all men be conscientious. Even though you go among barbarians, you may not relinquish these virtues.'

Tzu Kung asked: 'What must an official be like to merit his name?' 'If in his personal conduct,' replied the Master, 'he has a sensibility to dishonour, and wheresoever he be sent will not disgrace his prince's commission, he may be said to merit his title.'

'I would venture to ask who may be ranked lower,' said Tzu Kung. 'He whom his relatives commend as filial and whose neighbours commend as brotherly,' was the answer. 'I venture to ask the next lower,' said Tzu Kung. 'He is one who always stands by his word,' was the answer, 'and who persists in all he undertakes; he is a man of grit, though of narrow outlook; yet perhaps he may be taken as of the third class.' 'What would you say of the present-day government officials?' asked Tzu Kung. 'Faugh!' said the Master. 'A set of pecks and hampers, unworthy to be taken into account!'

The Master said: 'If I cannot obtain men of the Golden Mean to teach, those whom I must have, let them be the ambitious and the discreet; for the ambitious do make progress and take hold, and as to the discreet, there are things that they will refuse to sanction.'

The Master said: 'The true gentleman is friendly but not familiar; the inferior man is familiar but not friendly.' Tzu Kung asked: 'What would you say of the man who is liked by all his fellow townsmen?' 'That is not sufficient,' was the reply. 'Then what would you say of him who is hated by all his fellow townsmen?' 'Nor is that sufficient,' was the reply. 'What is better is that the good among his fellow townsmen like him, and the bad hate him.'

The Master said: 'The true gentleman is easy to serve, yet difficult to please. If you attempt to please him in any improper way, he will be displeased; but when it comes to appointing men in their work, he has regard to their capacity. The inferior man is hard to serve, yet easy to please. If you attempt to please him, even in an improper way, he will be pleased; but in appointing men their work, he expects them to be fit for everything.'

The Master said: 'The well-bred are dignified but not pompous. The ill-bred are pompous, but not dignified.'

The Master said: 'The firm of spirit, the resolute in character, the simple in manner, and the slow of speech are not far from virtue.'

Tzu Lu asked: 'What qualities must one possess to be entitled to be called an educated man?' 'He who is earnest in spirit, persuasive in speech, and withal of gracious bearing,' said the Master, 'may be called an educated man – earnest in spirit and persuasive of speech with his friends, and of gracious bearing towards his brothers.'

BOOK XIV

Chiefly
Concerning
Government and
Certain Rulers

When Hsien[36] asked the meaning of dishonour, the Master said: 'When his country is well-governed to be thinking only of pay, and when his country is ill-governed to be thinking only of pay – that is dishonour for a man.'

Hsien again asked: 'If a man refrains from ambition, boasting, resentment, and selfish desire, it may, I suppose, be counted to him for virtue.' 'It may be counted for difficult,' said the Master, 'but whether that alone is virtue, I know not.'

The Master said: 'The scholar whose regard is his comfort is unworthy to be deemed a scholar.'

The Master said: 'When law and order prevail in the land, a man may be bold in speech and bold in action; but when the land lacks law and order, though he may take bold action, he should lay restraint on his speech.'

The Master said: 'A man of principle is sure to have something good to say, but he who has something good to say is not necessarily a man of principle. A virtuous man is sure to be courageous, but a courageous man is not necessarily a man of virtue.'

Nan Kung Kua remarked to Confucius by way of inquiry: 'Is it not a fact that Prince I excelled as an archer, and Ao could propel a boat on dry land, yet neither died a natural death, while Yü and Chi, who took a personal interest in agriculture, became possessed of the empire?'[37]

The Master made no reply, but when Nan Kung Kua had withdrawn, he observed: 'A scholar indeed is such a man! Such a man has a true estimation of virtue!'

'There may perhaps be men of the higher type who fail in virtue, but there has never been one of the lower type who possessed virtue.'

The Master said: 'Can love be other than exacting, or loyalty refrain from admonition?'

The Master said: 'To be poor and not complain is difficult; to be rich and not arrogant is easy.'

When Tzu Lu asked what constituted the character of the perfect man, the Master replied: 'If he have the sagacity of Tsang Wu Chung, the purity of Kung Ch'o, the courage of Chuang Tzu of P'ien, and the skill of Jan Ch'iu,[38] and if he refines these with the arts of courtesy and harmony, then, indeed, he may be deemed a perfect man.'

'But what need is there,' he added, 'for the perfect man of the present day to be like this? Let him when he sees anything to his advantage think whether it be right; when he meets with danger be ready to lay down his life; and, however long-standing the undertaking, let him not belie the professions of his whole life: then he, too, may be deemed a perfect man.'

The Master put a question to Kung-ming Chia about Kung-shu Wen-tzu,[39] and said: 'Is it really true that your Master neither talks, nor laughs, nor accepts anything?'

'That arises from the exaggeration of reporters,' answered Kung-ming Chia. 'Our Master talks only at the right time, hence people do not tire of his talk; he only laughs when he is really pleased, hence people do not tire of his laughter; he only accepts things when it is right to do so, hence men do not tire of his accepting.'

'Is that so?' said the Master. 'Can that indeed be so?'

The Minister Chüan, formerly a retainer of Kung-shu Wen-tzu, afterwards went up to court in company with Wen-tzu. The Master on hearing of it observed: 'Wen well deserves to be considered "a promoter of culture".'

When the Master was speaking of the unprincipled character of Duke Ling of Wei,[40] K'ang-tzu observed: 'Such being the case, how is it he does not lose his throne?'

'Chung-shu Yü,' answered Confucius, 'has charge of the envoys; the Reader T'o has charge of the ancestral temple; Wang-sun Chia commands the forces – and, such being the case, how should he lose his throne?'

The Master said: 'He who speaks without modesty will perform with difficulty.'

When Tzu Lu asked what constituted a man's duty to his prince, the Master said: 'Never deceive him and then you may boldly withstand him.'

The Master said: 'The progress of the nobler-minded man is upwards, the progress of the inferior man is downwards.'

The Master said: 'The men of old studied for the sake of self-improvement; the men of the present day study for the approbation of others.'

Chü Po Yü[41] having sent a messenger to convey his respects to Confucius, Confucius made him sit down along with him and questioned him, asking: 'What is your master doing now?' The messenger replied: 'My master is seeking to make his faults fewer, but has not yet succeeded.'

When the messenger had withdrawn, the Master observed: 'What a messenger! What a messenger!'

The Master said: 'He who does not occupy the office does not discuss its policy.'

The Philosopher Tseng [Tzeng Tzu] said: 'A wise man, even in his thoughts, does not stray from his own duty.'

The Master said: 'The higher type of man is modest in what he says, but surpasses in what he does.'

The Master said: 'There are three characteristics of the noble man's life, to which I cannot lay claim: being virtuous he is free from care; possessing knowledge he is free from doubts; being courageous he is free from fear.'

'That is what you say of yourself!' replied Tzu Kung.

Tzu Kung being in the habit of making comparisons, the Master observed: 'How worthy Tzu must be! As for me, I have not the time to spare.'

The Master said: 'A wise man is not distressed that people do not know him; he is distressed at his own lack of ability.'

The Master said: 'Is not he a man of real worth who does not anticipate deceit nor imagine that people will doubt his word; and yet who has immediate perception thereof when present?'

Wei-sheng Mou,[42] sneering at Confucius, said: 'Ch'iu, what are you doing with this "perching here and perching there"? Are you not making a business of talking to please people?'

'I should not dare to talk only to please people,' replied Confucius; 'and I should hate to be obstinately immovable.'

The Master said: 'A good horse is not praised for its strength but for its character.'

Some one asked: 'What do you think about the principle of rewarding enmity with kindness?'

'With what, then, would you reward kindness?' asked the Master. 'Reward enmity with just treatment, and kindness with kindness.'

'No one knows me, alas!' exclaimed the Master. 'Why do you say, Master, that no one knows you?' said Tzu Kung. 'I make no complaint against Heaven,' replied the Master, 'nor blame men, for though my studies are lowly, my mind soars aloft; and does not Heaven know me?'

Kung-po Liao[43] having spoken against Tzu Lu to Chi-sun, Tzu-fu Ching-po informed Confucius thereof, and said: 'Our lord's mind is undoubtedly being disturbed by Kung-po Liao, but I am still strong enough to have his carcass exposed in the market-place.'

The Master replied: 'If my principles are going to prevail, it is so fated; if they are going to fail, it is so fated; what can Kung-po Liao do against Destiny?'

The Master said: 'Some good men withdraw from the world. Withdrawal from fatherland comes next in order; next is from uncongenial looks; and next is from uncongenial language.'

The Master said: 'There are seven men who have done this.'

On one occasion when Tzu Lu happened to spend the night at Stone Gate, the gate opener asked him, 'Where are you from?' 'Master K'ung's,' replied Tzu Lu.

'Is not he the one who knows he cannot succeed and keeps on trying to do so?' was the response.

Tzu Chang said: 'The *Book of History* says that when Kao Tsung[44] observed the imperial mourning he did not speak for three years. What may be the meaning of that?'

'Why need you specialize Kao Tsung? All the men of old did the same,' answered Confucius. 'When a prince died, all his officers attended to their several duties in obedience to the prime minister for three years.'

The Master said: 'When those in high position are fond of orderly behaviour, service from the people is easily commanded.'

When Tzu Lu asked what should be the character of a man of the nobler order, the Master replied: 'He should cultivate himself unfailingly to respect others.'

'Will it suffice to be like this?' asked Tzu Lu.

'He should cultivate himself so as to ease the lot of others,' was the reply.

'And is this sufficient?' asked Tzu Lu.

'He should cultivate himself so as to ease the lot of the people.

He should cultivate himself so as to ease the lot of the people – even Yao and Shun[45] ever remained assiduous about this!'

Yüan Jang[46] sat squatting and waiting as the Master approached, who said to him: 'When young being mannerless, when grown up doing nothing worthy of mention, when old not dying – this is being a rogue!' And with this he hit him on the shank with his staff.

A youth from the village of Ch'üeh was acting as messenger for Confucius, so some one said concerning him: 'He has made good progress, I suppose?' 'I notice,' replied the Master, 'that he occupies the seat of adult age, and I notice that he walks on a level with his seniors. It is not that he seeks to progress, he wants speedy arrival!'

BOOK XV

Chiefly on the Maintenance of Principles and Character

When Duke Ling of Wei[40] asked Confucius about military tactics, Confucius replied: 'With the appurtenances of worship I have indeed an acquaintance, but as to military matters I have never studied them.' Next day he straightway took his departure.

On the way in Ch'en their supplies failed, and his followers were so ill that they could not stand. Tzu Lu with some irritation sought an interview and said: 'Does a man of the higher order also have to suffer want?' 'The superior man bears want unshaken,' replied the Master, 'the inferior man in want becomes demoralized.'

'Tzu,' said the Master, 'You regard me as a man of multifarious study who retains all in mind, eh?'

'Yes,' answered he; 'but maybe it is not so?'

'No,' was the reply, 'I have one principle connecting all.'

'Yu,' said the Master, 'there are few who understand virtue.'

The Master said: 'May not Shun[45] be instanced as one who made no effort, yet the empire was well governed? For what effort did he make? Ordering himself in all seriousness, he did nothing but maintain the correct imperial attitude.'

When Tzu Chang asked how to succeed with others, the Master made answer: 'If you are sincere and truthful in what you say, and trustworthy and circumspect in what you do, then although you be in the land of the barbarians you will succeed with them. But if you are not sincere and truthful in what you say, and untrustworthy and not circumspect in what you do, are you likely to succeed even in your own country? When standing, see these principles there in front of you. When in your carriage, see them resting on the yoke. Then you will succeed everywhere.'

Tzu Chang inscribed these counsels on his sash.

The Master said: 'What a straight man was the recorder Yü![47] When the country was well governed, he was like an arrow; and when the country was ill governed, he was still straight as an arrow.

'What a noble man is Chü Po Yü! When the country is well governed, he holds office; but when the country is ill governed, he can roll up his portfolio and keep it in his bosom.'

'Not to enlighten one who can be enlightened is to waste a man; to enlighten one who cannot be enlightened is to waste words. The intelligent man neither wastes his man nor his words.'

The Master said: 'The resolute scholar and the virtuous man will not seek life at the expense of virtue. Some even sacrifice their lives to crown their virtue.'

When Tzu Kung asked about the practice of virtue, the Master replied: 'A workman who wants to do his work well must first sharpen his tools. In whatever state you dwell, take service with the worthiest of its ministers, and make friends of the most virtuous of its scholars.'

Yen Yüan once asked about the administration of a state.

The Master replied: 'Adopt the calendar of Hsia; ride in the state carriage of Yin; wear the cap of Chou; in music adopt the Shao dances; banish the songs of Cheng, and avoid specious men; for the songs of Cheng are licentious, and specious men dangerous.'[48]

The Master said: 'Who heeds not the future will find sorrow at hand.'

'It is all in vain!' said the Master. 'I have never yet seen a man as fond of virtue as of [female] beauty.'

The Master said: 'He who demands much from himself and little from others will avoid resentment.'

The Master said: 'If a man does not ask himself, "What am I to make of this?" "What am I to make of that?" – there is nothing whatever I can make of him.'

The Master said: 'Men who associate together the livelong day and whose conversation never rises to what is just and right, but whose delight is in deeds of petty shrewdness – how hard is their case!'

The Master said: 'The noble man takes the Right as his foundation principle, reduces it to practice with all courtesy, carries it out with modesty, and renders it perfect with sincerity. Such is the noble man.'

The Master remarked: 'The noble man is pained over his own incompetency; he is not pained that others ignore him.'

The Master said: 'The noble man seeks what he wants in himself; the inferior man seeks it from others.'

The Master said: 'The noble man upholds his dignity without striving for it; he is sociable without entering any clique.'

The Master said: 'The wise man does not appreciate a man because of what he says; nor does he depreciate what he says because of the man.'

'Is there any one word,' asked Tzu Kung, 'which could be adopted as a lifelong rule of conduct?' The Master replied: 'Is not Sympathy the word? Do not do to others what you would not like yourself.'

The Master said: 'In my treatment of men, whom have I unduly disparaged or whom have I unduly extolled? If there be one whom I have so extolled, there is that by which he has been tested.

'Thus and with such people the Three Dynasties pursued their straightforward course.'

The Master said: 'I can still go back to the days when a recorder left a temporary blank in his records, and when a man who had a horse would lend it to another to ride. Now, alas! such a condition no more exists.'

The Master said: 'Plausible words confound morals, and a trifling impatience may confound a great project.'

The Master said: 'Though all hate a man, one must investigate the cause; and though all like him, one must also investigate the cause.'

The Master said: 'A man can enlarge his principles; it is not his principles that enlarge the man.'

The Master said: 'To err and not reform may indeed be called error.'

The Master said: 'I have spent the whole day without food and the whole night without sleep in order to think. It was of no use. It is better to learn.'

The Master said: 'The wise man makes duty, not a living, his aim; for there is hunger even for a farmer, and sometimes emolument for a scholar! But the wise man is anxious about his duty, not about poverty.'

The Master said: 'If a man intellectually realizes a given principle, but if his moral character does not enable him to live up to it, even though he has reached it, he will decline from it. Though intellectually he has attained to it, and his moral character enables him to live up to it, if he does not govern people with dignity, they will not respect him. And though he has intellectually attained to it, his moral character enables him to live up to it, and he governs with dignity, if he instigates the people to act in a disorderly manner, he is still lacking in excellence.'

The Master said: 'A man of the higher type may not be distinguishable in minor responsibilities, but he can undertake great ones. An inferior man cannot undertake great responsibilities, but may be distinguished in minor ones.'

The Master said: 'Virtue is more to man than either water or fire. I have seen men die through walking into water or fire, but I have never seen a man die through walking the path of virtue.'

The Master said: 'He upon whom a moral duty devolves should not give way even to his master.'

The Master said: 'The wise man is intelligently, not blindly, loyal.'

The Master said: 'In serving one's prince, one should give careful attention to his business, and make the pay a secondary consideration.'

The Master said: 'In teaching there should be no class distinctions.'

The Master said: 'Those whose ways are different do not make plans together.'

The Master said: 'In language perspicuity is everything.'

The State Bandmaster Mien[49] once called to see him. On arriving at the steps the Master said, 'Here are the steps.' On coming to the mat, he said, 'Here is your mat.' When all were seated the Master informed him: 'So and so is here, so and so is there.'

When the Bandmaster had gone, Tzu Chang inquired: 'Is it the proper thing to tell a Bandmaster those things?' 'Yes,' answered the Master, 'undoubtedly it is the proper thing for a blind Bandmaster's guide to do so.'

BOOK XVI

Concerning Ministerial Responsibility et Alia

The chief of the House of Chi being about to invade the minor principality of Chuan-yü, Jan Yu and Chi Lu interviewed Confucius and said: 'Our chief is about to commence operations against Chuan-yü fief.' 'Ch'iu,' said Confucius, 'is not this misdeed yours? The Head of Chuan-yü was appointed by the ancient kings to preside over the sacrifices to the Eastern Meng; the fief also is within the boundaries of our state, and its ruler is direct sacrificial minister of the crown. What business has your chief with attacking it?'

'It is our master's wish,' said Jan Yu, 'neither of us two ministers wishes it.' 'Ch'iu,' replied Confucius, 'Chou Jen had a saying: "Let him who is allowed to use his ability retain his position, and let him who cannot retire. Of what use is he as a blind man's guide, who neither holds him up when tottering, nor supports him when falling?" Moreover, your remark is quite wrong, for when a tiger or a wild bull escapes from its cage, or when tortoise-shell or a precious stone is injured in its cabinet, whose fault is it?'

'But now,' said Jan Yu, 'Chuan-yü is strongly fortified and near to Pi. If our chief does not take it now it must hereafter become a cause of anxiety to his descendants.'

'Ch'iu,' replied Confucius, 'the man of honour detests those who decline to say plainly that they want a thing and insist on making excuses in regard thereto. I have heard that the ruler of a kingdom, or the chief of a house, is not concerned about his people being few, but about lack of equitable treatment; nor is he concerned over poverty, but over the presence of discontent;

for where there is equity there is no poverty, where concord prevails there is no lack of people, and where contentment reigns there are no upheavals. Such a state of things existing, then, if any outlying people are still unsubmissive he attracts them by the promotion of culture and morality, and when he has attracted them he makes them contented. But here are you two, Yu and Ch'iu, assisting your chief; for though an outlying people are unsubmissive, he cannot attract them; and though the state is disorganized and disrupted, he cannot preserve it. And yet he is planning to take up arms within his own state. I myself fear that Chi-sun's cause for anxiety does not lie in Chuan-yü, but within his own gate-screen [his palace]!'

Confucius said: 'When good government prevails in the empire, civil ordinances and punitive expeditions issue from the emperor. When good government fails in the empire, civil ordinance and punitive expeditions issue from the nobles. When they issue from a noble, it is rare if the empire be not lost within ten generations. When they issue from a noble's minister, it is rare if the empire be not lost within five generations. But when a minister's minister holds command in the kingdom, it is rare if it be not lost within three generations. When there is good government in the empire, its policy is not in the hands of ministers. And when there is good government in the empire, the people do not even discuss it.'

Confucius said: 'There are three kinds of friends that are beneficial, and three that are harmful. To make friends with the upright, with the faithful, with the well-informed, is beneficial. To make friends with the plausible, with the insinuating, with the glib, is harmful.'

Confucius said: 'There are three ways of pleasure-seeking that are beneficial, and there are three that are harmful. To seek pleasure in the refinements of manners and music, to seek pleasure in discussing the excellences of others, to seek pleasure in making many worthy friends – these are beneficial. To seek pleasure in unbridled enjoyment, to seek pleasure in looseness and gadding, to seek pleasure in conviviality – these are harmful.'

Confucius said: 'There are three errors to be avoided when in the presence of a superior: to speak before being called upon, which may be termed forwardness; not to speak when called upon, which may be termed timidity; and to speak before noting a superior's expression, which may be called blindness.'

Confucius said: 'There are three things the nobler type of man is on his guard against. In the period of youth, before his physical nature has settled down, he guards against lust. Having reached his prime, when his physical nature has now attained its mature strength, he guards against combativeness. When he has reached old age, and his physical nature is already decaying, he guards against acquisitiveness.'

Confucius said: 'The man of noble mind holds three things in awe. He holds the Divine Will in awe; he holds the great in awe; and he holds the precepts of the sages in awe. The baser man, not knowing the Divine Will, does not stand in awe of it; he takes liberties with the great; and makes a mock of the precepts of the sages.'

Confucius said: 'Those who have innate wisdom take highest rank. Those who acquire it by study rank next. Those who learn despite natural limitations come next. But those who are of limited ability and yet will not learn – these form the lowest class of men.'

Confucius said: 'The wise man has nine points of thoughtful care. In looking, his care is to observe distinctly; in listening, his care is to apprehend clearly; in his appearance, his care is to be kindly; in his manner, his care is to be courteous; in speaking, his care is to be conscientious; in his duties, his care is to be earnest; in doubt, his care is to seek information; in anger, he has a care for the consequences; and when he has opportunity for gain, his care is whether it be right.'

Confucius said: '"They look up at the good as if fearing not to reach it, and shrink from evil as if from scalding water." I have seen such men, as I have heard such sayings. "They dwell in seclusion to think out their aims, and practise right living in order to extend their principles" – I have heard such sayings, but I have never seen such men.'

Ch'en K'ang once asked Po Yü: 'Have you ever had any lesson different from the rest of us from the Master?'

'No,' was the reply, 'but he was once standing alone, and as I hastened across the hall, he remarked: "Have you studied the Odes?" "No," I replied. "If you do not study the Odes," he said, "you will have nothing to use in conversation." On going out I set myself to study the Odes.

'Another day, he was again standing alone, and as I hastened across the hall, he asked: "Have you studied the Rules of Ceremony?" "No," I replied. "If you do not study the Ceremonies, you will have no grounding." On going out I set myself to study the Ceremonies. These are the two lessons I have received.'

When Ch'en K'ang came away he remarked with delight, 'I asked one thing and obtained three – I have learnt about the Odes, I have learnt about the Ceremonies, and I have learnt that the Wise Man keeps his son at a distance.'

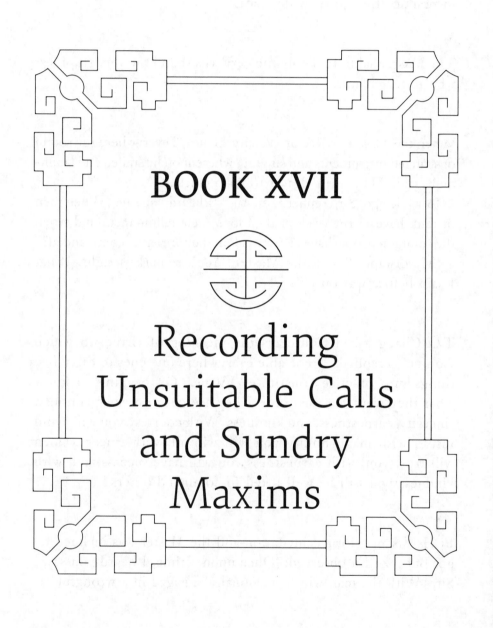

BOOK XVII

Recording Unsuitable Calls and Sundry Maxims

The Master said: 'By nature men nearly resemble each other; in practice they grow wide apart.'

The Master said: 'It is only the very wisest and the very stupidest who never change.'

When the Master arrived at Wu city, he heard everywhere the sound of stringed instruments and singing; whereupon he smiled and laughingly said, 'Why use a cleaver to kill a chicken?'

'A while ago, Sir,' replied Tzu Yu,[51] 'I heard you say: "When men of rank have learnt wisdom they love their fellow men; and when the common people have learnt wisdom they are easily commanded".'

'My disciples!' said the Master, 'Yen's remark is right. What I said before was only in jest.'

Tzu Chang asked Confucius the meaning of virtue, to which Confucius replied: 'To be able everywhere one goes to carry five things into practice constitutes Virtue.' On begging to know what they were, he was told: 'They are courtesy, magnanimity, sincerity, earnestness, and kindness. With courtesy you will avoid insult, with magnanimity you will win all, with sincerity men will trust you, with earnestness you will have success, and with kindness you will be well fitted to command others.'

Pi Hsi[52] sent a formal invitation and the Master was inclined to go. But Tzu Lu observed: 'Once upon a time, I heard you say, Sir, "With the man who is personally engaged in a wrongful enterprise, the man of honour declines to associate." Pi Hsi is holding Chung-mou in revolt, what will it be like, Sir, if you go there?'

'True,' said the Master, 'I did use those words; but is it not said of the really hard, that you may grind it and it will not grind down; also is it not said of the really white, that you may dye it but it will not turn black? Am I indeed a bitter gourd? Must I, like it, be hung up and never eaten?'

The Master said: 'Yu, have you ever heard of the six good words and the six things that obscure them?' 'Never,' was the reply. 'Sit down then, and I will tell you.' 'Love of kindness, without a love to learn, finds itself obscured by foolishness. Love of knowledge, without a love to learn, finds itself obscured by loose speculation. Love of honesty, without a love to learn, finds itself obscured by harmful candour. Love of straightforwardness, without a love to learn, finds itself obscured by misdirected judgement. Love of daring, without a love to learn, finds itself obscured by insubordination. And love for strength of character, without a love to learn, finds itself obscured by intractability.'

The Master said: 'My sons, my disciples, why do you not study the poets? Poetry is able to stimulate the mind, it can train to observation, it can encourage social intercourse, it can modify the vexations of life; from it the student learns to fulfil his more immediate duty to his parents, and his remoter duty to his prince; and in it he may become widely acquainted with the names of birds and beasts, plants and trees.'

The Master said to his son Po Yü: 'Have you studied the Chou Nan and the Chao Nan?[53] Is not the man who does not study the Chou Nan and the Chao Nan Odes like one who stands with his face hard up against a wall, eh?'

The Master said: 'He who shams a stern appearance while inwardly he is a weakling, can only be compared with the vulgar and low; indeed is he not like the thief who sneaks through or skulks over walls?'

The Master said: 'To proclaim on the road what you hear on the way is virtue thrown away.'

'These servile fellows!' said the Master. 'How is it possible to serve one's prince along with them? Before obtaining their position they are in anxiety to obtain it, and when they have it they are in anxiety lest they lose it; and if men are in anxiety about losing their position, there is no length to which they will not go.'

'In olden times,' said the Master, 'the people had three faults, which nowadays perhaps no longer exist. High spirit in olden times meant liberty in detail; the high spirit of today means utter looseness. Dignity of old meant reserve; dignity today means resentment and offence. Simple-mindedness of old meant straightforwardness; simple-mindedness today is nothing but a mask for cunning.'

The Master said: 'Artful address and an insinuating demeanour seldom accompany virtue.'

The Master said: 'Artful address and an insinuating demeanour seldom accompany virtue.'

'I wish I could do without speaking,' said the Master. 'If you did not speak, Sir,' said Tzu Kung, 'what should we disciples pass on to others?' 'What speech has Heaven?' replied the Master. 'The four seasons run their courses and all things flourish; yet what speech has Heaven?'

Ju Pei⁵⁴ wished to see Confucius, who excused himself on the grounds of sickness; but when the messenger had gone out at the door, he took up his harpsichord and began to sing, so that Ju Pei might hear it.

Tsai Wo, asking about the three years' mourning, suggested that one year was long enough. 'If,' said he, 'a well-bred man be three years without exercising his manners, his manners will certainly degenerate; and if for three years he make no use of music, his music will certainly go to ruin. In one year the last year's grain is finished and the new grain has been garnered, the seasonal friction-sticks have made their varying fires – a year would be enough.'

   'Would you, then, feel at ease in eating good rice and wearing fine clothes?' asked the Master.

   'I should,' was the reply.

   'If you would feel at ease, then do so; but a well-bred man, when mourning, does not relish good food when he eats it, does not enjoy music when he hears it, and does not feel at ease when in a comfortable dwelling; therefore he avoids those things. But now you would feel at ease, so go and do them.'

When Tsai had gone out, the Master said: 'The unfeelingness of Tsai Yü! Only when a child is three years old does it leave its parents' arms, and the three years' mourning is the universal mourning everywhere. And Yü – was not he the object of his parents' affection for three years?'

The Master said: 'How hard is the case of the man who stuffs himself with food the livelong day, never applying his mind to anything! Are there no checkers or chess to play? Even to do that is surely better than nothing at all.'

Tzu Lu once asked: 'Does a man of the nobler class hold courage in estimation?'

'Men of the nobler class,' said the Master, 'deem rectitude the highest thing. It is men of the nobler class, with courage but without rectitude, who rebel. It is men of the lower order, with courage but without rectitude, who become robbers.'

'Do men of the nobler class detest others?' asked Tzu Kung.

'They do detest others,' answered the Master. 'They detest men who divulge other people's misdeeds. They detest those low, base people who slander their superiors. They detest the bold and mannerless. They detest the persistently forward who are yet obtuse. And have you, Tzu, those whom you detest?' he asked.

'I detest those who count prying out information as wisdom. I detest those who count absence of modesty as courage. I detest those who count denouncing a man's private affairs as straightforwardness,' replied Tzu Kung.

The Master said: 'Of all people, maids and servants are hardest to keep in your house. If you are friendly with them they lose their deference; if you are reserved with them they resent it.'

The Master said: 'If a man reach forty and yet be disliked by his fellows, he will be so to the end.'

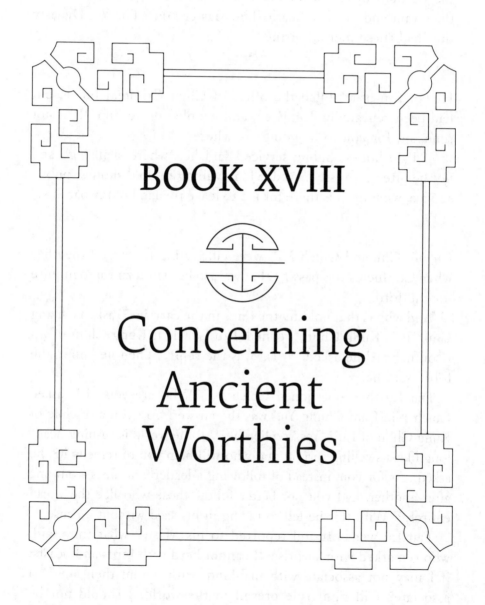

BOOK XVIII

Concerning Ancient Worthies

The viscount of Wei withdrew from serving the tyrant Chou;[55] the viscount of Chi was made a slave; Pi Kan remonstrated with the tyrant and suffered death. The Master said: 'The Yin Dynasty thus had three men of virtue.'

Hui of Liu-hsia[56] filled the office of Chief Criminal Judge, but had been repeatedly dismissed, and people said to him, 'Is it not time, sir, for you to be going elsewhere?'

'If I do honest public service,' said he, 'where shall I go and not be often dismissed? And if I am willing to do dishonest public service, what need is there for me to leave the land of my parents?'

Ch'ang Chü and Chieh Ni[57] were cultivating their land together when Confucius was passing that way, so he sent Tzu Lu to inquire for the ford.

'And who is that holding the reins in the carriage?' asked Ch'ang Chü. 'It is Kung Ch'iu,' replied Tzu Lu. 'Is it Kung Ch'iu of Lu [Confucius]?' he asked. 'It is,' was the reply. 'Then he knows the ford,' said he.

Tzu Lu then questioned Chieh Ni. 'Who are you, sir?' asked Chieh Ni. 'I am Chung Yu,' was the answer. 'Are you a disciple of Kung Ch'iu of Lu?' 'Yes,' replied he. 'All the world is rushing headlong like a swelling torrent and who will help you to remedy it?' he asked. 'As for you, instead of following a leader who flees from one after another, had you not better follow those who flee the world entirely?' With this he fell to raking in his seed without a pause.

Tzu Lu went off and reported to his Master what they said, who remarked with surprise: 'I cannot herd with birds and beasts; if I may not associate with mankind, with whom then am I to associate? Did right rule prevail in the world, I should not be taking part in reforming it.'

Once when Tzu Lu was following the Master on a journey he happened to fall behind. Meeting an old man carrying a basket on his staff, Tzu Lu asked him, 'Have you seen my Master, sir?' 'You,' said the old man, 'whose four limbs know not toil, and who cannot distinguish the five grains, who may your Master be?' With that he planted his staff in the ground and commenced weeding.

Tzu Lu joined his hands together in salutation and stood waiting. The old man kept Tzu Lu for the night, killed a fowl, prepared millet, and gave him to eat, introducing also his two sons.

Next morning Tzu Lu went his way and reported his adventure. 'He is a recluse,' said the Master, and sent Tzu Lu back again to see him, but on his arrival the old man had gone. Whereupon Tzu Lu said to the sons: 'It is not right to refuse to serve one's country. If the regulations between old and young in family life may not be set aside, how is it that your father sets aside the duty between a prince and his ministers? In his desire to maintain his own personal purity, he subverts one of the main principles of society. A wise man in whatever office he occupies, fulfils its proper duties, even though he is well aware that right principles have ceased to make progress.'

The men noted for withdrawal into private life were Po I, Shu Ch'i, Yü Chung, Yi Yi, Chu Chang, Hui of Liu-hsia, and Shao Lien.

The Master observed: 'Those of them who would neither abate their high purpose, nor abase themselves, it seems to me were Po I and Shu Ch'i.[58] Concerning Hui of Liu-hsia and Shao Lien, while they abated their high purpose and abased themselves, what they said made for social order, and what they did hit the mark of what men were anxious about: and that is all. Concerning Yü Chung and Yi Yi, though in their seclusion they were immoderate in their utterances, yet they sustained their personal purity, and their self-immolation had weighty purpose.

'But I am different from these. With me there is no inflexible "thou shalt" or "thou shalt not".'

The Duke of Chou[59] addressing his son, the Duke of Lu, said: 'The wise prince does not neglect his relatives; nor does he cause his chief ministers to be discontented at his not employing them; he does not dismiss old servants from office without some grave cause for it; nor does he expect one man to be capable of everything.'

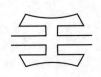

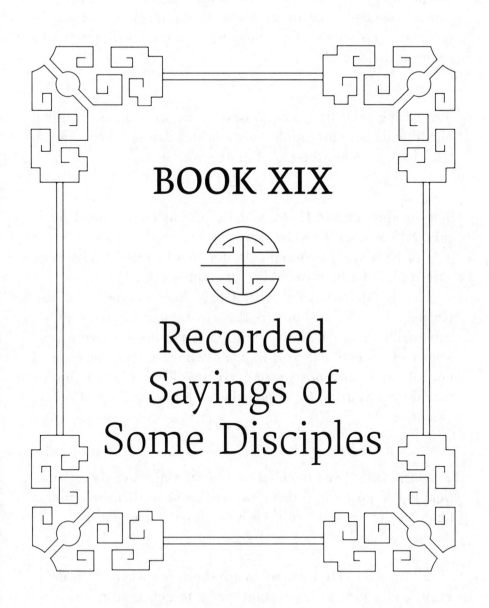

BOOK XIX

Recorded Sayings of Some Disciples

Tzu Chang said: 'A servant of the State, who in the presence of danger offers his life, whose first thought in presence of personal gain is whether it be right, whose first thought in sacrifice is reverence, and whose first thought in mourning is grief – he commands approval.'

Tzu Chang said: 'If a man possess virtue without its enlarging him, if he believe in truth but without steadfastness, how can you tell whether he has these qualities or not?'

The disciples of Tzu Hsia asked Tzu Chang concerning friendship. 'What does Tzu Hsia say?' he inquired.

'Tzu Hsia says,' they replied, 'if a man be suitable, associate with him, if he be unsuitable, turn him away.'

'This is different from what I have been taught,' said Tzu Chang. 'A wise man honours the worthy and tolerates all; he commends the good and commiserates the incompetent. Am I a man of exceptional worth? Then whom among men may I not tolerate? Am I not a man of worth? Then others would be turning me away. Why should there be this turning of others away then?'

Tzu Hsia said: 'Even the inferior arts certainly have their attraction; but to go far into them involves a risk of their becoming a hindrance to progress: so the wise man lets them alone.'

Tzu Hsia said: 'He who day by day finds out where he is deficient, and who month by month never forgets that in which he has become proficient, may truly be called a lover of learning.'

Tzu Hsia said: 'Broad culture and a steady will, earnest investigation and personal reflection – virtue is to be found therein.'

Tzu Hsia said: 'As the various craftsmen dwell in their workshops that they may do their work effectively, so the Wise Man applies himself to study that he may carry his wisdom to perfection.'

Tzu Hsia said: 'The inferior man always embellishes his mistakes.'

Tzu Hsia said: 'The Wise Man varies from three aspects. Seen from a distance he appears stern; when approached he proves gracious; as you listen to him you find him decided in opinion.'

Tzu Hsia said: 'The Wise Man obtains the people's confidence before imposing burdens on them, for without confidence they will think themselves oppressed. He also obtains the confidence of his prince before pointing out his errors, for before obtaining such confidence his prince would deem himself aspersed.'

Tzu Hsia said: 'He who does not overstep the threshold in the major virtues, may have liberty of egress and ingress in the minor ones.'

Tzu Hsia said: 'The occupant of office when his duties are finished should betake himself to study; and the student when his studies are finished should betake himself to office.'

Tzu Yu remarked: 'My friend Chang [Tzu Chang] does things hardly possible to others, but he is not yet perfect in virtue.'

Tseng Tzu said: 'What a stately manner Chang puts on! It must be hard to live the perfect life alongside him.'

Tseng Tzu said: 'I have heard the Master say: "Though a man may never before have shown what was in him, surely he will do so when he mourns his parents."'

Tseng Tzu said: 'I have heard the Master observe that the filial piety of Meng Chuang Tzu[60] might in other particulars be possible to other men, but his unaltered maintenance of his father's servants, and of his father's administration – these they would hardly find possible.'

When the Chief of the Meng family appointed Yang Fu[61] as chief criminal judge, the latter came to ask advice of Tseng Tzu who replied: 'The rulers have lost their principles, and for long the people have been disorganized; hence, when you discover evidence against a man, be grieved for and commiserate him and take no pleasure in your discovery.'

Tzu Kung said: 'The transgressions of the Wise Man are like eclipses of the sun or moon. When he transgresses all men look at him. When he recovers all men look up to him.'

Kung-sun Ch'ao of Wei once inquired of Tzu Kung: 'From whom did Chung Ni [Confucius] get his learning?' 'The doctrines of Wen and Wu[62] have never yet fallen to the ground,' replied Tzu Kung, 'but have remained amongst men. Gifted men have kept in mind their nobler principles, while others not so gifted have kept in mind the minor, so that nowhere have the doctrines of Wen and Wu been absent. From whom then, could our Master not learn? And, moreover, what need was there for him to have a regular teacher?'

Shu-sun Wu-shu,[63] talking to the high officers at Court, remarked: 'Tzu Kung is a superior man to Chung Ni [Confucius].' Tzu-fu Ching-po took and told this to Tzu Kung, who replied: 'One might illustrate the position with the boundary wall of a building. As to my wall, it only reaches to the shoulder, and with a peep you may see whatever is of value in the house and home. The Master's wall rises fathoms high, and unless you find the gate and go inside, you cannot see the beauties of the temple and the richness of its host of officers. But those who find the gate perhaps are few – indeed does not His Honour's remark confirm this view?'

Shu-sun Wu-shu having spoken disparagingly of Chung Ni, Tzu Kung observed: 'There is no use in doing that, for Chung Ni cannot be disparaged. The excellences of others are mounds and hillocks, which may nevertheless be climbed over, but Chung Ni! He is the sun, the moon, which there is no way of climbing over; and though a man may desire to cut himself off from them, what harm does he do to the sun or moon? He only shows that he has no idea of proportion.'

Ch'en Tzu Chin once said to Tzu Kung: 'You are too modest, Sir. How can Chung Ni be considered superior to you?'

'An educated man,' replied Tzu Kung, 'for a single expression is often deemed wise, and for a single expression is often deemed foolish; hence one should not be heedless in what one says. The impossibility of equalling our Master is like the impossibility of scaling a ladder and ascending to the skies. Were our Master to obtain control of a country, then, as has been said, "He raises his people and they stand; he leads them, and they follow; he gives them tranquillity and multitudes resort to him; he brings his influence to bear on them and they live in harmony; his life is glorious and his death bewailed" – how is it possible for him to be equalled?'

BOOK XX

Concerning Right Government

Yao[64] said: 'O, thou Shun! The celestial lineage rests in thy person. Faithfully hold to the golden mean. Should the land become lean, Heaven's bounties will forever end towards you.' And Shun in like terms charged Yü.

T'ang said: 'I thy child Li, Dare to use a black ox, And dare clearly to state to Thee, O Most August and Sovereign God, That the sinner I dare not spare, Nor keep Thy ministers, O God, in obscurity, As Thy heart, O God, discerns. If I have sinned, Let it not concern the country; If my country has sinned, Let the sin rest on me.'

Wu of Chou conferred great largesses, the good being enriched. 'Although,' said he, 'the tyrant Chou had his host of princes closely related to the throne, they compared not with my men of virtue; and it is upon me that the grievances of the people fell.'

He paid careful attention to the weights and measures, revised the laws and regulations, restored the disused offices; and universal government prevailed.

He re-established states that had been extinguished, restored the lines of broken succession, called to office men who had exiled themselves; and all the people gave him their hearts. What he laid stress on were the people's food, mourning for the dead, and sacrifices. By his magnanimity he won all, by his good faith he gained the people's confidence, by his diligence he achieved his ends, and by his justice all were gratified.

Tzu Chang inquired of Confucius, saying, 'How should a man act to achieve the proper administration of government?' The Master replied: 'Let him honour the five good and banish the four bad rules; then he will be a worthy administrator.'

'What is meant by the five good rules?' asked Tzu Chang. 'That the ruler,' replied the Master, 'be beneficent without expending the public revenue, that he exact service without arousing dissatisfaction, that his desires never degenerate to greed, that he be dignified but without disdain, and that he be commanding but not domineering.'

'What is meant by beneficence without expenditure?' asked Tzu Chang. The Master replied: 'To benefit the people by the development of their natural resources; is not this a public benefaction without expense to the revenue? If he selects suitable works to exact from them – who then will be dissatisfied? If his desires are for the good of others, and he secures it, how can he be greedy? The wise ruler without considering whether the persons concerned are many or few, or the affair small or great, never permits himself to slight them – is not this to be dignified without disdain? The wise ruler arrays himself properly in robe and cap, and throws a nobility into his looks, so that men looking upon him in his dignity stand in awe of him – and is not this commanding without being domineering?'

'What is the meaning of the four bad rules?' asked Tzu Chang. The Master replied, 'Putting men to death without having taught them their duty – which may be called cruelty; expecting the completion of works when no warning has been given – which may be called oppression; remissness in ordering and then demand for instant performance – which may be called robbery; and likewise, when giving rewards to men, offering them in grudging fashion – which may be called being merely an official.'

The Master said: 'He who does not know the divine law cannot become a noble man. He who does not know the laws of right conduct cannot form his character. He who does not know the force of words, cannot know men.'

NOTES

Confucius' disciples are referred to by more than one name in the *Analects*. These names are included in brackets at the first occurrence of a disciple's name in these notes, with the name most frequently used printed in italics.

BOOK I

1. Yu (Yu Juo, Yu Tzu, *Tzu Yu*); Tseng (Tseng Shen, Shen, *Tseng Tzu*); *Tzu Hsia* (Pu Shang, Shang); *Tzu Ch'in* (Ch'en K'ang), *Tzu Kung* (Tuan-mu Tzu, Tz'u): disciples of Confucius.

BOOK II

2. The Odes or *Shih Ching* are said to have been compiled by Confucius himself.
3. Meng I Tzu (Meng Sun): minister of Lu prior to Confucius' exile. Meng Wu Po: son of Meng I Tzu.
4. *Fan Ch'ih* (Fan Hsu); *Tzu Yu* (Yen Yen); *Hui* (Yen Hui, Yen Yüan); *Tzu Chang* (Tuan-sun Shih): disciples of Confucius. Hui was Confucius' favourite disciple.
5. Duke Ai: duke of Lu when Confucius returned from exile.
6. Chi K'ang Tzu (K'ang Tzu): minister to Duke Ai of Lu, he recalled Confucius and his disciples from exile.

BOOK III

7. A comment on the arrogance of Chi in adopting an Imperial rite.
8. *Lin Fang*: disciple of Confucius.
9. The Chou dynasty was founded by Duke Wen of Chou – sometimes called King Wen – who served as regent during the minority of his nephew, later King Wu. Confucius considered Wen the ideal of a good ruler.
10. Duke Ting of Lu: Confucius served as his minister before the exile.
11. *Tsai Wo* (Tsai Yü, Yü): disciple of Confucius.
12. Shao (Succession) and Wen (Overthrow) were musical forms associated

respectively with Shun and Wu, two rulers of ancient China. The former came to the throne through succession, the latter by over-throwing his rivals.

BOOK V

13. Several of Confucius' disciples are encountered for the first time in this book. They are, in order of appearance: *Kung Yeh Ch'ang*; Nan Yung (*Nan-Kung Kua*); *Tzu Chien* (Fu-Pu Ch'i); Yung (Jan Yung, *Chung Kung*); *Ch'i-tiao K'ai*; *Shen Ch'eng* (Ch'eng); *Tzu Lu* (Chung Yu, Chi Lu).
14. K'ung Tzu: a Counsellor of Wei. Given the posthumous title 'Wen' (meaning 'cultured') and referred to in later books of the *Analects* by his full name of Kung-shu Wen-tzu.
15. The people named in Book V from here onwards are ministers or officers of state, apart from one paragraph which concerns disciples of Confucius.

BOOK VI

16. *Jan Ch'iu* (Jan Yu, Ch'iu): disciple of Confucius.
17. Yao and Shun: legendary rulers of ancient China, renowned for their wisdom, moral character and benevolence.

BOOK VII

18. The *Book of Changes*: also known as the *I Ching*, one of the classic texts of ancient China, is variously described as a book of divination, philosophy or cosmological processes. According to tradition, Confucius wrote a commentary on it.
19. *Kung-hsi Hua* (Kung-hsi Ch'ih, Ch'ih): disciple of Confucius.

BOOK VIII

20. Meng Ching Tzu: son of Meng Wu Po (*see* note 3).
21. Shun and Yü: legendary emperors from the 23rd century BCE.

BOOK IX

22. When Confucius came to K'uang during the exile, he found himself in danger because he was mistaken for somebody else.
23: Lao (Chi'in Chang): disciple of Confucius.
24: The hypothetical 'jewel' to which Tzu Kung refers is Confucius' teaching.

BOOK X

25. K'ang Tzu (Chi K'ang Tzu): minister to Duke Ai of Lu. It was polite custom to acknowledge edible presents by tasting them at once.

BOOK XI

26. Confucius is referring back to his period in exile and the disciples who were with him then. Mentioned for the first time here are *Min Tzu Ch'ien* (Min Tzu); Jan Niu (Jan Keng, *Po Niu*); *Jan Yu.*
27. Yu = Tzu Lu. He trained as a soldier and was killed in battle, fighting for his lord.
28. Shih = Tzu Chang; Shang = Tzu Hsia (Pu Shang).
29. Ch'ai = Kao Ch'ai (Tzu Kao); Shen = Tseng Tzu (Tseng Shen); Shih = Tzu Chang; Yu = Tzu Lu. Confucius is describing the character of these disciples when they first came to him.
30. Hui = Yen Yüan; T'zu = Tzu Kung.
31. Chi Tzu-jan: younger brother of the minister Chi K'ang Tzu (*see* note 25). They were thinking of doing away with their prince.

BOOK XII

32. Ssu-ma Niu's brother, Huan T'ui, had tried to kill Confucius.
33. Chi Tzu-Ch'eng: an official who questions the value of art and self-refinement.

BOOK XIII

34. She: a small state.
35. Chü-fu: a city in Lu.

BOOK XIV

36. Hsien (Yüan Hsien, *Yüan Ssu*): disciple of Confucius.
37. Prince I, Ao, Yü and Chi: legendary figures from antiquity. Prince I and Ao were famed for their individual heroic feats whereas Yü and Chi were noted for their contribution to wider society: because Yü successfully tamed China's Great Flood, the legendary emperor Shun considered him a worthy successor and abdicated in his favour; in turn, Yü appointed his son Chi as his successor and thus established China's first recorded dynasty, the Hsia dynasty.
38. Tsang Wu Chung and Kung Ch'o were both counsellors in Lu; Chuang Tzu of P'ien was said to have killed two tigers in one day; Jan Ch'iu

(Confucius' disciple Tzu Yu) served under Chi K'ang Tzu, a minister in Lu, and was instrumental in the Master being recalled from exile.

39. Kung-shu Wen-tzu: an official in Wei, who was also a philosopher (*see* note 14).

40. Duke Ling of Wei: an unprincipled ruler who retained his throne only through the proficiency of his ministers. Chi K'ang Tzu: a minister in Lu.

41. Chü Po Yü: an official in Wei and former disciple of Confucius.

42. Wei-sheng Mou: an elderly recluse. Ch'iu = Confucius.

43. Kung-po Liao: a disciple of Confucius. Chi-sun = Chi K'ang Tzu, the Lu minister. Tzu-fu Ching-po: a prominent official in Lu.

44. Kao Tsung: emperor of the Shang dynasty.

45. Yao and Shun: legendary emperors.

46. Yüan Jang: an elderly scoundrel, said to have been an old friend of Confucius.

BOOK XV

47. Yü and Chü Po Yü: officials in Wei (*see also* note 41).

48. The Hsia calendar mirrored the harmonious cosmological relationship of the heavens, earth and humankind; the state carriage of Yin was a simple wooden carriage, devoid of ornamentation; the cap of Chou was used for sacred rites; the gestures of the Shao dances were stately and ordered; the songs of Cheng were considered frivolous by Confucius.

49. In Confucius' time, the musical profession was open only to those who were blind.

BOOK XVI

50. Po Yü: Confucius' son.

BOOK XVII

51. Tzu Yu (Yen Yen): disciple of Confucius and administrator in Wu where he had worked hard to put in to effect the Master's principles of government. He mistakenly interpreted Confucius' playful remark as a criticism of his zeal.

52. Pi Hsi: steward of the fiefdom of Chung-mou in the state of Chin.

53. Chou Nan and Chao Nan: the first two books of *The Odes*.

54. Ju Pei: former disciple of Confucius.

BOOK XVIII

55. Chou: a brutal tyrant, last of the Shang emperors, 1153–1122BCE. Pi Kan and the viscounts of Wei and Chi were his relatives, yet when they tried to persuade Chou to change his ways he punished them.
56. Hui of Liu-hsia: an incorruptible judge.
57. Ch'ang Chü and Chieh Ni: two recluses.
58. Po I and Shu Ch'i: two princes who withdrew from court and died of starvation rather than betray their principles. Hui Liu-hsia, *see* note 56.
59. Duke of Chou: acted as regent for his son, the Duke of Lu.

BOOK XIX

60. Meng Chuang Tzu: a minister of Lu.
61. Yang Fu: a disciple of Tseng Tzu (disciple of Confucius).
62. Wen and Wu: a reference to Kings Wen and Wu, founders of the Chou dynasty (*see* note 9).
63. Shu-sun Wu-shu: a high official of Lu.

BOOK XX

64. The first section of this book records sayings and actions attributed to the founders of the great dynasties.

THE WAY
OF THE
SAMURAI

CONTENTS

DEDICATION

TO MY BELOVED UNCLE TOKITOSHI OTA
WHO TAUGHT ME TO REVERE THE PAST
AND TO ADMIRE THE DEEDS OF THE SAMURAI
I DEDICATE THIS LITTLE BOOK

'There are, if I may so say, three powerful spirits, which have from time to time, moved on the face of the waters, and given a predominant impulse to the moral sentiments and energies of mankind. These are the spirits of liberty, of religion, and of honour.'

Hallam, *Europe in the Middle Ages*

'Chivalry is itself the poetry of life.'

Schlegel, *Philosophy of History*

PREFACE

About ten years ago, while spending a few days under the hospitable roof of the distinguished Belgian jurist, the lamented M. de Laveleye, our conversation turned, during one of our rambles, to the subject of religion. 'Do you mean to say,' asked the venerable professor, 'that you have no religious instruction in your schools?' On my replying in the negative he suddenly halted in astonishment, and in a voice which I shall not easily forget, he repeated 'No religion! How do you impart moral education?' The question stunned me at the time. I could give no ready answer, for the moral precepts I learned in my childhood days were not given in schools; and not until I began to analyze the different elements that formed my notions of right and wrong, did I find that it was Bushido[1] that breathed them into my nostrils.

The direct inception of this little book is due to the frequent queries put by my wife as to the reasons why such and such ideas and customs prevail in Japan.

In my attempts to give satisfactory replies to M. de Laveleye and to my wife, I found that without understanding Feudalism and Bushido, the moral ideas of present Japan are a sealed volume.

Taking advantage of enforced idleness on account of long illness, I put down in the order now presented to the public some of the answers given in our household conversation. They consist mainly of what I was taught and told in my youthful days, when Feudalism was still in force.

Between Lafcadio Hearn and Mrs. Hugh Fraser on one side and Sir Ernest Satow and Professor Chamberlain on the other, it is indeed discouraging to write anything Japanese in English. The only advantage I have over them is that I can assume the attitude of a personal defendant, while these distinguished writers are at best solicitors and attorneys. I have often thought, 'Had I their gift of language, I would present the cause of Japan in more eloquent terms!' But one who speaks in a borrowed tongue should be thankful if he can just make himself intelligible.

All through the discourse I have tried to illustrate whatever points I have made with parallel examples from European history and literature, believing that these will aid in bringing the subject nearer to the comprehension of foreign readers.

Should any of my allusions to religious subjects and to religious workers be thought slighting, I trust my attitude towards Christianity itself will not be questioned. It is with ecclesiastical methods and with the forms which obscure the teachings of Christ, and not with the teachings themselves, that I have little sympathy. I believe in the religion taught by Him and handed down to us in the New Testament, as well as in the law written in the heart. Further, I believe that God hath made a testament which may be called 'old' with every people and nation – Gentile or Jew, Christian or Heathen. As to the rest of my theology, I need not impose upon the patience of the public.

In concluding this preface, I wish to express my thanks to my friend Anna C. Hartshorne for many valuable suggestions.

INAZO NITOBE

CHAPTER 1

BUSHIDO AS AN
ETHICAL SYSTEM

Chivalry is a flower no less indigenous to the soil of Japan than its emblem, the cherry blossom; nor is it a dried-up specimen of an antique virtue preserved in the herbarium of our history. It is still a living object of power and beauty among us; and if it assumes no tangible shape or form, it not the less scents the moral atmosphere, and makes us aware that we are still under its potent spell. The conditions of society which brought it forth and nourished it have long disappeared; but as those far-off stars which once were and are not, still continue to shed their rays upon us, so the light of chivalry, which was a child of feudalism, still illuminates our moral path, surviving its mother institution. It is a pleasure to me to reflect upon this subject in the language of Burke, who uttered the well-known touching eulogy over the neglected bier of its European prototype.

It argues a sad defect of information concerning the Far East, when so erudite a scholar as Dr. George Miller did not hesitate to affirm that chivalry, or any other similar institution, has never existed either among the nations of antiquity or among the modern Orientals[2]. Such ignorance, however, is amply excusable, as the third edition of the good Doctor's work appeared the same year that Commodore Perry was knocking at the portals of our exclusivism. More than a decade later, about the time that our feudalism was in the last throes of existence, Karl Marx, writing his *Capital*, called the attention of his readers to the peculiar advantage of studying the social and political institutions of feudalism, as then to be seen in living form only in Japan. I would likewise invite the Western historical and ethical student to the study of chivalry in the Japan of the present.

Enticing as is a historical disquisition on the comparison between European and Japanese feudalism and chivalry, it is not the purpose of this paper to enter into it at length. My attempt is rather to relate, *firstly*, the origin and sources of our chivalry; *secondly*, its character and teaching; *thirdly*, its influence among the masses; and, *fourthly*, the continuity and permanence of its influence. Of these several points, the first will be only brief and cursory, or else I should have to take my readers into the devious paths of our national history; the second will be dwelt upon at greater length, as being most likely to interest students of International Ethics and Comparative Ethology in our ways of thought and action; and the rest will be dealt with as corollaries.

The Japanese word which I have roughly rendered Chivalry, is, in the original, more expressive than Horsemanship. *Bu-shi-do* means literally Military-Knight-Ways – the ways which fighting nobles should observe in their daily life as well as in their vocation; in a word, the 'Precepts of Knighthood,' the *noblesse oblige* of the warrior class. Having thus given its literal significance, I may be allowed henceforth to use the word in the original. The use of the original term is also advisable for this reason, that a teaching so circumscribed and unique, engendering a cast of mind and character so peculiar, so local, must wear the badge of its singularity on its face; then, some words have a national *timbre* so expressive of race characteristics that the best of translators can do them but scant justice, not to say positive injustice, and grievance. Who can improve by translation what the German *Gemüth* signifies, or who does not feel the difference between the two words verbally so closely allied as the English *gentleman* and the French *gentilhomme*?

Bushido, then, is the code of moral principles which the knights were required or instructed to observe. It is not a written code; at best it consists of a few maxims handed down from mouth to mouth or coming from the pen of some well-known warrior or savant. More frequently it is a code unuttered and unwritten, possessing all the more the powerful sanction of veritable deed, and of a law written on the fleshly tablets of the heart. It was founded not on the creation of one brain, however able, or on the life of a single personage, however renowned. It was an organic growth of decades and centuries of military career. It, perhaps, fills the same position in the history of ethics that the English Constitution does in political history; yet it has had nothing to compare with the Magna Carta or the Habeas Corpus Act. True, early in the seventeenth century Military Statutes (*Buké Hatto*) were promulgated; but their thirteen short articles were taken up mostly with marriages, castles, leagues, etc., and didactic regulations were but meagrely touched upon. We cannot, therefore, point out any definite time and place and say, 'Here is its fountain head.' Only as it attains consciousness in the feudal age, its origin, in respect to time, may be identified with feudalism. But feudalism itself is woven of many threads, and Bushido shares its intricate nature. As in England the political institutions of feudalism may be said to date from the Norman Conquest, so we may say that in Japan its rise was simultaneous with the ascendancy of Yoritomo, late in the twelfth century. As, however, in England, we find the social elements of feudalism far back in the period previous to William the Conqueror, so, too, the germs of feudalism in Japan had been long existent before the period I have mentioned.

Again, in Japan as in Europe, when feudalism was formally inaugurated, the professional class of warriors naturally came into prominence. These were known as *samurai*, meaning literally, like the old English *cniht* (knecht, knight), guards or attendants – resembling in character the *soldurii* whom Caesar mentioned as existing in Aquitania, or the *comitati*, who, according to Tacitus, followed Germanic chiefs in his time; or, to take a still later parallel, the *milites medii* that one reads about in the history of Medieval Europe. A Sinico-Japanese word *Bu-ké* or *Bu-shi* (Fighting Knights) was also adopted in common use. They were a privileged class, and must originally have been a rough breed who made fighting their vocation. This class was naturally recruited, in a long period of constant warfare, from the manliest and the most adventurous, and all the while the process of elimination went on, the timid and the feeble being sorted out, and only 'a rude race, all masculine, with brutish strength,' to borrow Emerson's phrase, surviving to form families and the ranks of the *samurai*. Coming to profess great honour and great privileges, and correspondingly great responsibilities, they soon felt the need of a common standard of behaviour, especially as they were always on a belligerent footing and belonged to different clans. Just as physicians limit competition among themselves by professional courtesy, just as lawyers sit in courts of honour in cases of violated etiquette, so must also warriors possess some resort for final judgment on their misdemeanours.

Fair play in fight! What fertile germs of morality lie in this primitive sense of savagery and childhood. Is it not the root of all military and civic virtues? We smile (as if we had outgrown it!) at the boyish desire of the small Britisher, Tom Brown, 'to leave behind him the name of a fellow who never bullied a little boy or turned his back on a big one.' And yet, who does not know that this desire is the cornerstone on which moral structures of mighty dimensions can be reared? May I not go even so far as to say that the gentlest and most peace-loving of religions endorses this aspiration? This desire of Tom's is the basis on which the greatness of England is largely built, and it will not take us long to discover that *Bushido* does not stand on a lesser pedestal. If fighting in itself, be it offensive or defensive, is, as Quakers rightly testify, brutal and wrong, we can still say with Lessing, 'We know from what failings our virtue springs.' 'Sneaks' and 'cowards' are epithets of the worst opprobrium to healthy, simple natures. Childhood begins life with these notions, and knighthood also; but, as life grows larger and its relations many-sided, the early faith seeks sanction from higher authority and more rational sources for its own justification, satisfaction and development. If military interests had operated alone, without higher moral support, how far short of chivalry would the ideal of knighthood have fallen! In Europe, Christianity, interpreted with concessions convenient to chivalry, infused it nevertheless with spiritual data. 'Religion, war and glory were the three souls of a perfect Christian knight,' says Lamartine. In Japan there were several sources of Bushido.

CHAPTER 2

SOURCES OF BUSHIDO

I may begin with Buddhism. It furnished a sense of calm trust in Fate, a quiet submission to the inevitable, that stoic composure in sight of danger or calamity, that disdain of life and friendliness with death. A foremost teacher of swordsmanship, when he saw his pupil master the utmost of his art, told him, 'Beyond this my instruction must give way to Zen teaching.' 'Zen' is the Japanese equivalent for the Dhyâna, which 'represents human effort to reach through meditation zones of thought beyond the range of verbal expression.'[3] Its method is contemplation, and its purport, as far as I understand it, to be convinced of a principle that underlies all phenomena, and, if it can, of the Absolute itself, and thus to put oneself in harmony with this Absolute. Thus defined, the teaching was more than the dogma of a sect, and whoever attains to the perception of the Absolute raises himself above mundane things and awakes, 'to a new Heaven and a new Earth.'

What Buddhism failed to give, Shintoism offered in abundance. Such loyalty to the sovereign, such reverence for ancestral memory, and such filial piety as are not taught by any other creed, were inculcated by the Shinto doctrines, imparting passivity to the otherwise arrogant character of the samurai. Shinto theology has no place for the dogma of 'original sin.' On the contrary, it believes in the innate goodness and God-like purity of the human soul, adoring it as the adytum from which divine oracles are proclaimed. Everybody has observed that the Shinto shrines are conspicuously devoid of objects and instruments of worship, and that a plain mirror hung in the sanctuary forms the essential part of its furnishing. The presence of this article is easy to explain: it typifies the human heart, which, when perfectly placid and clear, reflects the very image of the Deity. When you stand, therefore, in front of the shrine to worship, you see your own image reflected on its shining surface, and the act of worship is tantamount to the old Delphic injunction, 'Know Thyself.' But self-knowledge does not imply, either in the Greek or Japanese teaching, knowledge of the physical part of man, not his anatomy or his psycho-physics; knowledge was to be of a moral kind, the introspection of our moral nature. Mommsen, comparing the Greek and the Roman, says that when the former worshipped he raised his eyes to heaven, for his prayer was contemplation, while the latter veiled his head, for his was reflection. Essentially like the Roman conception of religion, our reflection brought into prominence not so much the moral as the national consciousness of the individual. Its nature-worship endeared the country to our inmost souls, while its ancestor-worship, tracing from lineage to lineage, made the Imperial family the fountain-head of the whole nation. To us the country is more than land and soil from which to mine gold or to reap grain – it is the sacred abode of the gods, the spirits of our forefathers: to us the Emperor is more than the Arch Constable of a *Rechtsstaat*, or even the Patron of a *Culturstaat* – he is the bodily representative of Heaven on earth, blending in his person its power and its mercy. If what M. Boutmy[4] says is true of English royalty – that it 'is not only the image of authority, but the author and symbol of national unity,' as I believe it to be, doubly and trebly may this be affirmed of royalty in Japan.

The tenets of Shintoism cover the two predominating features of the emotional life of our race – Patriotism and Loyalty. Arthur May Knapp very truly says: 'In Hebrew literature it is often difficult to tell whether the writer is speaking of God or of the Commonwealth; of heaven or of Jerusalem; of the Messiah or of the nation itself.'[5]

A similar confusion may be noticed in the nomenclature of our national faith. I said confusion, because it will be so deemed by a logical intellect on account of its verbal ambiguity; still, being a framework of national instinct and race feelings, Shintoism never pretends to a systematic philosophy or a rational theology. This religion – or, is it not more correct to say, the race emotions which this religion expressed? – thoroughly imbued Bushido with loyalty to the sovereign and love of country. These acted more as impulses than as doctrines; for Shintoism, unlike the Medieval Christian Church, prescribed to its votaries scarcely any *credenda*, furnishing them at the same time with *agenda* of a straightforward and simple type.

As to strictly ethical doctrines, the teachings of Confucius were the most prolific source of Bushido. His enunciation of the five moral relations between master and servant (the governing and the governed), father and son, husband and wife, older and younger brother, and between friend and friend, was but a confirmation of what the race instinct had recognized before his writings were introduced from China. The calm, benignant, and worldly-wise character of his politico-ethical precepts was particularly well suited to the samurai, who formed the ruling class. His aristocratic and conservative tone was well adapted to the requirements of these warrior statesmen. Next to Confucius, Mencius exercised an immense authority over Bushido. His forcible and often quite democratic theories were exceedingly taking to sympathetic natures, and they were even thought dangerous to, and subversive of, the existing social order, hence his works were for a long time under censure. Still, the words of this mastermind found permanent lodgment in the heart of the samurai.

The writings of Confucius and Mencius formed the principal text-books for youths and the highest authority in discussion among the old. A mere acquaintance with the classics of these two sages was held, however, in no high esteem. A common proverb ridicules one who has only an intellectual knowledge of Confucius, as a man ever studious but ignorant of *Analects*. A typical samurai calls a literary savant a book-smelling sot. Another compares learning to an ill-smelling vegetable that must be boiled and boiled before it is fit for use. A man who has read a little smells a little pedantic, and a man who has read much smells yet more so; both are alike unpleasant. The writer meant thereby that knowledge becomes really such only when it is assimilated in the mind of the learner and shows in his character.

Bushido made light of knowledge as such. It was not pursued as an end in itself, but as a means to the attainment of wisdom. Hence, he who stopped short of this end was regarded no higher than a convenient machine, which could turn out poems and maxims at bidding. Thus, knowledge was conceived as identical with its practical application in life; and this Socratic doctrine found its greatest exponent in the Chinese philosopher, Wan Yang Ming, who never wearies of repeating, 'To know and to act are one and the same.'

I beg leave for a moment's digression while I am on this subject, inasmuch as some of the noblest types of *bushi* were strongly influenced by the teachings of this sage. Western readers will easily recognize in his writings many parallels to the New Testament. Making allowance for the terms peculiar to either teaching, the passage, 'Seek ye first the kingdom of God and his righteousness; and all these things shall be added unto you,' conveys a thought that may be found on almost any page of Wan Yang Ming. A Japanese disciple[6] of his says – 'The lord of heaven and earth, of all living beings, dwelling in the heart of man, becomes his mind (*Kokoro*); hence a mind is a living thing, and is ever luminous': and again, 'The spiritual light of our essential being is pure, and is not affected by the will of man. Spontaneously springing up in our mind, it shows what is right and wrong: it is then called conscience; it is even the light that proceedeth from the god of heaven.' How very much do these words sound like some passages from Isaac Pennington or other philosophic mystics! I am inclined to think that the Japanese mind, as expressed in the simple tenets of the Shinto religion, was particularly open to the reception of Yang Ming's precepts. He carried his doctrine of the infallibility of conscience to extreme transcendentalism, attributing to it the faculty to perceive, not only the distinction between right and wrong, but also the nature of psychical facts and physical phenomena.

Thus, whatever the sources, the essential principles which *Bushido* imbibed from them and assimilated to itself, were few and simple. Few and simple as these were, they were sufficient to furnish a safe conduct of life even through the unsafest days of the most unsettled period of our nation's history. The wholesome, unsophisticated nature of our warrior ancestors derived ample food for their spirit from a sheaf of commonplace and fragmentary teachings, gleaned as it were on the highways and byways of ancient thought, and, stimulated by the demands of the age, formed from these gleanings a new and unique type of manhood. An acute French *savant*, M. de la Mazelière, thus sums up his impressions of the sixteenth century: 'Toward the middle of the sixteenth century, all is confusion in Japan, in the government, in society, in the church. But the civil wars, the manners returning to barbarism, the necessity for each to execute justice for himself – these formed men comparable to those Italians of the sixteenth century, in whom Taine praises "the vigorous initiative, the habit of sudden resolutions and desperate undertakings, the grand capacity to do and to suffer." In Japan as in Italy "the rude manners of the Middle Ages" made of man a superb animal, "wholly militant and wholly resistant." And this is why the sixteenth century displays in the highest degree the principal quality of the Japanese race, that great diversity which one finds there between minds (*esprits*) as well as between temperaments. While in India and even in China men seem to differ chiefly in degree of energy or intelligence, in Japan they differ by originality of character as well.'

To the pervading characteristics of the men of whom M. de la Mazelière writes, let us now address ourselves. I shall begin with Rectitude.

CHAPTER 3

RECTITUDE OR JUSTICE

Here we discern the most cogent precept in the code of the samurai. Nothing is more loathsome to him than underhand dealings and crooked undertakings. The conception of Rectitude may be erroneous – it may be narrow. A well-known bushi defines it as a power of resolution; 'Rectitude is the power of deciding upon a certain course of conduct in accordance with reason, without wavering – to die when it is right to die, to strike when to strike is right.' Another speaks of it in the following terms: 'Rectitude is the bone that gives firmness and stature. As without bones the head cannot rest on the top of the spine, nor hands move nor feet stand, so without rectitude neither talent nor learning can make of a human frame a samurai. With it the lack of accomplishments is as nothing.' Mencius calls Benevolence man's mind, and Rectitude or Righteousness his path. 'How lamentable,' he exclaims, 'is it to neglect the path and not pursue it, to lose the mind and not know to seek it again! When men's fowls and dogs are lost, they know to seek for them again, but they lose their mind and do not know to seek for it.' Righteousness, according to Mencius, is a straight and narrow path which a man ought to take to regain the lost paradise.

Even in the latter days of feudalism, when the long continuance of peace brought leisure into the life of the warrior class, and with it dissipations of all kinds and gentle accomplishments, the epithet *Gishi* (a man of rectitude) was considered superior to any name that signified mastery of learning or art. The Forty-seven Faithfuls – of whom so much is made in our popular education – are known in common parlance as the Forty-seven *Gishi*.

In times when cunning artifice was liable to pass for military tact and downright falsehood for *ruse de guerre*, this manly virtue, frank and honest, was a jewel that shone the brightest and was most highly praised. Rectitude is a twin brother to Valour, another martial virtue. But before proceeding to speak of Valour, let me linger a little while on what I may term a derivation from Rectitude, which, at first deviating slightly from its original, became more and more removed from it, until its meaning was perverted in the popular acceptance. I speak of *Gi-ri*, literally the Right Reason, but which came in time to mean a vague sense of duty which public opinion expected an incumbent to fulfil. In its original and unalloyed sense, it meant duty, pure and simple – hence, we speak of the *Giri* we owe to parents, to superiors, to inferiors, to society at large, and so forth. In these instances *Giri* is duty; for what else is duty than what Right Reason demands and commands us to do. Should not Right Reason be our categorical imperative?

Giri primarily meant no more than duty, and I dare say its etymology was derived from the fact that in our conduct, say to our parents, though love should be the only motive, lacking that, there must be some other authority to enforce filial piety; and they formulated this authority in *Giri*. Very rightly did they formulate this authority – *Giri* – since if love does not rush to deeds of virtue, recourse must be had to man's intellect and his reason must be quickened to convince him of the necessity of acting aright. The same is true of any other moral obligation. The instant Duty becomes onerous, Right Reason steps in to prevent our shirking it. *Giri* thus understood is a severe taskmaster, with a birch-rod in his hand to make sluggards perform their part. It is a secondary power in ethics; as a motive it is infinitely inferior to the Christian doctrine of love, which should be *the* law. I deem it a product of the conditions of an artificial society – of a society in which accident of birth and unmerited favour instituted class distinctions, in which the family was the social unit, in which seniority of age was of more account than superiority of talents, in which natural affections had often to succumb before arbitrary man-made customs. Because of this very artificiality, *Giri* in time degenerated into a vague sense of propriety called up to explain this and sanction that – as, for example, why a mother must, if need be, sacrifice all her other children in order to save the first-born; or why a daughter must sell her chastity to get funds to pay for the father's dissipation, and the like. Starting as Right Reason, *Giri* has, in my opinion, often stooped to casuistry. It has even degenerated into cowardly fear of censure. I might say of *Giri* what Scott wrote of patriotism, that 'as it is the fairest, so it is often the most suspicious, mask of other feelings.' Carried beyond or below Right Reason, *Giri* became a monstrous misnomer. It harboured under its wings every sort of sophistry and hypocrisy. It might easily have been turned into a nest of cowardice, if Bushido had not a keen and correct sense of courage, the spirit of daring and bearing.

CHAPTER 4

COURAGE, THE SPIRIT
OF DARING AND BEARING

Courage was scarcely deemed worthy to be counted among virtues, unless it was exercised in the cause of Righteousness. In his *Analects* Confucius defines Courage by explaining, as is often his wont, what its negative is. 'Perceiving what is right,' he says, 'and doing it not, argues lack of courage.' Put this epigram into a positive statement, and it runs, 'Courage is doing what is right.' To run all kinds of hazards, to jeopardize one's self, to rush into the jaws of death – these are too often identified with Valour, and in the profession of arms such rashness of conduct – what Shakespeare calls, 'valour misbegot' – is unjustly applauded; but not so in the Precepts of Knighthood. Death for a cause unworthy of dying for, was called a 'dog's death.' 'To rush into the thick of battle and to be slain in it,' says a Prince of Mito, 'is easy enough, and the merest churl is equal to the task; but,' he continues, 'it is true courage to live when it is right to live, and to die only when it is right to die,' and yet the Prince had not even heard of the name of Plato, who defines courage as 'the knowledge of things that a man should fear and that he should not fear.' A distinction which is made in the West between moral and physical courage has long been recognized among us. What samurai youth has not heard of 'Great Valour' and the 'Valour of a Villain'?

Valour, Fortitude, Bravery, Fearlessness, Courage, being the qualities of soul which appeal most easily to juvenile minds, and which can be trained by exercise and example, were, so to speak, the most popular virtues, early emulated among the youth. Stories of military exploits were repeated almost before boys left their mother's breast. Does a little booby cry for any ache? The mother scolds him in this fashion: 'What a coward to cry for a trifling pain! What will you do when your arm is cut off in battle? What when you are called upon to commit *hara kiri*?' We all know the pathetic fortitude of a famished little boy-prince of Sendai, who in the drama is made to say to his little page, 'Seest thou those tiny sparrows in the nest, how their yellow bills are opened wide, and now see! there comes their mother with worms to feed them. How eagerly and happily the little ones eat! but for a samurai, when his stomach is empty, it is a disgrace to feel hunger.' Anecdotes of fortitude and bravery abound in nursery tales, though stories of this kind are not by any means the only method of early imbuing the spirit with daring and fearlessness. Parents, with sternness sometimes verging on cruelty, set their children to tasks that called forth all the pluck that was in them. 'Bears hurl their cubs down the gorge,' they said. Samurai's sons were let down the steep valleys of hardship, and spurred to Sisyphus-like tasks. Occasional deprivation of food or exposure to cold, was considered a highly efficacious test for inuring them to endurance. Children of tender age were sent among utter strangers with some message to deliver, were made to rise before the sun, and before breakfast attend to their reading exercises, walking to their teacher with bare feet in the cold of winter; they frequently – once or twice a month, as on the festival of a god of learning – came together in small groups and passed the night without sleep, in reading aloud by turns. Pilgrimages to all sorts of uncanny places – to execution grounds, to graveyards, to houses reputed to be haunted, were favourite pastimes of the young. In the days when decapitation was public, not only were small boys sent to witness the ghastly scene, but they were made to visit alone the place in the darkness of night and there to leave a mark of their visit on the trunkless head.

Does this ultra-Spartan system of 'drilling the nerves' strike the modern pedagogist with horror and doubt – doubt whether the tendency would not be brutalizing, nipping in the bud the tender emotions of the heart? Let us see what other concepts Bushido had of Valour.

The spiritual aspect of valour is evidenced by composure – calm presence of mind. Tranquillity is courage in repose. It is a statical manifestation of valour, as daring deeds are a dynamical. A truly brave man is ever serene; he is never taken by surprise; nothing ruffles the equanimity of his spirit. In the heat of battle he remains cool; in the midst of catastrophes he keeps level his mind. Earthquakes do not shake him, he laughs at storms. We admire him as truly great, who, in the menacing presence of danger or death, retains his self-possession; who, for instance, can compose a poem under impending peril or hum a strain in the face of death. Such indulgence betraying no tremor in the writing or in the voice, is taken as an infallible index of a large nature – of what we call a capacious mind (*yoyu*), which, far from being pressed or crowded, has always room for something more.

There is even a sportive element in a courageous nature. Things which are serious to ordinary people, may be but play to the valiant. Hence in old warfare it was not at all rare for the parties to a conflict to exchange repartee or to begin a rhetorical contest. Combat was not solely a matter of brute force; it was, as well, an intellectual engagement.

The sorrow which overtook Antony and Octavius at the death of Brutus, has been the general experience of brave men. Kenshin, who fought for fourteen years with Shingen, when he heard of the latter's death, wept aloud at the loss of 'the best of enemies.' Nietzsche spoke for the samurai heart when he wrote, 'You are to be proud of your enemy; then, the success of your enemy is your success also.' Indeed valour and honour alike required that we should own as enemies in war only such as prove worthy of being friends in peace. When valour attains this height, it becomes akin to Benevolence.

CHAPTER 5

BENEVOLENCE,
THE FEELING OF DISTRESS

Love, magnanimity, affection for others, sympathy and pity, were ever recognized to be supreme virtues, the highest of all the attributes of the human soul. It was deemed a princely virtue in a twofold sense: princely among the manifold attributes of a noble spirit; princely as particularly befitting a princely profession. We needed no Shakespeare to feel – though, perhaps, like the rest of the world, we needed him to express it – that mercy became a monarch better than his crown, that it was above his sceptred sway. How often both Confucius and Mencius repeat the highest requirement of a ruler of men to consist in benevolence. Confucius would say, 'Let but a prince cultivate virtue, people will flock to him; with people will come to him lands; lands will bring forth for him wealth; wealth will give him the benefit of right uses. Virtue is the root, and wealth an outcome.' Again, 'Never has there been a case of a sovereign loving benevolence, and the people not loving righteousness.' Mencius follows close at his heels and says, 'Instances are on record where individuals attained to supreme power in a single state, without benevolence, but never have I heard of a whole empire falling into the hands of one who lacked this virtue. Also, it is impossible that any one should become ruler of the people to whom they have not yielded the subjection of their hearts.' Both defined this indispensable requirement in a ruler by saying, 'Benevolence – benevolence is Man.'

Under the regime of feudalism, which could easily degenerate into militarism, it was to benevolence that we owed our deliverance from despotism of the worst kind. An utter surrender of 'life and limb' on the part of the governed would have left nothing for the governing but self-will, and this has for its natural consequence the growth of that absolutism so often called 'oriental despotism,' as though there were no despots of occidental history!

Let it be far from me to uphold despotism of any sort; but it is a mistake to identify feudalism with it. When Frederick the Great wrote that 'Kings are the first servants of the State,' jurists thought rightly that a new era was reached in the development of freedom. Strangely coinciding in time, in the backwoods of North-western Japan, Yozan of Yonézawa made exactly the same declaration, showing that feudalism was not all tyranny and oppression. A feudal prince, although unmindful of owing reciprocal obligations to his vassals, felt a higher sense of responsibility to his ancestors and to Heaven. He was a father to his subjects, whom Heaven entrusted to his care. According to the ancient Chinese *Book of Poetry*, 'Until the house of Yin lost the hearts of the people, they could appear before Heaven.' And Confucius in his *Great Learning* taught: 'When the prince loves what the people love and hates what the people hate, then is he what is called the parent of the people.' Thus are public opinion and monarchical will or democracy and absolutism merged one in the other. Thus also, in a sense not usually assigned to the term, Bushido accepted and corroborated paternal government – paternal also as opposed to the less interested avuncular government. (Uncle Sam's, to wit!) The difference between a despotic and a paternal government lies in this, that in the one the people obey reluctantly, while in the other they do so with 'that proud submission, that dignified obedience, that subordination of heart which kept alive, even in servitude itself, the spirit of exalted freedom.'[7]

Virtue and absolute power may strike the Anglo-Saxon mind as terms which it is impossible to harmonise. Pobyedonostseff has clearly set forth before us the contrast in the foundations of English and other European communities; namely, that these were organized on the basis of common interest, while that was distinguished by a strongly developed independent personality. What this Russian statesman says of the personal dependence of individuals on some social alliance and in the end of ends on the State, among the continental nations of Europe and particularly among Slavonic peoples, is doubly true of the Japanese. Hence not only is a free exercise of monarchical power not felt as heavily by us as in Europe, but it is generally moderated by paternal consideration for the feelings of the people. 'Absolutism,' says Bismarck, 'primarily demands in the ruler impartiality, honesty, devotion to duty, energy and inward humility.' If I may be allowed to make one more quotation on this subject, I will cite from the speech of the German Emperor at Coblenz, in which he spoke of 'Kingship, by the grace of God, with its heavy duties, its tremendous responsibilities to the Creator alone, from which no man, no minister, no parliament, can release the monarch.'

We knew benevolence was a tender virtue and mother-like. If upright Rectitude and stem justice were peculiarly masculine, Mercy had the gentleness and the persuasiveness of a feminine nature. We were warned against indulging in indiscriminate charity, without seasoning it with justice and rectitude. Masamuné expressed it well in his oft-quoted aphorism – 'Rectitude carried to excess hardens into stiffness; benevolence indulged beyond measure sinks into weakness.' Fortunately mercy was not so rare as it was beautiful, for it is universally true that 'The bravest are the tenderest, the loving are the daring.' *'Bushi no nasaké'* – the tenderness of a warrior – had a sound which appealed at once to whatever was noble in us; not that the mercy of a samurai was generically different from the mercy of any other being, but because it implied mercy where mercy was not a blind impulse, but where it recognized due regard to justice, and where mercy did not remain merely a certain state of mind, but where it was backed with power to save or kill. As economists speak of demand as being effectual or ineffectual, similarly we may call the mercy of Bushi effectual, since it implied the power of acting for the good or detriment of the recipient.

Priding themselves as they did in their brute strength and privileges to turn it into account, the samurai gave full consent to what Mencius taught concerning the power of love. 'Benevolence,' he says, 'brings under its sway whatever hinders its power, just as water subdues fire: they only doubt the power of water to quench flames who try to extinguish with a cupful a whole burning waggon-load of fagots.' He also says that 'the feeling of distress is the root of benevolence,' therefore a benevolent man is ever mindful of those who are suffering and in distress. Thus did Mencius long anticipate Adam Smith, who founds his ethical philosophy on sympathy.

It is indeed striking how closely the code of knightly honour of one country coincides with that of others; in other words, how the much-abused oriental ideas of morals find their counterparts in the noblest maxims of European literature. If the well-known lines,

> *Hae tibi erunt artes – pacisque imponere morem,*
> *Parcere subjectis, et debellare superbos,*[8]

were shown to a Japanese gentleman, he might readily accuse the Mantuan bard of plagiarizing from the literature of his own country.

Benevolence to the weak, the down-trodden or the vanquished, was ever extolled as peculiarly becoming to a samurai. Lovers of Japanese art must be familiar with the representation of a priest riding backwards on a cow. The rider was once a warrior who in his day made his name a by-word of terror. In that terrible battle of Sumano-ura (AD 1184), which was one of the most decisive in our history, he overtook an enemy and in single combat had him in the clutch of his gigantic arms. Now the etiquette of war required that on such occasions no blood should be spilt, unless the weaker party proved to be a man of rank or ability equal to that of the stronger. The grim combatant would have the name of the man under him; but he refusing to make it known, his helmet was ruthlessly torn off, when the sight of a juvenile face, fair and beardless, made the astonished knight relax his hold. Helping the youth to his feet, in paternal tones he bade the stripling go: 'Off, young prince, to thy mother's side! The sword of Kumagayé shall never be tarnished by a drop of thy blood. Haste and flee o'er yon pass before thine enemies come in sight!' The young warrior refused to go and begged Kumagayé, for the honour of both, to dispatch him on the spot. Above the hoary head of the veteran gleams the cold blade, which many a time before has sundered the chords of life, but his stout heart quails; there flashes athwart his mental eye the vision of his own boy, who this self-same day marched to the sound of bugle to try his maiden arms; the strong hand of the warrior quivers; again he begs his victim to flee for his life. Finding all his entreaties vain and hearing the approaching steps of his comrades, he exclaims: 'If thou art overtaken, thou mayst fall at a more ignoble hand than mine. O thou Infinite! receive his soul!' In an instant the sword flashes in the air, and when it falls it is red with adolescent blood. When the war is ended, we find our soldier returning in triumph, but little cares he now for honour or fame; he renounces his warlike career, shaves his head, dons a priestly garb, devotes the rest of his days to holy pilgrimage, never turning his back to the West where lies the Paradise whence salvation comes and whither the sun hastes daily for his rest.

Critics may point out flaws in this story, which is casuistically vulnerable. Let it be: all the same it shows that Tenderness, Pity, and Love were traits which adorned the most sanguinary exploits of a samurai. It was an old maxim among them that 'It becometh not the fowler to slay the bird which takes refuge in his bosom.'

This in a large measure explains why the Red Cross movement, considered so peculiarly Christian, so readily found a firm footing among us. Decades before we heard of the Geneva Convention, Bakin, our greatest novelist, had familiarized us with the medical treatment of a fallen foe. In the principality of Satsuma, noted for its martial spirit and education, the custom prevailed for young men to practise music; not the blast of trumpets or the beat of drums – 'those clamorous harbingers of blood and death' – stirring us to imitate the actions of a tiger, but sad and tender melodies on the *biwa*,[9] soothing our fiery spirits, drawing our thoughts away from scent of blood and scenes of carnage.

Nor was Satsuma the only place in Japan where gentleness was inculcated among the warrior class. A Prince of Shirakawa jots down his random thoughts, and among them is the following: 'Though they come stealing to your bedside in the silent watches of the night, drive not away, but rather cherish these – the fragrance of flowers, the sound of distant bells, the insect hummings of a frosty night.' And again, 'Though they may wound your feelings, these three you have only to forgive, the breeze that scatters your flowers, the cloud that hides your moon, and the man who tries to pick quarrels with you.'

It was ostensibly to express, but actually to cultivate, these gentler emotions that the writing of verses was encouraged. Our poetry has therefore a strong undercurrent of pathos and tenderness. A well-known anecdote of a rustic samurai illustrates the case in point. When he was told to learn versification, and 'The Warbler's Notes'[10] was given him for the subject of his first attempt, his fiery spirit rebelled and he flung at the feet of his master this uncouth production, which ran:

'The brave warrior keeps apart
The ear that might listen
To the warbler's song.'

His master, undaunted by the crude sentiment, continued to encourage the youth, until one day the music of his soul was awakened to respond to the sweet notes of the *uguisu*, and he wrote:

'Stands the warrior, mailed and strong,
To hear the uguisu's song,
Warbled sweet the trees among.'

We admire and enjoy the heroic incident in Korner's short life, when, as he lay wounded on the battlefield, he scribbled his famous *Farewell to Life*. Incidents of a similar kind were not at all unusual in our warfare. Our pithy, epigrammatic poems were particularly well suited to the improvization of a single sentiment. Everybody of any education was either a poet or a poetaster. Not infrequently a marching soldier might be seen to halt, take his writing utensils from his belt, and compose an ode – and such papers were found afterward in the helmets or the breastplates when these were removed from their lifeless wearers.

What Christianity has done in Europe toward rousing compassion in the midst of belligerent horrors, love of music and letters has done in Japan. The cultivation of tender feelings breeds considerate regard for the sufferings of others. Modesty and complaisance, actuated by respect for others' feelings, are at the root of politeness.

CHAPTER 6

POLITENESS

Courtesy and urbanity of manners have been noticed by every foreign tourist as a marked Japanese trait. Politeness is a poor virtue, if it is actuated only by a fear of offending good taste, whereas it should be the outward manifestation of a sympathetic regard for the feelings of others. It also implies a due regard for the fitness of things, therefore due respect to social positions; for these latter express no plutocratic distinctions, but were originally distinctions for actual merit.

In its highest form, politeness almost approaches love. We may reverently say, politeness 'suffereth long, and is kind; envieth not, vaunteth not itself, is not puffed up; doth not behave itself unseemly, seeketh not her own, is not easily provoked, taketh not account of evil.' Is it any wonder that Professor Dean, in speaking of the six elements of Humanity, accords to politeness an exalted position, inasmuch as it is the ripest fruit of social intercourse?

While thus extolling politeness, far be it from me to put it in the front rank of virtues. If we analyze it, we shall find it correlated with other virtues of a higher order; for what virtue stands alone? While – or rather because – it was exalted as peculiar to the profession of arms, and as such esteemed in a degree higher than its deserts, there came into existence its counterfeits. Confucius himself has repeatedly taught that external appurtenances are as little a part of propriety as sounds are of music.

When propriety was elevated to the *sine qua non* of social inter-course, it was only to be expected that an elaborate system of etiquette should come into vogue to train youth in correct social behaviour. How one must bow in accosting others, how he must walk and sit, were taught and learned with utmost care. Table manners grew to be a science. Tea serving and drinking were raised to a ceremony. A man of education is, of course, expected to be master of all these.

I have heard slighting remarks made by Europeans upon our elaborate discipline of politeness. It has been criticized as absorbing too much of our thought and in so far a folly to observe strict obedience to it. I admit that there may be unnec-essary niceties in ceremonious etiquette, but whether it partakes as much of folly as the adherence to ever-changing fashions of the West, is a question not very clear to my mind. Even fashions I do not consider solely as freaks of vanity; on the contrary, I look upon these as a ceaseless search of the human mind for the beautiful. Much less do I consider elaborate ceremony as alto-gether trivial; for it denotes the result of long observation as to the most appropriate method of achieving a certain result. If there is anything to do, there is certainly a best way to do it, and the best way is both the most economical and the most graceful. Mr. Spencer defines grace as the most economical manner of motion. The tea ceremony presents certain definite ways of manipulating a bowl, a spoon, a napkin, etc. To a novice it looks tedious. But one soon discovers that the way prescribed is, after all, the most saving of time and labour; in other words, the most economical use of force – hence, according to Spencer's dictum, the most graceful.

I have said that etiquette was elaborated into the finest niceties, so much so that different schools advocating different systems, came into existence. But they all united in the ultimate essential, and this was put by a great exponent of the best known school of etiquette, the Ogasawara, in the following terms: 'The end of all etiquette is to so cultivate your mind that even when you are quietly seated, not the roughest ruffian can dare make onset on your person.' It means, in other words, that by constant exercise in correct manners, one brings all the parts and faculties of his body into perfect order and into such harmony with itself and its environment as to express the mastery of spirit over the flesh. What a new and deep significance the French word *bienséance*[11] comes thus to contain!

If the premise is true that gracefulness means economy of force, then it follows as a logical sequence that a constant practice of graceful deportment must bring with it a reserve and storage of force. Fine manners, therefore, mean power in repose.

As an example of how the simplest thing can be made into an art and then become spiritual culture, I may take *Cha-no-yu*, the tea ceremony. Tea-sipping as a fine art! Why should it not be? In the children drawing pictures on the sand, or in the savage carving on a rock, was the promise of a Raphael or a Michelangelo. How much more is the drinking of a beverage, which began with the transcendental contemplation of a Hindoo anchorite, entitled to develop into a handmaid of Religion and Morality? That calmness of mind, that serenity of temper, that composure and quietness of demeanour, which are the first essentials of *Cha-no-yu*, are without doubt the first conditions of right thinking and right feeling. The scrupulous cleanliness of the little room, shut off from sight and sound of the madding crowd, is in itself conducive to direct one's thoughts from the world. The bare interior does not engross one's attention like the innumerable pictures and bric-a-brac of a Western parlour; the presence of *kakémono*[12] calls our attention more to grace of design than to beauty of colour. The utmost refinement of taste is the object aimed at; whereas anything like display is banished with religious horror. The very fact that it was invented by a contemplative recluse, in a time when wars and the rumours of wars were incessant, is well calculated to show that this institution was more than a pastime. Before entering the quiet precincts of the tea-room, the company assembling to partake of the ceremony laid aside, together with their swords, the ferocity of the battlefield or the cares of government, there to find peace and friendship.

Cha-no-yu is more than a ceremony – it is a fine art; it is poetry, with articulate gestures for rhythm: it is a *modus operandi* of soul discipline. Its greatest value lies in this last phase. Not infrequently the other phases preponderated in the mind of its votaries, but that does not prove that its essence was not of a spiritual nature.

Politeness will be a great acquisition, if it does no more than impart grace to manners; but its function does not stop here. For propriety, springing as it does from motives of benevolence and modesty, and actuated by tender feelings toward the sensibilities of others, is ever a graceful expression of sympathy. Its requirement is that we should weep with those that weep and rejoice with those that rejoice. Such didactic requirement, when reduced into small everyday details of life, expresses itself in little acts scarcely noticeable, or, if noticed, is, as one missionary lady of twenty years' residence once said to me, 'awfully funny.' You are out in the hot glaring sun with no shade over you; a Japanese acquaintance passes by; you accost him, and instantly his hat is off – well, that is perfectly natural, but the 'awfully funny' performance is, that all the while he talks with you his parasol is down and he stands in the glaring sun also. How foolish! – Yes, exactly so, provided the motive were less than this: 'You are in the sun; I sympathize with you; I would willingly take you under my parasol if it were large enough, or if we were familiarly acquainted; as I cannot shade you, I will share your discomforts.' Little acts of this kind, equally or more amusing, are not mere gestures or conventionalities. They are the 'bodying forth' of thoughtful feelings for the comfort of others.

Another 'awfully funny' custom is dictated by our canons of politeness; but many superficial writers on Japan have dismissed it by simply attributing it to the general topsy-turvyness of the nation. Every foreigner who has observed it will confess the awkwardness he felt in making proper reply upon the occasion. In America, when you make a gift, you sing its praises to the recipient; in Japan we depreciate or slander it. The underlying idea with you is, 'This is a nice gift: if it were not nice I would not dare give it to you; for it will be an insult to give you anything but what is nice.' In contrast to this, our logic runs: 'You are a nice person, and no gift is nice enough for you. You will not accept anything I can lay at your feet except as a token of my good will; so accept this, not for its intrinsic value, but as a token. It will be an insult to your worth to call the best gift good enough for you.' Place the two ideas side by side; and we see that the ultimate idea is one and the same. Neither is 'awfully funny.' The American speaks of the material which makes the gift; the Japanese speaks of the spirit which prompts the gift.

It is perverse reasoning to conclude, because our sense of propriety shows itself in all the smallest ramifications of our deportment, to take the least important of them and uphold it as the type, and pass judgment upon the principle itself. Which is more important, to eat or to observe rules of propriety about eating? A Chinese sage answers, 'If you take a case where the eating is all-important, and observing the rules of propriety is of little importance, and compare them together, why merely say that the eating is of the more importance?' 'Metal is heavier than feathers,' but does that saying have reference to a single clasp of metal and a wagon-load of feathers? Take a piece of wood a foot thick and raise it above the pinnacle of a temple, none would call it taller than the temple. To the question, 'Which is the more important, to tell the truth or to be polite?' the Japanese are said to give an answer diametrically opposite to what the American will say – but I forbear any comment until I come to speak of veracity and sincerity.

CHAPTER 7

VERACITY AND SINCERITY

Without veracity and sincerity, politeness is a farce and a show. 'Propriety carried beyond right bounds,' says Masamuné, 'becomes a lie.' An ancient poet has outdone Polonius in the advice he gives: 'To thyself be faithful: if in thy heart thou strayest not from truth, without prayer of thine the Gods will keep thee whole.' The apotheosis of Sincerity to which Confucius gives expression in the *Doctrine of the Mean*, attributes to it transcendental powers, almost identifying them with the Divine. 'Sincerity is the end and the beginning of all things; without Sincerity there would be nothing.' He then dwells with eloquence on its far-reaching and long-enduring nature, its power to produce changes without movement and by its mere presence to accomplish its purpose without effort. From the Chinese ideogram for Sincerity, which is a combination of 'Word' and 'Perfect,' one is tempted to draw a parallel between it and the Neo-Platonic doctrine of *Logos* – to such height does the sage soar in his unwonted mystic flight.

Lying or equivocation were deemed equally cowardly. The bushi held that his high social position demanded a loftier standard of veracity than that of the tradesman and peasant. *Bushi no ichi-gon* – the word of a samurai, or in exact German equivalent *ein Ritterwort* – was sufficient guaranty of the truthfulness of an assertion. His word carried such weight with it that promises were generally made and fulfilled without a written pledge, which would have been deemed quite beneath his dignity. Many thrilling anecdotes were told of those who atoned by death for *ni-gon*, a double tongue.

The regard for veracity was so high that, unlike the generality of Christians who persistently violate the plain commands of the Teacher not to swear, the best of samurai looked upon an oath as derogatory to their honour. I am well aware that they did swear by different deities or upon their swords; but never has swearing degenerated into wanton form and irreverent interjection. To emphasize our words a practice was sometimes resorted to of literally sealing with blood. For the explanation of such a practice, I need only refer my readers to Goethe's *Faust*.

A recent American writer is responsible for this statement, that if you ask an ordinary Japanese which is better, to tell a falsehood or be impolite, he will not hesitate to answer 'to tell a falsehood!' Dr. Peery[13] is partly right and partly wrong; right in that an ordinary Japanese, even a samurai, may answer in the way ascribed to him, but wrong in attributing too much weight to the term he translates 'falsehood.' This word (in Japanese, *uso*) is employed to denote anything which is not a truth (*makoto*) or fact (*honto*). Lowell tells us that Wordsworth could not distinguish between truth and fact, and an ordinary Japanese is in this respect as good as Wordsworth. Ask a Japanese, or even an American of any refinement, to tell you whether he dislikes you or whether he is sick at his stomach, and he will not hesitate long to tell falsehoods and answer, 'I like you much,' or, 'I am quite well, thank you.' To sacrifice truth merely for the sake of politeness was regarded as an 'empty form' (*kyo-rei*) and 'deception by sweet words.'

I own I am speaking now of the Bushido idea of veracity; but it may not be amiss to devote a few words to our commercial integrity, of which I have heard much complaint in foreign books and journals. A loose business morality has indeed been the worst blot on our national reputation; but before abusing it or hastily condemning the whole race for it, let us calmly study it and we shall be rewarded with consolation for the future.

Of all the great occupations of life, none was farther removed from the profession of arms than commerce. The merchant was placed lowest in the category of vocations – the knight, the tiller of the soil, the mechanic, the merchant. The samurai derived his income from land and could even indulge, if he had a mind to, in amateur farming; but the counter and abacus were abhorred. We know the wisdom of this social arrangement. Montesquieu has made it clear that the debarring of the nobility from mercantile pursuits was an admirable social policy, in that it prevented wealth from accumulating in the hands of the powerful. The separation of power and riches kept the distribution of the latter more nearly equable. Professor Dill, the author of *Roman Society in the Last Century of the Western Empire*, has brought afresh to our mind that one cause of the decadence of the Roman Empire, was the permission given to the nobility to engage in trade, and the consequent monopoly of wealth and power by a minority of the senatorial families.

Commerce, therefore, in feudal Japan did not reach that degree of development which it would have attained under freer conditions. The obloquy attached to the calling naturally brought within its pale such as cared little for social repute. 'Call one a thief and he will steal.' Put a stigma on a calling and its followers adjust their morals to it, for it is natural that 'the normal conscience,' as Hugh Black says, 'rises to the demands made on it, and easily falls to the limit of the standard expected from it.' It is unnecessary to add that no business, commercial or otherwise, can be transacted without a code of morals. Our merchants of the feudal period had one among themselves, without which they could never have developed, as they did in embryo, such fundamental mercantile institutions as the guild, the bank, the bourse, insurance, checks, bills of exchange, etc.; but in their relations with people outside their vocation, the tradesmen lived too true to the reputation of their order.

This being the case, when the country was opened to foreign trade, only the most adventurous and unscrupulous rushed to the ports, while the respectable business houses declined for some time the repeated requests of the authorities to establish branch houses. Was Bushido powerless to stay the current of commercial dishonour? Let us see.

Those who are well acquainted with our history will remember that only a few years after our treaty ports were opened to foreign trade, feudalism was abolished, and when with it the samurai's fiefs were taken and bonds issued to them in compensation, they were given liberty to invest them in mercantile transactions. Now you may ask, 'Why could they not bring their much-boasted veracity into their new business relations and so reform the old abuses?' Those who had eyes to see could not weep enough, those who had hearts to feel could not sympathize enough, with the fate of many a noble and honest samurai who signally and irrevocably failed in his new and unfamiliar field of trade and industry, through sheer lack of shrewdness in coping with his artful plebeian rival. When we know that eighty per cent of the business houses fail in so industrial a country as America, is it any wonder that scarcely one among a hundred samurai who went into trade could succeed in his new vocation? It will be long before it will be recognized how many fortunes were wrecked in the attempt to apply Bushido ethics to business methods; but it was soon patent to every observing mind that the ways of wealth were not the ways of honour. In what respects, then, were they different?

Of the three incentives to veracity that Lecky enumerates, viz., the industrial, the political, and the philosophical, the first was altogether lacking in Bushido. As to the second, it could develop little in a political community under a feudal system. It is in its philosophical and, as Lecky says, in its highest aspect, that honesty attained elevated rank in our catalogue of virtues. With all my sincere regard for the high commercial integrity of the Anglo-Saxon race, when I ask for the ultimate ground, I am told that 'honesty is the best policy' – that it *pays* to be honest. Is not this virtue, then, its own reward? If it is followed because it brings in more cash than falsehood, I am afraid Bushido would rather indulge in lies!

If Bushido rejects a doctrine of *quid pro quo* rewards, the shrewder tradesman will readily accept it. Lecky has very truly remarked that veracity owes its growth largely to commerce and manufacture; as Nietzsche puts it, honesty is the youngest of the virtues – in other words, it is the foster-child of modern industry. Without this mother, veracity was like a blue-blood orphan whom only the most cultivated mind could adopt and nourish. Such minds were general among the samurai, but, for want of a more democratic and utilitarian foster-mother, the tender child failed to thrive. Industries advancing, veracity will prove an easy, nay, a profitable virtue to practise. Just think – as late as November, 1880, Bismarck sent a circular to the professional consuls of the German Empire, warning them of 'a lamentable lack of reliability with regard to German shipments *inter alia,* apparent both as to quality and quantity.' Nowadays we hear comparatively little of German carelessness and dishonesty in trade. In twenty years her merchants have learned that in the end honesty pays. Already our merchants have found that out.

Often have I wondered whether the veracity of Bushido had any motive higher than courage. In the absence of any positive commandment against bearing false witness, lying was not condemned as sin, but simply denounced as weakness, and, as such, highly dishonourable. As a matter of fact, the idea of honesty is so intimately blended, and its Latin and its German etymology so identified with honour, that it is high time I should pause a few moments for the consideration of this feature of the Precepts of Knighthood.

CHAPTER 8

HONOUR

The sense of honour, implying a vivid consciousness of personal dignity and worth, could not fail to characterize the samurai, born and bred to value the duties and privileges of their profession. Though the word ordinarily given nowadays as the translation of honour was not used freely, yet the idea was conveyed by such terms as *na* (name) *men-moku* (countenance), *guai-bun* (outside hearing), reminding us respectively of the biblical use of 'name,' of the evolution of the term 'personality' from the Greek mask, and of 'fame.' A good name – one's reputation, 'the immortal part of one's self, what remains being bestial' – assumed as a matter of course, any infringement upon its integrity was felt as shame, and the sense of shame (*Ren-chi-shin*) was one of the earliest to be cherished in juvenile education. 'You will be laughed at,' 'It will disgrace you,' 'Are you not ashamed?' were the last appeal to correct behaviour on the part of a youthful delinquent. Such a recourse to his honour touched the most sensitive spot in the child's heart, as though it had been nursed on honour while he was in his mother's womb; for most truly is honour a pre-natal influence, being closely bound up with strong family consciousness. 'In losing the solidarity of families,' says Balzac, 'society has lost the fundamental force which Montesquieu named Honour.' Indeed, the sense of shame seems to me to be the earliest indication of the moral consciousness of the race. The first and worst punishment which befell humanity in consequence of tasting 'the fruit of that forbidden tree' was, to my mind, not the sorrow of childbirth, nor the thorns and thistles, but the awakening of the sense of shame. Few incidents in history excel in pathos the scene of the first mother plying, with heaving breast and tremulous fingers, her crude needle on the few fig leaves which her dejected husband plucked for her. This first fruit of disobedience clings to us with a tenacity that nothing else does. All the sartorial ingenuity of mankind has not yet succeeded in sewing an apron that will efficaciously hide our sense of shame. That samurai was right who refused to compromise his character by a slight humiliation in his youth; 'because,' he said, 'dishonour is like a scar on a tree, which time, instead of effacing, only helps to enlarge.'

Mencius had taught centuries before, in almost the identical phrase, what Carlyle has latterly expressed – namely, that 'Shame is the soil of all Virtue, of good manners and good morals.'

The fear of disgrace was so great that if our literature lacks such eloquence as Shakespeare puts into the mouth of Norfolk, it nevertheless hung like Damocles' sword over the head of every samurai and often assumed a morbid character. In the name of honour, deeds were perpetrated which can find no justification in the code of Bushido. At the slightest, nay – imaginary insult – the quick-tempered braggart took offence, resorted to the use of the sword, and many an unnecessary strife was raised and many an innocent life lost. The story of a well-meaning citizen who called the attention of a bushi to a flea jumping on his back, and who was forthwith cut in two, for the simple and questionable reason, that inasmuch as fleas are parasites which feed on animals, it was an unpardonable insult to identify a noble warrior with a beast – I say, stories like these are too frivolous to believe. Yet, the circulation of such stories implies three things: (1) that they were invented to overawe common people; (2) that abuses were really made of the samurai's profession of honour; and (3) that a very strong sense of shame was developed among them. It is plainly unfair to take an abnormal case to cast blame upon the precepts, any more than to judge of the true teachings of Christ from the fruits of religious fanaticism and extravagance – inquisitions and hypocrisy. But, as in religious monomania there is something touchingly noble as compared with the delirium tremens of a drunkard, so in that extreme sensitiveness of the samurai about their honour do we not recognize the substratum of a genuine virtue?

The morbid excess into which the delicate code of honour was inclined to run was strongly counterbalanced by preaching magnanimity and patience. To take offence at slight provocation was ridiculed as 'short-tempered.' The popular adage said: 'To bear what you think you cannot bear is really to bear.' The great Iyéyasu left to posterity a few maxims, among which are the following: 'The life of man is like going a long distance with a heavy load upon the shoulders. Haste not... Reproach none, but be forever watchful of thine own short-comings... Forbearance is the basis of length of days.' He proved in his life what he preached. A literary wit put a characteristic epigram into the mouths of three well-known personages in our history: to Nobunaga he attributed, 'I will kill her, if the nightingale sings not in time'; to Hidéyoshi, 'I will force her to sing for me'; and to Iyéyasu, 'I will wait till she opens her lips.'

Patience and long-suffering were also highly commended by Mencius. In one place he writes to this effect: 'Though you denude yourself and insult me, what is that to me? You cannot defile my soul by your outrage.' Elsewhere he teaches that anger at a petty offence is unworthy of a superior man, but indignation for a great cause is righteous wrath.

To what height of unmartial and unresisting meekness Bushido could reach in some of its votaries, may be seen in their utterances. Take, for instance, this saying of Ogawa: 'When others speak all manner of evil things against thee, return not evil for evil, but rather reflect that thou wast not more faithful in the discharge of thy duties.' Take another of Kumazawa: 'When others blame thee, blame them not; when others are angry at thee, return not anger. Joy cometh only as Passion and Desire part.' Still another instance I may cite from Saigo, upon whose overhanging brows 'Shame is ashamed to sit': 'The Way is the way of Heaven and Earth; Man's place is to follow it; therefore make it the object of thy life to reverence Heaven. Heaven loves me and others with equal love; therefore with the love wherewith thou lovest thyself, love others. Make not Man thy partner but Heaven, and making Heaven thy partner do thy best. Never condemn others; but see to it that thou comest not short of thine own mark.' Some of these sayings remind us of Christian expostulations, and show us how far in practical morality natural religion can approach the revealed. Not only did these sayings remain as utterances, but they were really embodied in acts.

It must be admitted that very few attained this sublime height of magnanimity, patience and forgiveness. It was a great pity that nothing clear and general was expressed as to what constitutes honour, only a few enlightened minds being aware that it 'from no condition rises,' but that it lies in each acting well his part; for nothing was easier than for youths to forget in the heat of action what they had learned in Mencius in their calmer moments. Said this sage: ''Tis in every man's mind to love honour; but little doth he dream that what is truly honourable lies within himself and not elsewhere. The honour which men confer is not good honour. Those whom Châo the Great ennobles, he can make mean again.' For the most part, an insult was quickly resented and repaid by death, as we shall see later, while honour – too often nothing higher than vainglory or worldly approbation – was prized as the *summum bonum* of earthly existence. Fame, and not wealth or knowledge, was the goal toward which youths had to strive. Many a lad swore within himself as he crossed the threshold of his paternal home, that he would not recross it until he had made a name in the world; and many an ambitious mother refused to see her sons again unless they could 'return home,' as the expression is, 'caparisoned in brocade.' To shun shame or win a name, samurai boys would submit to any privations and undergo the severest ordeals of bodily or mental suffering. They knew that honour won in youth grows with age. In the memorable seige of Osaka, a young son of Iyéyasu, in spite of his earnest entreaties to be put in the vanguard, was placed at the rear of the army. When the castle fell, he was so chagrined and wept so bitterly that an old councillor tried to console him with all the resources at his command; 'Take comfort, Sire,' said he, 'at the thought of the long future before you. In the many years that you may live, there will come divers occasions to distinguish yourself.' The boy fixed his indignant gaze upon the man and said, 'How foolishly you talk! Can ever my fourteenth year come round again?' Life itself was thought cheap if honour and fame could be attained therewith: hence, whenever a cause presented itself which was considered dearer than life, with utmost serenity and celerity was life laid down.

Of the causes in comparison with which no life was too dear to sacrifice, was the duty of loyalty, which was the key-stone making feudal virtues a symmetrical arch.

CHAPTER 9

THE DUTY OF LOYALTY

Feudal morality shares other virtues in common with other systems of ethics, with other classes of people, but this virtue – homage and fealty to a superior – is its distinctive feature. I am aware that personal fidelity is a moral adhesion existing among all sorts and conditions of men – a gang of pickpockets owe allegiance to a Fagin; but it is only in the code of chivalrous honour that loyalty assumes paramount importance.

In spite of Hegel's criticism[14] that the fidelity of feudal vassals, being an obligation to an individual and not to a commonwealth, is a bond established on totally unjust principles, a great compatriot of his made it his boast that personal loyalty was a German virtue. Bismarck had good reasons to do so, not because the *Treue* he boasts of was the monopoly of his Fatherland or of any single nation or race, but because this favoured fruit of chivalry lingers latest among the people where feudalism has lasted longest. In America, where 'everybody is as good as anybody else,' and, as the Irishman added, 'better too,' such exalted ideas of loyalty as we feel for our sovereign may be deemed 'excellent within certain bounds,' but preposterous as encouraged among us. Montesquieu complained long ago that right on one side of the Pyrenees was wrong on the other, and the recent Dreyfus trial[15] proved the truth of his remark, save that the Pyrenees were not the sole boundary beyond which French justice finds no accord. Similarly, loyalty as we conceive it may find few admirers elsewhere, not because our conception is wrong, but because it is, I am afraid, forgotten, and also because we carry it to a degree not reached in any other country. Griffis[16] was quite right in stating that whereas in China Confucian ethics made obedience to parents the primary human duty, in Japan precedence was given to loyalty. At the risk of shocking some of my good readers, I will relate of one 'who could endure to follow a fall'n lord' and who thus, as Shakespeare assures, 'earned a place i' the story.'

The story is of one of the greatest characters of our history, Michizané, who, falling a victim to jealousy and calumny, is exiled from the capital. Not content with this, his unrelenting enemies are now bent upon the extinction of his family. Strict search for his son – not yet grown – reveals the fact of his being secreted in a village school kept by one Genzo, a former vassal of Michizané. When orders are dispatched to the schoolmaster to deliver the head of the juvenile offender on a certain day, his first idea is to find a suitable substitute for it. He ponders over his school-list, scrutinizes with careful eyes all the boys, as they stroll into the class-room, but none among the children born of the soil bears the least resemblance to his protégé. His despair, however, is but for a moment; for, behold, a new scholar is announced – a comely boy of the same age as his master's son, escorted by a mother of noble mien.

No less conscious of the resemblance between infant lord and infant retainer, were the mother and the boy himself. In the privacy of home both had laid themselves upon the altar; the one his life – the other her heart, yet without sign to the outer world. Unwitting of what had passed between them, it is the teacher from whom comes the suggestion.

Here, then, is the scapegoat! The rest of the narrative may be briefly told. On the day appointed, arrives the officer commissioned to identify and receive the head of the youth. Will he be deceived by the false head? The poor Genzo's hand is on the hilt of the sword, ready to strike a blow either at the man or at himself, should the examination defeat his scheme. The officer takes up the gruesome object before him, goes calmly over each feature, and in a deliberate, business-like tone, pronounces it genuine. That evening in a lonely home awaits the mother we saw in the school. Does she know the fate of her child? It is not for his return that she watches with eagerness for the opening of the wicket. Her father-in-law has been for a long time a recipient of Michizané's bounties, but since his banishment, circumstances have forced her husband to follow the service of the enemy of his family's benefactor. He himself could not be untrue to his own cruel master; but his son could serve the cause of the grandsire's lord. As one acquainted with the exile's family, it was he who had been entrusted with the task of identifying the boy's head. Now the day's – yea, the life's – hard work is done, he returns home and as he crosses its threshold, he accosts his wife, saying: 'Rejoice, my wife, our darling son has proved of service to his lord!'

'What an atrocious story!' I hear my readers exclaim. 'Parents deliberately sacrificing their own innocent child to save the life of another man's!' But this child was a conscious and willing victim: it is a story of vicarious death – as significant as, and not more revolting than, the story of Abraham's intended sacrifice of Isaac. In both cases was obedience to the call of duty, utter submission to the command of a higher voice, whether given by a visible or an invisible angel, or heard by an outward or an inward ear; but I abstain from preaching.

The individualism of the West, which recognizes separate interests for father and son, husband and wife, necessarily brings into strong relief the duties owed by one to the other; but Bushido held that the interest of the family and of the members thereof is intact – one and inseparable. This interest it bound up with affection – natural, instinctive, irresistible; hence, if we die for one we love with natural love (which animals themselves possess), what is that? 'For if ye love them that love you, what reward have ye? Do not even the publicans the same?'

In his great history, Sanyo relates in touching language the heart struggle of Shigemori concerning his father's rebellious conduct. 'If I be loyal, my father must be undone; if I obey my father, my duty to my sovereign must go amiss.' Poor Shigemori! We see him afterward praying with all his soul that kind Heaven may visit him with death, that he may be released from this world where it is hard for purity and righteousness to dwell.

Many a Shigemori has his heart torn by the conflict between duty and affection. Indeed, neither Shakespeare nor the Old Testament itself contains an adequate rendering of *ko*, our conception of filial piety, and yet in such conflicts Bushido never wavered in its choice of loyalty. Women, too, encouraged their offspring to sacrifice all for the king. Even as resolute as Widow Windham and her illustrious consort, the samurai matron stood ready to give up her boys for the cause of loyalty.

Since Bushido, like Aristotle and some modern sociologists, conceived the state as antedating the individual – the latter being born into the former as part and parcel thereof – he must live and die for it or for the incumbent of its legitimate authority. Readers of *Crito* will remember the argument with which Socrates represents the laws of the city as pleading with him on the subject of his escape. Among others he makes them (the laws or the state) say: 'Since you were begotten and nurtured and educated under us, dare you once to say you are not our offspring and servant, you and your fathers before you?' These are words which do not impress us as any thing extraordinary; for the same thing has long been on the lips of Bushido, with this modification, that the laws and the state were represented with us by a personal being. Loyalty is an ethical outcome of this political theory.

I am not entirely ignorant of Mr. Spencer's view according to which political obedience – loyalty – is accredited with only a transitional function.[17] It may be so. Sufficient unto the day is the virtue thereof. We may complacently repeat it, especially as we believe that day to be a long space of time, during which, so our national anthem says, 'tiny pebbles grow into mighty rocks draped with moss.'

Political subordination, Mr. Spencer predicts, will give place to loyalty, to the dictates of conscience. Suppose his induction is realized – will loyalty and its concomitant instinct of reverence disappear forever? We transfer our allegiance from one master to another, without being unfaithful to either: from being subjects of a ruler that wields the temporal sceptre we become servants of the monarch who sits enthroned in the penetralia of our hearts. A few years ago a very stupid controversy, started by the misguided disciples of Spencer, made havoc among the reading class of Japan. In their zeal to uphold the claim of the throne to undivided loyalty, they charged Christians with treasonable propensity in that they avow fidelity to their Lord and Master. They arrayed forth sophistical arguments without the wit of Sophists, and scholastic tortuosities minus the niceties of the Schoolmen. Little did they know that we can, in a sense, 'serve two masters without holding to the one or despising the other,' 'rendering unto Caesar the things that are Caesar's and unto God the things that are God's.' Did not Socrates, all the while he unflinchingly refused to concede one iota of loyalty to his *daemon*, obey with equal fidelity and equanimity the command of his earthly master, the State? His conscience he followed, alive; his country he served, dying. Alack the day when a state grows so powerful as to demand of its citizens the dictates of their conscience!

Bushido did not require us to make our conscience the slave of any lord or king. Thomas Mowbray was a veritable spokesman for us when he said:

> 'Myself I throw, dread sovereign, at thy foot.
> My life thou shall command, but not my shame.
> The one my duty owes; but my fair name,
> Despite of death, that lives upon my grave,
> To dark dishonour's use, thou shall not have.'

A man who sacrificed his own conscience to the capricious will or freak or fancy of a sovereign was accorded a low place in the estimate of the Precepts. Such a one was despised as *nei-shin*, a cringeling, who makes court by unscrupulous fawning, or as *chô-shin*, a favourite who steals his master's affections by means of servile compliance; these two species of subjects corresponding exactly to those which Iago describes – the one, a duteous and knee-crooking knave, doting on his own obsequious bondage, wearing out his time much like his master's ass; the other trimming in forms and visages of duty, keeping yet his heart attending on himself. When a subject differed from his master, the loyal path for him to pursue was to use every available means to persuade him of his error, as Kent did to King Lear. Failing in this, let the master deal with him as he wills. In cases of this kind, it was quite a usual course for the samurai to make the last appeal to the intelligence and conscience of his lord by demonstrating the sincerity of his words with the shedding of his own blood.

Life being regarded as the means whereby to serve his master, and its ideal being set upon honour, the whole education and training of a samurai were conducted accordingly.

CHAPTER 10

THE EDUCATION AND TRAINING OF A SAMURAI

The first point to observe in knightly pedagogics was to build up character, leaving in the shade the subtler faculties of prudence, intelligence and dialectics. We have seen the important part aesthetic accomplishments played in his education. Indispensable as they were to a man of culture, they were accessories rather than essentials of samurai training. Intellectual superiority was, of course, esteemed; but the word *Chi*, which was employed to denote intellectuality, meant wisdom in the first instance and gave knowledge only a very subordinate place. The tripod which supported the framework of Bushido was said to be *Chi*, *Jin*, *Yu*, respectively, Wisdom, Benevolence, and Courage. A samurai was essentially a man of action. Science was without the pale of his activity. He took advantage of it in so far as it concerned his profession of arms. Religion and theology were relegated to the priests; he concerned himself with them in so far as they helped to nourish courage. Like an English poet the samurai believed ''tis not the creed that saves the man; but it is the man that justifies the creed.' Philosophy and literature formed the chief part of his intellectual training; but even in the pursuit of these, it was not objective truth that he strove after – literature was pursued mainly as a pastime, and philosophy as a practical aid in the formation of character, if not for the exposition of some military or political problem.

From what has been said, it will not be surprising to note that the curriculum of studies, according to the pedagogics of Bushido, consisted mainly of the following: fencing, archery, *jiujutsu*[18] or *yawara*, horsemanship, the use of the spear, tactics, calligraphy, ethics, literature, and history. Of these, *jiujutsu* and calligraphy may require a few words of explanation. Great stress was laid on good writing, probably because our logograms, partaking as they do of the nature of pictures, possess artistic value, and also because chirography was accepted as indicative of one's personal character. *Jiujutsu* may be briefly defined as an application of anatomical knowledge to the purpose of offence or defence. It differs from wrestling, in that it does not depend upon muscular strength. It differs from other forms of attack in that it uses no weapons. Its feat consists in clutching or striking such part of the enemy's body as will make him numb and incapable of resistance. Its object is not to kill, but to incapacitate one for action for the time being.

A subject of study which one would expect to find in military education and which is rather conspicuous by its absence in the Bushido course of instruction, is mathematics. This, however, can be readily explained in part by the fact that feudal warfare was not carried on with scientific precision. Not only that, but the whole training of the samurai was unfavourable to fostering numerical notions.

Chivalry is uneconomical: it boasts of penury. It says with Ventidius that 'ambition, the soldier's virtue, rather makes choice of loss, than gain which darkens him.' Don Quixote takes more pride in his rusty spear and skin-and-bone horse than in gold and lands, and a samurai is in hearty sympathy with his exaggerated confrère of La Mancha. He disdains money itself – the art of making or hoarding it. It was to him veritably filthy lucre. The hackneyed expression to describe the decadence of an age was 'that the civilians loved money and the soldiers feared death.' Niggardliness of gold and of life excited as much disapprobation as their lavish use was panegyrized. 'Less than all things,' says a current precept, 'men must grudge money: it is by riches that wisdom is hindered.' Hence children were brought up with utter disregard of economy. It was considered bad taste to speak of it, and ignorance of the value of different coins was a token of good breeding. Knowledge of numbers was indispensable in the mustering of forces as well as in distribution of benefices and fiefs; but the counting of money was left to meaner hands. In many feudatories, public finance was administered by a lower kind of samurai or by priests. Every thinking bushi knew well enough that money formed the sinews of war; but he did not think of raising the appreciation of money to a virtue. It is true that thrift was enjoined by Bushido, but not for economical reasons so much as for the exercise of abstinence. Luxury was thought the greatest menace to manhood and severest simplicity of living was required of the warrior class, sumptuary laws being enforced in many of the clans.

We read that in ancient Rome the farmers of revenue and other financial agents were gradually raised to the rank of knights, the State thereby showing its appreciation of their service and of the importance of money itself. How closely this is connected with the luxury and avarice of the Romans may be imagined. Not so with the Precepts of Knighthood. It persisted in systematically regarding finance as something low – low as compared with moral and intellectual vocations.

Money and the love of it being thus diligently ignored, Bushido itself could long remain free from a thousand and one evils of which money is the root. This is sufficient reason for the fact that our public men have long been free from corruption; but alas! how fast plutocracy is making its way in our time and generation.

The mental discipline which would nowadays be chiefly aided by the study of mathematics, was supplied by literary exegesis and deontological discussions. Very few abstract subjects troubled the mind of the young, the chief aim of their education being, as I have said, decision of character. People whose minds were simply stored with information found no great admirers. Of the three services of studies that Bacon gives – for delight, ornament, and ability – Bushido had decided preference for the last, where their use was 'in judgment and the disposition of business.' Whether it was for the disposition of public business or for the exercise of self-control, it was with a practical end in view that education was conducted. 'Learning without thought,' said Confucius, 'is labour lost; thought without learning is perilous.'

When character and not intelligence, when the soul and not the head, is chosen by a teacher for the material to work upon and to develop, his vocation partakes of a sacred character. 'It is the parent who has borne me: it is the teacher who makes me man.' With this idea, therefore, the esteem in which one's preceptor was held was very high. A man to evoke such confidence and respect from the young, must necessarily be endowed with superior personality, without lacking erudition. He was a father to the fatherless, and an adviser to the erring. 'Thy father and thy mother' – so runs our maxim – 'are like heaven and earth; thy teacher and thy lord are like the sun and moon.'

The present system of paying for every sort of service was not in vogue among the adherents of Bushido. It believed in a service which can be rendered only without money and without price. Spiritual service, be it of priest or teacher, was not to be repaid in gold or silver, not because it was valueless but because it was invaluable. Here the non-arithmetical honour-instinct of Bushido taught a truer lesson than modern Political Economy; for wages and salaries can be paid only for services whose results are definite, tangible, and measurable, whereas the best service done in education – namely, in soul development (and this includes the services of a pastor) – is not definite, tangible, or measurable. Being immeasurable, money, the ostensible measure of value, is of inadequate use. Usage sanctioned that pupils brought to their teachers money or goods at different seasons of the year; but these were not payments but offerings, which indeed were welcome to the recipients as they were usually men of stern calibre, boasting of honourable penury, too dignified to work with their hands and too proud to beg. They were grave personifications of high spirits undaunted by adversity. They were an embodiment of what was considered as an end of all learning, and were thus a living example of that discipline of disciplines, self-control, which was universally required of samurai.

CHAPTER 11

SELF-CONTROL

The discipline of fortitude on the one hand, inculcating endurance without a groan, and the teaching of politeness on the other, requiring us not to mar the pleasure or serenity of another by expressions of our own sorrow or pain, combined to engender a turn of mind, and eventually to confirm it into a national trait of apparent stoicism. I say apparent stoicism, because I do not believe that true stoicism can ever become the characteristic of a whole nation, and also because some of our national manners and customs may seem to a foreign observer hard-hearted. Yet we are really as susceptible to tender emotion as any race under the sky.

I am inclined to think that in one sense we have to feel more than others – yes, doubly more – since the very attempt to restrain natural promptings entails suffering. Imagine boys – and girls, too – brought up not to resort to the shedding of a tear or the uttering of a groan for the relief of their feelings – and there is a physiological problem whether such effort steels their nerves or makes them more sensitive.

It was considered unmanly for a samurai to betray his emotions on his face. 'He shows no sign of joy or anger,' was a phrase used, in describing a great character. The most natural affections were kept under control. A father could embrace his son only at the expense of his dignity; a husband would not kiss his wife – no, not in the presence of other people, whatever he might do in private! There may be some truth in the remark of a witty youth when he said, 'American husbands kiss their wives in public and beat them in private; Japanese husbands beat theirs in public and kiss them in private.'

Calmness of behaviour, composure of mind, should not be disturbed by passion of any kind. I remember when, during the late war with China, a regiment left a certain town, a large concourse of people flocked to the station to bid farewell to the general and his army. On this occasion an American resident resorted to the place, expecting to witness loud demonstrations, as the nation itself was highly excited and there were fathers, mothers, wives, and sweethearts of the soldiers in the crowd. The American was strangely disappointed; for as the whistle blew and the train began to move, the hats of thousands of people were silently taken off and their heads bowed in reverential farewell; no waving of handkerchiefs, no word uttered, but deep silence in which only an attentive ear could catch a few broken sobs. In domestic life, too, I know of a father who spent whole nights listening to the breathing of a sick child, standing behind the door that he might not be caught in such an act of parental weakness! I know of a mother who, in her last moments, refrained from sending for her son, that he might not be disturbed in his studies. Our history and everyday life are replete with examples of heroic matrons who can well bear comparison with some of the most touching pages of Plutarch.

It is the same discipline of self-restraint which is accountable for the absence of more frequent revivals in the Christian churches of Japan. When a man or woman feels his or her soul stirred, the first instinct is quietly to suppress the manifestation of it. In rare instances is the tongue set free by an irresistible spirit, when we have eloquence of sincerity and fervour. It is putting a premium upon a breach of the third commandment to encourage speaking lightly of spiritual experience. It is truly jarring to Japanese ears to hear the most sacred words, the most secret heart experiences, thrown out in promiscuous audiences. 'Dost thou feel the soil of thy soul stirred with tender thoughts? It is time for seeds to sprout. Disturb it not with speech; but let it work alone in quietness and secrecy,' writes a young samurai in his diary.

To give in so many articulate words one's inmost thoughts and feelings – notably the religious – is taken among us as an unmistakable sign that they are neither very profound nor very sincere. 'Only a pomegranate is he' – so runs a popular saying 'who, when he gapes his mouth, displays the contents of his heart.'

It is not altogether perverseness of oriental minds that the instant our emotions are moved, we try to guard our lips in order to hide them. Speech is very often with us, as the Frenchman defines it, 'the art of concealing thought.'

Call upon a Japanese friend in time of deepest affliction and he will invariably receive you laughing, with red eyes or moist cheeks. At first you may think him hysterical. Press him for explanation and you will get a few broken commonplaces – 'Human life has sorrow'; 'They who meet must part'; 'He that is born must die'; 'It is foolish to count the years of a child that is gone, but a woman's heart will indulge in follies'; and the like. So the noble words of a noble Hohenzollern – *'Lerne zu leiden ohne klagen'*[19] – had found many responsive minds among us long before they were uttered.

Indeed, the Japanese have recourse to risibility whenever the frailties of human nature are put to the severest test. I think we possess a better reason than Democritus himself for our Abderian tendency, for laughter with us oftenest veils an effort to regain balance of temper when disturbed by any untoward circumstance. It is a counterpoise of sorrow or rage.

The suppression of feelings being thus steadily insisted upon, they find their safety-valve in poetical aphorisms. A poet of the tenth century writes 'In Japan and China as well, humanity, when moved by sorrow, tells its bitter grief in verse.' Another who tries to console her broken heart by fancying her departed child absent on his wonted chase after the dragon-fly hums,

> *'How far to-day in chase, I wonder,*
> *Has gone my hunter of the dragon-fly!'*

I refrain from quoting other examples, for I know I could do only scant justice to the pearly gems of our literature, were I to render into a foreign tongue the thoughts which were wrung drop by drop from bleeding hearts and threaded into beads of rarest value. I hope I have in a measure shown that inner working of our minds which often presents an appearance of callousness or of an hysterical mixture of laughter and dejection, and whose sanity is sometimes called in question.

It has also been suggested that our endurance of pain and indifference to death are due to less sensitive nerves. This is plausible as far as it goes. The next question is, why are our nerves less tightly strung? It may be our climate is not so stimulating as the American. It may be our monarchical form of government does not excite us so much as the Republic does the Frenchman. It may be that we do not read *Sartor Resartus* so zealously as the Englishman. Personally, I believe it was our very excitability and sensitiveness which made it a necessity to recognize and enforce constant self-repression; but whatever may be the explanation, without taking into account long years of discipline in self-control, none can be correct.

Discipline in self-control can easily go too far. It can well repress the genial current of the soul. It can force pliant natures into distortions and monstrosities. It can beget bigotry, breed hypocrisy, or hebetate affections. Be a virtue never so noble, it has its counterpart and counterfeit. We must recognize in each virtue its own positive excellence and follow its positive ideal, and the ideal of self-restraint is to keep the mind level – as our expression is – or, to borrow a Greek term, attain the state of euthymia, which Democritus called the highest good.

The acme and pitch of self-control is reached and best illustrated in the first of the two institutions which we shall now bring to view, namely, the institutions of suicide and redress.

CHAPTER 12

THE INSTITUTIONS
OF SUICIDE AND REDRESS

Of these two institutions (the former known as *hara-kiri* and the latter as *kataki-uchi*), many foreign writers have treated more or less fully.

To begin with suicide, let me state that I confine my observations only to *seppuku* or *kappuku*, popularly known as *hara-kiri* – which means self-immolation by disembowelment. 'Ripping the abdomen? How absurd!' – so cry those to whom the name is new. Absurdly odd as it may sound at first to foreign ears, it cannot be so very foreign to students of Shakespeare, who puts these words in Brutus's mouth – 'Thy [Caesar's] spirit walks abroad and turns our swords into our proper entrails.' Listen to a modern English poet[20] who, in his *Light of Asia*, speaks of a sword piercing the bowels of a queen; none blames him for bad English or breach of modesty. Or, to take still another example, look at Guercino's painting of Cato's death in the Palazzo Rossa, in Genoa. Whoever has read the swan-song which Addison makes Cato sing, will not jeer at the sword half-buried in his abdomen. In our minds this mode of death is associated with instances of noblest deeds and of most touching pathos, so that nothing repugnant, much less ludicrous, mars our conception of it. So wonderful is the transforming power of virtue, of greatness, of tenderness, that the vilest form of death assumes a sublimity and becomes a symbol of new life, or else the sign which Constantine beheld would not conquer the world!

Not for extraneous associations only does *seppuku* lose in our mind any taint of absurdity; for the choice of this particular part of the body to operate upon, was based on an old anatomical belief as to the seat of the soul and of the affections. When Moses wrote of Joseph's 'bowels yearning upon his brother,' or David prayed the Lord not to forget his bowels, or when Isaiah, Jeremiah, and other inspired men of old spoke of the 'sounding' or the 'troubling' of bowels, they all and each endorsed the belief prevalent among the Japanese that in the abdomen was enshrined the soul. The Semites habitually spoke of the liver and kidneys and surrounding fat as the seat of emotion and of life. The term '*hara*' was more comprehensive than the Greek *phren* or *thumos*, and the Japanese and Hellenese alike thought the spirit of man to dwell somewhere in that region. Such a notion is by no means confined to the peoples of antiquity. The French, in spite of the theory propounded by one of their most distinguished philosophers, Descartes, that the soul is located in the pineal gland, still insist in using the term *ventre* in a sense which, if anatomically too vague, is nevertheless physiologically significant. Similarly, *entrailles* stands in their language for affection and compassion. Nor is such a belief mere superstition, being more scientific than the general idea of making the heart the centre of the feelings. Without asking a friar, the Japanese knew better than Romeo 'in what vile part of this anatomy one's name did lodge.' Modern neurologists speak of the abdominal and pelvic brains, denoting thereby sympathetic nerve centres in those parts which are strongly affected by any psychical action. This view of mental physiology once admitted, the syllogism of *seppuku* is easy to construct. 'I will open the seat of my soul and show you how it fares with it. See for yourself whether it is polluted or clean.'

I do not wish to be understood as asserting religious or even moral justification of suicide, but the high estimate placed upon honour was ample excuse with many for taking one's own life. How many acquiesced in the sentiment expressed by Garth,

'When honour's lost, 't is a relief to die;
Death's but a sure retreat from infamy,'

and have smilingly surrendered their souls to oblivion! Death involving a question of honour, was accepted in Bushido as a key to the solution of many complex problems, so that to an ambitious samurai a natural departure from life seemed a rather tame affair and a consummation not devoutly to be wished for. I dare say that many good Christians, if only they are honest enough, will confess the fascination of, if not positive admiration for, the sublime composure with which Cato, Brutus, Petronius, and a host of other ancient worthies terminated their own earthly existence. Is it too bold to hint that the death of the first of the philosophers was partly suicidal? When we are told so minutely by his pupils how their master willingly submitted to the mandate of the state – which he knew was morally mistaken – in spite of the possibilities of escape, and how he took the cup of hemlock in his own hand, even offering libation from its deadly contents, do we not discern, in his whole proceeding and demeanour, an act of self-immolation? No physical compulsion here, as in ordinary cases of execution. True, the verdict of the judges was compulsory: it said, 'Thou shalt die – and that by thine own hand.' If suicide meant no more than dying by one's own hand, Socrates was a clear case of suicide. But nobody would charge him with the crime; Plato, who was averse to it, would not call his master a suicide.

Now my readers will understand that *seppuku* was not a mere suicidal process. It was an institution, legal and ceremonial. An invention of the middle ages, it was a process by which warriors could expiate their crimes, apologize for errors, escape from disgrace, redeem their friends, or prove their sincerity. When enforced as a legal punishment, it was practised with due ceremony. It was a refinement of self-destruction, and none could perform it without the utmost coolness of temper and composure of demeanour, and for these reasons it was particularly befitting the profession of bushi.

Antiquarian curiosity, if nothing else, would tempt me to give here a description of this obsolete ceremony; but seeing that such a description was made by a far abler writer, whose book is not much read nowadays, I am tempted to make a somewhat lengthy quotation. Mitford, in his *Tales of Old Japan*, after giving a translation of a treatise on *seppuku* from a rare Japanese manuscript, goes on to describe an instance of such an execution of which he was an eye-witness:

> '*We (seven foreign representatives) were invited to follow the Japanese witnesses into the* hondo *or main hall of the temple, where the ceremony was to be performed. It was an imposing scene. A large hall with a high roof supported by dark pillars of wood. From the ceiling hung a profusion of those huge gilt lamps and ornaments peculiar to Buddhist temples. In front of the high altar, where the floor, covered with beautiful white mats, is raised some three or four inches from the ground, was laid a rug of scarlet felt. Tall candles placed at regular intervals gave out a dim mysterious light, just sufficient to let all the proceedings be seen. The seven Japanese took their places on the left of the raised floor, the seven foreigners on the right. No other person was present.*
>
> '*After the interval of a few minutes of anxious suspense, Taki Zenzaburo, a stalwart man thirty-two years of age, with a noble air, walked into the hall attired in his dress of ceremony, with the peculiar* hempen-cloth *wings which are worn on great occasions. He was accompanied by a* kaishaku *and three officers, who wore the* jimbaori *or war surcoat with gold tissue facings. The word* kaishaku, *it should be observed, is one to which our word executioner is no equivalent term.*

The office is that of a gentleman; in many cases it is performed by a kinsman or friend of the condemned, and the relation between them is rather that of principal and second than that of victim and executioner. In this instance, the kaishaku *was a pupil of Taki Zenzaburo, and was selected by friends of the latter from among their own number for his skill in swordsmanship.*

'With the kaishaku *on his left hand, Taki Zenzaburo advanced slowly toward the Japanese witnesses, and the two bowed before them, then drawing near to the foreigners they saluted us in the same way, perhaps even with more deference; in each case the salutation was ceremoniously returned. Slowly and with great dignity the condemned man mounted on to the raised floor, prostrated himself before the high altar twice, and seated*[21] *himself on the felt carpet with his back to the high altar, the* kaishaku *crouching on his left-hand side. One of the three attendant officers then came forward, bearing a stand of the kind used in the temple for offerings, on which, wrapped in paper, lay the* wakizashi, *the short sword or dirk of the Japanese, nine inches and a half in length, with a point and an edge as sharp as a razor's. This he handed, prostrating himself, to the condemned man, who received it reverently raising it to his head with both hands, and placed it in front of himself.*

'After another profound obeisance, Taki Zenzaburo, in a voice which betrayed just so much emotion and hesitation as might be expected from a man who is making a painful confession, but with no sign of either in his face or manner, spoke as follows: –

'"I, and I alone, unwarrantably gave the order to fire on the foreigners at Kobe, and again as they tried to escape. For this crime I disembowel myself, and I beg you who are present to do me the honour of witnessing the act."

'Bowing once more, the speaker allowed his upper garments to slip down to his girdle, and remained naked to the waist. Carefully, according to custom, he tucked his sleeves under his knees to prevent himself from falling backward; for a noble Japanese gentleman should die falling* *forwards. Deliberately, with a steady hand he took the dirk that lay before him; he looked at it wistfully, almost affectionately; for a moment he seemed to collect his thoughts for the last time, and then stabbing himself deeply below the waist in the left-hand side, he drew the dirk slowly across to his right side, and turning it in the wound, gave a slight cut upwards. During this sickeningly painful operation he never moved a muscle of his face. When he drew out the dirk, he leaned forward and stretched out his neck; an expression of pain for the first time crossed his face, but he uttered no sound. At that moment the kaishaku, who, still crouching by his side, had been keenly watching his every movement, sprang to his feet, poised his sword for a second in the air; there was a flash, a heavy, ugly thud, a crashing fall; with one blow the head had been severed from the body.*

'*A dead silence followed, broken only by the hideous noise of the blood throbbing out of the inert heap before us, which but a moment before had been a brave and chivalrous man. It was horrible.*

'*The* kaishaku *made a low bow, wiped his sword with a piece of paper which he had ready for the purpose, and retired from the raised floor; and the stained dirk was solemnly borne away, a bloody proof of the execution.*

'*The two representatives of the Mikado then left their places, and crossing over to where the foreign witnesses sat, called to us to witness that the sentence of death upon Taki Zenzaburo had been faithfully carried out. The ceremony being at an end, we left the temple.*'

The glorification of *seppuku* offered, naturally enough, no small temptation to its unwarranted committal. For causes entirely incompatible with reason, or for reasons entirely undeserving of death, hot-headed youths rushed into it as insects fly into fire; mixed and dubious motives drove more samurai to this deed than nuns into convent gates. Life was cheap – cheap as reckoned by the popular standard of honour. The saddest feature was that honour, which was always in the *agio*, so to speak, was not always solid gold, but alloyed with baser metals. No one circle in the Inferno will boast of greater density of Japanese population than the seventh, to which Dante consigns all victims of self-destruction!

And yet, for a true samurai to hasten death or to court it, was alike cowardice. A typical fighter, when he lost battle after battle and was pursued from plain to hill and from bush to cavern, found himself hungry and alone in the dark hollow of a tree, his sword blunt with use, his bow broken and arrows exhausted – did not the noblest of the Romans fall upon his own sword in Philippi under like circumstances? – deemed it cowardly to die, but, with a fortitude approaching a Christian martyr's, cheered himself with an impromptu verse:

> 'Come! evermore come,
> Ye dread sorrows and pains!
> And heap on my burden'd back;
> That I not one test may lack
> Of what strength in me remains!'

This, then, was the Bushido teaching – Bear and face all calamities and adversities with patience and a pure conscience; for, as Mencius[22] taught, 'When Heaven is about to confer a great office on anyone, it first exercises his mind with suffering and his sinews and bones with toil; it exposes his body to hunger and subjects him to extreme poverty: and it confounds his undertakings. In all these ways it stimulates his mind, hardens his nature, and supplies his incompetencies.' True honour lies in fulfilling Heaven's decree and no death incurred in so doing is ignominious, whereas, death to avoid what Heaven has in store is cowardly indeed! In that quaint book of Sir Thomas Browne's, *Religio Medici*, there is an exact English equivalent for what is repeatedly taught in our Precepts. Let me quote it: 'It is a brave act of valour to contemn death, but where life is more terrible than death, it is then the truest valour to dare to live.' A renowned priest of the seventeenth century satirically observed – 'Talk as he may, a samurai who ne'er has died is apt in decisive moments to flee or hide.' Again – 'Him who once has died in the bottom of his breast, no spears of Sanada nor all the arrows of Tametomo can pierce.' How near we come to the portals of the temple whose Builder taught, 'He that loseth his life for my sake shall find it'! These are but a few of the numerous examples that tend to confirm the moral identity of the human species, notwith-standing an attempt so assiduously made to render the distinction between Christian and Pagan as great as possible.

We have thus seen that the Bushido institution of suicide was neither so irrational nor barbarous as its abuse strikes us at first sight. We will now see whether its sister institution of Redress – or call it Revenge, if you will – has its mitigating features. I hope I can dispose of this question in a few words, since a similar institution, or call it custom, if that suits you better, prevailed among all peoples and has not yet become entirely obsolete, as attested by the continuance of duelling and lynching. Why, has not an American captain recently challenged Esterhazy, that the wrongs of Dreyfus be avenged? Among a savage tribe which has no marriage, adultery is not a sin, and only the jealousy of a lover protects a woman from abuse; so in a time which has no criminal court, murder is not a crime, and only the vigilant vengeance of the victim's people preserves social order. 'What is the most beautiful thing on earth?' said Osiris to Horus. The reply was, 'To avenge a parent's wrongs,' to which a Japanese would have added 'and a master's.'

In revenge there is something which satisfies one's sense of justice. The avenger reasons: 'My good father did not deserve death. He who killed him did great evil. My father, if he were alive, would not tolerate a deed like this: Heaven itself hates wrongdoing. It is the will of my father; it is the will of Heaven that the evil-doer cease from his work. He must perish by my hand; because he shed my father's blood, I, who am his flesh and blood, must shed the murderer's. The same Heaven shall not shelter him and me.' The ratiocination is simple and childish (though we know Hamlet did not reason much more deeply); nevertheless it shows an innate sense of exact balance and equal justice. 'An eye for an eye, a tooth for a tooth.' Our sense of revenge is as exact as our mathematical faculty, and until both terms of the equation are satisfied we cannot get over the sense of something left undone.

In Judaism, which believed in a jealous God, or in Greek mythology, which provided a Nemesis, vengeance may be left to superhuman agencies; but common sense furnished Bushido with the institution of redress as a kind of ethical court of equity, where people could take cases not to be judged in accordance with ordinary law. The master of the forty-seven Ronins was condemned to death; he had no court of higher instance to appeal to; his faithful retainers addressed themselves to vengeance, the only Supreme Court existing; they in their turn were condemned by common law – but the popular instinct passed a different judgment, and hence their memory is still kept as green and fragrant as are their graves at Sengakuji to this day.

Though Lâo-tse taught to recompense injury with kindness, the voice of Confucius was very much louder, which taught that injury must be recompensed with justice – and yet revenge was justified only when it was undertaken in behalf of our superiors and benefactors. One's own wrongs, including injuries done to wife and children, were to be borne and forgiven. A samurai could therefore fully sympathize with Hannibal's oath to avenge his country's wrongs, but he scorns James Hamilton for wearing in his girdle a handful of earth from his wife's grave, as an eternal incentive to avenge her wrongs on the Regent Murray.

Both of these institutions of suicide and redress lost their *raison d'être* at the promulgation of the Criminal Code. No more do we hear of romantic adventures of a fair maiden as she tracks in disguise the murderer of her parent. No more can we witness tragedies of family vendetta enacted. The knight errantry of Miyamoto Musashi is now a tale of the past. The well-ordered police spies out the criminal for the injured party and the law metes out justice. The whole state and society will see that wrong is righted. The sense of justice satisfied, there is no need of *kataki-uchi*. If this had meant that 'hunger of the heart which feeds upon the hope of glutting that hunger with the life blood of the victim,' as a New England divine has described it, a few paragraphs in the Criminal Code would not so entirely have made an end of it.

As to *seppuku*, though it too has no existence *de jure*, we still hear of it from time to time, and shall continue to hear, I am afraid, as long as the past is remembered. Many painless and time-saving methods of self-immolation will come in vogue, as its votaries are increasing with fearful rapidity throughout the world; but Professor Morselli will have to concede to *seppuku* an aristocratic position among them. He maintains that 'when suicide is accomplished by very painful means or at the cost of prolonged agony, in ninety-nine cases out of a hundred, it may be assigned as the act of a mind disordered by fanaticism, by madness, or by morbid excitement.'[23] But a normal *seppuku* does not savour of fanaticism, or madness or excitement, utmost *sang froid* being necessary to its successful accomplishment. Of the two kinds into which Dr. Strahan[24] divides suicide, the Rational or Quasi, and the Irrational or True, *seppuku* is the best example of the former type.

From these bloody institutions, as well as from the general tenor of Bushido, it is easy to infer that the sword played an important part in social discipline and life. The saying passed as an axiom which called the sword the soul of the samurai.

CHAPTER 13

THE SWORD, THE SOUL OF THE SAMURAI

Bushido made the sword its emblem of power and prowess. When Mahomet proclaimed that 'the sword is the key of Heaven and of Hell,' he only echoed a Japanese sentiment. Very early the samurai boy learned to wield it. It was a momentous occasion for him when at the age of five he was apparelled in the paraphernalia of samurai costume, placed upon a *go*-board[25] and initiated into the rights of the military profession, by having thrust into his girdle a real sword instead of the toy dirk with which he had been playing. After this first ceremony of *adoptio per arma*, he was no more to be seen outside his father's gates without this badge of his status, even though it was usually substituted for everyday wear by a gilded wooden dirk. Not many years pass before he wears constantly the genuine steel, though blunt, and then the sham arms are thrown aside and with enjoyment keener than his newly acquired blades, he marches out to try their edge on wood and stone. When he reaches man's estate, at the age of fifteen, being given independence of action, he can now pride himself upon the possession of arms sharp enough for any work. The very possession of the dangerous instrument imparts to him a feeling and an air of self-respect and responsibility. 'He beareth not the sword in vain.' What he carries in his belt is a symbol of what he carries in his mind and heart – loyalty and honour. The two swords, the longer and the shorter – called respectively *daito* and *shoto* or *katana* and *wakizashi* – never leave his side. When at home, they grace the most conspicuous place in the study or parlour; by night they guard his pillow within easy reach of his hand. Constant companions, they are beloved, and proper names of endearment given them. Being venerated, they are well-nigh worshipped. The Father of History has recorded as a curious piece of information that the Scythians sacrificed to an iron scimitar. Many a temple and many a family in Japan hoards a sword as an object of adoration. Even the commonest dirk has due respect paid to it. Any insult to it is tantamount to personal affront. Woe to him who carelessly steps over a weapon lying on the floor!

So precious an object cannot long escape the notice and the skill of artists nor the vanity of its owner, especially in times of peace, when it is worn with no more use than a crosier by a bishop or a sceptre by a king. Sharkskin and finest silk for hilt, silver and gold for guard, lacquer of varied hues for scabbard, robbed the deadliest weapon of half its terror; but these appurtenances are playthings compared with the blade itself.

The swordsmith was not a mere artisan but an inspired artist and his workshop a sanctuary. Daily he commenced his craft with prayer and purification, or, as the phrase was, 'he committed his soul and spirit into the forging and tempering of the steel.' Every swing of the sledge, every plunge into water, every friction on the grindstone, was a religious act of no slight import. Was it the spirit of the master or of his tutelary god that cast a formidable spell over our sword? Perfect as a work of art, setting at defiance its Toledo and Damascus rivals, there was more than art could impart. Its cold blade, collecting on its surface the moment it is drawn the vapour of the atmosphere; its immaculate texture, flashing light of bluish hue; its matchless edge, upon which histories and possibilities hang; the curve of its back, uniting exquisite grace with utmost strength – all these thrill us with mixed feelings of power and beauty, of awe and terror. Harmless were its mission, if it only remained a thing of beauty and joy! But, ever within reach of the hand, it presented no small temptation for abuse. Too often did the blade flash forth from its peaceful sheath. The abuse sometimes went so far as to try the acquired steel on some harmless creature's neck.

The question that concerns us most is, however – Did Bushido justify the promiscuous use of the weapon? The answer is unequivocally, no! As it laid great stress on its proper use, so did it denounce and abhor its misuse. A dastard or a braggart was he who brandished his weapon on undeserved occasions. A self-possessed man knows the right time to use it, and such times come but rarely. Let us listen to the late Count Katsu, who passed through one of the most turbulent times of our history, when assassinations, suicides, and other sanguinary practices were the order of the day. Endowed as he once was with almost dictatorial powers, chosen repeatedly as an object of assassination, he never tarnished his sword with blood. In relating some of his reminiscences to a friend he says, in a quaint, plebeian way peculiar to him: 'I have a great dislike for killing people and so I haven't killed one single man. I have released those whose heads should have been chopped off. A friend said to me one day, "You don't kill enough. Don't you eat pepper and egg-plants?" Well, some people are no better! But you see that fellow was slain himself. My escape may be due to my dislike of killing. I had the hilt of my sword so tightly fastened to the scabbard that it was hard to draw the blade. I made up my mind that though they cut me, I would not cut. Yes, yes! some people are truly like fleas and mosquitoes and they bite – but what does their biting amount to? It itches a little, that's all; it won't endanger life.' These are the words of one whose Bushido training was tried in the fiery furnace of adversity and triumph. The popular apothegm – 'To be beaten is to conquer,' meaning true conquest consists in not opposing a riotous foe; and 'The best won victory is that obtained without shedding of blood,' and others of similar import – will show that after all the ultimate ideal of knighthood was peace.

It was a great pity that this high ideal was left exclusively to priests and moralists to preach, while the samurai went on practising and extolling martial traits. In this they went so far as to tinge the ideals of womanhood with Amazonian character. Here we may profitably devote a few paragraphs to the subject of the training and position of woman.

CHAPTER 14

THE TRAINING AND POSITION OF WOMAN

The female half of our species has sometimes been called the paragon of paradoxes, because the intuitive working of its mind is beyond the comprehension of men's 'arithmetical understanding.' The Chinese ideogram denoting 'the mysterious,' 'the unknowable,' consists of two parts, one meaning 'young' and the other 'woman,' because the physical charms and delicate thoughts of the fair sex are above the coarse mental calibre of our sex to explain.

In the Bushido ideal of woman, however, there is little mystery and only a seeming paradox. I have said that it was Amazonian, but that is only half the truth. Ideographically the Chinese represent wife by a woman holding a broom – certainly not to brandish it offensively or defensively against her conjugal ally, neither for witchcraft, but for the more harmless uses for which the besom was first invented – the idea involved being thus not less homely than the etymological derivation of the English wife (weaver) and daughter (*duhitar*, milkmaid). Without confining the sphere of woman's activity to *Küche, Kirche, Kinder,*[26] as the present German Kaiser is said to do, the Bushido ideal of womanhood was preeminently domestic. These seeming contradictions – domesticity and Amazonian traits – are not inconsistent with the Precepts of Knighthood, as we shall see.

Bushido being a teaching primarily intended for the masculine sex, the virtues it prized in woman were naturally far from being distinctly feminine. Winckelmann remarks that 'the supreme beauty of Greek art is rather male than female,' and Lecky adds that it was true in the moral conception of the Greeks as in their art. Bushido similarly praised those women most 'who emancipated themselves from the frailty of their sex and displayed an heroic fortitude worthy of the strongest and the bravest of men.'[27] Young girls, therefore, were trained to repress their feelings, to indurate their nerves, to manipulate weapons – especially the long-handled sword called *nagi-nata*, so as to be able to hold their own against unexpected odds. Yet the primary motive for exercise of this martial character was not for use in the field; it was twofold – personal and domestic. Woman owning no suzerain of her own, formed her own body-guard. With her weapon she guarded her personal sanctity with as much zeal as her husband did his master's. The domestic utility of her warlike training was in the education of her sons, as we shall see later.

Fencing and similar exercises, if rarely of practical use, were a wholesome counterbalance to the otherwise sedentary habits of women. But these exercises were not followed only for hygienic purposes. They could be turned into use in times of need. Girls, when they reached womanhood, were presented with dirks (*kai-ken*, pocket poniards), which might be directed to the bosom of their assailants, or, if advisable, to their own. The latter was very often the case; and yet I will not judge them severely. Even the Christian conscience with its horror of self-immolation, will not be harsh with them, seeing Pelagia and Dominina, two suicides, were canonized for their purity and piety. When a Japanese Virginia saw her chastity menaced, she did not wait for her father's dagger. Her own weapon lay always in her bosom. It was a disgrace to her not to know the proper way in which she had to perpetrate self-destruction. For example, little as she was taught in anatomy, she must know the exact spot to cut in her throat; she must know how to tie her lower limbs together with a belt so that, whatever the agonies of death might be, her corpse be found in utmost modesty with the limbs properly composed. Is not a caution like this worthy of the Christian Perpetua or the Vestal Cornelia? I would not put such an abrupt interrogation were it not for a misconception, based on our bathing customs and other trifles, that chastity is unknown among us.[28] On the contrary, chastity was a pre-eminent virtue of the samurai woman, held above life itself.

It would be unfair to give my readers an idea that masculinity alone was our highest ideal for woman. Far from it! Accomplishments and the gentler graces of life were required of them. Music, dancing, and literature were not neglected. Some of the finest verses in our literature were expressions of feminine sentiments; in fact, woman played an important role in the history of Japanese *belles-lettres*. Dancing was taught (I am speaking of samurai girls and not of *geisha*) only to smooth the angularity of their movements. Music was to regale the weary hours of their fathers and husbands; hence it was not for the technique, the art as such, that music was learned; for the ultimate object was purification of heart, since it was said that no harmony of sound is attainable without the player's heart being in harmony with itself. Here again we see the same idea prevailing which we notice in the training of youths – that accomplishments were ever kept subservient to moral worth. Just enough of music and dancing to add grace and brightness to life, but never to foster vanity and extravagance.

The accomplishments of our women were not acquired for show or social ascendancy. They were a home diversion; and if they shone in social parties, it was as the attributes of a hostess – in other words, as a part of the household contrivance for hospitality. Domesticity guided their education. It may be said that the accomplishments of the women of Old Japan, be they martial or pacific in character, were mainly intended for the home; and, however far they might roam, they never lost sight of the hearth as the centre. It was to maintain its honour and integrity that they slaved, drudged, and gave up their lives. Night and day, in tones at once firm and tender, brave and plaintive, they sang to their little nests. As daughter, woman sacrificed herself for her father, as wife for her husband, and as mother for her son. Thus from earliest youth she was taught to deny herself. Her life was not one of independence, but of dependent service. Man's help-meet, if her presence is helpful she stays on the stage with him: if it hinders his work, she retires behind the curtain. Not infre-quently does it happen that a youth becomes enamoured of a maiden who returns his love with equal ardour, but, when she realizes his interest in her makes him forgetful of his duties, disfigures her person that her attractions may cease. Adzuma, the ideal wife in the minds of samurai girls, finds herself loved by a man who is conspiring against her husband. Upon pretence of joining in the guilty plot, she manages in the dark to take her husband's place, and the sword of the lover-assassin descends upon her own devoted head.

Woman's surrender of herself to the good of her husband, home, and family, was as willing and honourable as the man's self-surrender to the good of his lord and country. Self-renunciation, without which no life-enigma can be solved, was the key-note of the loyalty of man as well as of the domesticity of woman. She was no more the slave of man than was her husband of his liege-lord, and the part she played was recognized as *naijo*, 'the inner help.' In the ascending scale of service stood woman, who annihilated herself for man, that he might annihilate himself for the master, that he in turn might obey Heaven. I know the weakness of this teaching and that the superiority of Christianity is nowhere more manifested than here, in that it requires of each and every living soul direct responsibility to its Creator. Nevertheless, as far as the doctrine of service is concerned, Bushido was based on eternal truth.

My readers will not accuse me of undue prejudice in favour of slavish surrender of volition. I accept in a large measure the view advanced and defended with breadth of learning and profundity of thought by Hegel, that history is the unfolding and realization of freedom. The point I wish to make is that the whole teaching of Bushido was so thoroughly imbued with the spirit of self-sacrifice, that it was required not only of woman but of man. Hence, until the influence of its precepts is entirely done away with, our society will not realize the view rashly expressed by an American exponent of woman's rights, who exclaimed, 'May all the daughters of Japan rise in revolt against ancient customs!' Can such a revolt succeed? Will it improve the female status? Will the rights they gain by such a summary process repay the loss of that sweetness of disposition, that gentleness of manner, which are their present heritage? Was not the loss of domesticity on the part of Roman matrons followed by moral corruption too gross to mention? Can the American reformer assure us that a revolt of our daughters is the true course for their historical development to take? These are grave questions. Changes must and will come without revolts! In the meantime let us see whether the status of the fair sex under the Bushido regimen was really so bad as to justify a revolt.

Mr. Spencer tells us that in a militant society (and what is feudal society if not militant?) the position of woman is necessarily low, improving only as society becomes more industrial. The military class in Japan was restricted to the samurai, comprising nearly two million souls. Above them were the military nobles, the *daimio*, and the court nobles, the *kugé* – these higher, sybaritical nobles being fighters only in name. Below them were masses of the common people – mechanics, tradesmen, and peasants – whose life was devoted to arts of peace. Thus what Herbert Spencer gives as the characteristics of a militant type of society may be said to have been exclusively confined to the samurai class, while those of the industrial type were applicable to the classes above and below it. This is well illustrated by the position of woman;

for in no class did she experience less freedom than among the samurai. Strange to say, the lower the social class – as, for instance, among small artisans – the more equal was the position of husband and wife. Among the higher nobility, too, the difference in the relations of the sexes was less marked, chiefly because there were few occasions to bring the differences of sex into prominence, the leisurely nobleman having become literally effeminate. Thus Spencer's dictum was fully exemplified in Old Japan.

I shall be guilty of gross injustice to historical truth if my words give one a very low opinion of the status of woman under Bushido. I do not hesitate to state that she was not treated as man's equal; but, until we learn to discriminate between differences and inequalities, there will always be misunderstandings upon this subject.

In view of the manifold variety of requisites for making each sex fulfil its earthly mission, the standard to be adopted in measuring its relative position must be of a composite character; or to borrow from economic language, it must be a multiple standard. Bushido had a standard of its own and it was binomial. It tried to gauge the value of woman on the battlefield and by the hearth. There she counted for very little; here for all. The treatment accorded her corresponded to this double measurement – as a social-political unit not much, while as wife and mother she received highest respect and deepest affection. While fathers and husbands were absent in field or camp, the government of the household was left entirely in the hands of mothers and wives. The education of the young, even their defence, was entrusted to them. The warlike exercises of women, of which I have spoken, were primarily to enable them intelligently to direct and follow the education of their children.

I have noticed a rather superficial notion prevailing among half-informed foreigners, that because the common Japanese expression for one's wife is 'my rustic wife' and the like, she is despised and held in little esteem. When it is told that such phrases as 'my foolish father,' 'my swinish son,' 'my awkward self,' etc., are in current use, is not the answer clear enough?

To me it seems that our idea of marital union goes in some ways farther than the so-called Christian. 'Man and woman shall be one flesh.' The individualism of the Anglo-Saxon cannot let go of the idea that husband and wife are two persons; hence when they disagree, their separate rights are recognized, and when they agree, they exhaust their vocabulary in all sorts of silly pet-names and nonsensical blandishments. It sounds highly irrational to our ears, when a husband or wife speaks to a third party of his or her other half – better or worse – as being lovely, bright, kind, and what not. Is it good taste to speak of one's self as 'my bright self,' 'my lovely disposition,' and so forth? We think praising one's own wife is praising a part of one's own self, and self-praise is regarded, to say the least, as bad taste among us – and I hope, among Christian nations too! I have diverged at some length because the polite debasement of one's consort was a usage most in vogue among the samurai.

The Teutonic races beginning their tribal life with a superstitious awe of the fair sex, and the Americans beginning their social life under the painful consciousness of the numerical insufficiency of women[29] (who, now increasing, are, I am afraid, fast losing the prestige their colonial mothers enjoyed), the respect man pays to woman has in Western civilization become the chief standard of morality. But in the martial ethics of Bushido, the main watershed dividing the good and the bad was sought elsewhere. It was located along the line of duty which bound man to his own divine soul and then to other souls in the five relations I have mentioned in the early part of this paper. Of these, we have brought to our reader's notice loyalty, the relation between one man as vassal and another as lord. Upon the rest, I have only dwelt incidentally as occasion presented itself; because they were not peculiar to Bushido. Being founded on natural affections, they could but be common to all mankind, though in some particulars they may have been accentuated by conditions which its teachings induced.

It is not surprising, however, that the virtues and teachings unique in the Precepts of Knighthood did not remain circumscribed to the military class. This makes us hasten to the consideration of the influence of Bushido on the nation at large.

CHAPTER 15

THE INFLUENCE OF BUSHIDO

Thus far we have brought into view only a few of the more prominent peaks which rise above the range of knightly virtues, in themselves so much more elevated than the general level of our national life. As the sun in its rising first tips the highest peaks with russet hue, and then gradually casts its rays on the valley below, so the ethical system which first enlightened the military order drew in course of time followers from amongst the masses. Democracy raises up a natural prince for its leader, and aristocracy infuses a princely spirit among the people. Virtues are no less contagious than vices. 'There needs but one wise man in a company, and all are wise, so rapid is the contagion,' says Emerson. No social class or caste can resist the diffusive power of moral influence.

Prate as we may of the triumphant march of Anglo-Saxon liberty, rarely has it received impetus from the masses. Was it not rather the work of the squires and *gentlemen*? Very truly does M. Taine say, 'These three syllables, as used across the channel, summarize the history of English society.' Democracy may make self-confident retorts to such a statement and fling back the question – 'When Adam delved and Eve span, where then was the gentleman?' All the more pity that a gentleman was not present in Eden! The first parents missed him sorely and paid a high price for his absence.

What Japan was she owed to the samurai. They were not only the flower of the nation, but its root as well. All the gracious gifts of Heaven flowed through them. Though they kept themselves socially aloof from the populace, they set a moral standard for them and guided them by their example. I admit Bushido had its esoteric and exoteric teachings; these were eudemonic, looking after the welfare and happiness of the commonalty; those were aretaic, emphasizing the practice of virtues for their own sake.

In the most chivalrous days of Europe, knights formed numerically but a small fraction of the population, but, as Emerson says, 'In English literature half the drama and all the novels, from Sir Philip Sidney to Sir Walter Scott, paint this figure (gentleman).' Write in place of Sidney and Scott, Chikamatsu and Bakin, and you have in a nutshell the main features of the literary history of Japan.

The innumerable avenues of popular amusement and instruction – the theatres, the story-tellers' booths, the preacher's dais, the musical recitations, the novels – have taken for their chief theme the stories of the samurai. The peasants around the open fire in their huts never tire of repeating the achievements of Yoshitsuné and his faithful retainer Benkéi, or of the two brave Soga brothers; the dusky urchins listen with gaping mouths until the last stick burns out and the fire dies in its embers, still leaving their hearts aglow with the tale that is told. The clerks and the shop boys, after their day's work is over and the *amado*[30] of the store are closed, gather together to relate the story of Nobunaga and Hidéyoshi far into the night, until slumber overtakes their weary eyes and transports them from the drudgery of the counter to the exploits of the field. The very babe just beginning to toddle is taught to lisp the adventures of Momotaro, the daring conqueror of ogreland. Even girls are so imbued with the love of knightly deeds and virtues that, like Desdemona, they would seriously incline to devour with greedy ear the romance of the samurai.

The samurai grew to be the *beau ideal* of the whole race. 'As among flowers the cherry is queen, so among men the samurai is lord,' so sang the populace. Debarred from commercial pursuits, the military class itself did not aid commerce; but there was no channel of human activity, no avenue of thought, which did not receive in some measure an impetus from Bushido. Intellectual and moral Japan was directly or indirectly the work of Knighthood.

How the spirit of Bushido permeated all social classes is also shown in the development of a certain order of men, known as *otoko-daté*, the natural leaders of democracy. Staunch fellows were they, every inch of them strong with the strength of massive manhood. At once the spokesmen and the guardians of popular rights, they had each a following of hundreds and thousands of souls who proffered, in the same fashion that samurai did to *daimio*, the willing service of 'limb and life, of body, chattels, and earthly honour.' Backed by a vast multitude of rash and impetuous working men, these born 'bosses' formed a formidable check to the rampancy of the two-sworded order.

In manifold ways has Bushido filtered down from the social class where it originated, and acted as leaven among the masses, furnishing a moral standard for the whole people. The Precepts of Knighthood, begun at first as the glory of the elite, became in time an aspiration and inspiration to the nation at large; and though the populace could not attain the moral height of those loftier souls, yet *Yamato Damashii*, the Soul of Japan, ultimately came to express the *Volksgeist* of the Island Realm. If religion is no more than 'Morality touched by emotion,' as Matthew Arnold defines it, few ethical systems are better entitled to the rank of religion than Bushido. Motoöri has put the mute utterance of the nation into words when he sings:

'Isles of blest Japan!
Should your Yamato spirit
Strangers seek to scan,
Say – scenting morn's sunlit air,
Blows the cherry wild and fair!'

Yes, the *sakura*[31] has for ages been the favourite of our people and the emblem of our character. Mark particularly the terms of definition which the poet uses, the words *the wild cherry flower scenting the morning sun.*

The Yamato spirit is not a tame, tender plant, but a wild – in the sense of natural – growth; it is indigenous to the soil; its accidental qualities it may share with the flowers of other lands, but in its essence it remains the original, spontaneous outgrowth of our clime. But its nativity is not its sole claim to our affection. The refinement and grace of its beauty appeal to our aesthetic sense as no other flower can. We cannot share the admiration of the Europeans for their roses, which lack the simplicity of our flower. Then, too, the thorns that are hidden beneath the sweetness of the rose, the tenacity with which she clings to life, as though loth or afraid to die rather than drop untimely, preferring to rot on her stem; her showy colours and heavy odours – all these are traits so unlike our flower, which carries no dagger or poison under its beauty, which is ever ready to depart life at the call of nature, whose colours are never gorgeous, and whose light fragrance never palls. Beauty of colour and of form is limited in its showing; it is a fixed quality of existence, whereas fragrance is volatile, ethereal as the breathing of life. So in all religious ceremonies frankincense and myrrh play a prominent part. There is something spirituelle in redolence. When the delicious perfume of the sakura quickens the morning air, as the sun in its course rises to illumine first the isles of the Far East, few sensations are more serenely exhilarating than to inhale, as it were, the very breath of beauteous day.

When the Creator Himself is pictured as making new resolutions in His heart upon smelling a sweet savour (Gen. 8:21), is it any wonder that the sweet-smelling season of the cherry blossom should call forth the whole nation from their little habitations? Blame them not, if for a time their limbs forget their toil and moil and their hearts their pangs and sorrows. Their brief pleasure ended, they return to their daily task with new strength and new resolutions. Thus in ways more than one is the sakura the flower of the nation.

Is, then, this flower, so sweet and evanescent, blown whithersoever the wind listeth, and, shedding a puff of perfume, ready to vanish forever, is this flower the type of the Yamato-spirit? Is the soul of Japan so frailly mortal?

CHAPTER 16

IS BUSHIDO STILL ALIVE?

Has Western civilization, in its march through our land, already wiped out every trace of its ancient discipline? It were a sad thing if a nation's soul could die so fast. That were a poor soul that could succumb so easily to extraneous influences.

The aggregate of psychological elements which constitute a national character is as tenacious as the 'irreducible elements of species, of the fins of the fish, of the beak of the bird, of the tooth of the carnivorous animal.' In his recent book, full of shallow asseverations and brilliant generalizations, M. LeBon[32] says: 'The discoveries due to the intelligence are the common patrimony of humanity; qualities or defects of character constitute the exclusive patrimony of each people: they are the firm rock which the waters must wash day by day for centuries before they can wear away even its external asperities.' These are strong words and would be highly worth pondering over, provided there were qualities and defects of character which *constitute the exclusive patrimony* of each people. Schematizing theories of this sort had been advanced long before LeBon began to write his book, and they were exploded long ago by Theodor Waitz and Hugh Murray. In studying the various virtues instilled by Bushido, we have drawn upon European sources for comparison and illustrations, and we have seen that no one quality of character was its *exclusive patrimony*. It is true the aggregate of moral qualities presents a quite unique aspect. It is this aggregate which Emerson names a 'compound result into which every great force enters as an ingredient.' But, instead of making it, as LeBon does, an exclusive patrimony of a race or people, the Concord philosopher calls it 'an element which unites the most forcible persons of every country; makes them intelligible and agreeable to each other; and is somewhat so precise that it is at once felt if an individual lack the Masonic sign.'

The character which Bushido stamped on our nation and on the samurai in particular, cannot be said to form 'an irreducible element of species,' but nevertheless as to the vitality which it retains there is no doubt. Were Bushido a mere physical force, the momentum it has gained in the last seven hundred years could not stop so abruptly. Were it transmitted only by heredity, its influence must be immensely widespread. Just think, as M. Cheysson, a French economist, has calculated, that, supposing there be three generations in a century, 'each of us would have in his veins the blood of at least twenty millions of the people living in the year AD1000.' The merest peasant that grubs the soil, 'bowed by the weight of centuries,' has in his veins the blood of ages, and is thus brother to us as much as 'to the ox.'

An unconscious and irresistible power, Bushido has been moving the nation and individuals. It was an honest confession of the race when Yoshida Shôin, one of the most brilliant pioneers of Modern Japan, wrote on the eve of his execution the following stanza:

> '*Full well I knew this course must end in death;*
> *It was Yamato spirit urged me on*
> *To dare whate'er betide.*'

Unformulated, Bushido was and still is the animating spirit, the motor force of our country.

Mr. Ransome says that 'there are three distinct Japans in existence side by side today – the old, which has not wholly died out; the new, hardly yet born except in spirit; and the transition, passing now through its most critical throes.' While this is very true in most respects, and particularly as regards tangible and concrete institutions, the statement, as applied to fundamental ethical notions, requires some modification; for Bushido, the maker and product of Old Japan, is still the guiding principle of the transition and will prove the formative force of the new era.

The great statesmen who steered the ship of our state through the hurricane of the Restoration and the whirlpool of national rejuvenation, were men who knew no other moral teaching than the Precepts of Knighthood. Some writers[33] have lately tried to prove that the Christian missionaries contributed an appreciable quota to the making of New Japan. I would fain render honour to whom honour is due; but this honour can as yet hardly be accorded to the good missionaries. More fitting it will be to their profession to stick to the scriptural injunction of preferring one another in honour, than to advance a claim in which they have no proofs to back them. For myself, I believe that Christian missionaries are doing great things for Japan – in the domain of education, and especially of moral education: – only, the mysterious though not the less certain working of the Spirit is still hidden in divine secrecy. Whatever they do is still of indirect effect. No, as yet Christian missions have effected but little visible in moulding the character of New Japan. No, it was Bushido, pure and simple, that urged us on for weal or woe. Open the biographies of the makers of Modern Japan – of Sakuma, of Saigo, of Okubo, of Kido, not to mention the reminiscences of living men such as Ito, Okuma, Itagaki, etc. – and you will find that it was under the impetus of samuraihood that they thought and wrought. When Mr. Henry Norman declared, after his study and observation of the Far East, that the only respect in which Japan differed from other oriental despotisms lay in 'the ruling influence among her people of the strictest, loftiest, and the most punctilious codes of honour that man has ever devised,' he touched the mainspring which has made New Japan what she is, and which will make her what she is destined to be.[34]

The transformation of Japan is a fact patent to the whole world. Into a work of such magnitude various motives naturally entered; but if one were to name the principal, one would not hesitate to name Bushido. When we opened the whole country to foreign trade, when we introduced the latest improvements in every department of life, when we began to study Western politics and sciences, our guiding motive was not the development of our physical resources and the increase of wealth; much less was it a blind imitation of Western customs.

A close observer of oriental institutions and peoples has written:

> *'We are told every day how Europe has influenced Japan, and forget that the change in those islands was entirely self-generated, that Europeans did not teach Japan, but that Japan of herself chose to learn from Europe methods of organization, civil and military, which have so far proved successful. She imported European mechanical science, as the Turks years before imported European artillery. That is not exactly influence,' continues Mr. Townsend, 'unless, indeed, England is influenced by purchasing tea in China. Where is the European apostle,' asks our author, 'or philosopher or statesman or agitator, who has re-made Japan?'*[35]

Mr. Townsend has well perceived that the spring of action which brought about the changes in Japan lay entirely within our own selves; and if he had only probed into our psychology, his keen powers of observation would easily have convinced him that this spring was no other than Bushido. The sense of honour which cannot bear being looked down upon as an inferior power – that was the strongest of motives. Pecuniary or industrial considerations were awakened later in the process of transformation.

The influence of Bushido is still so palpable that he who runs may read. A glimpse into Japanese life will make it manifest. Read Hearn, the most eloquent and truthful interpreter of the Japanese mind, and you see the working of that mind to be an example of the working of Bushido. The universal politeness of the people, which is the legacy of knightly ways, is too well known to be repeated anew. The physical endurance, fortitude, and bravery that 'the little Jap' possesses, were sufficiently proved in the Chino-Japanese war.[36] 'Is there any nation more loyal and patriotic?' is a question asked by many; and for the proud answer, 'There is not,' we must thank the Precepts of Knighthood.

On the other hand, it is fair to recognize that for the very faults and defects of our character, Bushido is largely responsible. Our lack of abstruse philosophy – while some of our young men have already gained international reputation in scientific researches, not one has achieved anything in philosophical lines – is traceable to the neglect of metaphysical training under Bushido's regimen of education. Our sense of honour is responsible for our exaggerated sensitiveness and touchiness; and if there is the conceit in us with which some foreigners charge us, that, too, is a pathological outcome of honour.

Deep-rooted and powerful as is still the effect of Bushido, I have said that it is an unconscious and mute influence. The heart of the people responds, without knowing a reason why, to any appeal made to what it has inherited, and hence the same moral idea expressed in a newly translated term and in an old Bushido term, has a vastly different degree of efficacy. A backsliding Christian, whom no pastoral persuasion could help from downward tendency, was reverted from his course by an appeal made to his loyalty, the fidelity he once swore to his Master. The word 'Loyalty' revived all the noble sentiments that were permitted to grow lukewarm. A party of unruly youths engaged in a long-continued 'students' strike' in a college, on account of their dissatisfaction with a certain teacher, disbanded at two simple questions put by the Director – 'Is your professor a worthy character? If so, you ought to respect him and keep him in the school. Is he weak? If so, it is not manly to push a falling man.' The scientific incapacity of the professor, which was the beginning of the trouble, dwindled into insignificance in comparison with the moral issues hinted at. By arousing the sentiments nurtured by Bushido, moral renovation of great magnitude can be accomplished.

One cause of the failure of mission work is that most of the missionaries are entirely ignorant of our history – 'What do we care for heathen records?' some say – and consequently estrange their religion from the habits of thought we and our forefathers have been accustomed to for centuries past. Mocking a nation's history? – as though the career of any people even of the lowest African savages possessing no record – were not a page in the general history of mankind, written by the hand of God Himself. Ignoring the past career of a people, missionaries claim that Christianity is a new religion, whereas, to my mind, it is an 'old, old story,' which, if presented in intelligible words – that is to say, if expressed in the vocabulary familiar in the moral development of a people – will find easy lodgment in their hearts, irrespective of race or nationality. Christianity in its American or English form – with more of Anglo-Saxon freaks and fancies than grace and purity of its Founder – is a poor scion to graft on Bushido stock. Should the propagator of the new faith uproot the entire stock, root, and branches, and plant the seeds of the Gospel on the ravaged soil? Such a heroic process may be possible – in Hawaii, where, it is alleged, the Church militant had complete success in amassing spoils of wealth itself, and in annihilating the aboriginal race; such a process is most decidedly impossible in Japan – nay, it is a process which Jesus Himself would never have adopted in founding His kingdom on earth.

It behoves us to take more to heart the following words of a saintly man, devout Christian, and profound scholar:

'Men have divided the world into heathen and Christian, without considering how much good may have been hidden in the one or how much evil may have been mingled with the other. They have compared the best part of themselves with the worst of their neighbours, the ideal of Christianity with the corruption of Greece or of the East. They have not aimed at impartiality, but have been contented to accumulate all that could be said in praise of their own, and in dispraise of other forms of religion.'[37]

But, whatever may be the error committed by individuals, there is little doubt that the fundamental principle of the religion they profess is a power which we must take into account in reckoning the future of Bushido, whose days seem to be already numbered. Ominous signs are in the air that betoken its future. Not only signs, but redoubtable forces are at work to threaten it.

CHAPTER 17

THE FUTURE OF BUSHIDO

Few historical comparisons can be more judiciously made than between the Chivalry of Europe and the Bushido of Japan, and, if history repeats itself, it certainly will do with the fate of the latter what it did with that of the former. The particular and local causes for the decay of chivalry which St. Palaye gives, have, of course, little application to Japanese conditions; but the larger and more general causes that helped to undermine knighthood and chivalry in and after the Middle Ages are as surely working for the decline of Bushido.

One remarkable difference between the experience of Europe and of Japan is, that whereas in Europe, when chivalry was weaned from feudalism and was adopted by the Church, it obtained a fresh lease of life, in Japan no religion was large enough to nourish it; hence, when the mother institution, feudalism, was gone, Bushido, left an orphan, had to shift for itself. The present elaborate military organization might take it under its patronage, but we know that modern warfare can afford little room for its continuous growth. Shintoism, which fostered it in its infancy, is itself superannuated. The hoary sages of ancient China are being supplanted by the intellectual parvenu of the type of Bentham and Mill. Moral theories of a comfortable kind, flattering to the Chauvinistic tendencies of the time, and therefore thought well adapted to the need of this day, have been invented and propounded; but as yet we hear only their shrill voices echoing through the columns of yellow journalism.

Principalities and powers are arrayed against the Precepts of Knighthood. Already, as Veblen says, 'the decay of the ceremonial code – or, as it is otherwise called, the vulgarization of life – among the industrial classes proper, has become one of the chief enormities of latter-day civilization in the eyes of all persons of delicate sensibilities.' The irresistible tide of triumphant democracy, which can tolerate no form or shape of trust – and Bushido was a trust organized by those who monopolized reserve capital of intellect and culture, fixing the grades and value of moral qualities – is alone powerful enough to engulf the remnant of Bushido. The present societary forces are antagonistic to petty class spirit, and chivalry is, as Freeman severely criticizes, a class spirit. Modern society, if it pretends to any unity, cannot admit 'purely personal obligations devised in the interests of an exclusive class.'[38] Add to this the progress of popular instruction, of industrial arts and habits, of wealth and city-life – then we can easily see that neither the keenest cuts of samurai sword nor the sharpest shafts shot from Bushido's boldest bows can aught avail. The state built upon the rock of Honour and fortified by the same – shall we call it the *Ehrenstaat*, or, after the manner of Carlyle, the Heroarchy? – is fast falling into the hands of quibbling lawyers and gibbering politicians armed with logic-chopping engines of war. The words which a great thinker used in speaking of Theresa and Antigone may aptly be repeated of the samurai, that 'the medium in which their ardent deeds took shape is forever gone.'

Alas for knightly virtues! alas for samurai pride! Morality ushered into the world with the sound of bugles and drums, is destined to fade away as 'the captains and the kings depart.'

If history can teach us anything, the state built on martial virtues – be it a city like Sparta or an Empire like Rome – can never make on earth a 'continuing city.' Universal and natural as is the fighting instinct in man, fruitful as it has proved to be of noble sentiments and manly virtues, it does not comprehend the whole man. Beneath the instinct to fight there lurks a diviner instinct – to love. We have seen that Shintoism, Mencius, and Wan Yang Ming, have all clearly taught it; but Bushido and all other militant types of ethics, engrossed doubtless, with questions of immediate practical need, too often forgot duly to emphasize this fact. Life has grown larger in these latter times. Callings nobler and broader than a warrior's claim our attention today. With an enlarged view of life, with the growth of democracy, with better knowledge of other peoples and nations, the Confucian idea of benevolence – dare I also add the Buddhist idea of pity? – will expand into the Christian conception of love. Men have become more than subjects, having grown to the estate of citizens; nay, they are more than citizens – being men. Though war clouds hang heavy upon our horizon, we will believe that the wings of the angel of peace can disperse them. The history of the world confirms the prophecy that 'the meek shall inherit the earth.' A nation that sells its birthright of peace, and backslides from the front rank of industrialism into the file of filibusterism, makes a poor bargain indeed!

When the conditions of society are so changed that they have become not only adverse but hostile to Bushido, it is time for it to prepare for an honourable burial. It is just as difficult to point out when chivalry dies, as to determine the exact time of its inception. Dr. Miller says that chivalry was formally abolished in the year 1559, when Henry II of France was slain in a tournament. With us, the edict formally abolishing feudalism in 1870 was the signal to toll the knell of Bushido. The edict, issued five years later, prohibiting the wearing of swords, rang out the old, 'the unbought grace of life, the cheap defence of nations, the nurse of manly sentiment and heroic enterprise,' it rang in the new age of 'sophisters, economists, and calculators.'

It has been said that Japan won her late war with China[39] by means of Murata guns and Krupp cannon; it has been said the victory was the work of a modern school-system; but these are less than half-truths. Does ever a piano, be it of the choicest workmanship of Ehrbar or Steinway burst forth into the Rhapsodies of Liszt or the Sonatas of Beethoven, without a master's hand? Or, if guns win battles, why did not Louis Napoleon beat the Prussians with his *Mitrailleuse*, or the Spaniards with their Mausers the Filipinos, whose arms were no better than the old-fashioned Remingtons? Needless to repeat what has grown a trite saying – that it is the spirit that quickeneth, without which the best of implements profiteth but little. The most improved guns and cannon do not shoot of their own accord; the most modern educational system does not make a coward a hero. No! What won the battles on the Yalu, in Korea and Manchuria, were the ghosts of our fathers, guiding our hands and beating in our hearts. They are not dead, those ghosts, the spirits of our warlike ancestors. To those who have eyes to see, they are clearly visible. Scratch a Japanese of the most advanced ideas, and he will show a samurai. The great inheritance of honour, of valour, and of all martial virtues is, as Professor Cramb very fitly expresses it, 'but ours on trust, the fief inalienable of the dead and of the generations to come,' and the summons of the present is to guard this heritage, nor to bate one jot of the ancient spirit; the summons of the future will be so to widen its scope as to apply it in all walks and relations of life.

It has been predicted – and predictions have been corroborated by the events of the last half-century – that the moral system of Feudal Japan, like its castles and its armouries, will crumble into dust, and new ethics rise phoenix-like to lead New Japan in her path of progress. Desirable and probable as the fulfilment of such a prophecy is, we must not forget that a phoenix rises only from its own ashes, and that it is not a bird of passage, neither does it fly on pinions borrowed from other birds. 'The Kingdom of God is within you.' It does not come rolling down the mountains, however lofty; it does not come sailing across the seas, however broad. 'God has granted,' says the Koran, 'to every people a prophet in its own tongue.' The seeds of the Kingdom, as vouched for and apprehended by the Japanese mind, blossomed in Bushido. Now its days are closing – sad to say, before its full fruition – and we turn in every direction for other sources of sweetness and light, of strength and comfort, but among them there is as yet nothing found to take its place.

Bushido as an independent code of ethics may vanish, but its power will not perish from the earth; its schools of martial prowess or civic honour may be demolished, but its light and its glory will long survive their ruins. Like its symbolic flower, after it is blown to the four winds, it will still bless mankind with the perfume with which it will enrich life. Ages after, when its customaries will have been buried and its very name forgotten, its odours will come floating in the air as from a far-off, unseen hill, 'the wayside gaze beyond'; – then in the beautiful language of the Quaker poet,

> 'The traveller owns the grateful sense
> Of sweetness near, he knows not whence,
> And, pausing, takes with forehead bare
> The benediction of the air.'

ENDNOTES

1 Pronounced *Boó-shee-doh*.
2 *History Philosophically Illustrated*, (3rd Edition, 1853), Volume 2, page 2.
3 Lafcadio Hearn, *Exotics and Retrospectives*, page 84.
4 *The English People*, page 188.
5 *Feudal and Modern Japan*, Volume 1, page 183.
6 Miwa Shissai.
7 Burke, *French Revolution*.
8 'These shall be thy arts: to impose the law of peace, / To spare the conquered, and to defeat the proud.' From *Aeneid VI*, Virgil (Ed.)
9 A musical instrument, resembling the guitar.
10 The *uguisu* or warbler, sometimes called the nightingale of Japan.
11 Literally 'well-seatedness.'
12 Hanging scrolls, which may be either paintings or ideograms, used for decorative purposes.
13 Peery, *The Gist of Japan*, p. 86.
14 *Philosophy of History* (English translation by Sibree), Part 4, section 2, chapter 1.
15 In 1894 Alfred Dreyfus, a Jewish captain in the French army, was falsely convicted of treason for espionage and exiled to a penal colony. When the real culprit came to light, the military authorities refused to exonerate Dreyfus, leading to accusations of anti-Semitism and a full-blown political furore that exposed deep political divisions in the French Republic. (Ed.)
16 *Religions of Japan*.
17 *Principles of Ethics*, Vol. 1, Part 2, chapter 10.
18 The same word as that misspelled jiu-jitsu in common English parlance. It is the gentle art. It 'uses no weapon.'
19 'Learn to suffer without complaint.' (Ed.)

20 Edwin Arnold.

21 Seated himself – that is, in the Japanese fashion, his knees and toes touching the ground and his body resting on his heels. In this position, which is one of respect, he remained until his death.

22 I use Dr. Legge's translation verbatim.

23 *Morselli, Suicide*, page 314.

24 *Suicide and Insanity.*

25 The game of *go* is sometimes called Japanese checkers, but is much more intricate than the English game. The *go*-board contains 361 squares and is supposed to represent a battle-field – the object of the game being to occupy as much space as possible.

26 Kitchen, Church, Children. (Ed.)

27 Lecky, *History of European Morals*, 2, page 383.

28 For a very sensible explanation of nudity and bathing see Finck's *Lotos Time in Japan*, pages 286–97.

29 I refer to those days when girls were imported from England and given in marriage for so many pounds of tobacco, etc.

30 Outside shutters.

31 *Cerasus pseudo-cerasus*, Lindley.

32 *The Psychology of Peoples*, page 33.

33 Speer: *Missions and Politics in Asia*, Lecture 4, pages 189–92; Dennis: *Christian Missions and Social Progress*, Volume 1, page 32, Volume 2, page 70 etc.

34 *The Far East*, page 375.

35 Meredith Townsend, *Asia and Europe*, page 28.

36 Among other works on the subject, read Eastlake and Yamada on *Heroic Japan*, and Diosy on *The New Far East*.

37 Jowett, *Sermons on Faith and Doctrine*, 2.

38 *Norman Conquest*, Volume 5, page 482.

39 The First Sino-Japanese War, 1894–5. (Ed.)

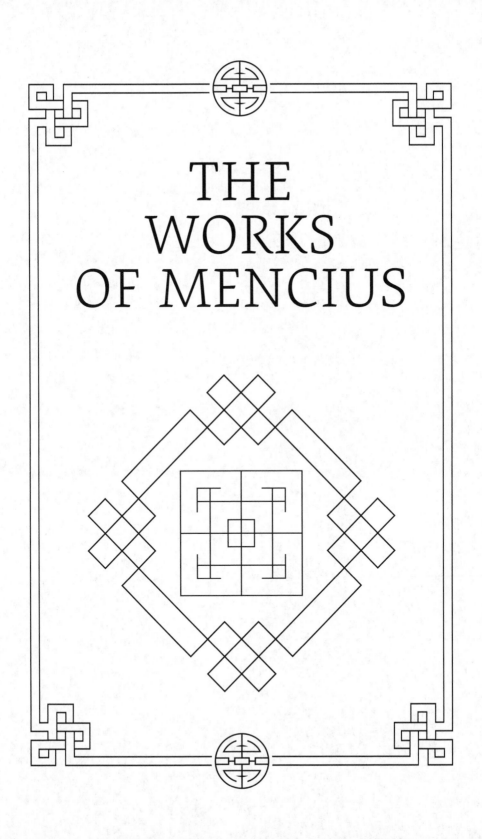

THE
WORKS
OF MENCIUS

CONTENTS

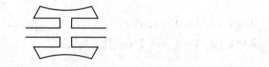

BOOK I

King Hwuy
of Lëang

Part I

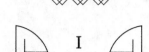

I

1   Mencius [went to] see king Hwuy of Lëang.

2   The king said, 'Venerable Sir, since you have not counted it far to come here, a distance of a thousand *le*, may I presume that you are likewise provided with [counsels] to profit my kingdom?'

3   Mencius replied, 'Why must your Majesty use that word "profit"? What I am likewise provided with are [counsels to] benevolence and righteousness; and these are my only topics.

4   'If your Majesty say, "What is to be done to profit my kingdom?' the great officers will say, 'What is to. be done to profit our families?" and the [inferior] officers and the common people will say, "What is to be done to profit our persons?" Superiors and inferiors will try to take the profit the one from the other, and the kingdom will be endangered. In the kingdom of ten thousand chariots, the murderer of his ruler will be [the chief of] a family of a thousand chariots. In the State of a thousand chariots, the murderer of his ruler will be [the chief of] a family of a hundred chariots. To have a thousand in ten thousand, and a hundred in a thousand, cannot be regarded as not a large allowance; but if righteousness be put last and profit first, they will not be satisfied without snatching all.

5   'There never was a man trained to benevolence who neglected his parents. There never was a man trained to righteousness who made his ruler an after-consideration.

6 'Let your Majesty likewise make benevolence and righteousness your only themes; – why must you speak of profit?'

II

1 When Mencius [another day] was seeing king Hwuy of Lëang, the king [went and] stood [with him] by a pond, and, looking round on the wild geese and deer, large and small, said, 'Do wise and good [princes] also take pleasure in these things?'

2 Mencius replied, 'Being wise and good, they then have pleasure in these things. If they are not wise and good, though they have these things, they do not find pleasure.

3 'It is said in the Book of Poetry: –

"When he planned the commencement of the Marvellous
    tower,
He planned it, and defined it,
And the people in crowds undertook the work,
And in no time completed it.
When he planned the commencement, [he said], 'Be not in a
    hurry;'
But the people came as if they were his children.
The king was in the Marvellous park.
Where the does were lying down, –
The does so sleek and fat;
With the white birds glistening.

The king was by the Marvellous pond; –
How full was it of fishes leaping about!"

'King Wăn used the strength of the people to make his tower and pond, and the people rejoiced [to do the work], calling the tower "the Marvellous tower" and the pond "the Marvellous pond" and being glad that he had his deer, his fishes, and turtles. The ancients caused their people to have pleasure as well as themselves, and therefore they could enjoy it.

4   'In the Declaration of T'ang it is said, "O sun, when wilt thou expire? We will die together with thee.' The people wished [for Kĕeh's death, though] they should die with him. Although he had his tower, his pond, birds and animals, how could he have pleasure alone?'

III

1   King Hwuy of Lëang said, 'Small as my virtue is, in [the government of] my kingdom, I do indeed exert my mind to the utmost. If the year be bad inside the Ho, I remove [as many of] the people [as] I can to the east of it, and convey grain to the country inside. If the year be bad on the east of the river, I act on the same plan. On examining the governmental methods of the neighbouring kingdoms, I do not find there is any [ruler] who exerts his mind as I do. And yet the people of the neighbouring kings do now decrease, nor do my people increase; – how is this?'

2   Mencius replied, 'Your Majesty loves war; allow me to take an illustration from war. [The soldiers move forward at] the sound of the drum; and when the edges of their weapons have been crossed, [on one side] they throw away their buff-coats, trail their weapons behind them, and run. Some run a hundred paces and then stop; some run fifty paces and stop. What would you think if these, because [they had run but] fifty paces, should laugh at [those who ran] a hundred paces?' The king said, 'They cannot do so. They only did not run a hundred paces; but they also ran.' [Mencius] said, "Since your Majesty knows this, you have no ground to expect that your people will become more numerous than those of the neighbouring kingdoms.

3   'If the seasons of husbandry be not interfered with, the grain will be more than can be eaten. If close nets are not allowed to enter the pools and ponds, the fish and turtles will be more than can be consumed. If the axes and bills enter the hill-forests [only] at the proper times, the wood will be more than can be used. When the grain and fish and turtles are more than can be eaten, and there is more wood than can be used, this enables the people to nourish their living and do all offices for their dead, without any feeling against any. [But] this condition, in which [the people] nourish their living, and do all offices to their dead without having any feeling against any, is the first step in the Royal way.

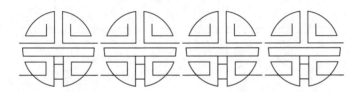

4 'Let mulberry-trees be planted about the homesteads with their five acres, and persons of fifty years will be able to wear silk. In keeping fowls, pigs, dogs, and swine, let not their times of breeding be neglected, and persons of seventy years will be able to eat flesh. Let there not be taken away the time that is proper for the cultivation of the field-allotment of a hundred acres, and the family of several mouths will not suffer from hunger. Let careful attention be paid to the teaching in the various schools, with repeated inculcation of the filial and fraternal duties, and grey-haired men will not be seen upon the roads, carrying burdens on – their backs or on their heads. It has never been that [the ruler of a State] where these results were seen, persons of seventy wearing silk and eating flesh, and the black-haired people suffering neither from hunger nor cold, did not attain to the Royal dignity.

5 'Your dogs and swine eat the food of men, and you do not know to store up [of the abundance]. There are people dying from famine on the roads, and you do not know to issue [your stores for their relief]. When men die, you say, "It is not owing to me; it, is owing to the year." In what does this differ from stabbing a man and killing him, and then saying, "It was not I; it was the weapon"? Let your Majesty cease to lay the blame on the year, and instantly the people, all under the sky, will come to you.'

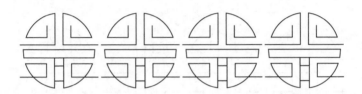

IV

1   King Hwuy of Lëang said, 'I wish quietly to receive your instructions.'

2   Mencius replied, 'Is there any difference between killing a man with a stick and with a sword?' 'There is no difference' was the answer.

3   [Mencius continued,] 'Is there any difference between doing it with a sword and with governmental measures?' 'There is not,' was the answer [again].

4   [Mencius then] said, 'In [your] stalls there are fat beasts; in [your] stables there are fat horses. [But] your people have the look of hunger, and in the fields there are those who have died of famine. This is leading on beasts to devour men.

5   'Beasts devour one another, and men hate them [for doing so]. When he who is [called] the parent of the people conducts his government so as to be chargeable with leading on beasts to devour men, where is that parental relation to the people?

6   'Chung-ne said, "Was he not without posterity who first made wooden images [to bury with the dead]?" [So he said,] because that man made the semblances of men and used them [for that purpose]; – what shall be thought of him who causes his people to die of hunger?'

V

1   King Hwuy of Lëang said, 'There was not in the kingdom a stronger State than Ts'in, as you, venerable Sir, know. But since it descended to me, on the east we were defeated by Ts'e, and then my eldest son perished; on the west we lost seven hundred *le* of territory to Ts'in; and on the south we have sustained disgrace at the hands of Ts'oo. I have brought shame on my departed predecessors, and wish on their account to wipe it away once for all. What course is to be pursued to accomplish this?'

2   Mencius replied, 'With a territory [only] a hundred *le* square it has been possible to obtain the Royal dignity.

3   'If your Majesty will [indeed] dispense a benevolent govern-ment to the people, being sparing in the use of punishments and fines, and making the taxes and levies of produce light, [so causing that] the fields shall be ploughed deep, and the weeding well attended to, and that the ablebodied, during their days of leisure, shall cultivate their filial piety, fraternal duty, faithfulness, and truth, serving thereby, at home, their fathers and elder brothers, and, abroad, their elders and super-iors; you will then have a people who can be employed with sticks which they have prepared to oppose the strong buff-coats and sharp weapons of [the troops of] Ts'in and Ts'oo.

4   '[The rulers of] those [States] rob their people of their time, so that they cannot plough and weed their fields in order to support their parents. Parents suffer from cold and hunger; elder and younger brothers, wives and children, are separated and scattered abroad.

5   'Those [rulers] drive their people into pitfalls or into the water; and your Majesty will go to punish them. In such a case, who will oppose your Majesty?

6   'In accordance with this is the saying, – 'The benevolent has no enemy!' I beg your Majesty not to doubt what I said].'

VI

1   Mencius had an interview with king Sëang of Lëang.

2   When he came out, he said. to some persons, 'When I looked at him from a distance, he did not appear like a ruler; when I drew near to him, I saw nothing venerable about him. Abruptly he asked me, "How can the kingdom, all under the sky, be settled?"

3   'I replied, "It will be settled by being united under one [sway]."

4   '"Who can so unite it?" [he asked].

5   'I replied, "He who has no pleasure in killing men can so unite it."

6   '"Who can give it to him?" [he asked].

7 'I replied, "All under heaven will give it to him. Does your Majesty know the way of the growing grain? During the seventh and eighth months, when drought prevails, the plants become dry. Then the clouds collect densely in the heavens, and send down torrents of rain, so that the grain erects itself as if by a shoot. When it does so, who can keep it back? Now among those who are shepherds of men throughout the kingdom, there is not one who does not find pleasure in killing men. If there were one who did not find pleasure in killing men, all the people under the sky would be looking towards him with outstretched necks. Such being indeed the case, the people would go to him as water flows downwards with a rush, which no one can repress."'

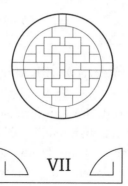

VII

1 King Seuen of Ts'e asked, saying, 'May I be informed by you of the transactions of Hwan of Ts'e and Wăn of Tsin?'

2 Mencius replied, 'There were none of the disciples of Chung-ne who spoke about the affairs of Hwan and Wăn, and therefore they have not been transmitted to [these] after-ages; your servant has not heard of them. If you will have me speak, let it be about [the principles of attaining to] the Royal sway?'

3   [The king] said, 'Of what kind must his virtue be who can [attain to] the Royal sway?'[Mencius] said, 'If he loves and protects the people, it is impossible to prevent him from attaining it.'

4   [The king] said, 'Is such an one as poor I competent to love and protect the people?' 'Yes,' was the reply. 'From what do you know that I am competent to that?' 'I have heard,' said [Mencius], 'from Hoo Heih the following incident: – "The king," said he, "was sitting aloft in the hall, when some people appeared leading a bull past below it. The king saw it, and asked where the bull was going, and being answered that they were going to consecrate a bell with its blood, he said, 'Let it go, I cannot bear its frightened appearance as if it were an innocent person going to the place of death.' They asked in reply whether, if they did so, they should omit the consecration of the bell; but [the king] said, 'How can that be omitted? Change it for a sheep.'" I do not know whether this incident occurred.'

5   'It did,' said [the king], and [Mencius] replied, 'The heart seen in this is sufficient to carry you to the Royal sway. The people all supposed that your Majesty grudged [the animal], but your servant knows surely that it was your Majesty's not being able to bear [the sight of the creature's distress which made you do as you did].'

6   The king said, 'You are right; and yet there really was [an appearance of] what the people imagined. [But] though Ts'e be narrow and small, how should I grudge a bull? Indeed it was because I could not bear its frightened appearance, as if it were an innocent person going to the place of death, that therefore I changed it for a sheep.'

7   Mencius said, 'Let not your Majesty deem it strange that the people should think you grudged the animal. When you changed a large one for a small, how should they know [the true reason]? If you felt pained by its [being led] without any guilt to the place of death, what was there to choose between a bull and a sheep?' The king laughed and said, 'What really was my mind in the matter? I did not grudge the value of the bull, and yet I changed it for a sheep! There was reason in the people's saying that I grudged [the creature].'

8   [Mencius] said, 'There is no harm [in their saying so]. It was an artifice of benevolence. You saw the bull, and had not seen the sheep, So is the superior man affected towards animals, that, having seen them alive, he cannot bear to see them die, and, having heard their [dying] cries, he cannot bear to eat their flesh. On this account he keeps away from his stalls and kitchen.'

9   The king was pleased and said, 'The Ode says,

"What other men have in their minds,
I can measure by reflection."

This might be spoken of you, my Master. I indeed did the thing, but when I turned my thoughts inward and sought for it, I could not discover my own mind. When you, Master, spoke those words, the movements of compassion began to work in my mind. [But] how is it that his heart has in it what is equal to the attainment of the Royal sway?'

10 [Mencius] said, 'Suppose a man were to make this statement to your Majesty, "My strength is sufficient to lift three thousand catties, but it is not sufficient to lift one feather; my eyesight is sharp enough to examine the point of an autumn hair, but I do not see a waggon-load of faggots," would your Majesty allow what he said?' 'No,' was the [king's] remark, [and Mencius proceeded], 'Now here is kindness sufficient to reach to animals, and yet no benefits are extended from it to the people; – how is this? is an exception to be made here? The truth is, the feather's not being lifted is because the strength was not used; the waggon-load of firewood's not being seen is because the eyesight was not used; and the people's not being loved and protected is because the kindness is not used. Therefore your Majesty's not attaining to the Royal sway is because you do not do it, and not because you are not able do it.'

11 [The king] asked, 'How may the difference between him who does not do [a thing] and him who is not able to do it be graphically set forth?' [Mencius] replied, 'In such a thing as taking the T'ae mountain under your arm, and leaping with it over the North sea, if you say to people, "I am not able to do it," that is a real case of not being able. In such a matter as breaking off a branch from a tree at the order of a superior, if you say to people, "I am not able to do it," it is not a case of not being able to do it. And so your Majesty's not attaining to the Royal sway is not such a case as that of taking the T'ae mountain under your arm and leaping over the North sea with it; but it is a case like that of breaking off a branch from a tree.

12 'Treat with the reverence due to age the elders in your own family, so that those in the families of others shall be similarly treated; treat with the kindness due to youth the young in your own family, so that those in the families of others shall be similarly treated: – do this and the kingdom may be made to go round in your palm. It is said in the Book of Poetry,

"His example acted on his wife,
Extended to his brethren,
And was felt by all the clans and States;"

telling us how [King Wăn] simply took this [kindly] heart, and exercised it towards those parties. Therefore the carrying out the [feeling of] kindness [by a ruler] will suffice for the love and protection of all within the four seas; and if he do not carry it out, he will not be able to protect his wife and children. The way in which the ancients came greatly to surpass other men was no other than this, that they carried out well what they did, so as to affect others. Now your kindness is sufficient to reach to animals, and yet no benefits are extended to the people. How is this? Is an exception to be made here?

13 'By weighing we know what things are light, and what heavy. By measuring we know what things are long, and what short. All things are so dealt with, and the mind requires specially to be so. I beg your Majesty to measure it.

14 'Your Majesty collects your equipments of war, endangers your soldiers and officers, and excites the resentment of the various princes: – do these things cause you pleasure in your mind?'

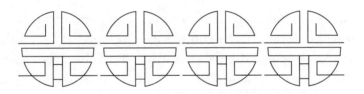

15 The king said, 'No. How should I derive pleasure from these things? My object in them is to seek for what I greatly desire.'

16 [Mencius] said, 'May I hear from you what it is that your Majesty greatly desires?' The king laughed, and did not speak. [Mencius] resumed, '[Are you led to desire it], because you have not enough of rich and sweet [food] for your mouth? or because you have not enough of light and warm [clothing] for your body? or because you have not enough of beautifully coloured objects to satisfy your eyes? or because there are not voices and sounds enough to fill your ears? or because you have not enough of attendants and favourites to stand before you and receive your orders? Your Majesty's various officers are sufficient to supply you with all these things. How can your Majesty have such a desire on account of them?' 'No' said the king, 'my desire is not on account of them.'[Mencius] observed, 'Then, what your Majesty greatly desires can be known. You desire to enlarge your territories, to have Ts'in and Ts'oo coming to your court, to rule the Middle States, and to attract to you the barbarous tribes that surround them. But to do what you do in order to seek for what you desire is like climbing a tree to seek for fish.'

17 'Is it so bad as that?' said [the king]. 'I apprehend it is worse,'
was the reply. 'If you climb a tree to seek for fish, although
you do not get the fish, you have no subsequent calamity.
But if you do what you do in order to seek for what you
desire, doing it even with all your heart, you will assuredly
afterwards meet with calamities.' The king said, 'May I hear
[what they will be]?' [Mencius] replied, 'If the people of
Tsow were fighting with the people of Ts'oo, which of them
does your Majesty think would conquer?' 'The people of
Ts'oo would conquer,' was the answer, and [Mencius]
pursued, 'So then, a small State cannot contend with a great,
few cannot contend with many, nor can the weak contend
with the strong. The territory within the seas would embrace
nine divisions, each of a thousand le square. All Ts'e together
is one of them. If with one part you try to subdue the other
eight, what is the difference between that and Tsow's
contending with Ts'oo? [With the desire which you have],
you must turn back to the proper course [for its attainment].

18 'Now if your Majesty will institute a government whose
action shall all be benevolent, this will cause all the offices
in the kingdom to wish to stand in your Majesty's court, the
farmers all to wish to plough in your Majesty's fields, the
merchants, both travelling and stationary, all to wish to store
their goods in your Majesty's market-places, travellers and
visitors all to wish to travel on your Majesty's roads, and all
under heaven who feel aggrieved by their rulers to wish to
come and complain to your Majesty. When they are so bent,
who will be able to keep them back?'

19 The king said, 'I am stupid, and cannot advance to this. [But] I wish you, my Master, to assist my intentions. Teach me clearly, and although I am deficient in intelligence and vigour, I should like to try at least [to institute such a government].'

20 [Mencius] replied, 'They are only men of education, who, without a certain livelihood, are able to maintain a fixed heart. As to the people, if they have not a certain livelihood, they will be found not to have a fixed heart. And if they have not a fixed heart, there is nothing which they will not do in the way of self-abandonment, of moral deflection, of depravity, and of wild license. When they have thus been involved in crime, to follow them up and punish, them, is to entrap the people. How can such a thing as entrapping the people be done under the rule of a benevolent man?'

21 'Therefore an intelligent ruler will regulate the livelihood of the people, so as to make sure that, above, they shall have sufficient wherewith to serve their parents, and below, sufficient wherewith to support their wives and children that in good years they shall always be abundantly satisfied, and that in bad years they shall not be in danger of perishing. After this he may urge them, and they will proceed to what is good, for in this case the people will follow after that with readiness.

22 'But now, the livelihood of the people is so regulated, that, above, they have not sufficient wherewith to serve their parents, and, below, they have not sufficient wherewith to support their wives and children; [even] in good years their lives are always embittered, and in bad years they are in danger of perishing. In such circumstances their only object is to escape from death, and they are afraid they will not succeed in doing so; – what leisure have they to cultivate propriety and righteousness?

23 'If your Majesty wishes to carry out [a benevolent government], why not turn back to what is the essential step [to its attainment]?

24 'Let mulberry-trees be planted about the homesteads with their five acres, and persons of fifty years will be able to wear silk. In keeping fowls, pigs, dogs, and swine, let not their times of breeding be neglected, and persons of seventy years will be able to eat flesh. Let there not be taken away the time that is proper for the cultivation of the field-allotment of a hundred acres, and the family of eight mouths will not suffer from hunger. Let careful attention be paid to the teaching in the various schools, with repeated inculcation of the filial and fraternal duties, and gray-haired men will not be seen upon the roads, carrying burdens on their backs or on their heads. It has never been that [the ruler of a State] where these results were seen, the old wearing silk and eating flesh, and the black-haired people suffering neither from hunger nor cold, did not attain to the Royal dignity.'

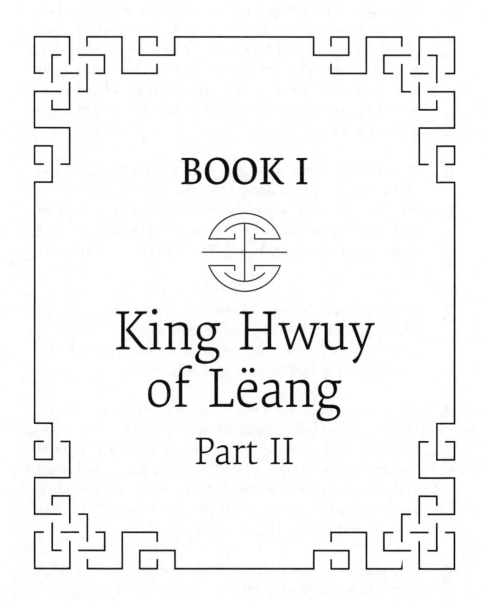

BOOK I

King Hwuy
of Lëang

Part II

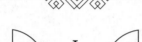

I

1 Chwang Paou, [having gone to] see Mencius, said to him, 'I had an audience of the king. His Majesty told me about his loving music, and I was not prepared with anything to reply to him. What do you pronounce concerning [that] love of music?' Mencius said, 'If the king's love of music were very great, the kingdom of Ts'e would be near to [being well governed]'

2 Another day, Mencius had an audience of the king, and said, 'Your Majesty, [I have heard,] told the officer Chwang about your love of music; – was it so?' The king changed colour, and said, 'I am unable to love the music of the ancient kings; I only love the music that suits the manners of the [present] age.'

3 [Mencius] said, 'If your Majesty's love of music were very great, Ts'e, I apprehend, would be near to [being well governed]. The music of the present day is just like the music of antiquity [for effecting that].'

4 [The king] said, 'May I hear [the proof of what you say]?' 'Which is the more pleasant,' was the reply, – 'to enjoy music by yourself alone, or to enjoy it along with others?' 'To enjoy it along with others,' said [the king]. 'And which is the more pleasant,' pursued [Mencius], – 'to enjoy music along with a few, or to enjoy it along with many?' 'To enjoy it along with many,' replied [the king].

5 [Mencius went on] 'Will you allow your servant to speak to your Majesty about music?

6 'Your Majesty is having music here. – The people hear the sound of your bells and drums, and the notes of your reeds and flutes, and they all, with aching heads, knit their brows, and say to one another, "That's how our king loves music! But why does he reduce us to this extremity [of distress]? Fathers and sons do not see one another; elder brothers and younger brothers, wives and children, are separated and scattered abroad." Again, your Majesty is hunting here. The people hear the noise of your carriages and horses, and see the beauty of your plumes and pennons, and they all, with aching heads, knit their brows, and say to one another, "That's how our king loves hunting! But why does lie reduce us to this extremity of distress? Fathers and sons do not see one another; elder brothers and younger brothers, wives and children, are separated and scattered abroad." This is from no other cause, but that you do not give the people to have pleasure as well as yourself.

7 'Your Majesty is having music here. – The people hear the sound of your bells and drums, and the notes of your reeds and flutes, and they all, delighted and with joyful looks, say to one another, "That sounds as if our king were free from all sickness! What fine music he is able to have!" Again, your Majesty is hunting here. – The people hear the noise of your carriages and horses, and see the beauty of your plumes and pennons, and they all, delighted and with joyful looks, say to one another, "That looks as if our king were free from all sickness! How he is able to hunt!" This is from no other reason but that you cause the people to have pleasure as well as yourself.

8 'If your Majesty now will make pleasure a thing common to the people and yourself, the Royal sway awaits you.'

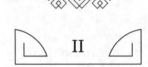

II

1   King Seuen of Ts'e asked, 'Was it so that the park of king Wan contained seventy square *le*?' Mencius replied, 'It is so in the Records.'

2   'Was it so large as that?' said [the king]. 'The people,' said [Mencius], 'still considered it small.' 'My park,' responded [the king], 'contains [only] forty square *le*, and the people still consider it large. How is this?' 'The park of king Wăn,' – said [Mencius], 'contained seventy square *le*, but the grass-cutters and fuel-gatherers [had the privilege of] resorting to it, and so also had the catchers of pheasants and hares. He shared it with the people, and was it not with reason that they looked on it as small?

3   'When I first arrived at your frontiers, I enquired about the great prohibitory regulations before I would venture to enter [the country]; and I heard that inside the border-gates there was a park of forty square *le*, and that he who killed a deer in it, whether large or small, was held guilty of the same crime as if he had killed a man. In this way those forty square *le* are a pit-fall in the middle of the kingdom. Is it not with reason that the people look upon [your park] as large?'

III

1   King Seuen of Ts'e asked, saying, 'Is there any way [to regulate one's maintenance] of intercourse with neighbouring States?' Mencius replied, 'There is. But it requires a benevolent [ruler] to be able with a great State to serve a small; – as, for instance, T'ang served Koh, and king Wăn served the hordes of the Keun. And it requires a wise [ruler] to be able with a small State to serve a great, – as, for instance, king T'ae served the Heun-yuh, and Kow-tsëen served Woo.

2   'He who with a great [State] serves a small is one who delights in Heaven; and he who with a small [State] serves a great is one who fears Heaven. He who delights in Heaven will affect with his love and protection all under the sky; and he who fears Heaven will so affect his own State.

3   'It is said in the Book of Poetry,

"I revere the majesty of Heaven,
And thus preserve its [favour]."'

4   The king said, 'A great saying! [But] I have an infirmity, – I love valour.'

5   [Mencius] replied, 'I beg your Majesty not to love small valour. If a man brandishes his sword, looks fierce, and says, "How dare he withstand me?" this is the valour of a common man, and can only be used against one individual. I beg your Majesty to change it into great valour.

6 'It is said in the Book of Poetry,

> "The king rose majestic in his wrath.
> He marshalled his troops,
> To stop the march to Keu;
> To consolidate the prosperity of Chow;
> To meet the expectations of all under heaven."

This was the valour of king Wăn. King Wăn, by one burst of his anger, gave repose to all the people under heaven.

7 'It is said in the Book of History, "Heaven, having produced the inferior people, made for them rulers, and made for them instructors, with the purpose that they should be aiding to God, and gave them distinction throughout the four quarters [of the land]. Whoever are offenders, and whoever are innocent, here am I [to deal with them]. How dare any under heaven give indulgence to their refractory wills?" One man was pursuing a violent and disorderly course in the kingdom, and king Woo was ashamed of it. This was the valour of king Woo, and he also, by one burst of his anger, gave repose to all the people under heaven.

8 'Let now your Majesty, in one burst of anger, give repose to all the people under heaven. The people are only afraid that your Majesty does not love valour.'

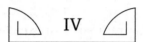

IV

1   King Seuen of Ts'e [went to] see Mencius in the Snow palace, and said to him, 'Do men of talents and virtue likewise find pleasure in [such a place as] this?' Mencius replied, 'They do. And if people [generally] do not get [similar pleasure], they condemn their superiors.

2   'For them, when they do not get that, to condemn their superiors is wrong; but when the superiors of the people do not make [such] pleasure a thing common to the people and themselves, they also do wrong.

3   'When [a ruler] rejoices in the joy of his people, they also rejoice in his joy; when he sorrows for the sorrow of his people, they also sorrow for his sorrow. When his joy extends to all under heaven, and his sorrow does the same, it never was that in such a case [the ruler] did not attain to the Royal sway.

4   'Formerly, duke King of Ts'e asked the minister Gan, saying, "I wish to make a tour to Chuen-foo and Chaouwoo, and then to bend my way southward, along the shore, till I come to Lang-yay. What shall I do specially, that my tour may be fit to be compared with those made by the former kings?"

5 'The minister Gan replied, "An excellent inquiry! When the son of Heaven visited the feudal princes, it was called a tour of inspection; that is, he surveyed the States tinder their care. When the princes attended at his court, it was called "a report of office; "that is, they reported [their administration of] their offices. [Thus] neither of those proceedings was without its proper object. [And moreover], in the spring they examined the ploughing, and supplied any deficiency [of seed]; in the autumn they examined the reaping, and assisted where there was any deficiency [of yield]. There is the saying of the Hëa dynasty,

'If our king go not from home,
Whence to us will comfort come?
If our king make not his round,
Whence to us will help be found?'

That excursion and that round were a pattern for the princes.

6 '"Now the state of things is different. A host marches [in attendance, on the ruler], and the provisions are consumed. The hungry are deprived of their food, and there is no rest for those who are called to toil. Maledictions are uttered by one to another with eyes askance, and the people proceed to the commission of wickedness. The [Royal] orders are violated and the people are oppressed; the supplies of food and drink flow away like water. The [rulers] yield themselves to the current; or they urge their way against it; they are wild; they are lost: – [these things proceed] to the grief of the [smaller] princes.

7 '"Descending along with the current, and forgetting to return," is what I call yielding to it. "Going against it, and forgetting to return," is what I called urging their way against it. "Pursuing the chase without satiety" is what I call being wild. "Delighting in spirits without satiety" is what I call being lost.

8 '"The former kings had no pleasures to which they gave themselves as on the flowing stream, no doings which might be so characterized as wild and lost.

9 '"It is for you, my ruler, to take your course."

10 'Duke King was pleased. He issued a grand proclamation through the State, and went out [himself] and occupied a shed in the suburbs. Prom that time he began to open [his granaries] for the relief of the wants [of the people], and, calling the grand music master, said to him, "Make for me music to suit a prince and his minister well pleased with each other." It was then that the Che Shaou and Kë'oh Shaou was made, in the poetry to which it was said

"What fault is it one's ruler to restrain?"

He who restrains his ruler loves him.'

1 King Seuen of Ts'e asked saying, 'People all tell me to pull down the Brilliant hall and remove it; shall I pull it down, or stop [the movement for that object]?'

2   Mencius replied, 'The Brilliant hall is the hall appropriate to the kings. If your Majesty wishes to practise Royal government, do not pull it down.'

3   The king said, 'May I hear from you what Royal government is?' 'Formerly' was the reply, 'king Wăn's government of K'e was the following: – From the husbandman [there was required the produce of] one ninth [of the land]; the descendants of officers were salaried; at the passes and in the markets, [strangers] were inspected, but goods were not taxed; there were no prohibitions respecting the ponds and weirs; the wives and children of criminals were not involved in their guilt. There were the old and wifeless, or widowers, the old and husbandless, or widows; the old and childless, or solitaries; and the young and fatherless, or orphans: – these four classes are the most destitute under heaven, and have none to whom they can tell [their wants], and king Wan, in the institution of his government with its benevolent action, made them the first objects of his regard. It is said in the Book of Poetry,

"The rich may get through,
But alas for the helpless and solitary!"'

4   The king said, 'Excellent words!' [Mencius] said, 'Since your Majesty deems them excellent, why do you not put them into practice?' 'I have an infirmity,' said the king; 'I am fond of substance.' 'Formerly,' replied [Mencius], 'duke Lëw was fond of substance. It is said in the Book of Poetry,

"He stored up [the produce] in the fields and in barns;
He tied up dried meat and grain
In bottomless bags and sacks;

That he might hold [his people] together, and glorify [his
    tribe].
Then with bows and arrows all ready,
With shields and spears, and axes, large and small.
He commenced his march."

In this way those who remained in their old seat had their
stores in the fields and in barns, and those who marched
had their bags of grain. It was not till after this that he
commenced his march. If your Majesty is fond of substance,
let the people have the opportunity to gratify the same
feeling, and what difficulty will there be in your attaining
to the Royal sway?'

5   The king said, 'I have an infirmity; I am fond of beauty.'
The reply was, 'Formerly king T'ae was fond of beauty, and
loved his wife. It is said in the Book of Poetry,

"The ancient duke T'an-foo
Came in the morning, galloping his horses,
Along the banks of the western rivers,
To the foot of Mount K'e;
And there he and the lady Këang
Came, and together looked out for a site on which to settle."

At that time, in the seclusion of the house, there were no
dissatisfied women, and, abroad, there were no unmarried
men. If your Majesty is fond of beauty, let the people be
able to gratify the same fueling, and what difficulty will
there be in your attaining to the Royal sway?'

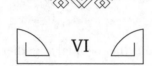

VI

1 Mencius said to king Seuen of Ts'e '[Suppose that] one of your Majesty's servants were to entrust his wife and children to the care of his friend, while he went [himself] into Ts'oo to travel, and that, on his return, [he should find] that [the friend] had caused his wife and children to suffer from cold and hunger, – how ought he to deal with him?' The king said, 'He should cast him off.'

2 [Mencius] proceeded, '[Suppose that] the chief criminal judge could not regulate the officers of justice under him, how should he be dealt with?' The king said, 'He should be dismissed.'

3 [Mencius again] said, 'When within the four borders [of your kingdom] there is not good government, what is to be done?' The king looked to the right and left, and spoke of other matters.

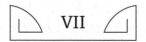

VII

1 Mencius, having [gone to] see king Seuen of Ts'e, said to him, 'When men speak of "an ancient kingdom" it is not meant thereby that it has lofty trees in it, but that it has ministers [sprang from families that have been noted in it] for generations. Your Majesty has no ministers with whom you are personally intimate. Those whom you advanced yesterday are gone to-day, and you do not know it.'

2   The king said, 'How shall I know that they have no ability, and avoid employing them at all?'

3   The reply was, 'A ruler advances to office [new] men of talents and virtue [only] as a matter of necessity. As he thereby causes the low to overstep the honourable and strangers to overstep his relatives, ought he to do so but with caution?

4   'When all those about you say [of a man], "He is a man of talents and virtue," do not immediately [believe them]. When your great officers all say, "He is a man of talents and virtue," do not immediately [believe them]. When your people all say, "He is a man of talents and virtue" then examine into his character; and, when you find that he is such indeed, then afterwards employ him. When all those about you say, "He will not do," do not listen to them. When your great officers all say, "He will not do," do not listen to them. When your people all say, "He will not do," then examine into his character; and when you find that he will not do, then afterwards send him away.

5   'When those about you all say [of a man], "He deserves death," do not listen to them. When your great officers all say, "He deserves death," do not listen to them. When your people all say, "He deserves death," then examine into his case; and when you find that he deserves death, then afterwards put him to death. In accordance with this we have the saying, "The people put him to death."

6   'Act in this way and you will be the parent of the people.'

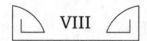

VIII

1 King Seuen of Ts'e asked, saying, 'Was it so that T'ang banished Këeh, and king Woo smote Chow?' Mencius replied, 'It is so in the Records.'

2 [The king] said, 'May a subject put his ruler to death?'

3 The reply was, 'He who outrages benevolence is called a ruffian; he who outrages righteousness is called a villain. The ruffian and villain we call a mere fellow. I have heard of the cutting off of the fellow Chow; I have not heard of the putting a ruler to death [in his case].'

IX

1 Mencius, [having gone to] see king Seuen of Ts'e, said, 'If you are going to build a large mansion, you will surely cause the Master of the workmen to look out for large trees; and when he has found them, your Majesty will be glad, thinking they will be fit for the object. Should the workmen hew them so as to make them too small, then you will be angry, thinking that they will not answer for the purpose. Now a man spends his youth in learning the principles of right government], and, when grown up to vigour, he wishes to put them in practice: – if your Majesty say to him, "For the present put aside what you have learned, and follow me," what shall we say?

2   'Here now you have a gem in the stone. Although it be worth 240,000 [taels], you will surely employ your chief lapidary to cut and polish it. But when you come to the government of your kingdom, you say, "For the present put aside what you have learned and follow me;" – how is it that you herein act differently from your calling in the lapidary to cut and polish the gem?'

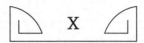

1   The people of Ts'e attacked Yen, and conquered it.

2   King Seuen asked, saying, 'Some tell me not to take possession of it, and some tell me to take possession of it. For a kingdom of ten thousand chariots to attack another of the same strength, and to complete the conquest of it in fifty days, is an achievement beyond [mere] human strength. If I do not take it, calamities from Heaven will surely come upon me: – what do you say to my taking possession of it?'

3   Mencius replied, "If the people of Yen will be pleased with your taking possession of it, do so. – Among the ancients there was [one] who acted in this way, namely king Woo. If the people of Yen will not be pleased with your taking possession of it, do not. Among the ancients there was one who acted in this way, namely king Wăn.

4   'When with [the strength of] your kingdom of ten thousand chariots you attacked another of the same strength, and they met your Majesty's army with baskets of rice and vessels of congee, was there any other reason for this but that they [hoped to] escape out of fire and water? If [you make] the water more deep and the fire more fierce, they will just in like manner make another revolution.'

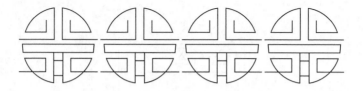

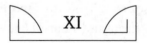 XI

1   The people of Ts'e having attacked Yen and taken possession of it, the [other] princes proposed to take measures to deliver Yen. King Seuen said, "As the princes are many of them consulting to attack me, how shall I prepare myself for them?" Mencius replied, "I have heard of one who with seventy le gave law to the whole kingdom, but I have not heard of [a ruler] who with a thousand le was afraid of others.

2 'The Book of History says, "When T'ang began his work of punishment, he commenced with Koh. All under heaven had confidence in him. When the work went on in the east, the wild tribes of the west murmured. When it went on in the south, those of the north murmured. They said, 'Why does he make us the last?' The looking of the people for him was like the looking in a time of great drought for clouds and rainbows. The frequenters of the markets stopped not; the husbandmen made no change [in their operations]. While he took off their rulers, he consoled the people. [His progress] was like the falling of seasonable rain, and the people were delighted." It is said [again] in the Book of History, "We have waited for our prince [long]; the prince's coming is our reviving."

3 'Now [the ruler of] Yen was tyrannizing over his people, and your Majesty went and punished him. The people supposed that you were going to deliver them out of the water and the fire, and with baskets of rice and vessels of congee they met your Majesty's host. But you have slain their fathers and elder brothers, and gut their sons and younger brothers in chains; you have pulled down the ancestral temple [of the rulers], and are carrying away its precious vessels: — how can such a course be admitted? [The other States of] the kingdom were afraid of the strength of Ts'e before; and now when with a doubled territory you do not exercise a benevolent government, this puts the arms of the kingdom in motion [against you].

4 'If your Majesty will make haste to issue an order, restoring [your captives] old and young, and stopping [the removal of] the precious vessels; [and if then] you will consult with the people of Yen, appoint [for them] a [new] ruler, and afterwards withdraw from the country: – in this way you may still be able to stop [the threatened attack].'

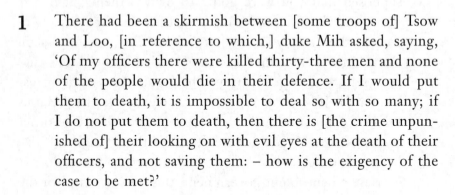

XII

1 There had been a skirmish between [some troops of] Tsow and Loo, [in reference to which,] duke Mih asked, saying, 'Of my officers there were killed thirty-three men and none of the people would die in their defence. If I would put them to death, it is impossible to deal so with so many; if I do not put them to death, then there is [the crime unpunished of] their looking on with evil eyes at the death of their officers, and not saving them: – how is the exigency of the case to be met?'

2   Mencius replied, 'In calamitous years and years of famine, the old and weak of your people who have been found lying in ditches and water-channels, and the able-bodied who have been scattered about to the four quarters, have amounted to thousands. All the while, your granaries, O prince, have been stored with rice and other grain, and your treasuries and arsenals have been full, and not one of your officers has told you [of the distress]; – so negligent have the superiors [in your State] been, and cruel to their inferiors. The philosopher Tsăng said, "Beware, beware. What proceeds from you will return to you." Now at last the people have had an opportunity to return [their conduct]; do not you, O prince, blame them.

3   'If you will practise a benevolent government, then the people will love all above them, and will die for their officers.'

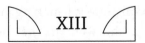

XIII

1   Duke Wăn of T'ăng asked, saying, 'T'ăng is a small State, and lies between Ts'e and Ts'oo. Shall I serve Ts'e? or shall I serve Ts'oo?'

2   Mencius replied, 'This is a matter in which I cannot counsel you. If you will have me speak, there is but one thing [I can suggest]. Dig [deep] your moats; build [strong] your walls; then guard them along with the people; be prepared to die [in their defence], and [have] the people [so that] they will not leave you; – this is a course which may be put in practice.'

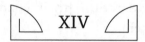

XIV

1   Duke Wăn of T'ăng asked, saying, 'The people of Ts'e are going to fortify Sĕeh, and [the movement] occasions me great alarm; what is the proper course for me to take in the case?'

2   Mencius replied, 'Formerly, when king T'ae dwelt in Pin, the Teih were [continually] making incursions upon it. He [therefore] left it, and went to the foot of Mount K'e, and there took up his residence. He did not take that situation as having selected it; – it was a matter of necessity.

3   'If you do good, among your descendants in future generations there shall be one who will attain to the Royal sway. The superior man lays the foundation of the inheritance, and hands down the beginning [which he has made], doing what can be continued [by his successors]. As to the accomplishment of the great result, that is with Heaven. What is that [Ts'e] to you, O prince? you have simply to make yourself strong to do good'

XV

1   Duke wăn of T'ăng asked, saying, 'T'ăng is a small State. I do my utmost to serve the great kingdoms [on either side of it], but I cannot escape [suffering from them]. What is the proper course for me to pursue in the case?' Mencius replied, 'Formerly, when king T'ae dwelt in Pin, the Teih were continually making incursions upon it. He served them with skins and silks, and still he suffered from them. He served them with dogs and horses, and still he suffered from them. He served them with pearls and pieces of jade, and still he suffered from them. On this he assembled his old men, and announced to them, saying, "What the Teih want is my territory. I have heard this, – that the superior man does not injure his people for that which he nourishes them with. My children, why should you be troubled about having no ruler. I will leave this." [Accordingly] he left Pin, crossed over Mount Lëang, [built] a town at the foot of Mount K'e, and dwelt there. The people of Pin said, "He is a benevolent man; – we must not lose him." Those who followed him [looked] like crowds going to market.

2   'On the other hand [a prince] may say, "[The country] has been held [by my ancestors] for generations, and is not what I can undertake to dispose of in my person. I will go to the death for it, and will not leave it."

3   'I beg you, O prince, to make your election between these two courses.'

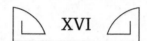

1   Duke P'ing of Loo was about to go out [one day when his favourite Tsang Ts'ang begged [to ask] him, saying, 'On other days, when your lordship has gone out, you have given instructions to the officers as to where you were going. But now the horses have been put to your carriage, and the officers do not yet know where you are going. I venture to request your orders.' The duke said, 'I am going to see the philosopher Măng.' 'What!' said the other. 'That you demean yourself, O prince, by what you are doing, to pay the first visit to a common man, is, I apprehend, because you think that he is a man of talents and virtue. [Our rules of] propriety and righteousness must have come from such men; but on the occasion of this Măng's second mourning, his observances exceeded those of the former. Do not go to see him, O prince.' The duke said, 'I will not.'

2   The officer Yoh-ching entered [the court], and had an audience. 'Prince,' said he, 'why have you not gone to see Măng K'o?' 'One told me,' was the reply, 'that on the occasion of Mr Mang's second mourning, his observances exceeded those of the former, and therefore I did not go to see him.' [Yoh-ching] said, 'How is this? By what your lordship calls "exceeding," you mean, I suppose, that on the former occasion he used the ceremonies appropriate to an inferior officer, and on the latter those appropriate to a great officer; that he first used three tripods, and afterwards five.' 'No,' said the duke, 'I refer to the greater excellence of the coffin, the shell, the grave-clothes, and the shroud.' [Yoh-ching] replied, 'That cannot be called "exceeding." That was the difference between being poor and being rich.'

3 [After this] the officer Yoh-ching [went to] see Mencius, and said, 'I told the ruler about you, and he was consequently coming to see you, when his favourite Tsang Ts'ang stopped him, and he did not carry his purpose into effect.' [Mencius] said, 'A man's advance is effected, it may be, by others, and the stopping him is, it may be, from the efforts of others. But to advance a man or to stop his advance is [really] beyond the power of other men. My not finding [the light prince in the marquis of Loo, is from Heaven. How could that scion of the Tsang family cause me not to find [the ruler that would suit me]?'

BOOK II

KUNG-SUN CH'OW

PART I

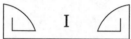

I

1 Kung-sun Ch'ow said, 'Master, if you were to obtain the ordering of the government in Ts'e, could you promise yourself the accomplishment of such successful results as were realized by Kwan Chung and the minister Gan?'

2 Mencius said, 'You, Sir, are indeed a [true] man of Ts'e. You know about Kwan Chung and the minister Gan, and nothing more.

3 'One asked Tsăng Se, saying, "To which, my [good] Sir, do you give the superiority, – to yourself or to Tsze-loo?" Tsăng Se looked uneasy, and said, "He was an object of veneration to my grandfather." "Then," pursued the man, "do you give the superiority to yourself, or to Kwan Chung?" Tsăng Se flushed with anger, was displeased, and said, "How do you compare me to Kwan Chung? Considering how entirely he possessed [the confidence of] his ruler, how long he had the direction of the government of the State, and how low [after all] was what he accomplished, how is it that you compare me to him?"

4 'Thus,' added Mencius, 'Tsăng Se would not play Kwan Chung, and is it what you desire for me, that I should do so?'

5 [Kung-sun Ch'ow] said, 'Kwan Chung raised his ruler to be the leader of all the other princes, and the minister Gan made his ruler illustrious; and do you still think that it would not be enough for you to do what they did?'

6 'To raise [the ruler of] Ts'e to the Royal dignity would [simply] be like turning round the hand,' was the reply.

7   'So!' returned the other. 'The perplexity of your disciple is hereby very much increased! And there was king Wăn, with all the virtue which belonged to him, and who did not die till he had reached a hundred years; yet his influence had not penetrated to all under heaven. It required king Woo and the duke of Chow to continue his course, before that influence greatly prevailed. And now you say that the Royal dignity may be so easily obtained: – is king Wăn then not worthy to be imitated?'

8   [Mencius] said, 'How can king Wăn be matched? From T'ang to Woo-ting there had arisen six or seven worthy and sage sovereigns; all under heaven had been long attached to Yin. The length of time made a change difficult, and Woo-ting gave audience to all the princes and possessed the whole kingdom, as if it had been a thing which he turned round in his palm. [Then] Chow was removed from Woo-ting by no great interval of time. There were still remaining some of the ancient families, and of the old manners, of the influence which had emanated [from the earlier sovereigns], and of their good government. Moreover, there were the viscount of Wei and his second son, his Royal Highness Pe-kan, the viscount of Ke, and Kaou Kih, all men of ability and virtue, who gave their joint assistance to Chow [in his government]. In consequence of these things it took him a long time to lose the kingdom. There was not a foot of ground which he did not possess; there was not one of all the people who was not his subject. So it was on his side, while king Wăn made his beginning from a territory of [only] a hundred square *le*, and therefore it was difficult for him [immediately to attain to the Royal dignity].

9 'The people of Ts'e have the saying, "A man may have wisdom and discernment, but that is not like embracing the favourable opportunity; a man may have [good] hoes, but that is not like waiting for the [favourable] seasons." The present time is one in which [the Royal dignity] may be easily attained.

10 'In the flourishing periods of the sovereigns of Hëa, of Yin, and of Chow, the [Royal] territory did not exceed a thousand *le* and Ts'e embraces as much. Cocks crow and dogs bark to one another all the way to its four borders, so that Ts'e also possesses the [requisite number of] people. No change is needed for the enlargement of its territory, nor for the collecting of a population. If [its ruler] will put in practice benevolent government, no power can prevent his attaining to the Royal sway.

11 'Moreover, never was there a time farther removed than this from the appearance of a true king; never was there a time when the sufferings of the people from oppressive government were more intense than this. The hungry are easily supplied with food, and the thirsty with drink.

12 'Confucius said, "The flowing progress of virtue is more rapid than the transmission of orders by stages and couriers."

13 'At the present time, in a country of ten thousand chariots, let a benevolent government be exercised, and the people will be delighted with it, as if they were relieved from hanging by the heels. With half the merit of the ancients, double their achievement is sure to be realized. It is only at this time that such could be the case.'

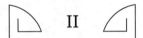

II

1 Kung-sun Ch'ow asked [Mencius], saying, 'Master, if you were to be appointed a high noble and prime minister of Ts'e, so as to carry your principles into practice, though you should thereupon [raise the ruler to be head of all the other princes or [even] to be king, it would not be to be wondered at; but in such a position would your mind be perturbed or not?' Mencius replied, 'No. At forty I attained to an unperturbed mind.'

2 [Ch'ow] said, 'Then, Master, you are far beyond Măng Pun.' '[The mere attainment of] that,' said [Mencius], 'is not difficult. The scholar Kaou attained to an unperturbed mind at an earlier period of life than I did.'

3 'Is there any [proper] way to an unperturbed mind?' asked [Chow]; and the reply was, 'Yes.

4 'Pih-kung Yëw had this way of nourishing his valour: – His flesh did not shrink [from a wound], and his eyes did not turn aside [from any thrusts at them]. He considered that to submit to have a hair pulled out by any one was as great [a disgrace] as to be beaten in the market-place, and that what he would not receive from [a common man in his] loose garments of hair-cloth, neither should he receive from the ruler of ten thousand chariots. He viewed stabbing the ruler of ten thousand chariots just as stabbing a fellow in cloth of hair. He feared not any of the princes. A bad word addressed to him he always returned.

5   'The valour which Măng She-shay nourished spoke on this wise: – 'I look upon conquering and not conquering in the same way. To measure the enemy and then advance; to calculate the chances of victory and then engage: – this is to stand in awe of the opposing force. How can I make certain of conquering? I can only rise superior to all fear.'

6   'Măng She-shay resembled the philosopher Tsăng, and Pih-kung Yëw resembled Tsze-hëa. I do not know to the valour of which the superiority should be ascribed; but Măng She-shay attended to what was of the greater importance.

7   'Formerly, the philosopher Tsăng said to Tsze-Seang, "Do you love valour? I heard an account of great valour from the Master, [who said that it speaks thus]: – 'If on self-examination I find that I am not upright, shall I not be afraid of [a common man in his] loose garments of haircloth; if on self-examination I find that I am upright, I will go forward against thousands and tens of thousands.'"

8   'What Măng She-shay maintained, however, was his physical energy merely, and was not equal to what the philosopher Tsăng maintained, which was [indeed] of the greater importance.'

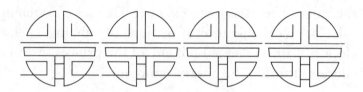

9 [Ch'ow] said, 'May I venture to ask [the difference between] your unperturbed mind. Master, and that of the scholar Kaou?' [Mencius] answered, 'Kaou says, "What you do not find in words, do not seek for in your mind; what you do not find in your mind, do not seek for by passion-effort." [This last] – not to seek by passion-effort for what you do not find in your mind – may be conceded; but not to seek in your mind for what you do not find in words ought not to be conceded. For the will is the leader of the passion nature; and the passion-nature pervades and animates the body. The will is [first and] chief, and the passion-nature is subordinate to it. Therefore [I] say. Maintain firm the will, and do no violence to the passion-nature.'

10 [Ch'ow observed], 'Since you say that the will is chief and the passion-nature subordinate to it, how do you also say. Maintain firm the will, and do no violence to the passion-nature?' The reply was, 'When the will is exclusively active, then it moves the passion-nature; and when the passion-nature is exclusively active, it moves the will. For instance now, the case of a man falling or running is an exertion of his passion-nature, and yet it moves his mind.'

11 'I venture to ask ' [said Ch'ow again], 'wherein you, Master, have the superiority.' [Mencius] said, 'I understand words. I am skilful in nourishing my vast, flowing, passion-nature.'

12 [Ch'ow pursued,] 'I venture to ask what you mean by your vast, flowing, passion-nature.' The reply was, 'It is difficult to describe it.

13 'This is the passion-nature: – It is exceedingly great, and exceedingly strong. Being nourished by rectitude and sustaining no injury, it fills up all between heaven and earth.

14 'This is the passion-nature: – It is the mate and assistant of righteousness and reason. Without this [man's nature] is in a state of starvation.

15 'It is produced by the accumulation of righteous deeds, and cannot be attained by incidental acts of righteousness. If the mind do not feel complacency in the conduct, [the nature becomes] starved. Hence it is that I say that Kaou has never understood righteousness, because he makes it something external.

16 'There must be the [constant] practice [of righteousness], but without the object [of thereby nourishing the passion-na-ture]. Let not the mind forget [its work], but let there be no assisting the growth. Let us not be like the man of Sung. There was a man at Sung who was grieved that his growing corn was not longer, and so he pulled it up. He then returned home, looking very stupid, and said to his people, "I am very tired to-day; I have been helping the corn to grow long." His son ran to look at it, and found the corn all withered. There are few people in the world who [do not deal with their passion-nature as if they] were thus assisting their corn to grow long. Some indeed consider it of no benefit to them, and neglect it; – they do not weed their corn. They who assist it to grow long pull out their corn. [What they do is] not only of no benefit [to the nature], but it also injures it.'

17 [Kung-sun Ch'ow further asked,] 'What do you mean by saying that you understand words?' [Mencius] replied, 'When speeches are one-sided, I know how [the mind of the speaker] is clouded over; when they are extravagant, I know wherein [the mind] is snared; when they are all-de-praved, I know how [the mind] has departed [from principle]; when they are evasive, I know how [the mind] is at its [wit's] end. [These evils], growing in the mind, injure the [princi-ples of the] government and, displayed in the government, are hurtful to the conduct of affairs. When a sage shall again arise, he will certainly agree with [these] my words.'

18 On this Ch'ow observed, 'Tsae Wo and Tsze-kung were clever in making speeches; Jen Nëw, the disciple Min, and Yen Yuen, while their words were good, were distinguished for their virtuous conduct. Confucius united both the qual-ities, [but still he] said, "In the matter of speeches I am not competent." – Then, Master, have you attained to be a sage?'

19 [Mencius] replied, 'Oh! what words are these? Formerly Tsze-kung asked Confucius, saying, "Master, are you a sage?" and was answered, "To be a sage is what I cannot [claim]; but I learn without satiety, and teach without being tired." Tsze-kung rejoined, "You learn without satiety; – that shows your wisdom. You teach without being tired; – that shows your benevolence. Benevolent and wise: – Master, you are a sage." Now, since Confucius would not accept the position of a sage, what words were those [you spake about me]?'

20 [Ch'ow said], 'Formerly, it seems to me, I have heard that Tsze-hëa, Tsze-yëw, and Tsze-chang had each one member of a sage, and that Jen Nëw, the disciple Min, and Yen Yuen had all the members, but in small proportions. I venture to ask with which of these you are pleased to rank yourself.'

21 [Mencius] replied, 'Let us drop [speaking about] these if you please.'

22 [Ch'ow then] asked, 'What do you say of Pih-e and E Yin?' 'Their ways' said [Mencius], 'were different [from mine]. Not to serve a prince nor employ a people whom he did not approve; in a time of good government to take office, and in a time of disorder to retire; – this was [the way of] Pih-e. [To say], "Whom may I not serve as my ruler? Whom may I not employ as my people?" In a time of good government to take office, and in a time of disorder to do the same: – this was [the way of] E Yin. When it was proper to go into office, then to go into office, and when it was proper to keep aloof from office, then to keep aloof; when it was proper to continue in it long, then to do so, and when it was proper to withdraw from it quickly, then so to withdraw: – that was [the way of] Confucius. These were all sages of antiquity, and I have not attained to do what they did; but what I wish to do is to learn to be like Confucius.'

23 [Ch'ow] said, 'Comparing Pih-e and E Yin with Confucius, are they to be placed in the same rank with him?' The reply was, 'No. Since there were living men until now, there never was [another] Confucius.'

24 'Then,' said [Ch'ow], 'did they have any points of agreement [with him]?' 'Yes,' said [Mencius]; 'if they had been rulers over a hundred *le* of territory, they would all of them have brought all the feudal princes to attend at their court, and would have possessed all under the sky. And none of them, to obtain that, would have committed one act of unright-eousness, or put to death one innocent person. In these points they agreed with him.'

25 [Ch'ow] said, 'I venture to ask wherein he differed from them.' [Mencius] replied, 'Tsae Wo, Tsze-kung, and Yew Joh had wisdom sufficient to know the sage. [Even if we rank them] low, they would not have demeaned themselves to flatter their favourite.

26 'Tsae Wo said, "According to my view of the Master, he is far superior to Yaou and Shun."

27 'Tsze-kung said, "By viewing the ceremonial ordinances [of a ruler] we know [the character of] his government; and by hearing his music we know [that of] his virtue. Along the distance of a hundred ages, I can arrange, [according to their merits], the line of their kings, so that not one can escape me; and from the birth of mankind downwards there has not been there has not been [another like our] Master."

28 'Yew Joh said, "Is it only among men that it is so? There is the *k'e-lin* among quadrupeds, the phoenix among birds, the T'ae mountain among ant-hills, the Ho and the sea among rain-pools. [Though different in degree], they are the same in kind. And so the sages among mankind are the same in kind. But they stand out from their fellows, and rise up above the crowd; and from the birth of mankind till now there never has been one so complete as Confucius."'

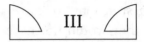

1 Mencius said, 'He who, using force, makes a pretence to benevolence becomes the leader of the princes, and he must be possessed of a large State. He who, using virtue, practises benevolence becomes the king, and he need not wait till he has a large State. T'ang did it with [only] seventy *le*, and king Wan with [only] a hundred *le*.

2 'When one by force subdues men they do not submit to him in heart, but because their strength is not adequate [to resist]. When one subdues men by virtue, in their hearts' core they are pleased, and sincerely submit, as was the case with the seventy disciples in their submission to Confucius. What is said in the Book of Poetry,

"From the west to the east,
From the south to the north,
There was not a thought but did him homage,"

is an illustration of this.'

1 Mencius said, 'Benevolence brings glory, and the opposite of it brings disgrace. For [the rulers of] the present day to hate disgrace, and yet live complacently doing what is not benevolent, is like hating moisture and yet living in a low situation.

2 'If [a ruler] hates disgrace, his best course is to esteem virtue and honour [virtuous] scholars, giving the worthiest of them places [of dignity] and the able offices [of trust]. When throughout the State there is leisure and rest [from external troubles], taking advantage of such a season, let him clearly digest the measures of his government with their penal sanctions, and even great States will stand in awe of him.

3 'It is said in the Book of Poetry,

"Before the sky was dark with rain,
I gathered the roots of the mulberry tree,
And bound round and round my window and door.
Now, ye people below,
Dare any of you despise my house?"

'Confucius said, "Did not he who made this ode understand the way [of governing]?" Who will dare to insult him who is able rightly to govern his State?

4 '[But] now [the rulers] take advantage of the time when throughout their States there is leisure and rest [from external troubles] to abandon themselves to pleasure and indolent indifference, – thus seeking calamities for themselves.

5 'Calamity and happiness are in all cases men's own seeking.

6   'This is illustrated by what is said in the Book of Poetry,

"Always strive to accord with the will [of heaven],
So shall you be seeking for much happiness;"

and by the passage of the T'ae-keah, "Calamities sent by Heaven may be avoided, but when we bring on the calamities ourselves, it is not possible to live."'

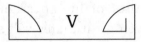

V

1   Mencius said, 'If [a ruler] give honour to men of talents and virtue and employ the able, so that offices shall all be filled by individuals of the highest distinction, then all the scholars of the kingdom will be pleased, and wish to stand in his court.

2   'If in the market-places he levy a ground-rent on the shops but do not tax the goods, or enforce the [proper] regulations without levying a ground-rent, then all traders of the kingdom will be pleased, and wish to store their goods in his market-places.

3   'If at the frontier-gates there be an inspection of the persons, but no charges levied, then all the travellers of the kingdom will be pleased, and wish to be found on his roads.

4 'If the husbandmen be required to give their material aid [in cultivating the public field], and no levies be made [of the produce of their own], then all the farmers in the kingdom will be pleased, and wish to plough in his fields.

5 'If from the [occupiers of the] people's dwellings he do not exact the cloth required from the individual [idler] or the quota for residences' then all the people in the kingdom will be pleased, and wish to be his people.

6 'If [a ruler] can truly practise these five things, then the people of neighbouring States will look up to him as a parent. From the first birth of mankind until now never has any one led children to attack their parents, and succeeded in his enterprise. Such [a ruler] will not have an enemy under the sky, and he who has no enemy under the sky is the minister of Heaven. Never has there been such a case where [the ruler] did not attain to the royal dignity.'

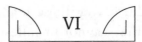

VI

1 Mencius said, 'All men have a mind which cannot bear [to see the sufferings of] others.

2 'The ancient kings had this commiserating mind, and they had likewise, as a matter of course, a commiserating government. When with a commiserating mind there was practised a commiserating government, to bring all under heaven to order was [as easy] as to make [a small thing] go round in the palm.

3   'The ground on which I say that all men have a mind which
cannot bear [to see the suffering of] others is this: – Even
now-a-days, when men suddenly see a child about to fall
into a well, they will all experience a feeling of alarm and
distress. They will feel so not that they may thereon gain
the favour of the child's parents; nor that they may seek the
praise of their neighbours and friends; nor from a dislike to
the reputation of [being unmoved by] such a thing.

4   'Looking at the matter from this case [we may see that] to be
without this feeling of distress is not human, and that it is not
human to be without the feeling of shame and dislike, or to
be without the feeling of modesty and complaisance, or to be
without the feeling of approving and disapproving.

5   'That feeling of distress is the principle of the benevolence
the feeling of shame and dislike is the principle of righteousness; the feeling of modesty and complaisance is the
principle of propriety; and the feeling of approving and
disapproving is the principle of knowledge.

6   'Men have these four principles just as they have their four
limbs. When men, having these four principles, yet say of
themselves that they cannot [manifest them], they play the
thief with themselves; and he who says of his ruler that he
cannot [manifest them], plays the thief with his ruler.

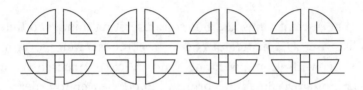

7 'Since we all have the four principles in ourselves, let us
know to give them all their development and completion,
and the issue will be like that of a fire which has begun to
burn, or of a spring which has begun to find vent. Let them
have their full development, and they will suffice to love
and protect all [within] the four seas; let them be denied
that development, and they will not suffice for a man to
serve his parents with.'

VII

1 Mencius said, 'Is the arrow-maker [naturally] more wanting
in benevolence than the maker of mail? [And yet], the
arrow-maker's only fear is lest [his arrows] should not wound
men, and the fear of the maker of mail is lest men should
be wounded. So it is as between the priest and the coffin-
maker. [The choice of] a profession therefore is a thing in
which it is very necessary to be careful.

2 'Confucius said, "The excellence of a neighbourhood consists
in its virtuous manners. If a man, in selecting a residence,
do not fix on one where such prevail, how can he be wise?"
Now benevolence belongs to the most honourable nobility
of Heaven, and is the quiet home where man should dwell.
Since no one can hinder us from being so, if we are not
benevolent, this shows our want of wisdom.

3   'He who is [thus] neither benevolent nor wise will be without propriety and righteousness, and must be the servant of [other] men. To be the servant of men and yet ashamed of such servitude is like a bow-maker's being ashamed to make bows, or an arrow-maker's being ashamed to make arrows.

4   'If [a man] be ashamed of being in such a case, his best course is to practise benevolence.

5   'He who [would be] benevolent is like the archer. The archer adjusts himself, and then shoots. If he shoot and do not hit, he does not murmur against those who surpass himself: – he simply turns round, and seeks the [cause of failure] in himself.'

VIII

1   Mencius said, 'When any one told Tsze-loo that he had a fault, he was glad.

2   'When Yu heard good words, he bowed [to the speaker].

3   'The great Shun had a [still] greater [quality]: – 'he regarded goodness as the common property of himself and others, giving up his own way to follow others, and delighting to copy [the example of] others, – in order to practise what was good.

4 'From the time that he ploughed and sowed, exercised the potter's art and was a fisherman, to that when he was emperor, he was always learning from others.

5 'To take example from others to practise what is good is to help men in the same practice. Therefore there is no attribute of the superior man greater than his helping men to practise what is good.'

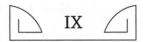

IX

1 Mencius said, 'Pih-e would not serve a ruler whom he did not approve, nor be friendly with any one whom he did not esteem. He would not stand in the court of a bad man, nor speak with a bad man. To stand in a bad man's court, or to speak with a bad man, would have been in his estimation the same as to stand with his court robes and court cap amid mire and charcoal. Pursuing our examination of his dislike to what was evil, [we find] that he thought it necessary, if he were standing with a villager whose cap was not rightly adjusted, to leave him with a high air as if he were going to be defiled. Hence it was, that, though some of the princes made application to him with very proper messages, he would not accept [their invitations]. That refusal to accept [their invitations] was because he counted it inconsistent with his purity to go to them.

2 'Hwuy of Lëw-hëa was not ashamed [to serve] an impure ruler, nor did he think it low to be in a small office. When called to employment, he did not keep his talents and virtue concealed, but made it a point to carry out his principles. When neglected and left out of office, he did not murmur; and when straitened by poverty, he did not grieve. Accordingly, he would say, "You are you, and I am I. Although you stand by my side with bare arms and breast, how can you defile me?" In this way, self-possessed, he associated with men indifferently, and did not feel that he lost himself. If pressed to remain in office, he would remain. He would remain in office when so pressed, because he did not feel that his purity required him to go away.'

3 Mencius said, 'Pih-e was narrow-minded, and Hwuy of Lëw-hëa was wanting in self-respect. The superior man will not follow either narrow-mindedness or the want of self-respect.'

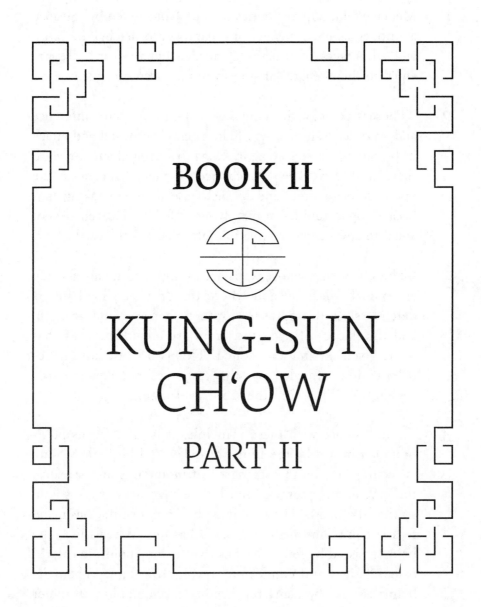

BOOK II

KUNG-SUN CH'OW

PART II

I

1   Mencius said, 'Opportunities of time [vouchsafed by] Heaven are not equal to advantages of situation [afforded by] the earth, and advantages of situation [afforded by] the earth are not equal to the strength [arising from the] accord of men.

2   '[There is a city], with an inner wall of three *le* in circumference and an outer wall of seven. [The enemy] surround and attack it, but are not able to take it. Now, to surround and attack it, there must have been vouchsafed to them by Heaven the opportunity of time, and in such case their not taking it is because opportunities of time [vouchsafed by] Heaven are not equal to advantages of situation [afforded by] the earth.

3   '[There is a city] whose walls are as high and moats as deep as could be desired, and where the arms and mail [of its defenders] are distinguished for their sharpness and strength, and the [stores of] rice and grain are abundant; yet it has to be given up and abandoned. This is because advantages of situation [afforded by] the earth are not equal to the [strength arising from the] accord of men.

4   'In accordance with these principles it is said, "A people is bounded in not by the limits of dykes and borders; a State is secured not by the strengths of mountains and streams, the kingdom is overawed not by the sharpness of arms [and strength] of mail." He who finds the proper course has many to assist him, and he who loses it has few. When this – the being assisted by few – reaches the extreme point, [a ruler's] own relatives and connexions revolt from him. When the being assisted by many reaches its extreme point, all under heaven become obedient [to the ruler].

5 'When one to whom all under heaven are prepared to become obedient attacks one from whom his own relatives and connexions are ready to revolt, [what must the result be?] Therefore the true ruler will [prefer] not [to] fight, but if he do fight, he is sure to overcome.'

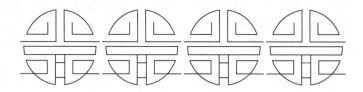

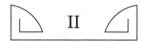

II

1 As Mencius was about to go to court to the king, the king sent a person to him with this message: – 'I was wishing to come and see you. But I have got a cold, and may not expose myself to the wind. In the morning I will hold my court. I do not know whether you will give me the opportunity of seeing you.' [Mencius] replied. 'Unfortunately I am unwell, and not able to go to court.'

2 Next day he went out to pay a visit of condolence to the Tung-kwoh family, when Kung-sun Ch'ow said to him, 'Yesterday you declined [going to the court] on the ground of being unwell, and to-day you are paying a visit of condolence: – may not this be regarded as improper?' 'Yesterday,' said [Mencius], 'I was unwell; to-day I am better: – why should I not pay this visit?'

3   [In the mean time] the king sent a messenger to inquire about his illness, and a physician [also] came [from the court]. Măng Chung replied to them, 'Yesterday, when the king's order came, he was feeling a little unwell, and could not go to the court. To-day he was a little better and hastened to go to court. I do not know whether he can have reached it [by this time] or not.' [Having said this,] he sent several men to intercept [Mencius] on the way, and say to him that he begged him, before he returned, to be sure and go to the court.

4   [On this, Mencius] felt himself compelled to go to King Ch'ow's, and there stop the night. The officer King said to him, 'In the family there is [the relation of] father and son; beyond it there is [that of] ruler and minister. These are the greatest relations among men. Between father and son the ruling principle is kindness; between ruler and minister the ruling principle is respect. I have seen the respect of the king to you, Sir, but I have not seen in what way you show respect to him.' The reply was, 'Oh! what words are these? Among the people of Ts'e there is no one who speaks to the king about benevolence and righteousness. Is it because they think that benevolence and righteousness are not admirable? No; but in their hearts they say, "This man is not fit to be spoken with about benevolence and right-eousness." Thus they manifest a disrespect than which there can be none greater. I do not dare to set forth before the king any but the ways of Yaou and Shun. There is therefore no man of Ts'e who respects the king so much as I do.'

5   King-tsze said, 'Not so; that was not what I meant. In the Book of Rites it is said, "When a father calls, the son must go to him without a moment's hesitation; when the prince's order calls, the carriage must not be waited for." You were certainly going to court, but when you heard the king's message, you did not carry the purpose out. This does seem as if your conduct were not in accordance with that rule of propriety.'

6   [Mencius] answered him, 'How can you give that meaning to my conduct? The philosopher Tsăng said, "The wealth of Tsin and Ts'oo cannot be equalled. Their [rulers] have their wealth, and I have my benevolence. They have their rank; and I have my righteousness. Wherein should I be dissatisfied [as inferior to them]?" Now were these sentiments not right? Seeing that the philosopher Tsăng gave expression to them, there is in them, I apprehend, a [real] principle. Under heaven there are three things universally acknowledged to be honourable: – rank; years; and virtue. In courts, rank holds the first place of the three; in villages, years; and for helping one's generation and presiding over the people, virtue. How can the possession of only one of them be presumed on to despise one who possesses the other two?

7   'Therefore, a prince who is to accomplish great deeds will certainly have ministers whom he does not call to go to him. When he wishes to consult with them, he goes to them. [The ruler] who does not honour the virtuous and delight in their ways of doing to this extent is not worth having to do with.

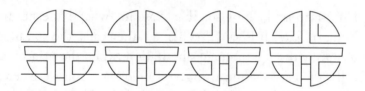

8   'Accordingly, so did T'ang behave to E Yin: – he learned of him, and then employed him as his minister, and so without difficulty he became king. And so did duke Hwan behave to Kwan Chung: – he learned of him, and then employed him as his minister, and so without difficulty he became leader of the princes.

9   'Now throughout the kingdom [the territories of] the princes are of equal extent and in their achievements they are on a level. Not one of them is able to exceed the others. This is from no other reason but that they love to make ministers of those whom they teach, and do not love to make ministers of those by whom they might be taught.

10 'So did T'ang behave to E Yin, and duke Hwan to Kwan Chung, that they would not venture to call them [to them]. If even Kwan Chung could not be called to him [by his ruler], how much less may he be called who would not play the part of Kwan Chung!'

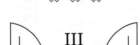

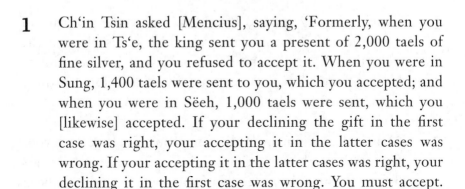

III

1 Ch'in Tsin asked [Mencius], saying, 'Formerly, when you were in Ts'e, the king sent you a present of 2,000 taels of fine silver, and you refused to accept it. When you were in Sung, 1,400 taels were sent to you, which you accepted; and when you were in Sëeh, 1,000 taels were sent, which you [likewise] accepted. If your declining the gift in the first case was right, your accepting it in the latter cases was wrong. If your accepting it in the latter cases was right, your declining it in the first case was wrong. You must accept. Master, one of these alternatives.'

2 Mencius said, 'I did right in all the cases.

3 'When I was in Sung, I was about to take a long journey. Travellers must be provided with what is necessary for their expenses. The [prince's] message was – "A present against travelling expenses." Why should I not have received it?

4 'When I was in Sëeh, I was apprehensive for my safety, and wished to take measures for my protection. The message [with the gift] was – "I have heard that you are apprehensive for your safety, and therefore I send you this to help you in procuring weapons." Why should I not have received it?

5 'But as to the case in Ts'e I had then no occasion for money. To send a man a gift, when he has no occasion for it, is to bribe him. How can one claim to be a superior man, and allow himself to be taken with a bribe?'

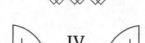

IV

1   Mencius, having gone to P'ing-luh, said to the governor of it, 'If [one of] your spearmen should lose his place in the ranks three times in one day, would you. Sir, put him to death or not?' 'I would not wait till he had done so three times,' was the reply.

2   [Mencius] continued, 'Well then, you, Sir, have lost your place in the ranks many times. In calamitous years and years of famine, the old and feeble of your people who have been found lying in ditches and water-channels, and the able-bodied who have been scattered about to the four quarters, have amounted to thousands.' 'This is not a case in which I, Keu-sin, can take it upon me to act.'

3   'Here,' said [Mencius], 'is a man who receives charge of the sheep and cattle of another, and undertakes to feed them for him; – of course he must seek for pasture-ground and grass for them. If, after seeking for these, he cannot find them, will he return his charge to the owner? or will he stand [by] and see them die?' 'Herein,' said [the governor], 'I am guilty.'

4   Another day Mencius had an audience of the king, and said to him, 'Of the governors of your Majesty's cities I am acquainted with five; but the only one who knows his fault is K'ung Keu-sin.' He then related to the king the conversation which he had had [with that officer], and the king said, 'In this matter I am the guilty one.'

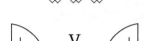

V

1   Mencius said to Ch'e Wa, 'There seemed to be reason in your declining [the governorship] of Ling-k'ëw, and requesting to be appointed chief criminal judge, because the [latter office] would afford you the opportunity of speaking your mind. But now several months have elapsed; and have you found nothing about which you might speak?'

2   [On this] Ch'e Wa remonstrated [on some matter] with the king; and, his counsel not being taken, he resigned his office, and went away.

3   The people of Ts'e said, 'In the course which he marked out for Ch'e Wa he did well; but as to the course which he pursues for himself, we do not know.'

4   His disciple Kung Too told him these remarks.

5   [Mencius] said, 'I have heard that when he, who is in charge of an office, is prevented from performing its duties, he should take his departure, and that he on whom is the responsibility of giving his opinions, when his words are disregarded, should do the same. [But] I am in charge of no office, and on me is no responsibility to speak out my views; – may not I act freely and without restraint either in going forward or in retiring?'

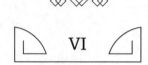

VI

1   Mencius, occupying the position of a high dignitary in Ts'e, went from it on a mission of condolence to T'ăng, and the king sent Wang Hwan, governor of Kah, [with him] as assistant commissioner. Wang Hwan, morning and evening, waited upon him, but, during all the way to T'ăng and back to Ts'e, [Mencius] never spoke to him about the affairs of the mission.

2   Kung-sun Ch'ow said [to Mencius], 'The position of a high dignitary of Ts'e is not a small one, and the way from Ts'e to T'ăng is not short; – "how was it that during all the way from Ts'e to T'ăng and back, you never spoke [to Hwan] about the affairs of the mission?' 'There were the proper parties to attend to them; why should I speak [to him about them]?'

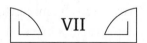

VII

1   Mencius [went] from Ts'e to bury [his mother] in Loo. When he returned to Ts'e, he stopped at Ying, and Ch'ung Yu begged [to put a question to] him, saying, 'Formerly, in ignorance of my incompetency, you employed me to superintend the business of making the coffin. As [you were then pressed by] the urgency [of the business], I did not venture to put any question to you; but now I wish to take the liberty to submit the matter. The wood, it appeared to me, was too good.'

2   [Mencius] replied, 'Anciently, there was no rule for [the thickness of] either the inner or the outer coffin. In middle antiquity, the inner coffin was made seven inches thick, and the outer the same. This was done by all from the son of Heaven down to the common people, and not simply for the beauty of the appearance, but because they thus satisfied [the natural feelings of] the human heart.

3   'If prevented [by statutory regulations] from making their coffins thus, men cannot have the feeling of pleasure; and if they have not the money [to make them thus], they cannot have that feeling. When they were not prevented, and had the money, the ancients all used this style; – why should I alone not do so?

4   'And moreover, is this alone no satisfaction to a man's heart – to prevent the earth from getting near to the bodies of his dead?

5   'I have heard that the superior man will not for all the world be niggardly to his parents.'

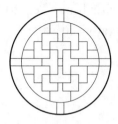

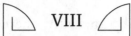

VIII

1   Shin T'ung, on his private authority, asked [Mencius], saying, 'May Yen be attacked?' Mencius said, 'It may. Tsze-k'wae had no right to give Yen to another man; and Tsze-che had no right to receive Yen from Tsze-k'wae. [Suppose] there were an officer here, with whom you. Sir, were pleased, and that, without announcing the matter to the king, you were privately to give to him your salary and rank, and [suppose that] this officer, also without the king's orders, were privately to receive them from you; – would [such a transaction] be allowable? And where is the difference between [the case of Yen and] this?'

2   The people of Ts'e attacked Yen, and some one asked [Mencius] saying, 'Is it true that you advised Ts'e to attack Yen?' He replied, 'No. Shin T'ung asked me whether Yen might be attacked, and I replied that it might, on which they proceeded to attack it. If he had asked me who might attack it, I would have answered him that the minister of Heaven might do so. Suppose the case of a murderer, and that one asked me, "May this man be put to death?" I would answer him, "He may." If he [further] asked me, "Who may put him to death?" I would answer him, "The chief criminal judge." But now with [one] Yen to attack [another] Yen: – how should I have advised this?'

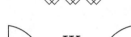

IX

1   The people of Yen having rebelled, the king said, 'I am very much ashamed [when I think] of Mencius.'

2   Ch'in Këa said [to him], 'Let not your Majesty be troubled. Whether does your Majesty consider yourself or the duke of Chow the more benevolent and wise?' The king replied, 'Oh! what words are these?' [Ch'in Këa] rejoined, 'The duke of Chow employed Kwan-shuh to oversee [the heir of] Yin, but Kwan-shuh rebelled with [the people of] Yin. If, knowing [that this would happen], he yet employed him, he was not benevolent. If he employed him without knowing it, he was not wise. The duke of Chow was [thus] not perfectly benevolent and wise, and how much less can your Majesty be expected to be so! I beg to [go and] see Mencius, and relieve [your Majesty] of that [feeling].'

3   [Accordingly] he saw Mencius, and asked him, saying, 'What kind of man was the duke of Chow?' 'An ancient sage,' was the reply. 'Is it true,' pursued [the other], 'that he employed Kwan-shuh to oversee [the heir of] Yin, and that Kwan-shuh rebelled with [the people of Yin?' 'It is,' said [Mencius]. [Ch'in Këa] asked, 'Did the duke of Chow know that he would rebel, and [thereupon] employ him?' 'He did not know it,' was the reply. 'Then though a sage, he still fell into error.' 'The duke of Chow,' said [Mencius], 'was the younger brother, and Kwan-shuh the elder. Was not the error of the duke of Chow reasonable?

4   'Moreover, when the superior men of old had errors, they reformed them; but when the superior men of the present day have errors, they persist in them. The errors of the superior men of old were like the eclipses of the sun and moon. All the people witness them; and when they have resumed their usual appearance, all the people look up to them [with their former admiration]. But do superior men of the present day merely persist [in their errors]? – they go on to make excuses for them as well.'

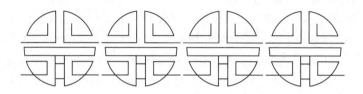

1   Mencius gave up his office [in Ts'e], and [was preparing to] return [to his native State].

2   The king went to see him, and said, 'Formerly I wished to see you, but found no opportunity to do so. When I got that opportunity, and stood by you in the same court, I was exceedingly glad. [But] now again you are abandoning me and returning home; – I do not know if hereafter I may have another opportunity of seeing you.' 'I do not venture to make any request,' was the reply, 'but indeed it is what I desire.'

3　Another day, the king said to the officer She, 'I wish to give Mencius a house in the centre of the kingdom, and to support his disciples with [an allowance of] 10,000 *chung*, so that all the great officers and people may have [such an example] to reverence and imitate. Had you not better tell him this for me?'

4　The officer She conveyed this message by means of the disciple Ch'in, who reported his words to Mencius.

5　Mencius said, 'Yes; but how should the officer She know that the thing may not be? Supposing that I wanted to be rich, having declined 100,000 *chung*, would my accepting 10,000 be the conduct of one desiring riches?

6　'Ke-sun said, "A strange man was Tsze-shuh E! Suppose that he himself was a high minister, if [his prince would] no longer employ him, he had to retire; but he would again [try to] get one of his younger relatives to be high minister. Who indeed is there of men that does not wish to be rich and noble, but he only, among the rich and noble, sought to monopolize the conspicuous mound."

7　'In old time the market-dealers exchanged the articles which they had for others which they had not, and simply had certain officers to keep them in order. There was a mean fellow, who made it a point to look out for a conspicuous mound, and get up upon it. Thence he looked right and left to catch in his net the whole gain of the market. People all thought his conduct mean, and therefore they proceeded to lay a tax upon his wares. The taxing of traders took its rise from this mean fellow.'

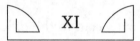

XI

1   Mencius, having left [the capital of] T'se, was passing the night in Chow.

2   A person who wished for the king to detain him [came and] sat down [to speak with him]. [Mencius] gave him no answer, but leant upon his stool and slept.

3   The stranger was displeased, and said, 'I have fasted for two days before I would venture to speak with you, and [now], Master, you sleep and do not listen to me. Allow me to request that I may not again presume to see you.' [Mencius] said, 'Sit down, and I will explain the matter clearly to you. Formerly, if duke Miih of Loo had not had persons [continually] by the side of Tsze-sze, he could not have kept Tsze-sze [in his State]; and if Sëeh Lëw and Shin Ts'ang had not had persons by the side of duke Muh, they would not have been able to feel at rest [in remaining in Loo].

4   'You, Sir, are concerned and plan about an old man like me, but I have not been treated as Tsze-sze was. Is it you. Sir, who cut me? Or is it I who cut you?'

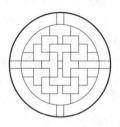

XII

1 Mencius having left Ts'e, Yin Sze spake about him to others, saying, 'If he did not know that the king could not be made a T'ang or a Woo, that showed his want of intelligence. If he knew that he could not be made such, and yet came [to Ts'e] notwithstanding, that he was seeking for favours. He came a thousand *le* to wait upon the king. Because he did not find in him the ruler he wished, he took his leave. Three nights he stayed, and then passed from Chow; – how dilatory and lingering [was his departure]! I am dissatisfied on account of this.'

2 The disciple Kaou informed [Mencius] of these remarks.

3 [Mencius] said, 'How should Yin Sze know me P When I came a thousand *le* to see the king, it was what I desired to do. When I went away, not finding in him the ruler that I wished, was that what I desired to do? I felt myself constrained to do it.

4 'When I stayed three nights before I passed from Chow, in my own mind I still considered my departure speedy. I was hoping that the king might change. If the king had changed, he would certainly have recalled me.

5 'When I passed from Chow, and the king had not sent after me, then, and only then, was my mind resolutely bent on returning [to Tsow]. But notwithstanding that, was I giving the king up? He is after all one who may be made to do what is good. If the king were to use me, would it be for the happiness of the people of Ts'e only? It would be for the happiness of all under heaven. Would the king but change! I am daily hoping for this.

6   'Am I like one of your little-minded people? They will remonstrate with their ruler, and when their remonstrance is not accepted, they get angry, and with their passion displayed in their countenance, they take their leave, and travel with all their strength for a whole day before they will stop for the night.'

7   When Yin Sze heard this [explanation], he said, 'I am indeed a small man.'

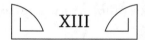

XIII

1   When Mencius left Ts'e, Ch'ung Yu questioned him on the way, saying, 'Master, you look like one who carries an air of dissatisfaction in his countenance. [But] formerly I heard yon say that the superior man does not murmur against Heaven, nor cherish a grudge against men.

2   [Mencius] said, 'That was one time, and this is another.

3   'It is a rule that a true sovereign should arise in the course of five hundred years, and that during that time there should be men illustrious in their generation.

4   'From the commencement of the Chow dynasty till now, more than seven hundred years have elapsed. Judging numerically, the date is passed. Considering the matter from the [character of the present] time, we might expect [a true king to arise].

5 'But Heaven does not yet wish that tranquillity and good order should prevail all under the sky. If it wished this, who is there besides me to bring it about? How should I be otherwise than dissatisfied?'

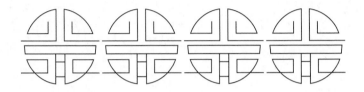

 XIV

1 When Mencius left Ts'e, he dwelt in Hëw. [There] Kung-sun Ch'ow asked him, 'Was it the way of the ancients to hold office without receiving salary?'

2 [Mencius] said, 'No. When I first saw the king in Ts'ung, it was my intention, on retiring from the interview, to go away. Because I did not wish to change this intention, I would not receive [any salary].

3 'Immediately after, orders were issued for [the collection of] troops, when it would have been improper for me to beg [permission to leave]. [But] to remain long in Ts'e was not my purpose.'

BOOK III

T'ĂNG WĂN KUNG

PART I

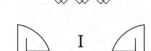

1 When duke Wăn of T'ang was heir-son, being on a journey to Ts'oo he passed by [the capital of] Sung, and had an interview with Mencius.

2 Mencius discoursed to him how the nature of man is good, and, in speaking, made laudatory appeal to Yaou and Shun.

3 When the heir-son was returning from Ts'oo, he again saw Mencius, when the latter said to him, 'Prince, do you doubt my words? The path is one, and only one.

4 'Ch'ing Kan said to duke King of Ts'e, "They were men, [and] I am a man; – why should I stand in awe of them?" Yeu Yuen said, "What kind of man was Shun? What kind of man am I? He who exerts himself will also become such as he was." Kung-ming E said, "King Wăn is my teacher and model; – how should the duke of Chow deceive me [by these words]?"

5 'Now T'ăng, taking its length with its breadth, will amount to about fifty square *le*. [Though small,] it may still be made a good kingdom. It is said in the Book of History, "If medicine do not distress the patient, it will not cure his sickness."'

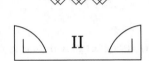

II

1   When duke Ting of T'ăng died, the heir-son said to Jen Yëw, 'Formerly, Mencius spoke with me in Sung, and I have never forgotten his words. Now, alas! this great affair [of the death of my father] has happened, and I wish to send you, Sir, to ask Mencius, and then to proceed to the services [connected with it].'

2   Jen Yëw [accordingly] proceeded to Tsow, and consulted Mencius. Mencius said, 'Is not this good? The mourning rites for parents are what men feel constrained to do their utmost in. The philosopher Tsăng said, "When parents are alive, they should be served according to [the rules of] propriety; when dead, they should be buried, and they should be sacrificed to, according to the same: – this may be called filial piety." I have not learned [for myself] the ceremonies to be observed by the feudal princes, but nevertheless I have heard these points: – Three years' mourning, with the wearing the garment of coarse cloth with its lower edge even, and the eating of thin congee, have been equally prescribed by the three dynasties, and are binding on all, from the son of Heaven to the common people.'

3   Jen Yëw reported the execution of his commission, and [the prince] determined that the three years' mourning should be observed. His uncles and elder cousins, and the body of the officers, did not wish it, and said, 'The former rulers of Loo, the State which we honour, have, none of them, observed this mourning, nor have any of our own former rulers observed it. For you to change their practice is improper; and moreover, the History says, "In mourning and sacrifice ancestors are to be followed," meaning that we have received those things from a [proper] source.'

4   [The prince again] said to Jen Yëw, 'Hitherto I have not given myself to the pursuit of learning, but have found my pleasure in driving my horses and in sword-exercise. Now my uncles and elder cousins and the body of officers are not satisfied with me. I am afraid I may not be able to carry out [this] great business; do you, Sir, [again go and] ask Mencius for me.' Jen Yëw went again to Tsow, and consulted Mencius, who said, 'Yes, but this is not a matter in which he has to look to any one but himself. Confucius said, "When a ruler died, his successor entrusted the administration to the prime minister. He sipped the congee, and his face looked very dark. He went to the [proper] place, and wept. Of all the officers and inferior employees there was not one who did not dare not to be sad, when [the prince thus] set them the example. What the superior loves, his inferiors will be found to love still more. The relation between superiors and inferiors is like that between the wind and the grass. The grass must bend when the wind blows upon it." The [whole thing] depends on the heir-son.'

5 Jen Yew returned with this answer to his commission, and the prince said, 'Yes; it does indeed depend on me.' For five months he dwelt in the shed, and did not issue an order or a caution. The body of officers and his relatives [said], 'He may be pronounced acquainted [with all the ceremonies].' When the time of interment arrived, they came from all quarters to see it, with the deep dejection of his countenance, and the mournfulness of his wailing and weeping. Those who [had come from other States to] condole with him were greatly pleased.

III

1 Duke Wăn of T'ăng asked [Mencius] about [the proper way of] governing a State.

2 Mencius said, 'The business of the people must not be remissly attended to. It is said in the Book of Poetry,

"In the daytime collect the grass.
And at night twist it into ropes.
Then get up quickly on our roofs: –
We shall have to recommence our sowing."

3　'The way of the people is this: – Those who have a certain livelihood have a fixed heart, and those who have not a certain livelihood have not a fixed heart. If they have not a fixed heart, there is nothing which they will not do in the way of self-abandonment, of moral deflection, of depravity, and of wild license. When they have thus been involved in crime, to follow them up and punish them is to entrap the people. How can such a thing as entrapping the people be done under the rule of a benevolent man?

4　'Therefore a ruler endowed with talents and virtue will be gravely complaisant and economical, showing a respectful politeness to his ministers, and taking from the people only according to definite regulations.

5　'Yang Hoo said, "He who seeks to be rich will not be benevolent; and he who seeks to be benevolent will not be rich."

6　'[Under] the sovereigns of Hëa, [each farmer received] fifty acres, and contributed [a certain tax]. [Under] those of Yin, [each farmer received] seventy acres, and [eight families] helped [to cultivate the public acres]. Under those of Chow, [each farmer received] a hundred acres, and [the produce] was allotted in shares. In reality what was paid in all these was a tithe. The share system means division; the aid system means mutual dependence.

7 'Lung-tsze said, "For regulating the land there is no better system than that of mutual aid, and none worse than that of contributing a certain tax. According to the tax system it was fixed by taking the average of several years. In good years, when the grain lies about in abundance, much might be taken without its being felt to be oppressive, and the actual exaction is small. In bad years, when [the produce] is not sufficient to [repay] the manuring of the fields, this system still requires the taking of the full amount. When he who should be the parent of the people causes the people to wear looks of distress, and, after the whole year's toil, yet not to be able to nourish their parents, and more over to set about borrowing to increase [their means of paying the tax], till their old people and children are found lying in the ditches and water-channels: – where [in such a case] is his parental relation to the people?"

8 'As to the system of hereditary salaries, that is already observed in T'ǎng.

9 'It is said in the Book of Poetry,

"May it rain first on our public fields,
And then come to our private!"

It is only in the system of mutual aid, that there are the public fields, and from this passage we perceive that even in the Chow dynasty this system has been recognized.

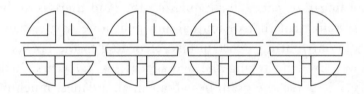

10 'Establish *ts'ëang*, *seu*, *hëoh*, and *hëaou*, – [all these educational institutions] – for the instruction [of the people]. The name *ts'ëang* indicates nourishing; *hëaou* indicates teaching; and *seu* indicates archery. By the Hea dynasty the name *hëaou* was used; by the Yin dynasty that of *seu*; and by the Chow dynasty that of *ts'ëang*. As to the *hëoh*, they belonged equally to the three dynasties, [and by that name]. The object of them all is to illustrate the [duties of the] human relations. When these are [thus] illustrated by superiors, mutual affection will prevail among the smaller people below.

11 'Should a [true] king arise, he will certainly come and take an example [from you], and thus you will be the teacher of the [true] king.

12 'It is said in the Book of Poetry,

"Although Chow was an old State,
The [favouring] appointment lighted on it recently."

That is said with reference to king Wăn. Do you practise those things with vigour, and you will also give a new history to your State.'

13 [The duke afterwards] sent Peih Chen to ask about the nine squares system of dividing the land. Mencius said to him, 'Since your ruler, wishing to put in practice a benevolent government, has made choice of you, and put you into this employment, you must use all your efforts, benevolent government must commence with the definition of the boundaries. If the boundaries be not defined correctly, the division of the land into squares will not be equal, and the produce [available for] salaries will not be evenly distributed. On this account, oppressive rulers and impure ministers are sure to neglect the defining of the boundaries. When the boundaries have been defined correctly, the division of the fields and the regulation of the salaries may be determined [by you] sitting [at your ease].

14 'Although the territory of T'ăng be narrow and small, there must be in it, I apprehend, men of a superior grade, and there must be in it country-men. If there were not men of a superior grade, there would be none to rule the countrymen; if there were not country-men, there would be none to support the men of superior grade.

15 'I would ask you, in the [purely] country districts, to observe the nine-squares division, having one square cultivated on the system of mutual aid; and in the central parts of the State, to levy a tenth, to be paid by the cultivators themselves.

16 'From the highest officers downwards, each one must have [his] holy field, consisting of fifty acres.

17 'Let the supernumerary males have [their] twenty-five acres.

18 'On occasions of death, or of removing from one dwelling to another, there will be no quitting the district. In the fields of a district, those who belong to the same nine-squares render all friendly offices to one another in their going out and coming in, aid one another in keeping watch and ward, and sustain one another in sickness. Thus the people will be led to live in affection and harmony.

19 'A square *le* covers nine squares of land, which nine squares contain nine hundred acres. The central square contains the public fields; and eight families, each having its own hundred acres, cultivate them together. And it is not till the public work is finished that they presume to attend to their private fields. [This is] the way by which the country-men are distinguished [from those of a superior grade].

20 'These are the great outlines [of the system]. Happily to modify and adapt them depends on your ruler and you.'

IV

1 There came from Ts'oo to T'ăng one Heu Hing, who gave out that he acted according to the words of Shinnung. Coming right to his gate, he addressed duke Wăn, saying, 'A man of a distant region, I have heard that you, ruler, are practising a benevolent government, and I wish to receive a site for a house, and to become one of your people.' Duke Wăn gave him a dwelling-place. His disciples, amounting to several tens, all wore clothes of hair-cloth, and made sandals of hemp and wove mats for a living.

2   Ch'in Sëang, a disciple of Ch'in Lëang, with his younger brother Sin, with their plough-handles and shares on their backs, came [at the same time] from Sung to T'ăng, saying, 'We have heard that you, ruler, are putting into practice the government of the [ancient] sages, [showing that] you are likewise a sage: we wish to be the subjects of a sage.'

3   When Ch'in Sëang saw Heu Hing, he was very much pleased with him, and, abandoning all which he had learned, he set about learning from him. Having an interview with Mencius, he repeated to him the words of Heu Hing to this effect: – 'The ruler of T'ăng is indeed a worthy prince, but nevertheless he has not yet heard the [real] ways [of antiquity]. Wise and able rulers should cultivate the ground equally and along with their people, and eat [the fruit of their own labour]. They should prepare their morning and evening meals [themselves], and [at the same time] carry on the business of government. But now [the ruler of] T'ăng has his granaries, treasuries, and arsenals, which is a distressing of the people to support himself; – how can he be deemed a [real] ruler of talents and virtue?'

4   Mencius said, 'Mr Heu, I suppose, sows grain and eats [the produce]' 'Yes' was the reply. 'I suppose he [also] weaves cloth, and wears his own manufacture.' 'No, he wears clothes of hair-cloth.' 'Does he wear a cap?' 'He wears a cap.' 'What kind of cap?' 'A plain cap.' 'Is it woven by himself?' 'No; he gets it in exchange for grain.' 'Why does he not weave it himself?' 'That would be injurious to his husbandry.' 'Does he cook his food with boilers and earthenware pans, and plough with an iron share?' 'Yes.' 'Does he make them himself?' 'No; he gets them in exchange for grain.'

5   [Mencius then said], 'The getting such articles in exchange for grain is not oppressive to the potter and founder; and are the potter and founder oppressive to the husbandman, when they give him their vigorous articles in exchange for grain? Moreover, why does Heu not act the potter and founder, and supply himself with the articles which he uses solely from his own establishment? Why does he go confusedly dealing and exchanging with the handicraftsmen? Why is he so indifferent to the trouble that he takes?'[Ch'in Sëang replied], 'The business of the handicraftsmen can by no means be carried on along with that of husbandry.'

6   [Mencius resumed], 'Then is it the government of all under heaven which alone can be carried on along with the business of husbandry? Great men have their proper business, and little men have theirs. Moreover, in the case of any single individual, [whatever articles he can require are] ready to his hand, being produced by the various handicraftsmen: – if he must first make them himself for his own use, this would keep all under heaven running about on the roads. Hence there is the saying, "Some labour with their minds, and some labour with their strength. Those who labour with their minds govern others, and those who labour with their strength are governed by others. Those who are governed by others support them, and those who govern others are supported by them." This is a thing of right universally recognized.

7   'In the time of Yaou, when the world had not yet been perfectly reduced to order, the vast waters, flowing out of their channels, made a universal inundation. Vegetation was luxuriant, and birds and beasts swarmed. The five kinds of grain could not be grown, and the birds and beasts pressed upon men. The paths marked by the feet of beasts and prints of birds crossed one another throughout the Middle States. To Yaou especially this caused anxious sorrow. He called Shun to office, and measures to regulate the disorder were set forth. Shun committed to Yih the direction of the fire to be employed, and he set fire to, and consumed, [the forests and vegetation on] the mountains and [in] the marshes, so that the birds and beasts fled away and hid themselves, Yu separated the nine [streams of the] Ho, cleared the courses of the Tse and the T'ah, and led them to the sea. He opened a vent for the Joo and the Han, removed the obstructions in the channels of the Hwae and the Sze, and led them to the Këang. When this was done, it became possible for [the people of] the Middle States to [cultivate the ground, and] get food [for themselves]. During that time, Yu was eight years away from his house, thrice passing by his door without entering it. Although he had wished to cultivate the ground, could he have done it?

8 'How-tseih taught the people to sow and reap, cultivating the five kinds of grain; and when these were brought to maturity, the people all enjoyed a comfortable subsistence. [But] to men there belongs the way [in which they should go]; and if they are well fed, warmly clad, and comfortably lodged, without being taught [at the same time], they become almost like the beasts. This also was a subject of anxious solicitude to the sage [Shun]; and he appointed Sëeh to be minister of Instruction, and to teach the relations of humanity! – how, between father and son, there should be affection; between ruler and subject, righteousness; between husband and wife, attention to their separate functions; between young and old, a proper distinction; and between friends, fidelity. Fang-heun said, "Encourage them; lead them on; rectify them; straighten them; help them; give them wings; causing them to become masters of their own [nature] for themselves." When the sages were exercising their solicitude for the people in this way, had they leisure to cultivate the ground?

9 'What Yaou felt as peculiarly giving him anxiety was the not getting Shun; and what Shun felt as peculiarly giving him anxiety was the not getting Yu and Kaou Yaou. But he whose anxiety is about his hundred acres' not being properly culti-vated is a [mere] husbandman.

10 'The imparting by a man to others of his wealth is called "a kindness." The teaching others what is good is called "an exercise of fidelity." The finding a man who shall benefit all under heaven is called "benevolence." Hence to give the kingdom to another man would be easy; to find a man who shall benefit it is difficult.

11 'Confucius said, "Great was Yaou as a ruler! Only Heaven is great, and only Yaou corresponded to it. How vast [was his virtue]! The people could find no name for it. Princely indeed was Shun! How majestic was he, possessing all under heaven, and yet seeming as if it were nothing to him!" In their governing all under heaven, had Yaou and Shun no subjects with which they occupied their minds? But they did not occupy them with their own cultivation of the ground.

12 'I have heard of men using [the ways of our] great land to change barbarians, but I have not yet heard of any being changed by barbarians. Ch'in Lëang was a native of Ts'oo. Pleased with the doctrines of the dukes of Chow and Chung-ne, he came north to the Middle States and learned them. Among the learners of the northern regions, there were perhaps none who excelled him; – he was what you call a scholar of high and distinguished qualities. You and your younger brother followed him for several tens of years, but on his death you forthwith turned the back on him.

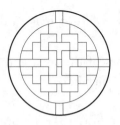

13 'Formerly, when Confucius died, after three years had elapsed the disciples put their baggage in order, intending to return to their homes. Having entered to take leave of Tsze-kung, they looked towards one another and wailed, till they all lost their voices. After this they returned to their homes, but Tsze-kung built another house for himself on the altar-ground, where he lived alone for [other] three years, after which he returned home. Subsequently, Tszehëa, Tsze-chang, and Tsze-yëw, thinking that Yëw Joh resembled the sage, wished to pay to him the same observances which they had paid to Confucius, and [tried to] force Tsăng-tsze [to join with them]. He said, [however], "The thing must not be done. What has been washed in the waters of the Keang and Han, and bleached in the autumn sun: – how glistening it is! Nothing can be added to it."

14 'Now here is this shrike-tongued barbarian of the south, whose doctrines are not those of the ancient kings. You turn your back on your [former] master, and learn of him; – different you are indeed from Tsăng-tsze.

15 'I have heard of [birds] leaving the dark valleys, and removing to lofty trees, but I have not heard of their descending from lofty trees, and entering the dark valleys.

16 'In the Praise-odes of Loo it is said,

"He smote the tribes of the west and the north;
He punished King and Shoo."

Thus the duke of Chow then smote those [tribes], and you are become a disciple of [one of] them; – the change which you have made is indeed not good.'

17 [Ch'in Sëang said], 'If Heu's doctrines were followed, there would not be two prices in the market, nor any deceit in the State. Though a lad of five cubits were sent to the market, nobody would impose on him. Linens and silks of the same length would be of the same price. So would it be with [bundles of] hemp and silk, being of the same weight; with the different kinds of grain, being the same in quantity; and with shoes which were of the same size.'

18 [Mencius] replied, 'It is in the nature of things to be of unequal quality. Some are twice, some five times, some ten times, some a hundred times, some a thousand times, some ten thousand times as valuable as others. If you reduce them all to the same standard, that would throw all under heaven into confusion. If large shoes and small shoes were of the same price, would people make them? If people were to follow the doctrines of Heu, they would [only] lead on one another to practise deceit; – how can they avail for the government of a State?'

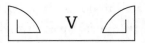

V

1 The Mihist E Che sought, through Seu Peih, to see Mencius. Mencius said, 'I indeed wished to see him; but at present I am still unwell. When I am better, I will myself go and see him; he need not come [to me].'

2   Next day, [E Che] again sought to see Mencius, who said, 'Yes, to-day I can see him. But if I do not correct [his errors], the [true] principles will not clearly appear; let me first correct him. I have heard that Mr E is a Mihist. Now Mih thinks that in the regulation of the rites of mourning a spare simplicity should be the rule. He thinks [with Mih's doctrines] to change [the customs of] all under heaven; but how does he [himself] regard them as if they were wrong, and not honour them? Thus when E buried his parents in a sumptuous manner, he was doing them service in a way which [his doctrines] discountenanced.'

3   The disciple Seu informed Mr E of these remarks. E said, '[Even according to] the principles of the learned, the ancients, [though sages, dealt with the people] as if they were loving and cherishing their children. What does this expression mean? To me it sounds that we are to love all without difference of degree, the manifestation of it [simply] beginning with our parents.' Seu reported this reply to Mencius, who said, 'Does Mr E really think that a man's affection for the child of his elder brother is [merely] like his affection for the child of his neighbour? What is to be taken hold of in that [expression] is simply this: – [that the people's offences are no more than] the guiltlessness of an infant, which, crawling, is about to fall into a well. Moreover, Heaven gives birth to creatures in such a way that they have [only] one root, while Mr E makes them to have two roots; – this is the cause [of his error].

4 'Indeed, in the most ancient times there were some who did not inter their parents, but [simply] took their dead bodies up and threw them into a ditch. Afterwards, when passing by them, [they saw] foxes and wild-cats devouring them, and flies and gnats gnawing at them. The perspiration started out upon their foreheads, and they looked away, because they could not bear the sight. It was not because of [what] other people [might say] that this perspiration flowed. The emotions of their hearts affected their faces and eyes, and so they went home, and returned with baskets and spades, and covered the [bodies]. If this covering them was indeed right, then filial sons and virtuous men must be guided by a certain principle in the burial of their parents.'

5 Seu informed Mr E of what Mencius had said. Mr E seemed lost in thought, and after a little said, 'He has instructed me.'

BOOK III

T'ĂNG WĂN KUNG

PART II

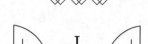

I

1   Ch'in Tae said [to Mencius], 'In not [going to] see any of the princes, you seem to me to be standing out on a small point. If now you were once to wait upon them, the result might be so great that you would make one of them king, or, if smaller, you might yet make one of them leader of the [other] princes. And moreover, the History says, "By bending only to the extent of one cubit, you make eight cubits straight." It appears to me like a thing which might be done.'

2   Mencius said, 'Formerly, duke King of Ts'e, [once] when he was hunting, called the forester to him by a flag. [The forester] would not come, and [the duke] was going to kill him. [With reference to this incident], Confucius said, "The resolute officer does not forget [that his end may be] in a ditch or stream; the brave officer does not forget that he may lose his head." What was it [in the forester] that Confucius thus approved? He approved his not going [to the duke], when summoned by an article that was not appropriate to him. If one go [to see the princes] without waiting to be called, what can be thought of him?

3   'Moreover, [that sentence,] "By bending to the extent of one cubit you make eight cubits straight," is spoken with reference to the gain [that may be got]. If gain be the rule, then we may seek it, I suppose, by bending to the extent of eight cubits to make one cubit straight.

4 'Formerly, the minister Chaou Këen made Wăng Lëang act as charioteer to his favourite He, and in the course of a whole day they did not get a single bird. The favourite He reported this result, saying, "He is the poorest charioteer in the world." Some one informed Wang Lëang of this, who said, "I beg to try again." By dint of pressing, he got this accorded to him, and in one morning they got ten birds. The favourite He [again] reported the result, saying, "He is the best charioteer in the world." The minister Këen said, "I will make him be the driver of your carriage;" but when he informed Wang Lëang of this, he refused, saying, "I [drove] for him, strictly observing the rules for driving, and in the whole day he did not get one bird. I [drove] for him so as deceitfully to intercept [the birds], and in one morning he got ten. The Book of Poetry says,

'No error in driving was committed,
And the arrows went forth like downright blows.'

I am not accustomed to drive for a mean man. I beg to decline the office."

5 '[Thus this] charioteer even was ashamed to bend improperly to the will of [such] an archer. Though by bending to it they would have caught birds and animals enough to form a hill, he would not do it. If I were to bend my principles and follow those [princes], of what course would my conduct be? Moreover you are wrong. Never has a man who has bent himself been able to make others straight.'

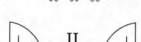

II

1   King Ch'un said [to Mencius], 'Are not Kung-sun Ten and Chang E really great men? Let them once be angry, and all the princes are afraid; let them live quietly, and the flames of trouble are extinguished throughout the kingdom.'

2   Mencius said, 'How can they be regarded as great men? Have you not read the Ritual [usages]; – "At the capping of a young man, his father admonishes him. At the marrying away of a daughter, her mother admonishes her, accompanying her to the door, and cautioning her in these words, 'You are going to your home. You must be respectful; you must be cautious. Do not disobey your husband.'" [Thus,] to look upon compliance as their correct course is the rule for concubines and wives.

3   'To dwell in the wide house of the world; to stand in the correct position of the world; and to walk in the great, path of the world; when he obtains his desire [for office], to practise his principles for the good of the people; and when that desire is disappointed, to practise them alone; to be above the power of riches and, honours to make dissipated, of poverty and mean condition to make swerve [from principle], and of power and force to make bend: – these characteristics constitute the great man.'

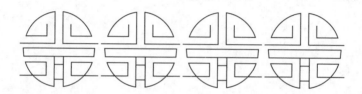

III

1 Chow Sëaou asked [Mencius], saying, 'Did superior men of old time take office?' Mencius said, 'They did.' The Record says, 'When Confucius was three months without [being employed by] some ruler, he looked disappointed and unhappy. When he passed over the boundary [of a State], he was sure to carry with him his proper gift of introduction.' Kung-ming E said, 'Among the ancients, when [an officer] was three months without [being employed by] some ruler, he was condoled with.'

2 [Sëaou said,] 'Did not this condoling, on being three months unemployed by a ruler, show a too great urgency?'

3 'The loss of his place,' was the reply, 'is to an officer like the loss of his State to a prince. It is said in the Book of Rites, "The prince ploughs [himself], and is afterwards assisted [by others], in order to supply the millet vessels [for sacrifice]. His wife keeps silk-worms and unwinds their cocoons, to make the robes [used in sacrificing]. If the victims be not perfect, the millet in the vessels not pure, and the robes not complete, he does not presume to sacrifice. And the scholar, who, [out of office], has no [holy] field, also does not sacrifice. The victims for slaughter, the vessels, and the robes, not being all complete, he does not presume to sacrifice, and then he does not presume to feel at ease and happy." Is there not in all this sufficient ground for condolence?'

4 [Sëaou again asked], 'What was the meaning of [Confucius'] always carrying his proper gift of introduction with him, when he passed over the boundary [of a State]?'

5 'An officer's being in office,' was the reply, 'is like the ploughing of a husbandman. Does a husbandman part with his plough because he goes from one State to another?'

6 [Sëaou] pursued, 'The kingdom of Tsin is one, as well as others, of official employments, but I have not heard of any being thus earnest about being in office in it. If there should be this urgency about being in office, why does a superior man make any difficulty about taking it?' [Mencius] replied, 'When a son is born, what is desired for him is that he may have a wife; and when a daughter is born, what is desired for her is that she may have a husband. This is the feeling of the parents, and is possessed by all men. [If the young people], without waiting for the orders of the parents and the arrangements of the go-betweens, shall bore holes to steal a sight of each other, or get over the wall to be with each other, then their parents and all other people will despise them. The ancients did indeed always desire to be in office, but they also hated being so by any but the proper way. To go [to see the princes] by any but the proper way is of a class with [young people's] boring holes.'

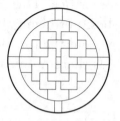

IV

1   P'ăng Kăng asked [Mencius], saying, 'Is it not an extravagant procedure to go from one prince to another and live upon them, followed by several tens of carriages and attended by several hundred men?' Mencius replied, 'If there be not a proper ground [for taking it], a single bamboo-cup of rice should not be received from a man; if there be such a ground for it, Shun's receiving from Yaou all under heaven is not to be considered excessive? Do you think it was excessive?'

2   [Kăng] said, 'No. [But] for a scholar performing no service to receive his support notwithstanding is improper.'

3   [Mencius] answered, 'If you do not have an intercommunication of the productions of labour and an interchange of [men's] services, so that [one from his] overplus may supply the deficiency of another, then husbandmen will have a superfluity of grain, and women a superfluity of cloth. If you have such an interchange, then cabinetmakers, builders, wheel-wrights, and carriage-builders may all get their food from you. Here is a man, who, at home, is filial, and, abroad, respectful to his elders; and who watches over the principles of the ancient kings to be ready for [the use of] future learners: – and yet he will not be able to get his support from you. How is it that you give honour to the cabinet-makers, and the others I have mentioned, and slight him who practises benevolence and righteousness.'

4   [P'ăng Kăng] said, 'The aim of the cabinet-maker and others of his class, is [by their trades] to seek for a living; – is it also the aim of the superior man, in his practice of the principles [you mention], to seek for a living?' 'What have you to do with his aim?' was the reply. 'He renders services to you. He deserves to be supported, and you support him? And [let me ask], – do you remunerate his man for his intention? or do you remunerate him for his service?' [To this Kang] replied, 'I remunerate him for his intention.'

5   [Mencius] said, 'There is a man here who breaks your tiles, and draws [unsightly] ornaments on your walls, his purpose being thereby to seek for his living; but will you indeed remunerate him?' 'No,' was the reply; and [Mencius then] concluded, Then, it is not for his purpose that you remunerate a man, but for the work done.'

1   Wan Chang said [to Mencius], 'Sung is a small State; but [its ruler] is now setting about to practise the [true] royal government, and Ts'e and Ts'oo hate and attack him; – what is to be done in the case?'

2 Mencius said, 'When T'ang dwelt in Poh, he adjoined to [the State of] Koh, the earl of which was living in a dissolute state, and neglecting [his proper] sacrifices. T'ang sent messengers to ask why he did not sacrifice, and when he said that he had no means of supplying the [necessary] victims, T'ang caused sheep and oxen to be sent to him. The earl, however, ate them, and still continued not to sacrifice. T'ang again sent messengers to ask him the same question as before, and when he said that he had no meatis of supplying the vessels of millet, T'ang sent the people of Poh to go and till the ground for him, while the old and feeble carried their food to them. The earl led his people to intercept those who were thus charged with spirits, cooked rice, millet and paddy, and took their stores from them, killing those who refused to give them up. There was a boy with millet and flesh for the labourers, who was thus killed and robbed. What is said in the Book of History, "The earl of Koh behaved as an enemy to the provision-carriers," has reference to this.

3 'Because of his murder of this boy, [T'ang] proceeded to punish him. All within the four seas said, "It is not because he desires the riches of the kingdom, but to avenge the common men and women."

4 'When T'ang began his work of executing justice, he commenced with Koh; and though he punished eleven [States], he had not an enemy under heaven. When he pursued his work in the east, the rude tribes in the west murmured. So did those in the north, when he pursued it in the south. Their cry was, "Why does he make us last?" The people's longing for him was like their longing for rain in a time of great drought. The frequenters of the markets stopped not; those engaged in weeding made no change [in their operations]. While he punished their rulers, he consoled the people. [His progress was] like the falling of opportune rain, and the people were delighted. It is said in the Book of History, "We have waited for our prince. When our prince comes, we shall escape the misery [under which we suffer]."

5 'There being some who would not become the subjects [of Chow, king Woo] proceeded to punish them on the east. He gave tranquillity to [their people, both] men and women, who [welcomed him] with baskets full of their dark and yellow silks, [saying,] "From henceforth [we shall serve] our king of Chow, and be made happy by him." So they gave in their adherence as subjects to the great State of Chow. The men of station [of Shang] took baskets full of dark and yellow silks, to meet the men of station [of Chow], and the lower classes of the one met those of the other with bamboo-cups of cooked rice and vessels of congee. [Woo] saved the people from the midst of fire and water, seizing only their oppressors, [and destroying them].

6 'It is said in "The Great Declaration:" – "My military prowess is displayed, and I enter his territories, and will seize the oppressor. My execution and punishment of him shall be displayed, more glorious than the work of T'ang."

7 '[Sung] is not practising royal government, as you say among other things about it. If it were practising royal government, all within the four seas would be lifting up their heads, and looking for [its king], wishing to have him for their ruler. Great as Ts'e and Ts'oo are, what would there we to fear from them?'

VI

1 Mencius said to Tae Puh-shing, 'Do you indeed, Sir, wish your king to be virtuous? Well, I will plainly tell you [how he may be made so]. Suppose that there is here a great officer of Ts'oo, who wishes his son to learn the speech of Ts'e, will he employ a man of Ts'e as his tutor, or a man of Ts'oo?' 'He will employ a man of Ts'e to teach him,' was the reply, and [Mencius] went on, 'If [but] one man of Ts'e be teaching him, and there be a multitude of men of Ts'oo shouting out about him, although [his father] beat him every day, wishing him to learn the speech of Ts'e, it will be impossible for him to do so. [But] in the same way, if he were to be taken and placed for several years in the Chwang [street], or the Yoh [quarter], although [his father] should beat him every day, wishing him to speak the language of Ts'oo, it would be impossible for him to do so.

2   'You say that Sëeh Keu-chow is a scholar of virtue, and you have got him placed in attendance on the king. If all that are in attendance on the king, old and young, high and low, were Sëeh Keu-chows, whom would the king have to do evil with? [But] if those that are in attendance on the king, old and young, high and low, are all not Sëeh Keu-chows, whom will the king have to do good with? What can one Sëeh Keu-chow do alone for the king of Sung?'

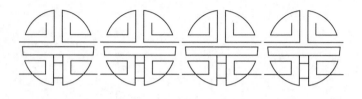

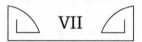

VII

1   Kung-sun Ch'ow asked [Mencius], saying, 'What is the point of righteousness in your not going to see the princes?' Mencius said, 'Anciently, if one had not been a minister [in the State], he did not go to see [the ruler].

2   'Twan Kan-muh leaped over a wall to avoid [the prince]; Sëeh Lëw shut the door and would not admit him. These two, however, [carried their scrupulosity] to excess. When a prince is urgent, it is not improper to see him.

3 'Yang Ho wished to get Confucius to go to see him, but disliked [that he should be charged himself with] any want of propriety. [As it was the rule, therefore, that] when a great officer sends a gift to a scholar, if the latter be not at home to receive it, he must go and make his acknowledgments at the gate of the other, Yang Ho watched when Confucius was out and sent him a steamed pig. Confucius, in his turn, watched when Ho was out, and went to pay his acknowledgments to him. At that time Yang Ho had taken the initiative; – how could [Confucius] avoid going to see him?

4 'The philosopher Tsăng said, "Those who shrug up their shoulders and laugh in a flattering way toil harder than the summer [labourer in the] fields." Tsze-loo said, "There are those who will talk with people with whom they have no agreement. If you look at their countenances, they are full of blushes, and are not such as I [care to] know." By looking at the matter in the light of these remarks, [the spirit] which the superior man nourishes may be known.'

VIII

1 Tae Ying-che said [to Mencius], 'I am not able at present and immediately to do with a tithe [only], and abolish [at the same time] the duties charged at the passes and in the markets. With your leave I will lighten all [the present extraordinary exactions] until next year, and then make an end of them. What do you think of such a course?'

2   Mencius said, 'Here is a man who every day appropriates the fowls of his neighbours that stray to his premises. Some one says to him, "Such is not the way of a good man," and he replies, "With your leave I will diminish my appropriations, and will take only one fowl a month, until next year, when I will make an end of the practice altogether."

3   'If you know that the thing is unrighteous, then put an end to it with all despatch; – why wait till next year?'

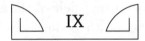

IX

1   The disciple Kung-too said [to Mencius], 'Master, people beyond [our school] all say that you are fond of disputing. I venture to ask why you are so.' Mencius replied, 'How should I be fond of disputing? But I am compelled to do it.

2   'A long period has elapsed since this world [of men] received its being, and there have been [along its history] now a period of good order, and now a period of confusion.

3   'In the time of Yaou, the waters, flowing out of their channels, inundated all through the States, snakes and dragons occupied the country, and the people had no place where they could settle themselves. In the low grounds they made [as it were] nests for themselves, and in the high grounds they made caves. It is said in the Book of History, "The vast waters filled me with dread." What are called "the vast waters" were those of the [above] great inundation.

4   '[Shun] employed Yu to reduce the waters to order. He dug open the ground [which impeded their flow], and led them to the sea. He drove away the snakes and dragons, and forced them into the grassy marshes. [On this] the waters pursued their course in their channels, – [the waters of] the Këang, the Hwae, the Ho, and the Han. The [natural] difficulties and obstructions being thus removed, and the birds and beasts which had injured the people having disappeared, men found the plains [available for them], and occupied them.

5   'After the death of Yaou and Shun, the principles of [those] sages fell into decay. Oppressive rulers arose one after another, who pulled down the houses [of the people] to make ponds and lakes, so that the people could nowhere rest in quiet, and threw fields out of cultivation to form gardens and parks, so that the people could not get clothes and food. [Afterwards], corrupt speakings and oppressive deeds also became rife; gardens and parks, ponds and lakes, thickets and marshes were numerous; and birds and beasts made their appearance. By the time of Chow, all under heaven was again in a state of great confusion.

6   'The duke of Chow assisted king Woo, and destroyed Chow. He attacked Yen, and in three years put its ruler to death. He drove Fei-lëen to a comer by the sea, and slew him. The States which he extinguished amounted to fifty. He drove far away the tigers, leopards, rhinoceroses, and elephants. All under heaven were greatly pleased. It is said in the Book of History, "How great and splendid were the plans of king Wǎn! How greatly were they carried out by the energy of king Woo. They are for the help and guidance of us their descendants, – all in principle correct, and deficient in nothing."

7 '[Again] the world fell into decay, and principles faded away. Perverse speakings and oppressive deeds again became rife. There were instances of ministers who murdered their rulers, and of sons who murdered their fathers.

8 'Confucius was afraid and made the Ch'un Ts'ëw. What the Ch'un Ts'ëw contains are matters proper to the son of Heaven. On this account Confucius said, "It is the Ch'un Ts'ëw which will make men know me, and it is the Ch'un Ts'ëw which will make men condemn me."

9 '[Once more] sage kings do not arise, and the princes of the States give the reins to their lusts. Unemployed scholars indulge in unreasonable discussions. The words of Yang Choo and Mih Teih fill the kingdom. [If you listen to] people's discourses throughout it, [you will find that] if they are not the adherents of Yang, they are those of Mih. Yang's principle is – "Each one for himself;" which leaves no place for duty to the ruler. Mih's principle is – "To love all equally" which leaves no place for the peculiar affection due to a father. But to acknowledge neither ruler nor father is to be in the state of a beast. Kung-ming E said "In their stalls there are fat beasts, and in their stables there are fat horses, but their people have the look of hunger, and in the fields there are those who have died of famine. This is leading on beasts to devour men." If the principles of Yang and Mih are not stopped, and the principles of Confucius are not set forth, then those perverse speakings will delude the people and stop up [the path of] benevolence and righteousness. When benevolence and righteousness are stopped up, beasts will be led on to devour men, and men will devour one another.

10 'I am alarmed by these things, and address myself to the defence of the principles of the former sages. I oppose Yang and Mih, and drive away their licentious expressions, so that such perverse speakers may not be able to show themselves. When [their errors] spring up in men's minds, they are hurtful to the conduct of affairs. When they are thus seen in their affairs, they are hurtful to their government. When a sage shall again arise, he will certainly not change [these] my words.

11 'Formerly, Yu repressed the vast waters [of the inundation], and all under the sky was reduced to order. The duke of Chow's achievements extended to the wild tribes of the east and north, and he drove away all ferocious animals, so that the people enjoyed repose. Confucius completed the Spring and Autumn, and rebellious ministers and villainous sons were struck with terror.

12 'It is said in the Book of Poetry,

"He smote the tribes of the west and the north;
He punished King and Shoo;
And no one dared to resist us."

These father-deniers and king-deniers would have been smitten by the duke of Chow.

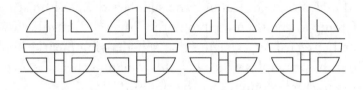

13 'I also wish to rectify men's hearts, and to put an end to [those] perverse speakings, to oppose their one-sided actions, and banish away their licentious expressions; – and thus carry on the [work of the] three sages. Do I do so because I am fond of disputing? I am constrained to do it.

14 'Whoever can by argument oppose Yang and Mih is a disciple of the sages.'

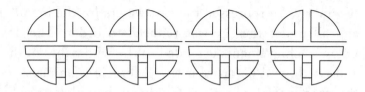

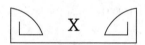

1 K'wang Chang said [to Mencius], 'Is not Mr Ch'in Chung a man of true self-denying purity? He was living in Woo-ling, and for three days was without food, till he could neither hear nor see. Over a well there grew a plum tree, a fruit of which had been, more than half of it, eaten by worms. He crawled to it, and tried to eat [some of this fruit], when, after swallowing three mouthfuls, he recovered his sight and hearing.'

2 Mencius replied, 'Among the scholars of Ts'e I must regard Chung as the thumb [among the fingers]. But still, how can he be regard od as having that self-denying purity? To carry out the principles which beholds, one must become an earth-worm, for so only can it be done.

3   'Now an earth-worm eats the dry mould above, and drinks the yellow spring below. Was the house in which Mr Chung lives built by a Pih-e? or was it built by a robber like Chih? Was the grain which he eats planted by a Pih-e? or was it planted by a robber like Chih? These are things which cannot be known.'

4   'But' said [Chang], 'what does that matter? He himself weaves sandals of hemp, and his wife twists hempen threads, which they exchange [for other things].'

5   [Mencius] rejoined, 'Mr Chung belongs to an ancient and noble family of Ts'e. His elder brother Tae received from Kah a revenue of 10,000 *chung*, but he considered his brother's emolument to be unrighteous, and would not dwell in the place. Avoiding his brother, and leaving his mother, he went and dwelt in Woo-ling. One day afterwards, he returned [to their house], when it happened that some one sent his brother a present of a live goose. He, knitting his brows, said, "What are you going to use that cackling thing for?" By-and-by, his mother killed the goose, and gave him some of it to eat. [Just then] his brother came into the house and said, "It's the flesh of that cackling thing," on which he went out, and vomited it.

6   'Thus what his mother gave him he would not eat, but what his wife gives him he eats. He will not dwell in his brother's house, but he dwells in Woo-ling. How can he in such circumstances complete the style of life which he professes? With such principles as Mr Chung holds, [a man must be] an earth-worm, and then he can carry them out.'

BOOK IV

LE LOW

PART I

I

1 Mencius said, 'The power of vision of Le Low, and the skill of hand of Kung-shoo, without the compass and square, could not form squares and circles. The acute ear of the [music]-master Kwang, without the pitch-tubes, could not determine correctly the five notes. The principles of Yaou and Shun, without a benevolent government, could not secure the tranquil order of the kingdom.

2 'There are now [princes] who have benevolent hearts and a reputation for benevolence, while yet the people do not receive any benefits from them, nor will they leave any example to future ages; – all because they do not put into practice the ways of the ancient kings.

3 'Hence we have the saying, "Goodness alone is not sufficient for the exercise of government; laws alone cannot carry themselves into practice."

4 'It is said in the Book of Poetry,

"Erring in nothing, forgetful of nothing,
Observing and following the old statutes."

Never has any one fallen into error who followed the laws of the ancient kings.

5   'When the sages had used all the power of their eyes, they called in to their aid the compass, the square, the level, and the line; and the ability to make things square, round, level, and straight was inexhaustible. When they had used all the power of their ears, they called in the aid of the pitch-tubes; and the ability to determine correctly the five notes was inexhaustible. When they had used all the thoughts of their hearts, they called in to their aid a government that could not bear [to witness the suffering of] men; and their benevolence overspread all under heaven.

6   'Hence we have the saying, "To raise a thing high we must begin from [the top of] a mound or a hill; to dig to a [great] depth, we must commence in [the low ground of] a stream or a marsh." Can he be pronounced wise who, in the exercise of government, does not start from the ways of the ancient kings.

7   'Therefore only the benevolent ought to be in high stations. When a man destitute of benevolence is in a high station, he thereby disseminates his wickedness among tie multitudes [below him].

8   'When the ruler has not principles by which he examines [his administration], and his ministers have no laws by which they keep themselves [in the discharge of their duties], then in the court obedience is not paid to principle, and in the office obedience is not paid to rule. Superiors violate [the laws of] righteousness, and inferiors violate the penal laws. It is only by a fortunate chance that a State in such a case is preserved.

9 'Therefore it is said, "It is not the interior and exterior walls being incomplete, nor the supply of weapons offensive and defensive not being large, which constitutes the calamity of a State. It is not the non-extension of the cultivable area, nor the non-accumulation of stores and wealth, which is injurious to a State." When superiors do not observe the rules of propriety, and inferiors do not learn [anything better], then seditious people spring up, and [that State] will perish in no time.

10 'It is said in the Book of Poetry,

"Heaven is now producing such movements; –
Do not be so indifferent."

11 '"Indifferent," that is, careless and dilatory.

12 'And so may [those officers] be deemed who serve their ruler without righteousness, who take office and retire from office without regard to propriety, and in their words disown the ways of the ancient kings.

13 'Therefore it is said, "To urge one's ruler to difficult achievements should be called showing respect for him; to set before him what is good and repress his perversities should be called showing reverence for him. [He who does not do these things, but says to himself], My ruler is incompetent to this, should be said to play the thief with him."'

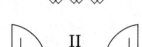

II

1   Mencius said, 'The compass and square produce perfect circles and squares. By the sages the human relations are perfectly exhibited.

2   'He who, as a ruler, would perfectly discharge the duties of a ruler, and he who, as a minister, would perfectly discharge the duties of a minister, have only to imitate, – the one Yaou, and the other Shun. He who does not serve his ruler as Shun served Yaou does not reverence his ruler, and he who does not rule the people as Yaou ruled them injures his people.

3   'Confucius said, "There are but two courses, that of benevolence and its opposite."

4   '[A ruler] who carries the oppression of his people to the highest pitch will himself be slain, and his State will perish. If one stop short of the highest pitch, his life will be in danger, and his State will be weakened. He will be styled "The Dark" or "The Cruel;" and though he may have filial sons and affectionate grandsons, they will not be able in a hundred generations to change [the designation].

5   'This is what is intended in the words of the Book of Poetry,

"The beacon of Yin is not far distant; –
It is in the age of the [last] sovereign of Hëa."'

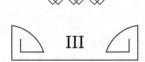

III

1   Mencius said, 'It was by benevolence that the three dynasties gained the kingdom, and by not being benevolent that they lost it.

2   'It is in the same way that the decaying and flourishing, the preservation and perishing, of States are determined.

3   'If the son of Heaven be not benevolent, he cannot preserve [all within] the four seas [from passing from him]. If a feudal prince be not benevolent, he cannot preserve his altars. If a noble or great officer be not benevolent, he cannot preserve his ancestral temple. If a scholar or common man be not benevolent, he cannot preserve his four limbs.

4   'Now they hate death and ruin, and yet delight in not being benevolent; – this is like hating to be drunk, and yet being strong [to drink] spirits.'

IV

1   Mencius said, 'If a man love others, and no [responsive] affection is shown to him, let him turn inwards and examine his own benevolence; if he [is trying to] rule others, and his government is unsuccessful, let him turn inwards and examine his own wisdom. If he treats others politely and they do not return his politeness, let him turn inwards and examine his own [feeling of] respect.

2   'If we do not by what we do realize [what we desire], we should turn inwards, and examine ourselves in every point. When a man is himself correct, all under heaven will turn to him [with recognition and submission].

3   'It is said in the Book of Poetry,

"Always strive to accord with the will [of Heaven];
So shall you be seeking for much happiness."'

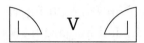

V

1   Mencius said. 'People have this common saying – "The kingdom, the State, the clan." The root of the kingdom is in the State; the root of the State is in the clan; the root of the clan is in the person.'

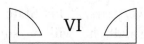

VI

1   Mencius said, 'The administration of government is not difficult; it lies in not offending against the great Houses. He whom the great Houses affect will be affected by the whole State; and he whom a whole State affects will be affected by all under heaven. When this is the case, [such an one's] virtue and teachings will spread over [all within] the four seas like the rush of water.'

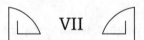

VII

1   Mencius said, 'When right government prevails throughout the kingdom, [princes of] little virtue are submissive to those of great, and [those of] little worth to [those of] great. When bad government prevails, the small are submissive to the large, and the weak to the strong. Both these cases are [the law of] Heaven. They who accord with Heaven are preserved; they who rebel against Heaven perish.

2   'Duke King of Ts'e said, "Not to be able to command [others], and further to refuse to receive their commands, is to cut one's-self off from all intercourse with them." His tears flowed forth, and he gave his daughter in marriage to [the prince of] Woo.

3   'Now the small States take for their models the large States, but are ashamed to receive their commands; – this is like scholars being ashamed to receive the commands of their master.

4   'For [a prince] who is ashamed of this, the best plan is to make king Wăn his model. Let one take king Wăn as his model and in five years, if his State be large, or in seven years, if it be small, he will be sure to give law to all under heaven.

5   'It is said in the Book of Poetry,

"The descendants of [the sovereigns of] Shang
Were more in number than a hundred thousand;
But when God gave the command,
They became subject to Chow.

'They became subject to Chow.
The appointment of Heaven is not constant.
The officers of Yin, admirable and alert,
Assist at the libations in our capital."

Confucius said, "As [against so] benevolent [a ruler, the multitudes] could not be deemed multitudes." If the ruler of a State love benevolence, he will have no opponent under heaven.

6 'Now-a-days, they wish to have no opponent under heaven, but [they do] not [seek to attain this] by being benevolent; – this is like trying to hold a heated substance, without having dipped it in water. It is said in the Book of Poetry,

"Who can hold anything hot?
Must he not dip it [first] in water?"'

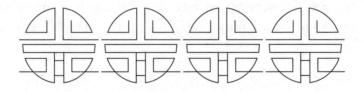

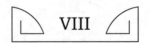

VIII

1 Mencius said, 'How is it possible to speak with [princes] who are not benevolent? Their perils they count safety, their calamities they count profitable, and they delight in the things by which they are going to ruin. If it were possible to talk with them who [so] violate benevolence, how should we have such ruin of States and destruction of families?

2   'There was a boy singing,

      "When the water of the Ts'ang-lang is clear,
      It does to wash the strings of my cap;
      When the water of the Ts'ang-lang is muddy,
      It does to wash my feet."

3   'Confucius said, "Hear what he says, my children: – when clear, to wash the cap strings; when muddy, to wash the feet." [This different application] is brought [by the water] on itself.

4   'A man must [first] despise himself, and then others will despise him. A family must [first] overthrow itself, and then others will overthrow it. A State must [first] smite itself, and then others will smite it.

5   'This is illustrated by the passage in the T'ae-këah, "Calamities sent by Heaven may be avoided; but when we bring on the calamities ourselves, it is not possible to live."'

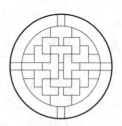

IX

1 Mencius said, 'Këeh and Chow's losing the kingdom arose from their losing the people; and to lose the people means to lose their hearts. There is a way to get the kingdom; – get the people, and the kingdom is got. There is a way to get the people; – get their hearts, and the people are got. There is a way to get their hearts; – 'it is simply to collect for them what they desire, and not to lay on them what they dislike.

2 'The people turn to a benevolent [rule] as water flows downwards, and as wild beasts run to the wilds.

3 'Accordingly [as] the otter aids the deep waters, driving the fish to them, and [as] the hawk aids the thickets, driving the little birds to them, [so] did Këeh and Chow aid T'ang and Woo, driving the people to them.

4 'If among the present rulers throughout the kingdom there were one who loved benevolence, all the [other] princes would aid him by driving the people to him. Although he wished not to exercise the royal sway, he could not avoid doing so.

5 'The case of [one of the] present [princes] wishing to attain to the royal sway is like the having to seek for mugwort three years old to cure a seven years' illness. If it have not been kept in store, the whole life may pass without getting it. If [the princes] do not set their minds on a benevolent [government], all their days will be in sorrow and disgrace, till they are involved in death and ruin.

6   'This is illustrated by what is said in the Book of Poetry,

"How can you [by your method] bring a good state of affairs
    about?
You [and your] advisers will sink together in ruin."ß'

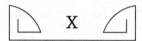

1   Mencius said, 'With those who do violence to themselves it
is impossible to speak. With those who throw themselves
away it is impossible to do anything. To disown in his conversation propriety and righteousness is what we mean by saying
of a man that he does violence to himself; that [he says], "I
am not able to dwell in benevolence and pursue the path of
righteousness is what we meant by saying of a man that he
throws himself away."

2   'Benevolence is the tranquil habitation of man, and righteousness is his straight path.

3   'Alas for those who leave the tranquil dwelling empty and
do not reside in it, and who neglect the straight path and
do not pursue it!'

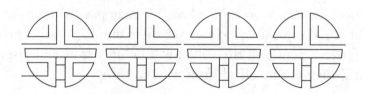

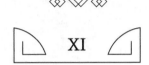

XI

1   Mencius said, 'The path [of duty] is in what is near, and [men] seek for it in what is remote. The work [of duty] is in what is easy, and [men] seek for it in what is difficult. If each man would love his parents, and show the due respect to his elders, all-under-heaven good order would prevail.'

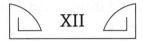

XII

1   When those occupying inferior situations do not obtain the confidence of their superior, they cannot succeed in governing the people. There is a way to obtain the confidence of the superior; – if one is not trusted by his friends, lie will not obtain the confidence of his superior. There is a way to being trusted by one's friends; – if one do not serve his parents so as to make them pleased, he will not be trusted by his friends. There is a way to make one's parents pleased; – if one on turning his thoughts inwards finds a want of sincerity, he will not give pleasure to his parents. There is a way to the attainment of sincerity in one's-self; – if a man do not understand what is good, he will not attain to sincerity in himself.

2   'Therefore sincerity is the way of Heaven; and to think [how] to be sincere is the way of man.'

3   'Never was there one possessed of complete sincerity who did not move [others]. Never was there one without sincerity who yet was able to move others.'

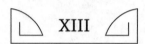

XIII

1 Mencius said, 'Pih-e, that he might avoid Chow, was dwelling on the coast of the northern sea. When he heard of the rise of king Wăn, he roused himself and said, "Why should I not attach myself to him? I have heard that the chief of the West knows well how to nourish the old." T'ae-kung, that he might avoid Chow, was dwelling on the west coast of the eastern sea. When he heard of the rise of king Wăn, he roused himself and said, "Why should I not attach myself to him? I have heard that the chief of the West knows well how to nourish the old."

2 'These two old men were the greatest old men in the kingdom. When they attached themselves to [king Wăn] it waft [like] all the fathers in the kingdom taking his side. When the fathers of the kingdom joined him, to whom could the sons go?

3 'Were any of the princes to practise the government of king Wăn, within seven years he would be sure to be giving law to all under heaven.'

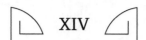

XIV

1   Mencius said, 'K'ëw acted as chief officer to the Head of the Ke family, whose [evil] ways he was unable to change, while he exacted from the people double the grain which they had formerly paid. Confucius said, "He is no disciple of mine. Little children, beat the drum and assail him."

2   'Looking at the subject from this case, [we perceive that] when a ruler who was not practising benevolent government, all [his ministers] who enriched him were disowned by Confucius; – how much more [would he have disowned] those who are vehement to fight [for their ruler]. Some contention about territory is the ground on which they fight, and they slaughter men till the fields are filled with them; or they fight for the possession of some fortified city, and slaughter men till the walls are covered with them. This is what is called "leading land on to devour human flesh." Death is not enough for such a crime.

3   'Therefore those who are skilful to fight should suffer the highest punishment. Next to them [should be punished] those who unite the princes in leagues; and next to them, those who take in grassy wastes, and impose the cultivation of the ground [upon the people].'

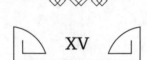

XV

1   Mencius said, 'Of all the parts of a man's [body] there is none more excellent thau the pupil of the eye. The pupil cannot [be used to] hide a man's wickedness. If within the breast [all] be correct, the pupil is bright; if within the breast [all] be not correct, the pupil is dull.

2   'Listen to a man's words, and look at the pupil of his eye; – how can a man conceal [his character]?'

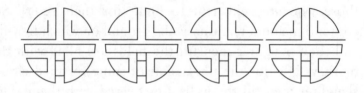

XVI

1   Mencius said, 'The courteous do not insult others, and the economical do not plunder others. The ruler who treats men with insult and plunders them is only afraid that they will not prove submissive to him; – how can he be regarded as courteous or economical? How can courtesy and economy be made out of tones of the voice and a smiling manner?'

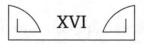

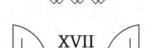

1 Shun-yu K'Wăn said, 'Is it the rule that males and females shall not allow their hands to touch in giving or receiving anything?' Mencius replied, 'It is the rule.' 'If a man's sister-in-law be drowning,' asked K'Wan, 'shall he rescue her by the hand?' [Mencius] said, 'He who would not [so] rescue his drowning sister-in-law would be a wolf. For males and females not to allow their hands to touch in giving and receiving is the [general] rule; to rescue by the hand a drowning sister-in-law is a peculiar exigency.'

2 [K'wăn] said, 'Now the whole kingdom is drowning; and how is it that you, Master, will not rescue it?'

3 [Mencius] replied, 'A drowning kingdom must be rescued by right principles, as a drowning sister-in-law has to be rescued by the hand. Do you. Sir, wish me to rescue the kingdom with my hand?'

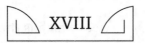

1 Kung-sun Ch'ow said, 'Why is it that the superior man does not [himself] teach his son?'

2 Mencius replied, 'The circumstances of the case forbid its being done. A teacher must inculcate what is correct. Doing this, and his lesson not being learned, he follows it up with being angry; and through thus being angry, he is offended, contrary to what should be, [with his pupil]. [At the same time, the pupil] says, "My master inculcates on me what is correct, and he himself does not proceed in a correct path." Thus father and son would be offended with each other, but when father and son come to be offended with each other, the case is evil.

3 'The ancients exchanged sons, and one taught the son of another.

4 'Between father and son there should be no reproving ' admonitions as to what is good. Such reproofs lead to alien-ation; and then alienation there is nothing more inauspicious.'

XIX

1 Mencius said, 'Of services which is the greatest? The service of parents is the greatest. Of charges which is the greatest? The charge of one's self is the greatest. That those who do not fail to keep themselves are able to serve their parents is what I have heard. [But] I have never heard of any who, having failed to keep themselves, were able [notwithstanding] to serve their parents.

2 'Everything [done] is a service, but the service of parents is the root of all others. Everything [obligatory] is a charge, but the charge of one's self is the root of all others.

3 'Tsăng-tsze, in nourishing Tsăng Seih, was always sure to have spirits and flesh provided. And when they were about to be removed, he would ask respectfully to whom [what was left] should be given. If [his father] asked whether there was anything left, he was sure to say, "There is." After the death of Tsăng Seih, when Tsăng Yuen came to nourish Tsăng-tsze, he was sure to have spirits and flesh provided; but when the things were about to be removed, he did not ask to whom [what was left] should be given, and if [his father] asked whether there was anything left, he would answer, "No"; – intending to bring them on again. This was what is called – "nourishing the mouth and body." We may call Tsăng-tsze's practice – "nourishing the will."

4 'To serve one's father as Tsăng-tsze served his may [be pronounced filial piety].'

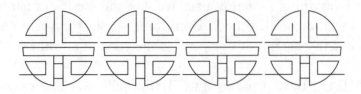

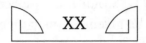

XX

1 Mencius said, 'It is not enough to reprove [a ruler] on account of [his mal-employment of] men, nor to blame [errors of] government. It is only the great man who can correct what is wrong in the ruler's mind. Let the ruler be benevolent, and all [his acts] will be benevolent. Let the ruler be righteous, and all [his acts] will be righteous. Let the ruler be correct, and everything will be correct. Once rectify the ruler, and the State will be firmly settled.'

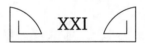

XXI

1 Mencius said, 'There are cases of praise which could not have been expected, and of reproach where the parties have been seeking to be perfect.'

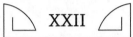

XXII

1 Mencius said, 'Men's being ready with their worries arises simply from their not having been reproved.'

2 Mencius said, 'The evil with men is that they like eachers of others.'

XXIV

1 The disciple Yoh-ching went in the train of Tsze-gaou to Ts'e.

2 He came to see Mencius, who said to him, 'Are you, Sir, also come to see me?' 'Master, why do you use such words?' was the reply. 'How many days have you been here?' asked [Mencius]. 'I came [only] yesterday,' said [the other]. 'Yesterday! Then is it not with reason that I thus speak?' 'My lodging-house was not arranged,' urged [Yoh-ching]. 'Have you heard,' said [Mencius] 'that a scholar's lodging-house must be arranged before he visits his master?'

3 [Yoh-ching] said, 'I have done wrong.'

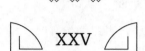

XXV

1   Mencius, addressing the disciple Yoh-ching, said, 'Your coming here in the train of Tsze-gaou was only [because of] the food and the drink [that you would so get]. I could not have thought that you, Sir, having learned the ways of the ancients, would have acted with a view to eating and drinking.'

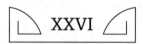

XXVI

1   Mencius said, 'There are three things which are unfilial, and to have no posterity is the greatest of them.

2   'Shun married without informing his parents because of this, – lest he should have no posterity. Superior men consider that his doing so was the same as if he had informed them.'

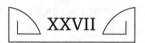

XXVII

1   Mencius said, 'The richest fruit of benevolence is this, – the service of one's parents. The richest fruit of righteousness is this, – the service of one's elder brother.

2   'The richest fruit of wisdom is this, – the knowing those two things and not departing from them. The richest fruit of propriety is this, – the ordering and adorning those two things. The richest fruit of music is this, – the joying in those two things. When joyed in, they grow. Growing, how can they be repressed? When they come to this state that they cannot be repressed, then unconsciously the feet begin to dance and the hands to move.'

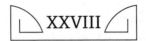

XXVIII

1   Mencius said, '[Suppose the case of] all under heaven turning with great delight to an individual to submit to him. To regard all under heaven [thus] turning to him with delight but as a bundle of grass; – only Shun was capable of this. [He considered that] if [one] could not get [the hearts of] his parents he could not be considered a man, and if he could not get to an entire accord with his parents, he could not be considered a son.

2   'By Shun's completely fulfilling the duty of serving parents, Koo-sow was brought to feel delight [in what was good]. When Koo-sow was brought to feel delight [in what was good], all under heaven were transformed. When Koo-sow was brought to feel delight [in what was good], all fathers and sons under heaven were established [in their respective duties]. This may well be called great filial piety.'

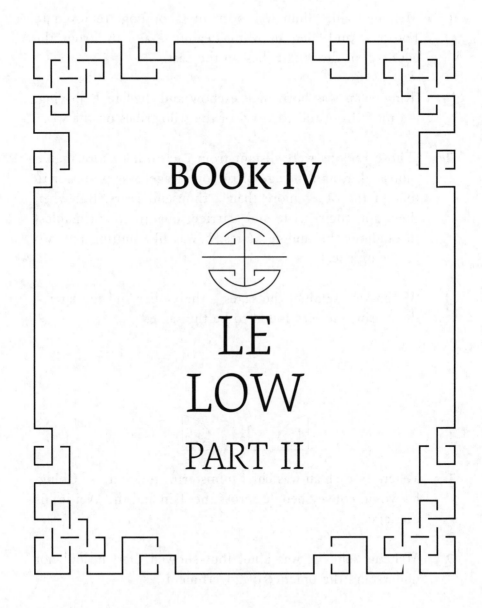

BOOK IV

LE
LOW

PART II

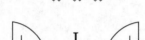

1   Mencius said, 'Shun was born in Choofung, removed to Foo-hea, and died in Ming-t'ëaou; – a man [from the country] of the wild tribes on the east.

2   'King Wăn was born in K'e-chow and died in Peih-ying; – a man [from the country] of the wild tribes on the west.

3   'Those regions were distant from each other more than a thousand *le*, and the age of the one [sage] was posterior to that of the other more than a thousand years. But when they got their wish and carried out [their principles] throughout the middle States, it was like uniting the two halves of a seal.

4   'When we examine] the sages – the earlier and the later – their principles are found to be the same.'

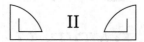

1   When Tsze-ch'an was chief minister of the State of Ch'ng, he would convey people across the Tsin and the Wei in his carriage.

2   Mencius said, 'It was kind, [but showed that] he did not understand the practice of government.

3 'In the eleventh month of the year the foot-bridges should be completed, and the carriage-bridges in the twelfth month, and the people will [then] not have the trouble of wading.

4 'Let a governor conduct his rule on the principles of equal justice, and he may cause people to be removed out of his path when he goes abroad; but how can he convey everybody across the rivers?

5 'Thus if a governor will [try] to please everybody, he will find the days not sufficient [for his work].'

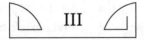

III

1 Mencius addressed himself to king Seuen of Ts'e, saying, 'When a ruler regards his ministers as his hands and feet, they regard him as their belly and heart; when he regards them as his dogs and horses, they regard him as they do any ordinary man; when he regards them as the ground or as grass, they regard him as a robber and an enemy.'

2 The king said, 'According to the rules of propriety, [a minister] should wear mourning [when he hears of the death of] a ruler whose service he had left; – how must [the ruler] have regarded him that [the minister] shall thus wear mourning for him?'

3 Mencius said, 'The admonitions [of a minister] having been followed and his advice listened to, so that blessings have descended on the people, if for some cause he leaves [the State], the ruler sends an escort to conduct him beyond the boundaries, and also sends before him [a recommendatory notice of him] to the State to which he is proceeding. When he has been gone three years and does not return, [only] then does he take back his fields and residence. This treatment is what we call "a thrice-repeated display of consideration." When a ruler acts thus, mourning will be worn [on hearing of his death].

4 'Now-a-days the remonstrances of a minister are not followed, and his advice is not listened to, so that no blessings descend on the people. When for any cause he leaves the State, the ruler tries to seize and hold him as a prisoner. He also pushes him to extremity in the State to which he has gone, and on the day of his departure he takes back his fields and residence. This treatment shows [the ruler] to be what we call "a robber and an enemy;" – how can mourning be worn for "a robber and an enemy"?'

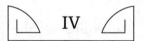

IV

1 Mencius said, 'When inferior officers are put to death, without any crime, it is [time] for the great officers to leave [the State]. When the people are slaughtered without any cause, it is [time] for the inferior officers to remove.'

1   Mencius said, 'If the ruler be benevolent, all will be benevolent; if the ruler be righteous, all will be righteous.'

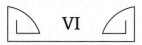

1   Mencius said, 'Acts of propriety which are not [really] proper, and acts of righteousness which are not [really] righteous, the great man does not do.'

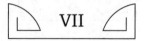

1   Mencius said, 'Those who keep the Mean train up those who do not, and those who have ability train up those who have not, and therefore men rejoice in having fathers and elder brothers of virtue and talent. If those who keep the Mean spurn those who do not, and those who have ability spurn those who have not, then the space between them – those who have the virtue and talents and those who are inferior to them – will not amount to an inch.'

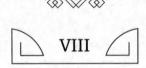

VIII

1 Mencius said, 'When men have what they will not do, they are prepared to act in what they do do [with effect].'

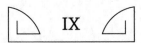

IX

1 Mencius said, 'What future misery are they sure to have to endure who talk of what is not good in others!'

X

1 Mencius said, 'Chung-ne did not do extraordinary things.'

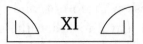

XI

1 Mencius said, 'The great man does not think before hand of his words that they shall be sincere, nor of his actions that they shall be resolute; – he simply [speaks and does] what is right.'

1 Mencius said, 'The great man is he who does not lose his child's heart.'

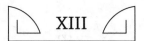

1 Mencius said, 'The nourishment of the living is not fit to be accounted the great thing. It is only in performing their obsequies when dead that we have what can be considered the great thing.'

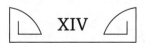

1 Mencius said, 'The superior man makes profound advances [in what he is learning], and by the proper course, wishing to get hold of it as in himself. Having got hold of it in himself, he abides in it quietly and firmly. Abiding in it quietly and firmly, he reposes a deep reliance on it. Reposing a deep reliance on it, he lays hold of it on the right and left, meeting with it as a fountain [from which things flow]. It is on this account that the. superior man wishes to get hold of [what he is learning] in himself.'

XV.

1   Mencius said, 'In learning extensively and setting forth minutely [what is learned], [the object of the superior man] is to go back and set forth in brief what is essential.'

XVI

1   Mencius said, 'Never has he who would by his excellence subdue men been able to subdue them. Let [a ruler seek] by his excellence to nourish men, and he will be able to subdue all under heaven. It is impossible that one should attain to the true royal sway to whom the hearts of all under heaven are not subject.'

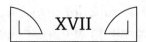
XVII

1   Mencius said, 'Words which are not true are [all] inauspicious, but those which are most truly obnoxious to the charge of being inauspicious are those which throw into the shade men of talents and virtue.'

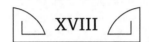

XVIII

1   The disciple Seu said, 'Chung-ne often praised water, saying, "O water! O water!" What did he find in water [to praise]?'

2   Mencius replied, 'How the water from a spring gushes out! It rests not day nor night. It fills up every hole, and then advances, flowing on to the four seas. Such is water having a spring. It was this which he found in it [to praise].

3   'But suppose that [the water] has no spring. In the seventh and eighth months the rain collects, and the channels in the fields are all filled, but their being dried up again may be expected in a short time. Thus it is that a superior man is ashamed of a reputation beyond the fact [of his merits].'

XIX

1   Mencius said, 'That whereby man differs from the animals is but small. The mass of men cast it away, while superior men preserve it.

2   'Shun clearly understood the multitude of things, and closely observed the relations of humanity. He walked along the path of benevolence and righteousness, and did not pursue [as by any effort] benevolence and righteousness.'

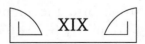

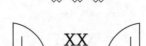

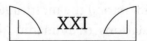
XX

1 Mencius said, 'Yu hated the pleasant wine, and loved good words.

2 'T'ang held fast the Mean, and employed men of talents and virtue wherever they came from.

3 'King Wan looked on the people as he would do with affectionate interest] on a man who was wounded; he looked towards the right path as [earnestly as] if he did not see it.

4 'King Woo did not disregard the near, nor forget the distant.

5 'The duke of Chow desired to unite in himself [the virtues of those] kings, [the founders of the] three [dynasties], that he might display in his practice [those] four things [which they did]. If [in his practice] there was anything which did not agree with them, he looked up and thought of it, from day-time into the night; and when he was fortunate enough to master [the difficulty], he sat waiting for the morning.'

XXI

1 Mencius said, 'The traces of true royal rule were extinguished, and [the royal] odes ceased to be produced. When those odes ceased to be produced, then the Ch'un Ts'ëw was made.

2 'The Shing of Tsin, the T'aou-wuh of Ts'oo, and the Ch'un Ts'ëw of Loo were [books] of the same character.

3 'The subjects [of the Ch'un Ts'ëw] are Hwan of Ts'e and Wan of Tsin, and its style is the historical. Confucius said, "Its righteous decisions I ventured to make."'

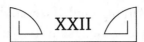

XXII

1 Mencius said, 'The influence of a sovereign sage terminates in the fifth generation. The influence of one who is merely a sage does the same.

2 'I could not be a disciple of Confucius himself, but I have endeavoured to cultivate my virtue by means of others [who were].'

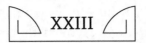

XXIII

1 Mencius said, 'When it appears proper to take [a thing], and [afterwards] not proper, to take it is contrary to moderation. When it appears proper to give [a thing], and [afterwards] not proper, to give it is contrary to kindness. When it appears proper to sacrifice one's life, and [afterwards] not proper, to sacrifice it is contrary to bravery.'

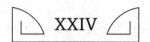

XXIV

1   P'ang Mung learned archery of E. When he had completely acquired all the method of E, thinking that under heaven only E was superior to himself, he slew him, Mencius said, 'In this case E also was to blame. Kungming E [indeed] said, "It would appear that E was not to be blamed," but he [only] meant that the blame attaching to him was slight; – how can he be held to have been without any blame?

2   'The people of Ch'ing sent Tsze-choh Yu-tsze to make an incursion into Wei, which. sent Tu Knng-sze to pursue him. Tsze-choh Tu-tsze said, "To-day I feel unwell, and cannot hold my bow; – I am a dead man." [At the same time] he asked his driver who was his pursuer; and being told that it was Yu Kung-sze, he said, "I shall live." The driver said, "Yu Kung-sze is the best archer of Wei, what do you mean by saying that you shall live?" "Yu Kung-sze," replied he, "learned archery from Yin Kung-t'o, who again learned it from me. Yin Kung-t'o is an upright man, and the friends of his selection must be upright [also]." When Yu Kung-sze came up, he said, "Master, why are you not holding your bow?" [Yu-tsze] answered, "To-day I am feeling unwell, and am unable to hold my bow." [Kung-sze] said, "I learned archery from Yin Kung-t'o, who again learned it from you. I cannot bear to injure you with your own science. The business of today, however, is my ruler's business, which I dare not neglect." He then took an arrow and knocked off the steel against his carriage-wheel. [In this way] he discharged four of them, and turned back.'

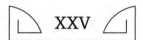

1 Mencius said, 'If the lady Se had been wearing a filthy head-dress, people would all have stopped their noses in passing her.

2 'Though a man be wicked, yet, if he adjust his thoughts, fast, and bathe, he may sacrifice to God.'

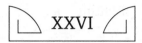

1 Mencius said, 'All who speak of the natures [of things], have in fact only their phenomena [to reason from], and the value of a phenomenon is in its being natural.

2 'What I hate in your wise men is their chiselling out [their conclusions]. If those wise men would act as Yu did when he conveyed away the waters, there would be nothing to dislike in their wisdom. The way in which Yu conveyed away the waters was by doing that which gave him no trouble. If your wise men would also do that which gave them no trouble, their wisdom would also be great.

3 'There is heaven so high; there are the stars and zodiacal spaces so distant. If we have investigated their phenomena, we may, while sitting [in our places], ascertain the solstices for a thousand years [past].'

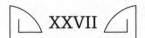

XXVII

1   The officer Kung-hăng having in hand the funeral of his son, the master of the Right went to condole with him. When [this noble] entered the door, some motioned to him to come to them, and spoke with him, and others went to his place and spoke with him.

2   Mencius did not speak with him, on which the master of the Right was displeased, and said, 'All the gentlemen have spoken with me. There is only Mencius who has not spoken with me, thereby slighting me.'

3   When Mencius heard of this remark, he said, 'According to the prescribed rules, in the court we must not change our places to speak with one another, and must not pass out of our own rank to bow to one another. I was wishing to observe these rules; – is it not strange that Tsze-gaou should think I Was thereby slighting him?'

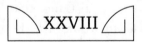

XXVIII

1   Mencius said, 'That wherein the superior man is different from other men is what he preserves in his heart; – namely, benevolence and propriety.

2   'The benevolent man loves others; the man of propriety shows respect to others.

3 'He who loves others is always loved by them, and he who respects others is always respected by them.

4 'Here is a man who treats me in a perverse and unreasonable manner; – [as] a superior man, I will turn round upon myself, [and say,] "I must have been wanting in benevolence; I must have been devoid of propriety; – how [else] should this have happened to [me]?"

5 'Having thus examined myself, I am [specially] benevolent, and [specially] observant of propriety. If the perversity and unreasonableness, of the other be still the same, [as] a superior man [I will say], "I must have been failing to do my utmost."

6 'I again turn round upon myself, and proceed to do my utmost. If the perversity and unreasonableness of the other be still the same, [as] a superior man, I will say, "This is a man utterly lost indeed. Since he conducts him so, there is nothing to choose between him and a beast; why should I go to trouble myself about a beast?"

7   'Thus it is that the superior man has a life-long anxiety, but not one morning's serious trouble. As to what is matter of anxiety to him, he has it [thus]: – "Shun," [he says,] "was a man, and I also am a man. Shun gave an example to all under heaven, and [his conduct] was fit to be handed down to future ages, while I am nothing better than a villager." This indeed is proper matter of anxiety to him; but in what way is he anxious? Simply that he maybe like Shun. As to what would be matter of serious trouble to a superior man, there is no such thing. He does nothing which is contrary to benevolence; he does nothing which is not according to propriety. Should there be one morning's trouble, as a superior man he does not reckon it a trouble.'

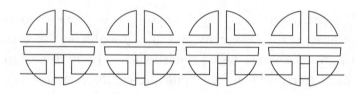

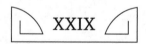

XXIX

1   Yu and Tseih, in an age of tranquillizing [government], thrice passed their doors without entering them. Confucius praised them.

2   Yen-tsze, in an age of disorder, dwelt in a mean narrow lane, having his single bamboo-dish of rice, and his single gourd-cup of water. Other men could not have endured the distress, but he did not allow his joy to be affected by it. Confucius [also] praised him.

3   Mencius said, 'Yu, Tseih, and Yen Hwuy agreed in the principles of their conduct.

4   'Yu thought that if any one under heaven were drowned, it was as if he himself drowned him. Tseih thought that if any one under heaven suffered hunger, it was as if he himself famished him. It was on this account that they were so earnest.

5   'If Yu and Tseih, and Yen-tsze could have exchanged places, they would have done each what the other did.

6   'Here now in the same apartment with you are people fighting; and [you wish to] part them. Though you were to part them with your cap tied on over your hair unbound, your conduct would be allowable.

7   'If the fighting were [only] in your village or neighbourhood, and you were to go to part them with your cap [so] tied on over your hair unbound, you would be in error. Though you were to shut your door [in such a case], your conduct would be allowable.'

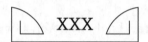

1   The disciple Kung-too said, 'Throughout the whole State, all pronounce K'wang Chang unfilial, and yet you, Master, keep company with him, and moreover treat him with politeness. I venture to ask why you do so.'

2   Mencius replied, 'There are five things which in the common parlance of the age are said to be unfilial. The first is laziness in the use of one's four limbs, so as not to attend to the maintenance of his parents. The second is gambling and chess-playing, and being fond of spirits, so as not to attend to the maintenance of one's parents. The third is being fond of goods and money, and being selfishly attached to one's wife and children, so as not to attend to the maintenance of one's parents. The fourth is following the desires of one's ears and eyes, so as to bring one's parents to disgrace. The fifth is being fond of bravery, fighting and quarrelling, so as to endanger his parents. Is Chang-tsze guilty of any one of these things?

3   'Between Chang-tsze and his father there arose disagreement, he, the son, reproving his father to urge him to what was good.

4   'To urge one another by reproofs to what is good is the way of friends. But such urging between father and son is the greatest injury to the kindly feeling [that should prevail between them].

5   'Did not Chang-tsze wish to have all that belongs to [the relationships] of husband and wife, child and mother? But because he had offended his father and was not permitted to approach him, he sent away his wife and draw forth his son, and would not for all [the rest of] his life receive any cherishing attentions from them. He settled it in his mind that, if he did not act in this way, his would be the greatest of crimes. Such and nothing more is the case of Chang-tsze.'

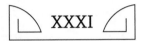

XXXI

1   When Tsăng-tsze dwelt in Woo-shing, there came [a band of] plunderers from Yueh. Some one said [to him], 'The plunderers are come; why not leave this?' [On this Tsăng-tsze left the city], saying [to the man in charge of his house], 'Do not let any one lodge in my house, lest he break and injure the plants and shrubs about it.' But when the plunderers were withdrawing [he sent word], saying, 'Repair the walls and roof of my house; I will return to it,' and when the plunderers had retired, he returned. His disciples said, 'Since our Master was treated with so much attention and respect, for him to be the first, on the arrival of the plunderers, to go away, so as to be observed by the people, and then, on their retiring, to return, seems to us to be improper.' Shin-yew Hăng said [to them], 'You do not understand this matter. Formerly, when [the house of us], the Shin-yëw, was exposed to the outbreak of the grass-carriers, there were seventy disciples in our Master's following, and none of them took any part in the matter.'

2   When Tsze-sze was living in Wei, there came plunderers from
Ts'e. Some one said to him, 'The plunderers are coming; why
not leave this?' [But] Tsze-sze said, 'If I go away, whom will
the ruler have with him to guard [the city]?'

3   Mencius said, 'Tsăng-tsze and Tsze-sze agreed in the principle of their conduct. Tsăng-tsze was a teacher; – in the
position of a father or elder brother. Tsze-sze was a minister;
– in a meaner position. If they could have exchanged places,
each would have done what the other did.'

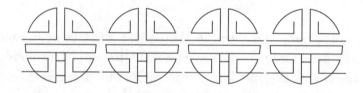

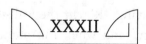

XXXII

1   The officer Ch'oo said [to Mencius], 'The king sent a person
to spy out whether you. Sir, were really different from other
men.' Mencius replied, 'How should I be different from other
men? Yaou and Shun were just the same as other men.'

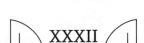

XXXII

1 'A man of Ts'e had a wife and a concubine, and lived together with them in his house. When their good-man went out, he was sure to get himself well filled with spirits and flesh and then return, and on his wife's asking him with whom he had been eating and drinking, they were sure to be all men of wealth and rank. The wife informed the concubine, saying, "When the good-man goes out, he is sure to come back having partaken plentifully of spirits and flesh, and when I ask him with whom he has been eating and drinking, they are all men of wealth and rank. And yet no men of distinction ever come [here]. I will spy out where our good-man goes." [Accordingly] she got up early in the morning, and privately followed the good-man to where he was going. All through the city there was nobody who stood and talked with him. At last he came to those who were sacrificing among the tombs outside the outer wall on the east, and begged what they had left. Not being satisfied, he looked round him and went to another party; – and this was the way in which he got himself satiated. His wife went home, and informed the concubine, saying, "It was to the good-man that we looked up in hopeful contemplation, and with whom our lot is cast for life; – and these are his ways." [On this] she and the concubine reviled their good-man, and wept together in the middle courtyard. [In the mean time] the good-man, knowing nothing of all this, came in with a jaunty air, carrying himself proudly to them.

2 'According to the view which a superior man takes of things,
as to the ways by which men seek for riches, honours, gain,
and advancement, there are few of their wives and concubines who might not be ashamed and weep together because
of them.'

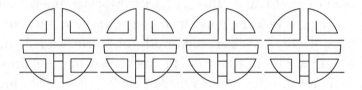

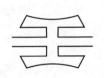

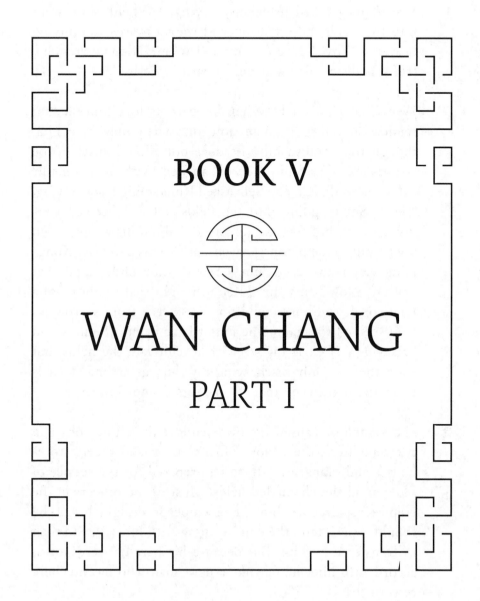

BOOK V

WAN CHANG

PART I

I

1 Wan Chang asked [Mencius], saying, '[When] Shun went into the fields, he cried out and wept towards the pitying heavens. Why did he cry out and weep?' Mencius replied, 'He was dissatisfied and full of earnest desire.'

2 Wan Chang pursued, 'When his parents love him, [a son] rejoices and forgets them not; and when they hate him, though they punish him, he does not allow himself to be dissatisfied. Was Shun then dissatisfied [with his parents]?' [Mencius said], 'Ch'ang Seih asked Kung-ming Kaou, saying, "As to Shun's going into the fields, I have received your instructions; but I do not understand about his weeping and crying out to the pitying heavens, and to his parents." Kung-ming Kaou answered him, "You do not understand that matter." Now Kung-ming Kaou thought that the heart of a filial son [like Shun] could not be so free from sorrow [as Seih seemed to imagine he might have been]. [Shun would be saying,] "I exert my strength to cultivate the fields, but I am thereby only discharging my duty as a son. What is there [wrong] in me that my parents do not love me?"

3 'The emperor caused his own [children], – nine sons and two daughters, the various officers, oxen and sheep, store-houses and granaries, [all] to be prepared for the service of Shun amid the channeled fields. Most of the officers in the empire repaired to him. The emperor designed that he should superintend the empire along with himself, and then to transfer it to him. But because his parents were not in accord with him, he felt like a poor man who has nowhere to turn to.

4 'To be an object of complacency to the officers of the empire is what men desire; but it was not sufficient to remove the sorrow of [Shun]. The possession of beauty is what men desire, – but though [Shun] had for his wives the two daughters of the emperor, it was not sufficient to remove his sorrow. Riches are what men desire, but though the empire was the rich property [of Shun], it was not enough to remove his sorrow. Honours are what men desire, but though [Shun] had the dignity of being the son of Heaven, it was not sufficient to remove his sorrow. The reason why his being the object of men's complacency, the possession of beauty, riches, and honours, could not remove his sorrow was because it could be removed only by his being in [entire] accord with his parents.

5 'The desire of a child is towards his father and mother, When he becomes conscious of [the attractions of] beauty, his desire is towards young and beautiful women. When he [comes to] have a wife and children, his desire is towards them. When he obtains office, his desire is towards his ruler; and if he cannot get the regard of his ruler, he burns within. [But] the man of great filial piety, all his life, has his desire towards his parents. In the great Shun I see the case of one whose desire was towards them when be was fifty years old.'

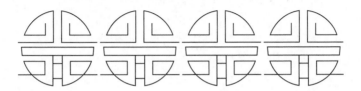

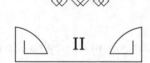

II

1   Wan Chang asked [Mencius], saying, 'It is said in the Book of Poetry,

"How do we proceed in taking a wife?
Announcement must [first] be made to our parents."

If [the rule] be indeed as thus expressed, no one ought to have illustrated it as well as Shun; – how was it that Shun's marriage took place without his informing [his parents]?' Mencius replied, 'If he had informed them, he would not have been able to marry. That mate and female dwell together is the greatest of human relations. If [Shun] had informed his parents, he must have made void this greatest of human relations, and incurred thereby their resentment. It was on this account that he did not inform them.'

2   Wan Chang said, 'As to Shun's marrying without making announcement [to his parents], I have heard your instructions. [But] how was it that the emperor gave him his daughters as wives without informing [his parents]?' [Mencius] said, 'The emperor also knew that, if he informed his parents, he could not have given him his daughters as wives.'

3   Wan Chang said, 'His parents set Shun to repair a granary, and then removed the ladder [by which he had ascended], [after which] Koo-sow set fire to it. They sent him to dig a well, [from which he managed to] get out; but they, [not knowing this,] proceeded to cover it up. [His brother] Sëang said, "Of this scheme to cover up the city-forming gentleman the merit is all mine. Let my parents have his oxen and sheep; let them have his granaries and storehouses. His shield and spear shall be mine; his lute shall be mine; his carved bow shall be mine; and I will make his two wives attend for me to my bed." Sëang then went away and entered Shun's house, and there was Shun upon a couch with his lute. Sëang said, "[I am come] simply because I was thinking anxiously about you," [and at the same time] he looked ashamed. Shun said to him, "There are all my officers; do you take the management of them for me." I do not know whether Shun was ignorant of Sëang's wishing to kill him.' [Mencius] replied, 'How could he be ignorant of it? But when Sëang was sorrowful, he was also sorrowful, and when Sëang was joyful, he was also joyful.'

4 [Wan Chang] continued, 'Then was Shun one who rejoiced hypocritically?' 'No,' was the reply. 'Formerly some one sent a present of a live fish to Tsze-ch'an of Ch'ing. Tsze-ch'an ordered his pond-keeper to feed it in the pond; but the man cooked it, and reported the execution of his commission, saying, "When I first let it go, it looked embarrassed. In a little it seemed to be somewhat at ease, and then it swam away as if delighted." "It had got into its element!" said Tsze-ch'an. "It had got into its element!" The pond-keeper went out and said, "Who calls Tsze-ch'an wise? When I had cooked and eaten the fish, he said, 'It has got into its element! It has got into its element!'" Thus a superior man may be imposed on by what seems to be as it ought to be, but it is difficult to entrap him by what is contrary to right principle. Sëang came in the way in which the love of his, elder brother would have made him come, and therefore Shun truly believed him, and rejoiced at it. What hypocrisy was there?'

III

1 Wan Chang said, 'Sëang made it his daily business to kill Shun; – why was it that, when [the latter] was raised to be the son of Heaven, he [only] banished him?' Mencius replied, 'He invested him with a State, and some have said that it was banishing him.'

2   Wan Chang said, 'Shun banished the superintendent of Works to Yëw-chow, sent away Hwan-tow to mount Ts'ung, slew the [prince of] San-mëaou in San-wei, and imprisoned K'wan on mount Yu. When those four criminals [were thus dealt with], all under heaven submitted to him; – it was a cutting off of men who were destitute of benevolence. But Sëang was [of all men] the most destitute of benevolence, and [Shun] invested him with the State of Pe; – of what crime had the people of Pe been guilty? Does a benevolent man really act thus? In the case of other men, he cut them off; in the case of his brother, he invested him with a State.' [Mencius] replied, 'A benevolent man does not lay up anger, nor cherish resentment, against his brother, but only regards him with affection and love. Regarding him with affection, he wishes him to enjoy honour; loving him, he wishes him to be rich. The investing him with Pe was to enrich and ennoble him. If while [Shun] himself was emperor, his brother had been a common man, could he have been said to regard him with affection and love?'

3   [Wan Chang said,] 'I venture to ask what is meant by some saying that it was a banishing [of Sëang]' [Mencius] replied, 'Sëang could do nothing [of himself] in his State. The emperor appointed all officer to manage its government, and to pay over its revenues to him; and therefore it was said that it was a banishing of him? How [indeed] could he be allowed the means of oppressing the people there? Nevertheless, [Shun] wished to be continually seeing him, and therefore he came unceasingly to court, as is signified in that expression, "He did not wait for the rendering of tribute, or affairs of government, to receive [the prince of] Pe."'

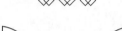

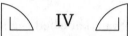

IV

1 Hëen-k'ëw Mung asked Mencius, saying, 'There is the old saying, – "An officer of complete virtue cannot be employed as a minister by his ruler, nor treated as a son by his father." Shun stood with his face to the south, and Yaou, at the head of all the feudal princes, appeared in his court with his face to the north. Koosow also appeared at Shun's court with his face to the north; and when Shun saw him, his countenance assumed a look of distress. Confucius said, "At this time the empire was in a perilous condition indeed! How unsettled was its state!" I do not know whether what is thus said really took place.' Mencius said, 'No. These are not the words of a superior man, but the sayings of an uncultivated person of the east of Ts'e. When Yaou was old, Shun took the management of affairs for him. It is said in the Canon of Yaou, "After twenty-eight years, Fang-heun demised, and the people mourned for him as for a parent three years. All within the four seas, the eight instruments of music were stopped and hushed." Confucius said, "There are not two suns in the sky, nor two sovereigns over the people. [If] Shun had already been [in the position of] the son of Heaven, and had moreover led on all the feudal princes of the empire to observe the three years' mourning for Yaou, there must in that case have been two sons of Heaven."'

2 Hëen-k'ëw Mung said, 'On the point of Shun's not employing Yaou as a minister, I have received your instructions. But it is said in the Book of Poetry,

"Under the wide heaven,
All is the king's land;

Within the sea-boundaries of the land,
All are the king's servants."

When Shun became emperor, I venture to ask how it was
that Koo-sow was not one of his servants.' [Mencius] replied,
'That ode is not to be understood in that way; – [it speaks
of] being laboriously engaged in the king's business, and not
being able to nourish one's parents, [as if the subject of it]
said, "This is all the king's business, but I alone am supposed
to have ability, and made to toil in it." Therefore those who
explain the odes must not insist on one term so as to do
violence to a sentence, nor on a sentence so as to do violence
to the general scope. They must try with their thoughts to
meet that scope, and then they will apprehend it. If we
simply take single sentences, there is that in the ode called
the "Yun Han,"

"Of the remnant of Chow, among the black-haired people,
There will not be half a man left."

If it had really been as thus expressed, then not an individual
of the people of Chow would have been left.

3   'Of all that a filial son can attain to, there is nothing greater
than his honouring his parents. Of what can be attained to
in honouring one's parents, there is nothing greater than
the nourishing them with the empire. To be the father of
the son of Heaven is the height of honour. To be nourished
with the empire is the height of nourishment. In this was
verified the sentiment in the Book of Poetry,

"Ever thinking how to be filial,
His filial mind was the model [which he supplied]."

4 'In the Book of History it is said, "With respectful service he appeared before Koo-sow, looking grave and awe-struck, till Koo-sow also was transformed by his example." This is the true case of [the scholar of complete virtue] not being treated as a son by his father.'

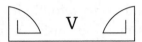

1 Wan Chang said, '[It is said that] Yaou gave the empire to Shun; was it so?' Mencius replied, 'No; the emperor cannot give the empire to another.'

2 'Yes; but Shun possessed the empire. Who gave it to him?' 'Heaven gave it to him' was the reply.

3 '"Heaven gave it to him;" did [Heaven] confer the appointment on him with specific injunctions?'

4 [Mencius] said, 'No; Heaven does not speak. It simply showed its will by his [personal] conduct, and by [his conduct of] affairs.'

5   '"It showed its will by his [personal] conduct, and by [his conduct of] affairs"' returned the other; – 'how was this?' [Mencius] said, 'The emperor can present a man to Heaven, but he cannot make Heaven give that man the empire. A feudal prince can present a man to the emperor [to take his place], but he cannot make the emperor give the princedom to that man. A great officer can present a man to his prince, but he cannot cause the prince to make that man a great officer [in his own room]. Anciently Yaou presented Shun to Heaven, and Heaven accepted him; he displayed him to the people, and the people accepted him. Therefore I say, "Heaven does not speak. It simply indicated its will by his [personal] conduct, and by [his conduct of] affairs."'

6   [Chang] said, 'I presume to ask how it was that [Yaou] presented Shun to Heaven, and Heaven accepted him, and displayed him to the people, and the people accepted him.' The reply was, 'He caused him to preside over the sacrifices, and all the Spirits were well pleased with them; thus it was that Heaven accepted him. He caused him to preside over the conduct of affairs, and affairs were well administered, so that all the people reposed under him; – thus it was that the people accepted him. Heaven gave [the empire] to him, and the people gave it to him. Therefore I said, "The emperor cannot give the empire to another."

7   'Shun assisted Yaou [in the government] for twenty and eight years; – this was more than man could have done, and was from Heaven. When the three years' mourning consequent on the death of Yaou were accomplished, Shun withdrew from the son of Yaou to the south of the southern Ho. The princes of the empire, however, repairing to court, went not to the son of Yaou, but to Shun. Litigants went not to the son of Yaou, but to Shun. Singers sang not the son of Yaou, but Shun. Therefore I said that it was Heaven [that gave him the empire]. It was after this that he went to the Middle State, and occupied the seat of the son of Heaven. If he had [before these things] taken up his residence in the palace of Yaou, and applied pressure to his son, it would have been an act of usurpation, and not the gift of Heaven.

8   'This view [of Shun's obtaining the empire] is in accordance with what is said in The Great Declaration, – "Heaven sees as my people see, Heaven hears as my people hear."'

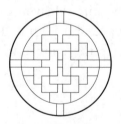

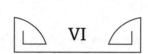

VI

1 Wan Chang said, 'People say, "When [the disposal of the empire] came to Yu, his virtue was inferior [to that of Yaou and Shun], and he did not transmit it to the worthiest, but to his son;" – was it so?'Mencius replied, 'No; it was not so. When Heaven gave [the empire] to the worthiest, it was given to the worthiest; when Heaven gave it to the son [of the preceding emperor], it was given to that son. Formerly Shun presented Yu to Heaven for [a period of] seventeen years; and when the three years' mourning, consequent on the death of Shun, were accomplished, Yu withdrew from the son of Yu to Yang-shing. The people of the empire followed him as, after the death of Yaou, they had not followed his son, but followed Shun. Yu presented Yih to Heaven for [a period of] seven years; and when the three years' mourning consequent on the death of Yu were accomplished, Yih withdrew from the son of Yu to the north of Mount Ke. [The princes] repairing to court, and litigants, went not to Yih, but to K'e, saying, "He is the son of our ruler." Singers did not sing Yih, but they sang K'o, saying, "He is the son of our ruler."

2   'That Tan-choo was not equal [to his father], and Shun's son also not equal [to his]; that Shun assisted Yaou, and Yu assisted Shun, for a period of many years, conferring benefits on the people for a long time; that K'e was virtuous and able, and could reverently enter into and continue the ways of Yu; that Yih assisted Yu for a period of few years, conferring benefits on the people not for a long time; that the length of time that Shun, Yu, and Yih [assisted in the government] was so different; and that the sons [of the emperors] were [one] a man of talents and virtue, and [the other two] inferior [to their fathers]: – all these things were from Heaven, and what could not be produced by man. That which is done without any one's [seeming] to do it is from Heaven. That which comes to pass without any one's [seeming] to bring it about is from Heaven.

3   'In the case of a private man's obtaining the empire, there must be in him virtue equal to that of Shun and Tu, and moreover there must be the presenting him to Heaven by the [preceding] emperor. It was on this [latter] account that Chung-ne did not obtain the kingdom.

4   'When the throne descends by natural succession, he who is displaced by Heaven must be like Keeh or Chow. It was on this account that Yih, E Yin, and the duke of Chow did not obtain the kingdom.

5 'E Yin assisted T'ang so that he became sovereign of the kingdom. After the demise of T'ang, T'ae-ting having died without being appointed [in his place], Waeping [reigned] two years, and Chung-jin four. T'ae-Këah [then] was turning upside down the canons and example of T'ang, and E Yin placed him in T'ung for three years. [There] he repented of his errors, was contrite, and reformed himself. In T'ung he came to dwell in benevolence and moved towards right-eousness, during those three years listening to the lessons given to him by E Yin, [after which] that minister again returned [with him] to Poh.

6 'The duke of Chow's not getting the kingdom was like that of Yih's not getting [the throne of] Hea, or E Yin's [that of] Yin.

7 'Confucius said, "T'ang and Yu resigned [the throne to the worthiest]; the founders of the Hëa, Yin, and Chow [dynas-ties] transmitted it to their sons. The principle of righteousness was the same in [all the cases]."'

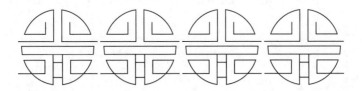

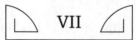

VII

1   Wan Chang asked [Mencius], saying, 'People say that E Yin sought [an introduction to] T'ang by his [knowledge of] cookery; – was it so?'

2   Mencius replied, 'No, it was not so. E Tin was farming in the lands of the State of Sin, delighting in the principles of Yaou and Shun. In any matter contrary to the righteousness which they prescribed, or to the course which they enjoined, though he had been salaried with the empire, he would not have regarded it; though there had been yoked for him a thousand teams, he would not have looked at them. In any matter contrary to the righteousness which they prescribed, or to the course which they enjoined, he would not have given nor taken [even] a single straw.

3   'T'ang sent persons with presents of silk to ask him to enter his service. With an air of indifference and self-satisfaction, he said, "What can I do with these silks with which T'ang invites me? Is it not best for me to abide in these channeled fields, and therein delight myself with the principles of Yaou and Shun?"

4 'T'ang thrice sent persons thus to invite him. After this, with the change of purpose displayed in his countenance, he spoke in a different style, saying, "Instead of abiding in the channeled fields, and therein delighting myself with the principles of Yaou and Shun; had I not better make this ruler one after the style of Yaou and Shun? had I not better make this people like the people of Yaou and Shun? had I not better in my own person see these things for myself?

5 '"Heaven's plan in the production of this people is this: – that they who are first informed, should instruct those who are later in being informed, and those who first apprehend [principles] should instruct those who are slower to do so. I am the one of Heaven's people who have first apprehended; I will take these principles and instruct this people in them. If I do not instruct them, who will do so?"

6 'He thought that among all the people of the kingdom, even the private men and women, if there were any that did not enjoy such benefits as Yaou and Shun conferred, it was as if he himself pushed them into a ditch. He took upon himself the heavy charge of all under Heaven in this way, and therefore he went to T'ang, and pressed upon him the duty of attacking Hëa, and saving the people.

7 'I have not heard of one who bent himself and at the same time made others straight; – how much less could one disgrace himself, and thereby rectify the whole kingdom? The actions of the sages have been different. Some have kept far away [from office], and others have drawn near to it; some have left [their offices], and others have not done so; that in which these different courses all meet, is simply the keeping of their persons pure.

8 'I have heard that E Yin sought [an introduction to] T'ang by the principles of Yaou and Shun; I have not heard that he did so by his [knowledge of] cookery.

9 'In the "Instructions of E" it is said, "Heaven, destroying [Këeh], commenced attacking him in the palace of Muh; we commenced in Poh."'

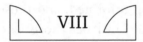

VIII

1 Wan Chang asked [Mencius], saying, 'Some say that Confucius in Wei lived with an ulcer-[doctor], and in Ts'e with Tseih Hwan, the chief of the eunuchs; was it so?' Mencius said, 'No, it was not so. Those are the inventions of men fond of [strange] things.

2 'In Wei he lived in the house of Yen Ch'ow-yëw. The wife of the officer Mei and the wife of Tsze-loo were sisters. Mei-tsze spoke to Tsze-loo, saying, "If Confucius will lodge with me, he may get to be a high noble of Wei."'Tsze-loo reported this to Confucius, who said, "That is as ordered [by Heaven]." Confucius advanced according to propriety, and retired according to righteousness. In regard to his obtaining [office and honour] or not obtaining them, he said "That is as ordered." But if he had lodged with an ulcer[-doctor] and with Tseih Hwan, the chief of the eunuchs, that would neither have been according to righteousness, nor any ordering [of Heaven].

3   'When Confucius, being dissatisfied in Loo and Wei, [had left those States], he met with the attempt of Hwan, the master of the Horse, in Sung, to intercept and kill him, so that he had to pass through Sung in the dress of a private man. At that time, [though] he was in circumstances of distress, he lodged in the house of Ching-tsze, the minister of works, who was [then] a minister of Chow, the marquis of Ch'in.

4   'I have heard that ministers in the service of a court may be known from those to whom they are hosts, and that ministers coming from a distance may be known from those with whom they lodge. If Confucius had lodged with an ulcer-[doctor] and with Tseih Hwan, the chief of the eunuchs, how could he have been Confucius?'

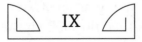

IX

1   Wan Chang asked [Mencius], saying, 'Some say that Pih-le He sold himself to a cattle-keeper of Ts'in for five sheep-skins, and fed his cattle for him, to seek an introduction to duke Muh of Ts'in; is this true?' Mencius said, 'No, it was not so. This is the invention of some one fond of [strange] things.

2   'Pih-le He was a man of Yu. The people of Ts'in by the inducement of a *peih* of Ch'uy-keih-and a team of Këuh-ch'an horses were asking liberty to march through Yu to attack Kwoh. Kung Che-k'e remonstrated [with the duke of Yu, asking him not to grant their request], but Pih-le He did not remonstrate.

3   'When he knew that the duke of Yu was not to be remonstrated with, and went in consequence from that State to Ts'in, he had reached the age of seventy. If by that time he did not know that it would be a disgraceful thing to seek for an introduction to duke Muh of Ts'in by feeding cattle, could he be called wise? But not remonstrating where it was of no use to remonstrate, could he be said not to be wise? Knowing that the duke of Yu would be ruined, and leaving his State before that event, he could not be said to be not wise. As soon as he was advanced in Ts'in, he knew that duke Muh was one with whom he could have a field for action, and became chief minister to him; – could he be said to be not wise? Acting as chief minister in Ts'in, he made his ruler distinguished throughout the kingdom, and worthy to be handed down to future ages; – if he had not been a man of talents and virtue, could he have done this? As to selling himself in order to bring about the destruction of his ruler, even a villager who had a regard for himself, would not do such a thing; – and shall we say that a man of talents and virtue did it?'

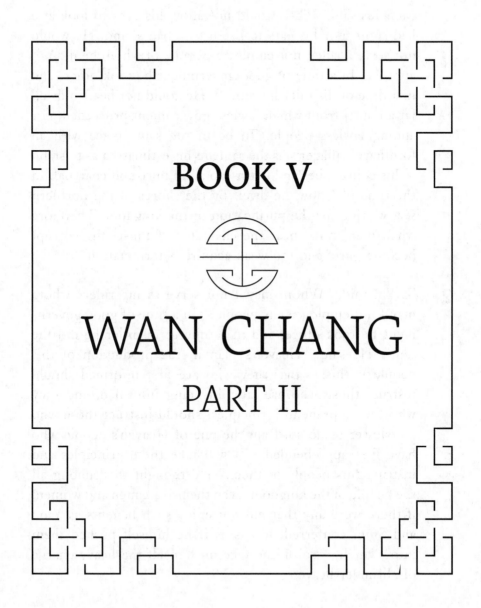

BOOK V

WAN CHANG

PART II

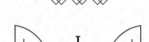

I

1   Mencius said, 'Pih-e would not allow his eyes to look at a bad sight, nor his ears to listen to a bad sound. He would not serve a ruler, nor employ a people, of whom he did not approve. In a time of good government he took office, and in a time of disorder he retired. He could not bear to dwell [at a court] from which lawless government proceeded, nor among lawless people. To be in the same place with an [ordinary] villager was the same in his estimation as to stand in his court robes and court cap amid mire and charcoal. In the time of Chow, he dwelt by the shores of the northern sea, waiting for the purification of the kingdom. Therefore when men [now] hear the character of Pih-e, the corrupt become pure, and the weak acquire determination.

2   'E Yin said, "Whom may I not serve as my ruler? whom may I not employ as my people?" In a time of good government he took office, and in a time of disorder he did the same. He said, "Heaven's plan in the production of this people is this: – that they who are first informed should instruct those who are later in being informed, and they who first apprehend [principles] should instruct those who are slower to do so. I am the one of Heaven's people who have first apprehended; – I will take these principles and instruct this people in them." He thought that among all the people of the kingdom, even the private men and women, if there were any that did not enjoy such benefits as Yaou and Shun conferred, it was as if he himself pushed them into a ditch; – so did he take on himself the heavy charge of all under heaven.

3   'Hwuy of Lëw-hëa was not ashamed to serve an impure ruler, nor did he decline a small office. When advanced to employment, he did not keep his talents and virtue concealed, but made it a point to carry out his principles. When neglected and left out of office, he did not murmur, and when straitened by poverty, he did not grieve. When in the company of village people, he was quite at ease and could not bear to leave them. [He would say], "You are you, and I am I. Though you stand by my side with bare arms and breast, how can you defile me?" Therefore when men [now] hear the character of Hwuy of Lëw-hëa, the mean become generous, and the niggardly become liberal.

4   'When Confucius was leaving Ts'e he took with his hands the water from the rice which was being washed in it, and went away [with the uncooked rice]. When he was about to leave Loo, he said, "I will go by and by;" – it was right he should leave the country of his parents in this way. When it was proper to go away quickly he did so; when it was proper to delay, he did so; when it was proper to keep in retirement, he did so; when it was proper to go into office, he did so; – this was Confucius.'

5   Mencius said, 'Pih-e among the sages was the pure one; E Yin was the one most inclined to take office; Hwuy of Lëw-hëa was the accommodating one; and Confucius was the timeous one.

6 'In Confucius we have what is called a complete concert. A complete concert is when the bell proclaims [the commencement of the music], and the [ringing] stone closes it. The metal sound commences the blended harmony [of all the instruments], and the winding up with the stone terminates that blended harmony. The commencing that harmony is the work of wisdom, and the terminating it is the work of sageness.

7 'As a comparison for wisdom, we may liken it to skill, and as a comparison for sageness, we may liken it to strength, as in the case of shooting at a mark a hundred paces distant. That you reach the mark is owing to your strength; his that you hit it is not owing to your strength.'

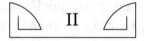

II

1 P'ih-kung E asked [Mencius], 'What was the arrangement of dignities and emoluments made by the House of Chow?'

2 Mencius said, 'The particulars of that arrangement cannot be learned, for the feudal princes, disliking them as injurious to themselves, have all made away with the records of them. Nevertheless I have learned the general outline of them.

3 'The SON OF HEAVEN was one dignity; the DUKE one; the MARQUIS one; the EARL one; and the VISCOUNT and BARON formed one, being of equal rank; – altogether making five degrees of dignity. The RULER was one dignity; the MINISTER one; the GREAT OFFICER one; the OFFICER OF THE FIRST CLASS one; the OFFICER OF THE SECOND CLASS one; and the OFFICER OF THE LOWEST CLASS one: – altogether making six grades.

4 'To the son of Heaven there was allotted a territory of a thousand *le* square; a duke and a marquis had each a hundred *le* square; an earl, seventy *le*; a viscount and a baron, fifty *le*. The assignments altogether were of four amounts. Where the territory did not amount to fifty *le*, the holder could not himself have access to the son of Heaven. His land was attached to some one of the feudal princes, and was called a FOO-YUNG.

5 'A high minister of the son of Heaven received an amount of territory equal to that of a marquis; a great officer, as much as an earl; and an officer of the first class, as much as a viscount or baron.

6 'In a great State, where the territory was a hundred *le* square, the ruler had ten times as much income as one of his high ministers; a high minister had four times as much as a great officer; a great officer twice as much as an officer of the first class; an officer of the first class, twice as much as one of the middle; and an officer of the middle class twice as much as one of the lowest. Officers of the lowest class, and such of the common people as were employed in the public offices, had the same emolument, – as much, namely, as what they would have made by tilling the fields.

7 'In a State of the next order, where the territory was seventy *le* square, the ruler had ten times as much income as one of his high ministers; a high minister, thrice as much as a great officer; a great officer, twice as much as an officer of the first class; an officer of the first class, twice as much as one of the second; and one of the second twice as much as one of the lowest. Officers of the lowest class and such of the common people as were employed in the public offices, had the same emolument, – as much, namely, as they would have made by tilling the fields.

8 'In a small State, where the territory was fifty *le* square, the ruler had ten times as much income as one of his high ministers; a high minister twice as much as a great officer; a great officer twice as much as an officer of the first class; an officer of the first class twice as much as one of the second; one of the second class twice as much as one of the lowest. Officers of the lowest class, and such of the common people as were employed in the public offices, had the same emol-ument, – as much, namely, as they would have made by tilling the fields.

9 'As to those who tilled the fields, each head of a family received a hundred *mow*. When these were manured, the [best] husbandmen of the first class supported nine individuals, and those ranking next to them supported eight. The [best] husbandmen of the second class supported seven men, and those ranking next to them supported six; while the lowest class [only] supported five. The salaries of the common people who were employed in the public offices, were regulated according to these differences.'

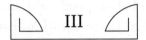

III

1 Wan Chang asked [Mencius], saying, 'I venture to ask about [the principles of] friendship.' Mencius replied, 'Friendship does not permit of any presuming on the ground of one's age, or station, or [the circumstances of] one's relations. Friendship [with a man] is friendship with his virtue, and there cannot be any presuming [on such things].

2 'The minister Măng Hëen was [chief of] a family of a hundred chariots, and he had five friends, – Yoh-ching K'ëw, Muh Ching and three [others whose names] I have forgotten. With these five men Hëen-tsze maintained a friendship, because they thought nothing about his family. If they had thought about his family, he would not have maintained his friendship with them.

3 'Not only has [the chief of] a family of a hundred chariots acted thus. The same has been exemplified even in the ruler of a small State. Duke Hwuy of Pe said, "I treat Tsze-sze as my master, and Yen Pan as my friend. As to Wang Shun and Ch'ang Seih, they serve me."'

4 'Not only has the ruler of a small State acted thus. The same thing has been exemplified by the ruler of a large State. There was Duke P'ing of Tsin with Hae T'ang: – when [T'ang] told him to come into his house, he came; when he told him to be seated, he sat; when he told him to eat, he ate. There might be only coarse rice, and soup of vegetables, but he always ate his fill, not daring to do otherwise. Here, however, [the duke] stopped, and went no farther. He did not call [T'ang] to share with him his Heavenly place, nor to administer with him his Heavenly office, nor to partake with him his Heavenly emolument. His conduct was a scholar's honouring of virtue and talent; not a king or a duke's honouring of them.

5 'Shun went up and had an interview with the emperor, and the emperor lodged him as his son-in-law in the second palace. He also partook of Shun's hospitality. He was host and guest alternately. This was the emperor maintaining friendship with a common man.

6 'Respect shown by inferiors to superiors is called giving to the noble the observance due to rank. Respect shown by superiors to inferiors is called giving honour to virtue and talents. The principle of righteousness is the same in both cases.'

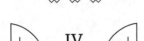

IV

1 Wan Chang asked [Mencius], saying, 'I venture to ask what [sentiment of the] mind is expressed in the gifts of courteous intercourse.' Mencius replied, '[The sentiment of] respect.'

2 'Why is it,' pursued the other, 'that to decline a gift decidedly is accounted disrespectful?' The answer was, 'When one of honourable rank presents a gift, to say [in the mind], "Was the way in which he got this righteous or not? I must know this before I receive it," – this is counted disrespectful, and therefore gifts are not declined.'

3 [Wan Chang] went on, 'Let me ask this: – If one do not in so many express words decline, the gift, but having declined it in his heart, saying, "He took it from the people, and it is not righteous," if he then assign some other reason for not receiving it, is not this a proper course?' Mencius said, 'When the donor offers it on the ground of reason, and his manner of doing so is according to propriety, in such a case Confucius would have received it.'

4   Wan Chang said, 'Here now is one who stops [and robs] people outside the city gates; – he offers his gift on a ground of reason, and presents it in accordance with propriety; – would the reception of the gift so acquired by robbery be proper?' [Mencius] said, 'It would not be proper. In the "Announcement to the Prince of K'ang" it is said "Where men kill others, or violently assault them, to take their property, being reckless and fearless of death, they are abhorred by all the people;" these are to be put to death without waiting to give them any lesson [or warning], Yin received [this rule] from Hea, and Chow received it from Yin; it cannot be questioned, and to the present day is clearly acknowledged. How can [the gift of a robber] be received?'

5   [Wan Chang] continued, 'The princes of the present day take from their people, as if they were [so many] robbers. But if they put a good face of propriety on their gifts, then the superior man receives them; – I venture to ask how you explain this?' [Mencius] replied, 'Do you think that if a true king were to arise, he would collect all the princes of the present day, and put them to death? Or would he admonish them, and then, when they did not change [their ways], put them to death? To say that [every one] who takes what does not properly belong to him is a robber is pushing a point of resemblance to the utmost, and insisting on the most refined idea of righteousness. When Confucius took office in Loo, the people struggled together for the game taken in hunting, and he also did the same. If that struggling for the captured game was allowable, how much more may the gifts [of the princes] be received!'

6   [Chang] urged, 'Then, when Confucius took office, was it not with the object that his principles should be carried into practice?' 'It was with that object,' was the reply. [The other said,] 'If the practice of his principles was his business, what had he to do with that struggling for the captured game?' [Mencius] answered, 'Confucius first rectified the vessels of sacrifice according to the registers, and [enacted] that being so rectified they should not be supplied with food gathered from every quarter.' 'But why did he not leave [the State]?' said [Chang]. [Mencius] replied, 'He would first make a trial [of carrying his principles into practice]. When this trial was sufficient [to show] they could be practised, and they were still not practised [on a larger scale], he would then go away. Thus it was that he never completed a residence [in any State] of three years.

7   'Confucius took office when he saw that the practice [of his principles] was possible; when the reception accorded to him was proper; and when he was supported by the State. In his relations with the minister Ke Hwan, he took office because he saw that the practice [of his principles] was possible. With the duke Ling of Wei he took office, because the reception accorded to him was proper. With duke Hëaou of Wei he took office, because he was maintained by the State.'

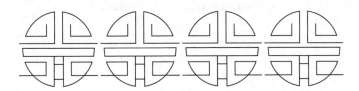

V

1   Mencius said, 'Office should not be [sought] on account of poverty, but there are times [when it may be sought] on that account. A wife should not be taken for the sake of being attended to by her, but there are times [when marriage may be entered on] with that view.

2   'He who takes office because of his poverty must decline an honourable situation, and occupy a poor one; he must decline riches and prefer a poor [sufficiency].

3   'What [office] will be in harmony with this declining an honourable situation and occupying a low one, with this declining riches and preferring a poor sufficiency? [Such an one] as that of being a gate-warder, or beating the watchman's stick.

4   'Confucius was once keeper of stores, and he [then] said, "My accounts must all be correct; that is all I have to think about." He was once in charge of the [ducal] lands, and he [then] said, "The oxen and sheep must be large, and fat, and superior. That is all I have to think about."

5   'When one is in a low station, to speak of high matters is a crime. To stand in the court of his prince, and his principles not be carried into practice, is a disgrace.'

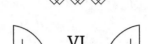

1   Wan Chang said, 'What is the reason that an officer [unemployed] does not look to a prince for his maintenance?' Mencius answered, 'He does not presume [to do so]. When one prince loses his State, and then throws himself on another for his maintenance, this is in accordance with propriety. But for [such an] officer to look to any of the princes for his maintenance is contrary to propriety.'

2   Wan Chang said, 'If the prince sends him a present of grain, will he receive it?' 'He will receive it,' was the answer. 'What is the principle of right in his receiving it?' [Mencius] said, 'Such is the relation between a ruler and his people that as a matter of course he should help them in their necessities.'

3   'What is the reason that [an officer unemployed will [thus] accept relief, but will not accept a [stated] bounty?' asked [Chang], and [Mencius] said, 'He does not presume [to do the latter].' 'Allow me to ask' urged the other, 'why he does not presume to do so.' The reply was, '[Even] the warder of a gate and the beater of a watchman's rattle have their regular duties for which they can take their support from their superiors; but he who without any regular office receives his superior's bounty must be deemed wanting in humility.'

4   [Chang again] said, 'When a ruler sends a present [to an officer unemployed], he accepts it; – I do not know whether this present may be constantly repeated.' [Mencius] answered, 'There was the way of duke Muh towards Tsze-sze: – He sent frequent inquiries after his health, and made frequent presents of cooked meat. Tsze-sze was displeased, and at last, having motioned to the messenger to go outside the great door, he bowed his head to the ground with his face to the north, then put his hands twice to the ground, and declined the present, saying, "From this time forth I shall know that the ruler supports me as a dog or a horse." And from this time an inferior officer was not sent with the present. When [a ruler] professes to be pleased with a man of talents and virtue, and can neither raise him to office nor support him [in the proper way], can he be said to be [really] pleased with his talents and virtue?'

5   [Chang] said, 'I venture to ask how the ruler of a State, when he wishes to support a superior man, must proceed that he may be said to do so [in the proper way].' [Mencius] answered, 'The present will [at first] be offered as by the ruler's commission, and [the superior man] will receive it, twice putting his hands to the ground, and then his head to the ground. After this, the store-keeper will continue to send grain, and the master of the kitchen to send meat, presenting it without any mention of the ruler's commission. Tsze-sze considered that the meat from the [ruler's] caldron, giving him the trouble of constantly doing obeisance, was not the way to support a superior man.

6 'There was the way of Yaou with Shun: – He caused his nine sons to serve him, and gave him his two daughters as wives; he caused the various officers, oxen and sheep, store-houses and granaries, [all] to be prepared to support Shun amid the channeled fields; and then he raised him to the most exalted station. Hence we have the expression – "The honouring of virtue and talents proper to a king or a duke."'

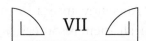

VII

1 Wan Chang said, 'I venture to ask what is the principle of right in not going to see the princes.' Mencius replied, '[A scholar unemployed], residing in the city, is called "a minister of the market-place and well"; one residing in the country is called "a minister of the grass and plants." In both cases he is a common man, and it is a rule of propriety that common men who have not presented the introductory present, and so become ministers [of the court], should not presume to have interviews with any of the princes.'

2 Wan Chang said, 'If a common man be called to perform any service, he goes and performs it. When a ruler wishes to see a scholar, and calls him, how is it that he does not go?' 'To go and perform the service is right; to go and see the ruler would not be right.

3 'And' [added Mencius] 'on what account is it that the prince wishes to see [the scholar]?' 'Because of his extensive information,' was the reply, 'or because of his talents and virtue.' 'If because of his extensive information,' said [Mencius], 'even the son of Heaven does not call [one thus fit to be] a teacher, and how much less may one of the princes do so! If because of his talents and virtue, I have not heard of any one's wishing to see a person with these qualities, and calling him to his presence.

4 'During the frequent interviews of duke Muh with Tsze-sze, he [once] said, "Anciently in States of a thousand chariots, their rulers, with all their resources, have been on terms of friendship with scholars; – what do you think of such cases?" Tsze-sze was displeased and said, "The ancients had a saying that, '[The scholar] should be served;' how should they have said merely that 'He should be made a friend of?' " Did not the displeasure of Tsze-sze say [in effect], "So far as station is concerned, you are ruler, and I am a subject; how should I presume to be on terms of friendship with my ruler? But in respect of virtue, you ought to make me your master; how can you be on terms of friendship with me?" [Thus], when a ruler of a thousand chariots sought to be on terms of friendship with a scholar, he could not obtain his wish, and how much less might he [presume to] call him [to his presence]!

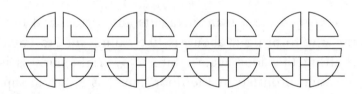

5   'Duke King of Ts'e [once] when he was hunting, called the forester to him with a flag. [The forester] refused to come, and the duke was going to kill him. [With reference to this incident, Confucius said,] "The resolute officer does not forget [that his end may be] in a ditch or in a stream; the bold officer does not forget that he may lose his head." What was it [in the forester] that Confucius [thus] approved? He approved his not going when summoned by an article which was not appropriate to him.'

6   [Chang] said, 'I venture to ask with what a forester should be called.' 'With a fur cap,' was the reply. 'A common man should be called with a plain banner; a scholar [who has taken office], with a flag having dragons embroidered on it; and a great officer, with one having feathers suspended from the top of the staff.

7   'When a forester is called with the article appropriate to the calling of a great officer, he would die rather than presume to go. When a common man is called with the article for the calling of a scholar [in office], how should he presume to go? How much more may we expect a man of talents and virtue to refuse to go, when he is called in a way unbecoming his character!

8 'To wish to see a man of talents and virtue, and not take the way to bring it about, is like calling him to enter and shutting the door against him. Now righteousness is the way, and propriety is the door, but it is only the superior man who can follow this way, and go out and in by this door. It is said in the Book of Poetry: –

"The way to Chow was like a whetstone
And straight as an arrow.
[So] the officers trod it,
And the common people looked on it."

9 Wan Chang said, 'When Confucius received his ruler's message calling him [to his presence], he went without waiting for his carriage to be yoked; did Confucius then do wrong?' [Mencius] replied, 'Confucius was in office, and had its appropriate duties devolving on him; and moreover he was called on the ground of his office.'

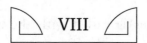

VIII

1 Mencius said to Wan Chang, 'The scholar whose excellence is most distinguished in a village will thereon make friends of the [other] excellent scholars of the village. The scholar whose excellence is most distinguished in a State will thereon make friends of the [other] excellent scholars of the State. The scholar whose excellence is most distinguished in the kingdom will thereon make friends of the [other] excellent scholars of the kingdom.

2 'When [a scholar] finds that his friendship with the excellent scholars of the kingdom is not sufficient [to satisfy him], he will ascend to consider the men of antiquity. He will repeat their poems, and read their books; and as he does not know whether they were as men all that was approvable, he will consider their history. This is to ascend and make friends [of the men of antiquity].'

IX

1 King Seuen of Ts'e asked about high ministers. Mencius said, 'Which high ministers is your Majesty asking about?' 'Are there differences among them?' said the king. 'Yes,' was the reply; 'there are high ministers who are noble, and relatives of the ruler, and there are those who are of a different surname from him.' 'Allow me to ask' said the king, 'about the high ministers who are noble, and relatives of the ruler.' [Mencius] answered, 'If the ruler have great faults, they ought to remonstrate with him; and if he do not listen to them, when they have done so again and again, they ought to appoint another in his place.'

2 The king looked moved, and changed countenance.

3 [Mencius] said, 'Let not your Majesty think [what I say] strange. You asked me, and I did not dare to reply but correctly.'

4   The king's countenance became composed, and he begged
     to ask about the high ministers who were of a different
     surname from the ruler. [Mencius] said, 'When the ruler
     has faults, they ought to remonstrate with him; and if he
     do not listen to them when they have done so again and
     again, they ought to leave [the State].'

BOOK VI

KAOU-TSZE

PART I

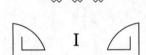

I

1 Kaou-tsze said, '[Man's] nature is like a willow tree, and righteousness is like a cup or a bowl. The fashioning benevolence and righteousness out of man's nature is like making cups and bowls from a willow tree.'

2 Mencius replied, 'Can you, in accordance with the nature of the willow tree, make cups and bowls from it? You will do violence and injury to the tree before you can make cups and bowls from it. If you will do violence and injury to the willow tree in order to make cups and bowls, will you also do violence and injury to a man, to fashion benevolence and righteousness [from him]? Your words, alas! would certainly with all men occasion calamity to benevolence and righteousness.'

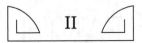

II

1 Kaou-tsze said, '[Man's] nature is like water whirling round [in a corner]. Open a passage for it on the east, and it will flow to the east; open a passage for it on the west, and it will flow to the west. Man's nature is indifferent to good and evil, just as water is indifferent to the east and west.'

2   Mencius replied, 'Water indeed will flow indifferently to the east or west, but will it flow indifferently up or down? The [tendency of] man's nature to goodness is like the [tendency of] water to flow downwards. There are none but have [this tendency to] goodness, [just as] water flows downwards.

3   'Now by striking water, and causing it to leap up, you may make it go over your forehead; and by damming and leading it, you may make it go up a hill; but are [such movements according to] the nature of water. It is the force applied which causes them. In the case of a man's being made to do what is not good, his nature is dealt with in this way.'

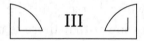

III

1   Kaou-tsze said, '[The phænomena of] life is what I call nature.'

2   Mencius replied, 'Do you say that life is nature just as you say that white is white?' 'Yes,' was the reply. [Mencius asked again], 'Is the whiteness of a white feather like the whiteness of white snow, and the whiteness of white snow like that of white jade?' 'Yes,' returned [the other].

3   Mencius retorted, 'Very well. Is the nature of a dog like the nature of an ox, and the nature of an ox like the nature of a man?'

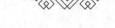
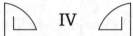

IV

1 Kaou-tsze said, '[To delight in] food and in sexual pleasure is nature. Benevolence is from within, and not from without; righteousness is from without and not from within.'

2 Mencius said, 'What is the ground of your saying that benevolence is from within, and righteousness from without?' [The other] replied, 'There is a man older than I, and I give honour to his age; – it is not that there is in me a principle of reverence for age. It is just as when there is a white man, and I consider him white; according as he is so externally to me. It is on this account that I say [of righteousness] that it is from without.'

3 [Mencius] said, 'There is no difference to us between the whiteness of a white horse, and the whiteness of a white man, but I do not know that there is no difference between the regard with which we acknowledge the age of an old horse, and that with which we acknowledge the age of a man older [than ourselves]? And what is it which we call righteousness? The fact of a man's being older [than we]? or the fact of our giving honour to his age?'

4 [Kaou] said, 'There is my younger brother; I love him. But the younger brother of a man of Ts'in I do not love; that is, it is [the relationship to] myself which, occasions my complacency, and therefore I say that benevolence is from within. I give the honour due to age to an old man of Ts'oo, and to an old man of my own [kindred]; that is, it is the age which occasions the complacency, and therefore I say that righteousness is from without.'

5 [Mencius]. answered him, 'Our enjoyment of meat broiled by a man of Ts'in does not differ from our enjoyment of meat broiled by [one of] our [own kindred]. Thus [what you insist on] takes place also in the case of [such] things; but is our enjoyment of broiled meat also from without?'

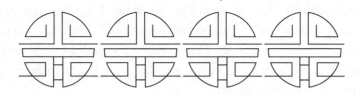

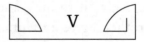

1 Mr Măng Ke asked the disciple Kung-too, saying, 'On what ground is it said that righteousness is from within?'

2 [Kung-too] replied. 'It is the acting out of our feeling of respect, and therefore it is said to be from within.'

3 [The other] said '[In the case of] a villager one year older than your elder brother, to which of them will yon show the [greater] respect?' 'To my brother,' was the reply. 'But for which would you pour out spirits first?' [Kuog-too] said, 'For the villager.' [Măng Ke then argued], 'Your feeling of respect rests on the one, but your reverence for age is rendered to the other; [righteousness] is certainly determined by what is without, and not by internal feeling.'

4   The disciple Kung-too was unable to reply, and reported [the conversation] to Mencius, who said, '[You should ask him], "Which do you respect more, your uncle, or your younger brother?" He will reply, "My uncle." [Ask him again], "If your younger brother be personating a deceased ancestor, to whom will you show respect more, – [to him or to your uncle]?" He will say, "To my younger brother." [You can go on], "But where is the [greater] respect due, as you said, to your uncle?" He will say, "[I show it to my younger brother,] because he is in the position [of the deceased ancestor]." And then you must say, "Because he is in that position; – and so ordinarily my respect is given to my elder brother, but a momentary respect is given to the villager."'

5   When Ke-tsze heard this, he observed, 'When respect is due to my uncle, I give it to him; and when respect is due to my younger brother, I give it to him. The thing is certainly determined by what is without us, and does not come from within.' Kung-too replied, 'In winter we drink things warm, but in summer we drink things cold; but is then our eating and drinking determined by what is external to us?'

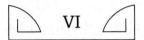

VI

1 The disciple Kung-too said, 'Kaou-tsze says, "[Man's] nature is neither good nor bad."

2 'Some say, "[Man's] nature may be made to do good, and it may be made to do evil; and accordingly, under Wan and Woo, the people loved what was good, and under Yëw and Le they loved what was cruel."'

3 'Some say, "The nature of some is good, and the nature of others is bad. Hence it was that under such a ruler as Yaou, there yet appeared Sëang; that with such a father as Koo-sow, there yet appeared Shun; and that, with Chow for their ruler and the son of their elder brother besides, there yet appeared K'e, the viscount of Wei, and prince Pe-kan."

4 'And now you say, "The nature is good." Then are all those wrong?'

5 Mencius replied, 'From the feelings proper to it, [we see] that it is constituted for the doing of what is good. This is what I mean in saying that [the nature] is good.

6 'If [men] do what is not good, the guilt cannot be imputed to their natural powers.

7 'The feeling of compassionate distress belongs to all men; so does that of shame and dislike; and that of modesty and respect; and that of approving and disapproving. The feeling of compassion and distress is the principle of benevolence; the feeling of shame and dislike is the principle of right-eousness; the feeling of modesty and respect is the principle of propriety; and the feeling of approving and disapproving is the principle of knowledge, benevolence, righteousness, propriety, and knowledge are not fused into us from without; they naturally belong to us, and [a different view] is simply from want of reflection. Hence it is said, "Seek, and you will find them; neglect, and you will lose them." [Men differ from one another in regard to them]; some as much again as others, some five times as much, and some to an incal-culable amount; it is because they cannot fully carry out their [natural] endowments.

8 'It is said in the Book of Poetry,

"Heaven in giving birth to the multitudes of the people,
To every faculty and relationship annexed its law:
The people possess this normal nature,
And they [consequently] love its normal virtue."

Confucius said, "The maker of this ode knew indeed the constitution [of our nature]." We may thus see that to every faculty and relationship there must belong its law, and that since the people possess this normal nature, they therefore love its normal virtue.'

VII

1 Mencius said, 'In good years the children of the people are most of them good, and in bad years they are most of them evil. It is not owing to their natural endowments conferred by Heaven, that they are thus different. It is owing to the circumstances in which they allow their minds to be ensnared and devoured that they appear so [as in the latter case].

2 'There now is barley. – Let the seed be sown and covered up; the ground being the same, and the time of sowing also the same, it grows luxuriantly, and when the full time is come it is all found to be ripe. Although there, may be inequalities [of produce], that is owing to [the difference of] the soil as rich or poor, to the [unequal] nourishment afforded by rain and dew, and to the different ways in which man has performed his business.

3 'Thus all things which are the same in kind are like to one another; –why should we doubt in regard to man, as if he were a solitary exception to this? The sage and we are the same in kind.

4 'In accordance with this, Lung-tsze said, "If a man make hempen sandals, without knowing [the size of people's] feet, yet I know that he will not make them like baskets." Sandals are like one another, because all men's feet are like one other.

5 'So with the mouth and flavours; – all mouths have the same relishes. Yih Ya [simply] appreciated before me what my mouth relishes. Suppose that his mouth, in its relish for flavours, were of a different nature from [the mouths of] other men, in the same way as dogs and horses are not of the same kind with us, how should all men be found following Yih Ya in their relishes? In the matter of tastes, the whole kingdom models itself after Yih Ya; that is, the mouths of all men are like one another.

6 'So it is with the ear also. In the matter of sounds, the whole kingdom models itself after the music-master Kwang; that is, the ears of all men are like one another.

7 'And so it is also with the eye. In the case of Tsze-too, there is no one under heaven but would recognize that he was beautiful. Any one who did not recognize the beauty of Taze-too would [be said to] have no eyes.

8 'Therefore [I] say, – [Men's] mouths agree in having the same relishes; their ears agree in enjoying the same sounds; their eyes agree in recognizing the same beauty: – shall their minds alone he without that which they similarly approve? What is it then of which their minds similarly approve? It is the principles [of things], and the [consequent determinations of] righteousness. The sages only apprehended before me that which I and other men agree in approving. Therefore the principles [of things] and [the determinations of] righteousness are agreeable to my mind just as [the flesh] of grass and grain-fed [animals] is agreeable to my mouth.'

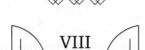

VIII

1   Mencius said, 'The trees of Nëw hill were once beautiful. Being situated, however, in the suburbs of [the capital of] a large State, they were hewn down with axes and bills; and could they retain their beauty? Still through the growth from the vegetative life day and night, and the nourishing influence of the rain and dew, they were not without buds and sprouts springing out. But then came the cattle and goats, and browsed upon them. To these things is owing the bare and stript appearance [of the hill]; and when people see this, they think it was never finely wooded. But is this the nature of the hill?

2   'And so even of what properly belongs to man; shall it be said that the mind [of any man] was without benevolence and righteousness. The way in which a man loses the proper goodness of his mind is like the way in which [those] trees were denuded by axes and bills. Hewn down day after day, can it retain its excellence? But there is some growth of its life day and night, and in the [calm] air of the morning, just between night and day, the mind feels in a degree those desires and aversions which are proper to humanity; but the feeling is not strong; and then it is fettered and destroyed by what the man does during the day. This fettering takes place again and again; the restorative influence of the night is not sufficient to preserve [the proper goodness]; and when this proves insufficient for that purpose, the [nature] becomes not much different from [that of] the irrational animals; and when people see this, they think that it never had those endowments [which I assert]. But does this condition represent the feelings proper to humanity?

3   'Therefore if it receive its proper nourishment, there is nothing which will not grow; if it lose its proper nourishment, there is nothing which will not decay away.

4   'Confucius said, "Hold it fast, and it remains with you; let it go, and you lose it. Its out-going and in-coming cannot be defined as to time and place." It was the mental nature of which this was said.'

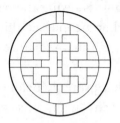

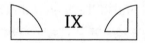

IX

1   Mencius said, 'It is not to be wondered at that the king is not wise!

2   'Suppose the case of the most easily growing thing in the world; – if you let it have one day's genial heat, and then expose it for ten days to cold, it will not be able to grow. It is but seldom that I have an audience [of the king], and when I retire, there come [all] those who act upon him like the cold. Though I succeed in bringing out some buds of goodness, of what avail is it?

3 'Now chess-playing is an art, though a small one; but without his whole mind being given, and his will bent to it, a roan cannot succeed in it. Chess Ts'ëw is the best chess-player in all the kingdom. Suppose that he is teaching two men to play; – the one gives all his mind to the game, and bends to it all his will, doing nothing but listen to Chess Ts'ëw; the other, though he [seems to] be listening to him, has his whole mind running on a swan which he thinks is approaching, and wishes to bend his bow, adjust the arrow to the string, and shoot it. Though the latter is learning along with the former, his progress is not equal to his. Is it because his intelligence is not equal? Not so.'

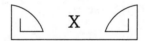

X

1 Mencius said, 'I like fish, and I also like bears' paws. If I cannot get both together, I will let the fish go, and take the bears' paws. So I like life, and I also like righteousness. If I cannot keep the two together, I will let life go, and choose righteousness.

2 'I like life indeed, but there is that which I like more than life; and therefore I will not seek to hold it by any improper ways. I dislike death indeed, but there is that which I dislike more than death, and therefore there are occasions when I will not avoid calamity [that may occasion death].

3   'If among the things which man likes there were nothing which he liked more than life, why should he not use all means by which he could preserve it? If among the things which man dislikes there were nothing which he disliked more than death, why should he not do everything by which he could avoid calamity [that might occasion it].

4   '[But as man is], there are cases when by a certain course men might preserve life, and yet they do not employ it; and when by certain things they might avoid calamity [that will occasion death], and yet they will not do them.

5   'Therefore men have that which they like more than life, and that which they dislike more than death. They are not men of talents and virtue only who have this mental nature. All men have it; – what belongs to such men is simply that they are able not to lose it.

6   'Here are a small basket of rice and a basin of soup; – and the case is one where the getting them will preserve life, and the want of them will be death. If they are offered to him in an insulting tone, [even] a tramper on the road will not receive them, or if you first tread upon them, [even] a beggar will not stoop to take them.

7   '[And yet] a man will accept of ten thousand *chung*, without any question as to the propriety and righteousness of his doing so. What can the ten thousand *chung* really add to him? [When he takes them], is it not that he may get beautiful mansions? or that he may secure the services of wives and concubines? or that the poor and needy of his acquaintance may be helped by him?

8 'In the former case, the [offered bounty] was not received, though it would have saved from death, and now the man takes [the emolument] for the sake of beautiful mansions. [The bounty] that would have saved from death was not received, and [the emolument] is taken to get the services of wives and concubines. [The bounty] that would have saved from death was not received and [the emolument] is taken that one's poor and needy acquaintances may be helped by him. Was it not possible then to decline [the emolument] in these instances? This is a case of what is called – losing the proper nature of one's mind.'

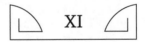

XI

1 Mencius said, 'Benevolence is [the proper quality of] man's mind, and righteousness is man's [proper] path.

2 'How lamentable is it to neglect this path and not pursue it, to lose this mind and not know to seek it [again].

3 'When men's fowls and dogs are lost, they know to seek them [again]; but they lose their mind, and do not know to seek it [again].

4 'The object of learning is nothing else but to seek for the lost mind.'

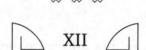

XII

1   Mencius said, 'Here is a man whose fourth finger is bent, and cannot be stretched out straight. It is not painful, nor does it incommode his business; but if there were any one who could make it straight, he would not think it far to go all the way from Ts'in to Ts'oo [to find him]; because his finger is not like those of other people.

2   'When a man's finger is not like other people's, he knows to feel dissatisfied; but when his mind is not like other people's, he does not know to feel dissatisfied. This is what is called – ignorance of the relative [importance of things].'

XIII

1   Mencius said, 'Anybody who wishes to cultivate a *t'ung* tree, or a *tsze*, which may be grasped with the two hands, [perhaps] with one, knows by what means to nourish it; but in the case of their own persons men.do not know by what means to nourish them. Is it to be supposed that their regard for their own persons is inferior to their regard for a *t'ung* or a *tsze*? Their want of reflection is extreme.'

XIV

1   Mencius said, 'Men love every part of their persons; and as they love every part, so they [should] nourish every part. There is not an inch of skin which they do not love, and so there is not an inch of skin which they will not nourish. For examining whether his [way of nourishing] be good or not, what other rule is there but simply this, that a man determine, [by reflecting] on himself, where it should be applied?

2   'Some parts of the body are noble, and some ignoble; some great, and some small. The great must not be injured for the small, nor the noble for the ignoble. He who nourishes the little belonging to him is a small man; he who nourishes the great is a great man.

3   'Here is a plantation-keeper, who neglects his *woo* and *këa*, and nourishes his small jujube trees; – he is a poor plantation-keeper.

4   'He who nourishes one of his fingers, neglecting his shoulders and back, without knowing that he is doing so, is a man [who resembles] a hurried wolf.

5   'A man who [only] eats and drinks is counted mean by others; because he nourishes what is little to the neglect of what is great.

6   'If a man, [fond of] eating and drinking, do [yet] not fail [in nourishing what in him is great], how should his mouth and belly be accounted as no more than an inch of skin?'

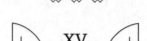

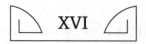

XV

1 The disciple Kung-too asked, saying, 'All are equally men, but some are great men, and others are little men; how is this?' Mencius replied, 'Those who follow that part of themselves which is great are great men; those who follow that part which is little are little men.'

2 Kung-too pursued, 'All are equally men; but some follow that part of themselves which is great, and some that which is little; how is this?' Mencius said, 'The ears and the eyes have it not in their office to think, and are [liable to be] obscured by things [affecting them]; and when one thing comes into contact with another, it simply leads it away. But it is in the office of the mind to think. By thinking, it gets [the right view of things]; when neglecting to think, it fails to do this. These – [the senses and the mind] – are what Heaven has given to us. Let a man first stand in [the supremacy of] the greater [and nobler] part of his constitution, and the smaller part will not be able to take it from him. It is simply this which makes the great man.'

XVI

1 Mencius said, 'There is a nobility of Heaven, and there is a nobility of man. Benevolence, righteousness, self-conse-cration, and fidelity, with unwearied joy in the goodness [of these virtues], – these constitute the nobility of Heaven. To be a duke, a minister, or a great officer, – this constitutes the nobility of man.

2   'The men of antiquity cultivated their nobility of Heaven, and the nobility of man came in its train.

3   'The men of the present day cultivate their nobility of Heaven in order to seek for the nobility of man, and when they have obtained this, they throw away the other; their delusion is extreme. The issue is simply this, that they must lose [that nobility of man] as well.'

XVII

1   Mencius said, 'To desire to be what is considered honourable is the common mind of men. And all I men have what is [truly] honourable in themselves; only they do not think of it.

2   'The honour which man confers is not the truly good honour. Those to whom Chaou-măng gave honourable rank he could make mean again.

3   'It is said in the Book of Poetry

"You have made us to drink to the full of your spirits;
You have satiated us with your kindness;"

meaning that [the guests] were filled with benevolence and righteousness, and therefore did not wish for the fat meat and fine millet of men. When a good reputation and far reaching; praise fall to [a man's] person, he does not desire the elegant embroidered garments of men.'

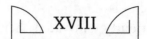

XVIII

1   Mencius said, 'Benevolence subdues its opposite just as water subdues fire. Those, however, who now-a-days practise benevolence [do it] as if with a cup of water they could save a whole waggon-load of faggots which was on fire, and when the flames were not extinguished were to say that water cannot subdue fire. Such a course, moreover, is the greatest aid to what is not benevolent.

2   'The final issue will simply be this, the loss [of that small amount of benevolence].'

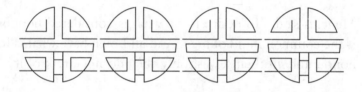

XIX

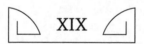

1   Mencius said, 'Of all seeds the best are the five kinds of grain, but if they are not ripe, they are not equal to the *t'e* or the *pae*. So the value of benevolence lies simply in its being brought to maturity.'

XX

1   Mencius said, 'E, in teaching men to shoot, made it a rule to draw the bow to the full, and his pupils were required to do the same.

2   'A masterworkman, in teaching others, must use the compass and square, and his pupils must do the same.'

BOOK VI

KAOU-TSZE

PART II

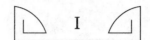

I

1 A man of Jin asked the disciple Uh-loo, saying, 'Is [an observance of] the rules of propriety [in regard to eating] or the eating the more important?' The answer was, '[The observance of] the rules of propriety is the more important.'

2 'Is [the gratifying] the appetite of sex or [the doing so only] according to the rules of propriety the more important?'

3 The answer [again] was, '[The observance of] the rules of propriety [in the matter] is the more important;' [and then the man] said, 'If the consequence of eating [only] according to the rules of propriety will be death from starvation, while by disregarding those rules one can get food, must he still observe them [in such a case]? If, according to the rule that he shall go in person to meet his bride, a man cannot get married, while by disregarding the rule he can get married, must he still hold to the rule [in such a case]?'

4 Uh-loo was unable to reply [to these questions], and next day he went to Tsow and told them to Mencius, who said, 'What difficulty is there in answering these inquiries?

5 'If you do not bring them together at the bottom, but only at their tops, a piece of wood an inch square may be made to be higher than the pointed ridge of a high building.

6 '"Metal is heavier than feathers;" – but does that saying have reference to a single clasp of metal and a waggon-load of feathers?

7 'If you take a case where the eating is all-important, and the observing the rules of propriety is of little importance, and compare them together, why merely say that the eating is the more important? [So,] taking the case where the gratifying the appetite of sex is all-important, and the observing the rules of propriety is of little importance, why merely say that the gratifying the appetite is the more important?

8 'Go and answer him thus: "If by twisting round your elder brother's arm, and snatching from him what he is eating, you can get food for yourself, while, if you do not do so, you cannot get such food, will you so twist round his arm? And if by getting over your neighbour's wall, and dragging away his virgin daughter, you can get a wife for yourself, while if you do not do so, you cannot get such wife, will you so drag her away?"'

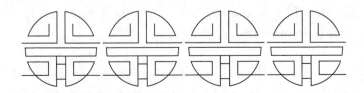

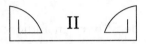 II

1 Këaou of Ts'aou asked, saying, '[It is said,] "All men may be Yaous and Shuns;" – is it so?' Mencius said, 'It is.'

2   [Kĕaou went on], 'I have heard that king Wăn was ten cubits high, and T'ang nine. Now I am nine cubits and four inches in height; but I can do nothing but eat my millet. What am I to do to realize that saying?'

3   The reply was, 'What has the thing to do with this, – [the question of size]? It all lies simply in acting as such. Here is a man whose strength was not equal to lift a duckling or a chicken, – he was [then] a man of no strength. [But] to-day he says, "I can lift three thousand catties;" he is [now] a man of strength. And so, he who can lift the weight which Woo Hwoh lifted is just another Woo Hwoh. Why should a man make a want of ability the subject of his grief? It is only that he will not do the thing.

4   'To walk slowly, keeping behind his elders, is to perform the part of a younger. To walk rapidly, going before his elders, is to violate the duty of a younger. But is walking slowly what any man can not do? it is [only] what he does not do. The course of Yaou and Shun was simply that of filial piety and fraternal duty.

5   'Do you wear the clothes of Yaou, repeat the words of Yaou, and do the actions of Yaou, and you will just be a Yaou. Aud if you wear the clothes of Kĕeh, repeat the words of Kĕeh, and do the actions of Kĕeh, you will just be a Kĕeh.'

6   [Kĕaou] said, 'When I have an audience of the ruler of Tsow, I can ask him to let me have a house to lodge in. I wish to remain here, and receive instruction at your gate.'

7 [Mencius] replied, 'The way [of truth] is like a great road; it is not difficult to know it. The evil is only that men will not seek for it. Do you go home, and seek it, and you will have abundance of teachers.'

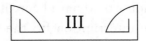

III

1 Kung-sun Ch'ow asked, saying, 'Kaou-tsze says that the *Sëaou pwan* is the ode of a small man; – [is it so?]' Mencius replied, 'Why does he say so?' and [the disciple] said, 'Because of the murmuring [which it expresses].'

2 [Mencius] answered, 'How stupid is that old Kaou in dealing with the ode! There is a man here, and a native of Yueh bends his bow to shoot him, while I will talk smilingly, and advise him [not to do so]; – for no other reason but that he is not related to me. [But] if my own elder brother be bending his bow to shoot the man, then I will advise him [not to do so], weeping and crying the while; – for no other reason but that he is related to me. The dissatisfaction expressed in the *Sëaou pwan* is the working of relative affection; and that affection shows benevolence. Stupid indeed is that old Kaou's criticism of the ode!'

3 [Ch'ow then] said, 'How is it that there is no murmuring in the *K'ae fung*?'

4   [Mencius] replied, 'The parent's fault referred to in the *K'ae fung* was small, while that referred to in the *Sëaou pwan* was great. Where the parent's fault was great, not to have murmured at it would have increased the alienation [between father and son]. Where the parent's fault was small, to have murmured at it would have been [like water which frets and foams about a rock that stands in its channel], unable to suffer the interruption to its course. To increase the want of natural affection would have been unfilial; to have refused to suffer such an interruption [to the flow of natural affection] would also have been unfilial.

5   'Confucius said, "Shun was indeed perfectly filial! Even when fifty, he was full of longing desire for [the affection of] his parents."'

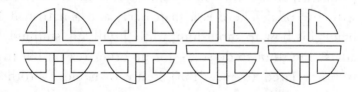

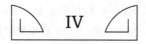

IV

1   Sung K'ăng being on his way to Ts'oo, Mencius met him in Shih-k'ëw.

2   'Where are you going, respected Sir?' said [Mencius].

3   [K'ăng] replied, 'I have heard that Ts'in and Ts'oo are fighting together, and I am going to see the king of Ts'oo, and advise him to cease hostilities. If he should not be pleased with my advice, I will go and see the king of Ts'in, and advise him in the same way. Of the two kings I shall [surely] find that I can succeed with one of them.'

4   [Mencius] said, 'I will not presume to ask the particulars, but I should like to hear the scope [of your plan]. What course will you take in advising them?' 'I will tell them,' was the reply, 'the unprofitableness [of their strife].' 'Your aim, Sir' rejoined [Mencius], 'is great, but your argument is not good.

5   'If you, respected Sir, starting from the point of profit, offer your counsels to the kings of Ts'in and Ts'oo, and they, being pleased with the consideration of profit, should stop the movements of their armies, then all belonging to those armies will rejoice in the cessation [of war], and find their pleasure in [the pursuit of] profit. Ministers will serve their rulers for the profit of which they cherish the thought; sons will serve their fathers, and younger brothers will serve their elder brothers, from the same consideration; and the issue will be that, abandoning benevolence and righteousness, ruler and minister, father and son, elder brother and younger, will carry on their intercourse with this thought of profit cherished in their breasts. But never has there been such a state [of society] without ruin being the result of it.

6 'If you. Sir, starting from the ground of benevolence and righteousness, offer your counsels to the kings of Ts'in and Ts'oo, and they, being pleased with benevolence and righteousness, should stop the movements of their armies, then all belonging to those armies will rejoice in the cessation [of war], and find their pleasure in benevolence and righteousness. Ministers will serve their rulers from the benevolence and righteousness of which they cherish the thought. Sons will serve their fathers, and younger brothers will serve their elder brothers, from the same; – and the issue will be that, abandoning [the thought of] profit, ruler and minister, father and son, elder brother and younger, will carry on their intercourse with benevolence and righteousness cherished in their breasts. But never has there been such a state [of society] without the result of it being the attainment of true Royal sway. Why must you speak of profit?'

1   When Mencius was residing in Tsow, the younger brother of [the ruler of] Jin, who was guardian of the State at the time, sent him a gift of [some] pieces of silk, which he received, without [going] to give thanks for it. When he was staying for a time in P'ing-luh, Ch'oo, who was prime-minister [of Ts'e], sent him [likewise] a gift of silks, which he received, without [going] to give thanks for it.

2   Subsequently, when he went from Tsow to Jin, he visited the younger brother of the ruler, but when he went from P'ing-luh to [the capital of] Ts'e, he did not visit the minister Ch'oo. The disciple Uh-loo was glad, and said, 'I have got an opportunity [to obtain some information].'

3   He asked accordingly, 'Master, when you went to Jin, you visited the ruler's younger brother. But when you went to [the capital of] Ts'e, you did not visit the minister Ch'oo; was it because he is [only] the minister?'

4   [Mencius] replied, 'No. It is said in the Book of History, "In offerings, there are many ceremonial observances. If the observances are not equal to the articles, it may be said that there is no offering, there being no service of the will in the offering."

5   '[This is] because the things [so presented] do not constitute an offering.'

6   Uh-loo was pleased; and when some one asked him what Mencius meant], he said, 'The younger brother [of the ruler of Jin] could not go to Tsow, but the minister Ch'oo could have gone to P'ing-luh.'

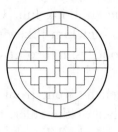

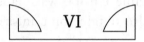

VI

1   Shun-yu K'wan, said, 'He who makes the fame and real service his first object acts from a regard to others; he who makes them only secondary objects acts from a regard to himself. You, Master, were ranked among the three high ministers of the kingdom, and before your fame and services had reached either to the ruler or the people, you went away. Is this indeed the way of the benevolent?'

2   Mencius replied, 'There was Pih-e; – he abode in an inferior position, and would not with his virtue and talents serve a degenerate ruler. There was E Yin; – he five times went to T'ang, and five times went to Këeh. There was Hwuy of Lëw-hëa; – he did not disdain to serve a vile ruler, nor did he decline a small office. The courses pursued by those three worthies were different, but their aim was one. And what was their one aim? We must answer – benevolence. And so it is simply after this that superior men strive; – why must they [all] pursue the same [course]?'

3   [K'wǎn] pursued, 'In the time of duke Muh of Loo, the government was in the hands of Kung-e, while Tsze-lëw and Tsze-sze were ministers. [And yet] the dismemberment of Loo increased exceedingly. Such was the case, – a specimen of how your men of talents and virtue are of no use to a State!'

4   [Mencius] replied, '[The duke of] Yu did not use Pih-le He, and [thereby] lost his State; duke Muh of Ts'in used him, and became chief of all the princes. The consequence of not employing mien of talents and virtue is ruin; – how can it end in dismemberment [merely]?'

5   [K'wǎn] urged [again], 'Formerly, when Wang Paou dwelt on the K'e, the people on the west of the Ho became skilful at singing in his abrupt manner. When Mëen K'eu dwelt in Kaou-t'ang, the people in the west of Ts'e became skilful at singing in his prolonged manner. The wives of Hwa Chow and K'e Lëang bewailed their husbands so skilfully that they changed the manners of the State. When there is [the gift] within, it is sure to manifest itself without. I have never seen the man who could do the deeds [of a worthy] and did not realize the work of one. Therefore there are [now] no men of talents and virtue; if there were, I should know them.'

6   [Mencius] replied, 'When Confucius was minister of crime in Loo, [the ruler] came not to follow [his counsels]. Soon after there was the [solstitial] sacrifice, and when a part of the flesh there presented did not come to him, he went away [even] without taking off his cap of ceremony. Those who did not know him supposed that [he went away] because the flesh [did not come to him]. Those who knew him [some-what] supposed that it was because of the neglect of the [usual] ceremony. The truth was that Confucius wished to go on occasion of some small offence, and did not wish to go without an apparent cause. All men cannot be expected to understand the conduct of a superior man.'

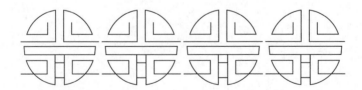

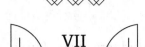

VII

1   Mencius said, 'The five presidents of the princes were sinners against the three kings. The princes of the present day are sinners against the five presidents. The great officers of the present day are sinners against the princes of the present day.

2   'When the son of Heaven visited the princes, it was called "A tour of inspection". When the princes attended at his court, it was called "A report of office". In the spring they examined the ploughing, and supplied any deficiency [of seed]; in the autumn they examined the reaping, and assisted where there was a deficiency [of yield]. When [the son of Heaven] entered the boundaries [of a State], if [new] ground was being reclaimed, and the old fields were well cultivated; if the old were nourished, and honour shown to men of talents and virtue; and if men of distinguished ability were placed in office: – then [the ruler] was rewarded, – rewarded with [an addition to his] territory. [On the other hand], if on his entering a State, the ground was found left wild or overrun with weeds; if the old were neglected, and no attention paid to men of talents and virtue; and if hard tax-gatherers were placed in office: – then [the ruler] was reprimanded. If [a prince] once omitted his attendance at court, he was punished by degradation of rank; if he did so a second time, he was deprived of a portion of his territory; and if he did so a third time, the royal armies [were set in motion], and he was removed [from his government]. Thus the son of Heaven commanded the punishment, but did not himself inflict it, while the various feudal princes inflicted the punishment, but did not command it. The five presidents, [however] dragged the princes of the States to attack other princes, and therefore I say that they were sinners against the three kings.

3   'Of the five presidents duke Hwan was the most distinguished. At the assembly of the princes in K'wei-k'ëw, they
bound the victim, and placed the writing [of the covenant]
upon it, but did not [slay it], and smear their mouths with
its blood. The first article in the covenant was: – "Slay the
unfilial; do not change the son who has been appointed heir;
do not exalt a concubine to the rank of wife." The second
was: – "Give honour to the worthy, and cherish the talented,
– to give distinction to the virtuous." The third was: –
"Reverence the old, and be kind to the young; be not
forgetful of visitors and travellers." The fourth was: – "Let
not offices be hereditary, nor let officers be pluralists; in the
selection of officers let the object be to get the proper men;
let not [a ruler] take it on himself to put a great officer to
death." The fifth was: – "Follow no crooked policy in making
embankments; do not restrict the sale of grain; do not grant
any investiture without [first] informing [the king, and
getting his sanction]." It was [then] said, "All we who have
united in this covenant shall hereafter maintain amicable
relations." The princes of the present day all violate those
five prohibitions, and therefore I say that they are sinners
against the five presidents.

4   'The crime of him who connives at and aids the wickedness
of his ruler is small, but the crime of him who anticipates
and excites that wickedness is great. The great officers of
the present day all are guilty of this latter crime, and I say
that they are sinners against the princes.'

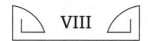

VIII

1 [The ruler of] Loo wanted to employ Shin-tsze in the command of an army.

2 Mencius said [to Shin], 'To employ an uninstructed people [in war] is what is called – destroying the people. A destroyer of the people was not tolerated in the age of Yaou and Shun.

3 'Though by a single battle you should vanquish Ts'e, and so get possession of Nan-yang, the thing ought not to be done'

4 Shin changed countenance, was displeased, and said, 'This is what I, Kuh-le, do not understand.'

5 [Mencius] said, 'I will lay the case plainly before you. The territory of the son of Heaven is a thousand *le* square; without a thousand *le*, he would not have enough for his entertainment of the princes. The territory of a prince [of the highest rank] is a hundred *le* square; – without a hundred *le*, he would not have enough wherewith to observe the statutes kept in his ancestral temple.

6 'When the duke of Chow was invested with [the marquisate of] Loo, it was a hundred *le* square. The territory was indeed enough, but it was limited to a hundred *le*. When T'ae-kung was invested with [the marquisate of] Ts'e, it was also a hundred *le* square; – sufficient indeed, but limited to that amount.

7 'Now Loo is five times a hundred *le* square. If a true king were to arise, whether do you think that Loo would be diminished or increased by him?

8 'If it were merely taking from one [State] to give to another, a benevolent person would not do it; how much less would he do so, when the thing has to be sought by the slaughter of men!

9 'The way in which a superior man serves his ruler is simply an earnest endeavour to lead him in the right path, and to direct his mind to benevolence.'

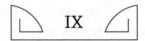

IX

1 Mencius said, 'Those who now-a-days serve their rulers, say, "We can for our ruler enlarge the limits of the cultivated ground, and fill his treasuries and arsenals." Such men are now-a-days called "Good ministers," but anciently they were called "Robbers of the people." If a ruler is not following the [right] path, nor has his mind bent on benevolence, to seek to enrich him is to enrich a Këeh.'

2   '[Or they will say], "We can for our ruler make engagements with our allied States, so that our battles must be successful." Such men are now-a-days called "Good ministers," but anciently they were called "Robbers of the people." If a ruler is not following the [right] path, nor has his mind bent on benevolence, to seek to make him stronger in battle is to help a Këeh.

3   'Although a [ruler], by the path of the present day, and with no change of its practices, were to have all under heaven given to him, he could not keep it for a single morning.'

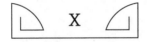

1   Pih Kwei said, 'I want to take [for the government] only a twentieth [of the produce]; what do you say to it?'

2   Mencius replied, 'Your way, Sir, would be that of the Mih.

3   'In a State of ten thousand families, would it do to have [only] one potter?' 'No,' said the other; 'the vessels would not be enough for use.'

4 [Mencius] went on, 'In Mih [all] the five kinds of grain are not grown; – it only produces the millet. There are no fortified cities with their walled suburbs, no great edifices, no ancestral temples, no ceremonies of sacrifice; there are no feudal princes requiring gifts of silk and entertainments; there is no system of officers with their various subordinates. On this account a tax of one twentieth of the produce is [there] sufficient.

5 'But now, [as] we live in the middle States, how can such a state of things be thought of, which would do away with the relationships of men, and have no officers of superior rank?

6 'A State cannot be made to subsist with but few potters; how much less can it be so without men of a superior rank to others!

7 'If we wish to make the taxation lighter than the system of Yaou and Shun, we shall have a great Mih and a small Mih. If we wish to make it heavier, we shall have the great Këeh and the small Këeh.'

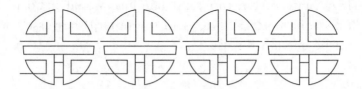

XI

1 Pih Kwei said, 'My management of the waters is superior to that of Yu.'

2 Mencius said, 'You are wrong. Sir. Yu's regulation of the waters was according to the laws of water.

3 'He therefore made the four seas their receptacle, while you now. Sir, make the neighbouring States their receptacle.

4 'When waters flow out of their natural channels, we have what is called an inundation. Inundating waters form a vast [waste] of water, and are what a benevolent man detests. You are wrong, my good Sir.'

XII

1 Mencius said, 'If a superior man have not confidence [in his views], how shall he take a firm hold [of things]?'

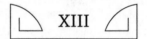

XIII

1 [The ruler of] Loo wishing to commit the administration of his government to the disciple Yoh-ching, Mencius said, 'When I heard of it, I was so glad that I could not sleep.'

2 Kung-sun Ch'ow said, 'Is Yoh-ching a man of vigour?' 'No.' 'Is he wise in council?' 'No.' 'Is he a man of much information?' 'No.'

3 'What then made you so glad that you could not sleep?'

4 'He is a man who loves what is good,' was the reply.

5 'Is the love of what is good sufficient?'

6 [Mencius] replied, 'The love of what is good is more than a sufficient qualification for the government of the whole kingdom; how much more is it so for the State of Loo!

7 'If [a minister] love what is good, then all within the four seas will think a thousand *le* but a small distance to come and lay [their thoughts about] what is good before him.

8 'If he do not love what is good, men will say, "How self-conceited he looks! [He is saying], 'I know it.'" The language and looks of that self-conceit will repel men to more than the distance of a thousand *le*. When good men stop more than a thousand le off, calumniators, flatterers, and sycophants will make their appearance. When [a minister] lives with calumniators, flatterers, and sycophants about him, though he may wish the State to be well governed, is it possible for it to be so?'

XIV

1   The disciple Ch'in said, 'What were the principles on which superior men of old took office?' Mencius said, 'There were three cases in which they accepted office, and three in which they left it.

2   'If received with the utmost respect and all courteous observances, and. they could say [to themselves] that [the ruler] would carry their words into practice, then they went to him [and took office], [Afterwards], though there might be no remission of the courteous observances, if their words were not carried into practice, they left him.

3   'The second case was that in which, though, [the ruler] could not [be expected] at once to carry their words into practice, yet being received by him with the utmost respect and all courteous observances, they went to him [and took office]. [But afterwards], if there was a remission of the courteous observances, they left him.

4   'The last case was that of [the superior man] who had nothing to eat either morning or evening, and was so famished that he could not move out of his door. If the ruler, on hearing of his state, said, "I must fail of the great point, – that of carrying his principles into practice, and moreover I cannot follow his words, but I am ashamed to allow him to starve in my country," and so assisted him, the help might be accepted in such a case, but not beyond what was sufficient to avert death.'

XV

1   Mencius said, 'Shun rose [to the empire] from among the channeled fields. Foo Tueh was called to office from the midst of his [building] frames and [earth-] beaters; Kaou Kih from his fish and salt; Kwan E-woo from the hands of the officer in charge of him; Sun Shuh-gaou from [his hiding by] the sea-shore; and Pih-le He from the market-place.

2   'Thus, when Heaven is about to confer a great office on any one, it first exercises his mind with suffering, and his sinews and bones with toil; it exposes his body to hunger, I and subjects him to extreme poverty; and it confounds his I undertakings. In all these ways it stimulates his mind, hardens his nature, and supplies his incompetencies.

3   'Men constantly err, but are afterwards able to reform. They are distressed in mind, and perplexed in thought, and then they arise to vigorous endeavour. When things have been evidenced in men's looks, and set forth in their words, then they understand them.

4   'If a ruler have not about his court families attached to the laws and able officers, and if abroad there are no hostile States or other external calamities, the State will generally come to ruin.

5   'From such things we see how life springs from sorrow and calamity, and death from ease and pleasure.'

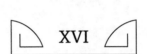

1 Mencius said, 'There are many arts in teaching. I refuse, as inconsistent with my character, to teach a man, but I am only thereby still teaching him.'

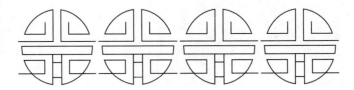

BOOK VII

TSIN SIN

PART I

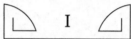

I

1　Mencius said, 'He who has exhaustively studied all his mental constitution knows his nature. Knowing his nature, he knows Heaven.

2　'To preserve one's mental constitution, and nourish one's nature, is the way to serve Heaven.

3　'When neither [the thought] of premature death nor [that] of long life causes a man any double-mindedness, but he waits in the cultivation of himself for whichever issue, – this is the way in which, he establishes his [Heaven-] ordained being.'

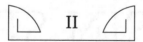

II

1　Mencius said, 'There is an appointment for everything. A man should submissively receive what is correctly ascribed thereto.

2　'Therefore, he who knows what is [Heaven's] appointment will not stand beneath a dangerous wall.

3　'Death sustained in the fulfilment. of one's proper course may correctly be ascribed to the appointment [of Heaven].

4　'Death under handcuffs and fetters cannot correctly be so ascribed.'

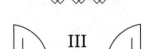

III

1   Mencius said, 'When we get by our seeking, and lose by our neglecting, in that case seeking is of use to getting; – the things sought are those which are in ourselves.

2   'When the seeking is according to the proper course, and the getting is [only] as appointed, in that case the seeking is of no use to getting; – the things sought are without ourselves.'

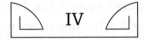

IV

1   Mencius said, 'All things are already complete in us.

2   'There is no greater delight than to be conscious of sincerity on self-examination.

3   'If one acts with a vigorous effort at the law of reciprocity, nothing, when he seeks for [the realization of] perfect virtue, can be closer than his approximation to it.'

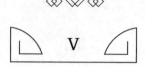

1   Mencius said, 'They do the thing, without clearly knowing
     [its propriety]; they practise the doing, without discrimi-
     nating [the reason of it]; they [thus] pursue the path all their
     life, without knowing its nature: – this is the case of
     multitudes.'

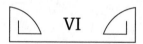

1   Mencius said, 'A man should not be without shame. When
     a man is ashamed of having been without shame, he will
     [afterwards] not have [occasion for] shame.'

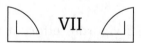

1   Mencius said, 'The sense of shame is to a man of great
     importance.

2   'Those who form contrivances and versatile schemes distin-
     guished for their artfulness do not allow their sense of shame
     to come into action.

3   'When one differs from other men in not having this sense
     of shame, what will he have in common with them?'

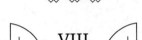

VIII

1 Mencius said, 'The able and virtuous monarchs of antiquity loved what was good and forgot [their own] power. And shall an exception be made of the able and virtuous scholars of antiquity – that they did not act in a similar way? They delighted in their own principles, and forgot the power [of princes]. Therefore, if kings and dukes did not cherish the utmost respect [for them] and observe all forms of ceremony, they were not permitted to see them frequently. If they found it not in their power to see them frequently, how much less could they get to employ them as ministers!'

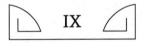

IX

1 Mencius said, to Sung Kow-tsëen, 'Are you fond, Sir, of travelling [to the different courts]? I will tell you about [such] travelling.

2 'If any [of the princes] acknowledge you. [and follow your counsels], look perfectly satisfied. If no one do so, still do the same.'

3 [The other] asked, 'What must I do that I may always wear this look of perfect satisfaction?' 'Honour virtue,' was the reply, 'and delight in righteousness; and so you may [always] appear to be perfectly satisfied.

4   'So it is that a scholar, though he may be poor, does not let go his righteousness, and, though prosperous, does not leave [his own] path.

5   'Poor and not letting go his righteousness; – it is thus that the scholar holds possession of himself. Prosperous, and not leaving [his own] path; – it is thus that the expectations of the people [from him] are not disappointed.

6   'When the men of antiquity realized their wishes, benefits accrued [from them] to the people. When they did not realize their wishes, they cultivated their personal character, and became illustrious in the world. When poor, they attended to the improvement of themselves in solitude when advanced to dignity, they prompted the improvement of all under heaven as well.'

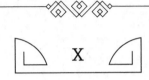

1 Mencius said, 'The mass of men wait for a king Wăn, and then receive a rousing impulse. Scholars distinguished from the mass, even without a king Wăn, rouse themselves.'

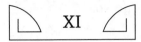

1 Mencius said, 'Add to a man [the wealth of] the families of Han and Wei, and, if he [still] look upon himself without being elated, he is far beyond [the mass of] men.'

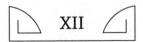

1 Mencius said, 'Let the people be employed in the way which is intended to secure their ease, and, though they be toiled, they will not murmur. Let them be put to death in the way which is intended to preserve their lives, and, though they die, they will not murmur.'

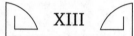

XIII

1   Mencius said, 'Under a president of the States, the people look brisk and cheerful; under a true king they have an air of deep contentment.

2   'Though he slay them, they do not murmur; when he benefits them, they do not think of his merit. From day to day they make progress towards what is good, without knowing who makes them do so.

3   'Wherever the superior man passes through, transformation follows; wherever he abides, his influence is of a spiritual nature. It flows abroad, above, and beneath like that of heaven and earth. How can it be said that he mends [society] but in a small way?'

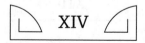

XIV

1   Mencius said, 'Kindly words do not enter into men so deeply as a reputation for kindness.

2   'Good government does not lay hold of the people so much as good instructions.

3   'Good government is feared by the people, [but] good instructions are loved by them. Good government gets the people's wealth, [but] good instructions get their hearts.'

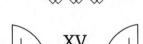

XV

1 Mencius said, 'The ability possessed by men without having been acquired by learning is their intuitive ability, and the knowledge possessed by them without the exercise of thought is their intuitive knowledge.

2 'Children carried in the arms all know to love their parents; and when they are grown [a little], they all know to respect their elder brothers.

3 'Filial affection for parents is benevolence; respect for elders is righteousness. There is no other [cause for these feelings]; – they belong to all under heaven.'

XVI

1 Mencius said, 'When Shun was living amidst the deep retired mountains, dwelling with the trees and rocks, and wandering with the deer and swine, the difference between him and the rude inhabitants of those remote hills was very small. But when he heard a single good word, or saw a single good action, he was like the Këang or the Ho, bursting its banks, and grandly flowing out in an irresistible flood.'

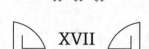

XVII

1   Mencius said, 'Let a man not do what [his sense of right-eousness tells him] not to do, and let him not desire what [the same sense tells him] not to desire: – to act thus is all that he has to do.'

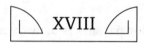

XVIII

1   Mencius said, 'When men are possessed of intelligent virtue and prudence in the management of affairs, it generally arises from their having been in distress.

2   'They are the friendless minister and the despised concu-bine's son who keep their hearts under a sense of peril, and use deep precautions against calamity. They become in consequence distinguished for their intelligence.'

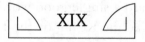

XIX

1   Mencius said, 'There are persons who serve the ruler; – they serve the ruler, that is, for the sake of his countenance and favour.

2   'There are ministers who seek the safety of the altars; – they find their pleasure in securing that tranquillity.

3   'There are those who are the people of Heaven; – [judging that], if they were in office, they could carry out [their principles] all under heaven, they proceed [so] to carry them out.

4   'There are those who are great men; – they rectify themselves, and [all] things are rectified.'

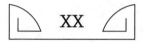

XX

1   Mencius said, 'The superior man has three things in which he delights, and to be sovereign over all under heaven is not one of them.

2   'That his father and mother are both alive, and that his brothers afford no cause [for distress of mind]; – this is his first delight.

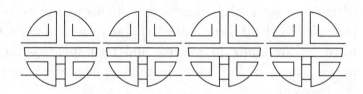

3   'That, when looking up, he has no occasion for shame before Heaven, and, below, he has no occasion to blush before men; – this is his second delight.

4   'That he gets hold of the individuals of the most superior abilities in the kingdom, and teaches and nourishes them; – this is his third delight.

5   'The superior man has three things in which he delights, and to be sovereign over all under heaven is not one of them.'

XXI

1   Mencius said, 'Wide territory and a numerous people are desired by the superior man, but what he delights in is not here.

2   'To stand in the centre of the kingdom and give tranquillity to the people within the four seas is an occasion of delight to the superior man; but [the highest element of] what belongs to him by his nature is not here.

3   'What belongs to the superior man by his nature cannot be increased by the largeness of his sphere of action, nor diminished by his being in poverty and retirement; – for this reason that it is determinately apportioned to him [by Heaven].

4   'What belong to the superior man are – benevolence, right-eousness, propriety, and knowledge, rooted in his heart. Their growth and manifestation are a mild harmony appearing in the countenance, a rich fulness in the back, and the character imparted to the four limbs. The four limbs understand [their several motions] without being told.'

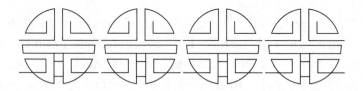

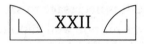

XXII

1   Mencius said, 'Pih-e, that he might avoid [the tyrant] Chow, was dwelling on the coast of the northern sea. When he heard of the rise of king Wăn, he roused himself and said, "Why should I not attach myself to him? I have heard that the chief of the West knows well how to nourish the old." T'ae-kung, that he might avoid Chow, was dwelling on the coast of the eastern sea. When he heard of the rise of king Wăn, he roused himself, and said, "Why should I not attach myself to him? I have heard that the chief of the West knows well how to nourish the old." If in the kingdom there were [now] a prince who knew well how to nourish the old, benevolent men would consider that he was the proper object for them to gather to.

2   'Around the homestead with its five *mow* the space at the foot of the walls was planted with mulberry trees, with which the [farmer's] wife nourished silkworms, and thus the old were able to have silk to wear. When the five brood-hens and the two brood-sows [of each family] were kept to their [breeding] seasons, the old were able to have flesh to eat. The husbandmen cultivated their fields of a hundred *mow*, and their families of eight mouths were secured against want.

3   'The expression, "The chief of the West knows well how to nourish the old," referred to his regulations about the fields and dwellings, his teaching [the farmers] to plant [the mulberry tree], and nourish [those animals]; his instructing their wives and children, so that they should nourish their aged. At fifty warmth cannot be maintained without silks; and at seventy flesh is necessary to satisfy the appetite. [The aged], not kept warm, nor well supplied with food, are said to be "starved and famished," but among the people of king Wăn there were no aged in that condition. – This was the meaning of that expression.'

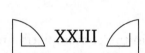

XXIII

1 Mencius said, 'Let it be seen to that their fields of grain and flax are well cultivated, and make the taxes on them light: – so the people may be made rich.

2 'Let [the people] use their resources of food seasonably and expend them [only] on the prescribed ceremonies: – so they will be more than can be consumed.

3 'The people cannot live without water and fire; yet, if you knock at a man's door in the dusk of the evening, and ask for water and fire, there is no one who will not give them, such is the great abundance of them. A sage would govern the kingdom so as to cause pulse and millet to be as abundant as fire and water. When pulse and millet are as abundant as fire and water, how shall there be among the people any that are not virtuous?'

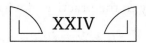

XXIV

1 Mencius said, 'Confucius ascended the eastern hill, and Loo appeared to him small. He ascended the T'ae mountain, and all beneath the heavens appeared to him small. So, he who has contemplated the sea finds it difficult to think anything of other waters; and he who has been a student in the gate of the sage finds it difficult to think anything of the words of others.

2   'There is an art in the contemplation of water; – it is necessary to contemplate its swelling waves. When the sun or the
moon is at its brightest, its light admitted [even] through
an orifice is sure to illuminate.

3   'Flowing water is a thing which does not proceed till it has
filled the hollows [in its course]. The student who has set his
mind on the doctrines [of the sage] does not come to the
understanding of them but by completing one lesson after
another.'

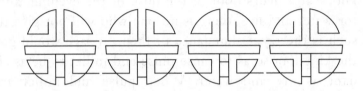

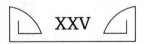 XXV

1   Mencius said, 'He who rises at cock-crow, and addresses
himself earnestly to the practice of what is good, is a disciple
of Shun.

2   'He who rises at cock-crow, and addresses himself earnestly
to the pursuit of gain, is a disciple of Chih.

3   'If you want to know what separated Shun from Chih it was
nothing but this, – the interval between [the thought of]
gain and [the thought of] goodness.'

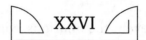

XXVI

1   Mencius said, 'The principle of Yang-tsze was – "Each one for himself." Though by plucking out one hair he might have benefited all under heaven, he would not have done it.

2   'Mih-tsze loves all equally. If, by rubbing [bare all his body] from the crown to the heel, he could have benefited all under heaven, he would have done it.

3   'Tsze-moh holds a medium [between these], and by holding that medium he is nearer the right. But by holding it without leaving room for the exigency of circumstances, it becomes like their holding their one point.

4   'What I dislike in that holding one point is the injury it does to the way [of right principle]. It takes up one point and disregards a hundred others.'

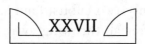

XXVII

1   Mencius said, 'The hungry think any food sweet, and the thirsty think the same of any drink; and thus they do not know the right [taste] of what they eat and drink. The hunger and thirst, [in fact,] injure [their palate]. And is it only the mouth and belly that are injured by hunger and thirst? Men's minds are also injured by them.

2   'If a man can prevent the injurious evils of hunger and thirst from doing any injury to his mind, there need be no anxiety about his not being up with other men.'

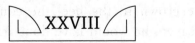

1   Mencius said, 'Hwuy of Lëw-hëa would not for the three highest offices at the royal court have changed his guiding plan of life.'

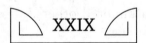

1   Mencius said, 'A man with definite aims to be accomplished may be compared to one digging a well. To dig the well to a depth of seventy-two cubits, [and stop] without reaching the spring, is after all throwing away the well.'

1   Mencius said, '[Benevolence and righteousness] were natural to yaou and Shun. T'ang and Woo made them their own. The five presidents of the States feigned them.

2   'Having borrowed them long and not retained them, how could it be known that they did not own them?'

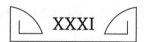

1   Kung-sun Ch'ow said, 'E Yin said, 'I cannot be near so disobedient a person,' and therewith he banished T'ae-këah to T'ung. The people were much pleased. When T'ae-këah became virtuous, he then brought him back; and the people were much pleased.

2   'When worthies are ministers, and their rulers are not virtuous, may they indeed banish them in this way?'

3   Mencius replied, 'If they have the mind of E Yin, they may. If they have not the mind, it would be usurpation.'

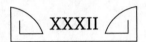

1 Kung-sun Ch'ow said, 'It is said in the Book of Poetry,

"He would not eat the bread of idleness!"

How is it that we see superior men eating without ploughing?' Mencius replied, 'When a superior man resides in any State, let its ruler employ his counsels, and he comes to tranquillity, wealth, honour, and glory. Let the young in it follow his instructions, and they become filial, obedient to their elders, true-hearted, and faithful. What greater example can there be than this of not eating the bread of idleness?'

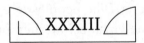

1 The king's son, Tëen, asked, saying, 'What is the business of the [unemployed] scholar?'

2 Mencius replied, 'To exalt his aim.'

3 'What do you mean by exalting the aim?' asked [the other]. The answer was, '[Setting it] simply on benevolence and righteousness. [The scholar thinks] how to put a single innocent person to death is contrary to benevolence; how to take what one has not [a right to] is contrary to righteousness; that one's dwelling-place should be benevolence, and one's path righteousness. When benevolence is the dwelling-place [of the mind], and righteousness the path [of the life], the business of the great man is complete.'

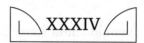

XXXIV

1 Mencius said, 'Supposing that the kingdom of Ts'e were offered, contrary to righteousness, to Chung-tsze, he would not receive it; and all men believe in him [as a man of the highest worth]. But this is [only] the righteousness which declines a small basket of rice and a dish of soup. A man can have no greater [crimes] than to disown his parents and relatives, and [the relations of] ruler and minister, superiors and inferiors. How can it be allowed to give a man credit for the great [excellences] because he possesses a small one.'

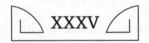

XXXV

1 T'aou Ying asked, saying, 'Shun being emperor, and Kaou Yaou chief minister of justice, if Koo-sow had murdered a man, what would have been done in the case?'

2 Mencius said, '[Kaou Yaou] would simply have apprehended him.'

3 'But would not Shun have forbidden such a thing?'

4 'Indeed,' was the reply, 'how could Shun have forbidden it? [The other] had received [the law] from a proper source.'

5 In that case what would Shun have done?'

6 [Mencius] said, 'Shun would have regarded abandoning all under heaven as throwing away a worn-out sandal. He would privately have taken [his father] on his back, and withdrawn into concealment, living somewhere on the seaboard. There he would have been all his life, cheerful and happy, forgetting the empire.'

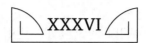

XXXVI

1 Mencius, going from Fan to [the capital of] Ts'e, saw the sons of the king of Ts'e at a distance, and said with a sigh, 'One's position alters the air, [just as] the nurture alters the body. Great is [the influence of position! Are not [we] all men's sons?'

2 Mencius said, 'The residences, the carriages and horses, and the dress of kings' sons, are mostly the same as those of other men. That the king's sons look so is occasioned by their position, – how much more should [a peculiar air distinguish] him whose position is in the wide house of the whole world!

3 'When the ruler of Loo went to Sung, he called out at the Tëeh-chih gate, the warder of which said, "This is not our ruler, but how like is his voice to our ruler's!" This was occasioned by nothing but the correspondence of their positions.'

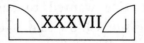

XXXVII

1 Mencius said, 'To feed [a scholar] and not love him is to treat him as a pig; to love him and not respect him is to keep him as a domestic animal.

2 'Honouring and respecting are what should exist before any offering of gifts.

3 'If there be honouring and respecting without [that] reality of them, a superior man cannot be retained by such empty [demonstrations].'

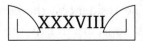

1 Mencius said, 'The bodily organs and the manifestations of sense belong to the heaven-conferred nature. But a man mast be a sage and then he may satisfy [the design of] his bodily organization.'

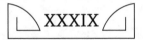

1 King Seuen of Ts'e wanted to shorten the period of mourning. Kung-sun Ch'ow said, 'To have a whole year's mourning is better than doing away with it altogether.'

2 Mencius said, 'That is just as if there were one twisting round the arm of his elder brother, and you were merely to say to him, "Gently, gently, if you please." Your only course should be to teach him filial piety and fraternal duty.'

3   [At that time] the mother of one of the king's sons had died, and his tutor asked for him that he might be allowed some months' mourning. Kung-sun Ch'ow said, 'What do you say to this?'

4   'This is a case,' was the reply, 'where the party wishes to complete the whole period, but finds it impossible to do so; the addition of a single day is better than not mourning at all. I spoke of the case where there was no hindrance and thing was not done.'

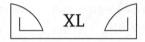

XL

1   Mencius said, 'There are five ways by which the superior man teaches.

2   'There are some on whom his transforming influence comes like seasonable rain.

3   'There are some whose virtue he perfects, and some to whose talents he gives their development.

4   'There are some whose inquiries he answers.

5   'There are some who privately make themselves good, and correct themselves [from his example and recorded lessons].

6   'These five are the ways by which the superior man teaches.'

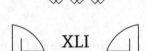

XLI

1   Kung-sun Ch'ow said, 'Lofty are your doctrines and admirable, but [to learn them] may well be likened to ascending the heavens; – they seem to be unattainable. Why not [adapt them] so as to make those [learners] consider them nearly within their reach, and so daily exert themselves?'

2   Mencius said, 'A great artificer does not, for the sake of a stupid workman, alter or do away with the marking-line. E did not, for the sake of a stupid archer, change his rule for drawing the bow to the full.

3   'The superior man draws the bow to the full, but does not discharge the arrow; – in a way, [however,] which makes the thing leap [before the learner]. [So] does he stand in the middle of the right path; – those who are able follow him.'

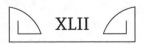

XLII

1   Mencius said, 'When right ways prevail throughout the kingdom, one's principles appear with one's person. When right ways disappear from the kingdom, one's person must vanish along with one's principles.

2   'I have not heard of one's principles being dependent for their manifestation on other men.'

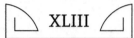

XLIII

1   The disciple Kung-too said, 'When Kăng of T'ăng appeared at your gate, it seemed proper that a polite consideration should be shown to him, and yet you did not answer him; – why was that?'

2   Mencius replied, 'I do not answer him who questions me presuming on his ability, nor him who presumes on his talents and virtue, nor him who presumes on his age, nor him who presumes on services performed to me, nor him who presumes on old acquaintance: – I answer in none of these cases. And Kăng of T'ăng was chargeable with two of them.'

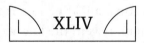

XLIV

1   Mencius said, 'He who stops short where stopping is not proper will stop short in everything. He who behaves shabbily to those whom he ought to treat well will behave shabbily to all.

2   'He who advances with precipitation will retire with speed.'

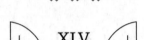

XLV

1   Mencius said, 'In regard to the [inferior] creatures, the superior man is loving, but does not show benevolence. In regard to people generally, he exercises benevolence but is not affectionate. He is affectionate to his parents, and exercises benevolence to people generally. He exercises benevolence to people generally, and is loving to [inferior] creatures.'

XLVI

1   Mencius said, 'The wise embrace all knowledge, but they are most earnest about what they ought to be most concerned about. The benevolent embrace all in their love, but to be earnest in cultivating an affection for the worthy is what most concerns them. [Even] the knowledge of Yaou and Shun did not extend to everything, but they were earnest about what first concerned them. The benevolence of Yaou and Shun did not show itself in [acts of] love to every man, but they were earnest in cultivating an affection for the worthy.

2   'Not to be able to keep the three years' mourning, and to be very particular about that of three months, or that of five months; to eat immoderately and swill down the drink, and [at the same time] to inquire about [the precept] not to tear off the flesh with the teeth; – such things illustrate what I say about not knowing what is most to be attended to.'

BOOK VII

TSIN SIN

PART II

I

1   Mencius said 'Opposite indeed of benevolent was king Hwuy of Lëang! The benevolent begin with what they [most] love, and proceed to what they do not [so naturally] love. Those who are not benevolent, beginning with what they do not [so naturally] love, proceed to what they [most] love'"

2   Kung-sun Ch'ow said, 'What do you mean?' [Mencius replied], 'King Hwuy of Lëang, for the matter of territory, tore and destroyed his people by employing them in fighting. Having sustained a great defeat, he wished to fight again; and, fearing lest the people should not be able to get the victory, he urged his son, a youth, whom he loved, [to take the command,] and sacrificed him with them. This is what I call – beginning with what they do not [so naturally] love, and proceeding to what they [most] love.'

II

1   Mencius said, 'In the "Spring and Autumn" there are no righteous wars. Instances indeed there are of one war better than another.

2   '"Punitive expeditions" are when the supreme authority smites its subjects. Hostile States conduct no punitive expeditions against one another.'

III

1   Mencius said, 'It would be better to be without the Book of History than to give entire credit to it.

2   'In the "Successful Completion of the War" I select two or three passages only, [and repose entire credit in them].

3   'The benevolent man has no enemy under heaven. When [the prince] the most benevolent was attacking him who was the most the opposite, how could the blood have flowed till it floated the pestles of the mortars?'

IV

1   Mencius said, 'There are some who say, "We are skilful at marshalling troops; we are skilful at conducting battles." They are great criminals.

2   'If the ruler of a State love benevolence, he will have no adversary under heaven.

3   'When [T'ang] was conducting his punitive expeditions in the south, the rude tribes on the north murmured. When he was doing so in the east, the rude tribes on the west murmured. Their cry was, – "Why does he make us last?"

4   'When king Woo attacked Yin, he had [only] three hundred chariots of war, and three thousand guards.

5 'The king said, "Do not fear. Let me give you repose. I am no enemy to the people." [On this] they bowed their heads to the ground, like the horns [of animals] falling off.

6 'The phrase "punitive expedition" has in it the meaning of correction. Each [State] wishing to have itself corrected, what need is there for fighting?'

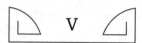

V

1 Mencius said, 'Cabinet-makers, builders, wheel-wrights, and carriage-builders can give to a man the compass and square, but they cannot make him skilful [in the use of them].'

VI

1 Mencius said, 'Shun ate [his] parched grain, and partook of [his] coarse herbs, as if he were to be doing so all his life. When he became emperor, and had the embroidered robes to wear, [his] lute to play on, and [Yaou's] two daughters to wait on him, he was as if those things belonged to him as a matter of course.'

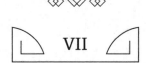

VII

1   Mencius said, 'From this time forth I know the heavy consequences of killing a man's near relations. When a man kills
another's father, that other will kill his father; when a man
kills another's elder brother, that other will kill his elder
brother. So he does not himself indeed do the act, but there
is only a [small] interval [between him and it].'

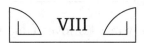

VIII

1   Mencius said, 'Anciently, the establishment of frontier-gates
was to guard against violence.

2   'Now-a-days, it is to exercise violence.'

IX

1   Mencius said, 'If a man do not himself walk in the right
way, it will not be walked in [even] by his wife and children.
If he order others but not according to the right way, he
will not be able to get the obedience [even] of his wife and
children.'

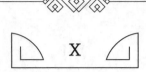

1   Mencius said, 'A bad year cannot prove the cause of death to him whose [stores of] what is needful are complete; an age of corruption cannot throw him into disorder whose [equipment of] virtue is complete.'

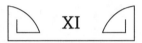

1   Mencius said, 'A man who loves fame may be able to decline a kingdom of a thousand chariots; but if he be not [really] the man [to do such a thing], it will appear in his countenance in the matter of a small basket of rice, or a dish of soup.'

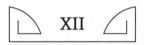

1   Mencius said, 'If the benevolent and worthy be not confided in, a State will become empty and void.

2   'Without the rules of propriety and distinctions of what is right, high and low will be thrown into confusion.

3   'Without the various business of government, there will not be resources sufficient for the expenditure.'

 XIII

1 Mencius said, 'There are instances of individuals without benevolence who have got possession of a [single] State, but there is no instance of the whole kingdom's being got by one without benevolence.'

 XIV

1 Mencius said, 'The people are the most important element [in a country]; the Spirits of the land and grain are the next; the ruler is the lightest.

2 'Therefore to gain the peasantry is the way to become the son of Heaven; to gain the son of Heaven is the way to become the prince of a State; to gain the prince of a State is the way to become a great officer.

3 'When the prince of a State endangers the altars of the Spirits of the land and grain, he is changed and another appointed [in his place].

4 'When the sacrificial victims have been perfect, the millet in its vessels all pure, and the sacrifices offered at their proper seasons, if there yet ensue drought or inundations, then the altars of the Spirits of the land and grain are changed, and others appointed.'

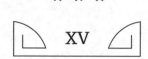

XV

1 Mencius said, 'A sage is the teacher of a hundred generations; – this is true of Pih-e and Hwuy of Lëw-hëa. Therefore when men [now] hear the character of Pih-e, the corrupt become pure, and the weak acquire determination. When they hear the character of Hwuy of Lëw-hëa, the mean become generous, and the niggardly become liberal. [Those two] made themselves distinguished a hundred generations back, and, a hundred generations after them, those who hear of them are all aroused [in this manner]. Could such effects be produced by them if they had not been sages? And how much more did they affect those who were in contiguity with them and warned by them!'

XVI

1 Mencius said, 'By benevolence is meant [the distinguishing characteristic of] man. When it is embodied in man's conduct, we have what we call the path [of duty].'

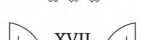

XVII

1 Mencius said, 'When Confucius was about to leave Loo, he said, "I will go by and by;" – it was right that he should leave the State of his parents in this way. When he was leaving Ts'e, he took with his hands the water from the rice which was being washed in it, and went away [with the rice uncooked]; – it was right he should leave another State in this way.'

XVIII

1 Mencius said, 'The reason why the superior man was reduced to straits between Ch'in and Ts'ae was because none of the rulers or of their ministers communicated with him.'

XIX

1 Mih K'e said, 'Greatly am I without anything to depend on from the mouths [of men].'

2 Mencius replied, 'There is no harm in that. Scholars suffer more than others from the mouths of people.

3   'It is said in the Book of Poetry,

"My anxious heart is full of trouble;
I am hated by the herd of mean people."

[Such was the case of] Confucius. And again,

"Though he could not prevent the rage [of his foes],
He did not let fall his own fame."

[Such was the case of] king Wăn.'

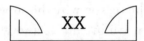

XX

1   Mencius said, '[Anciently], men of virtue and talents by
means of their own enlightenment made others enlightened. Now-a-days, [those who would be deemed such, seek]
by means of their own darkness to make others
nlightened.'

1   Mencius said to Kaou-tsze, 'There are the narrow foot-paths along the hills; – if suddenly they be used, they become roads, and if in a short space they are [again] disused, the wild grass fills them up. Now the wild grass is filling up your mind. Sir.'

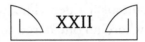

1   Kaou-tsze said, 'The music of Yu was better than that of king Wăn.'

2   Mencius asked, 'On what ground do you say so?' and the other replied, 'Because the knob of [Yu's] bells is nearly worn through.'

3   Mencius rejoined, 'How can that be a sufficient proof? Have the ruts at a city-gate been made [merely] by the two-horsed carriage?'

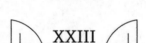

XXIII

1 There was a famine in Ts'e, and Ch'in Tsin said [to Mencius], 'The people are all thinking that you, Master, will again obtain for them the opening of [the granary of] T'ang, but I apprehend you will not do so a second time.'

2 [Mencius] replied, 'To do so would be to act like Fung Foo. There was a man of that name in Tsin, distinguished for his skill in seizing tigers. He afterwards became a scholar of reputation, and going once into the wild country, he found a crowd in pursuit of a tiger. The tiger took refuge in a corner of a hill, where no one dared to attack him; but when the people descried Fung Foo, they ran and met him. He [immediately] bared his arms, and descended from his carriage. The multitude were pleased with him but those who were scholars laughed at him.'

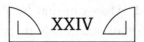

XXIV

1 Mencius said, 'For the mouth to desire tastes, the eye colours, the ear sounds, the nose odours, and the four limbs ease and rest; – these things are natural. But there is the appointment [of Heaven in connexion with them]; and the superior man does not say [in his pursuit of them], "It is my nature."

2 '[The exercise of] love between father and son, [the observance of] righteousness between ruler and minister, the rules
of ceremony between guest and host, [the display of] knowledge in [recognizing] the able and virtuous, and the
[fulfilling the whole] heavenly course by the sage: – these
are appointed [by Heaven and may be realized in different
degrees]. But there is [an adaptation of our] nature [for
them], and the superior man does not say [in reference to
them], "There is a [limiting] appointment [of Heaven]."'

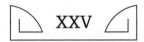

XXV

1 Haou-Săng Puh-hae asked, saying, 'What sort of man is
Yoh-ching?' Mencius replied, 'He is a good man, a real man.'

2 'What do you mean by "A good man?" What do you mean
by "A real man?"'

3 The reply was, 'A man who commands our liking is what is
called *good*.

4 'He whose [goodness] is part of himself is what is called *a
real man*.

5 'He whose [goodness] is accumulated in full measure is what
is called *a beautiful man*.

6   'He whose completed [goodness] is brightly displayed is what is called *a great man*.

7   'When this great man exercises a transforming influence, lie is what is called *a sage*.

8   'When the sage is beyond our knowledge, he is what is called *a spirit-man*.

9   'Yoh-ching is between the [first] two characters, and below the [last] four.'

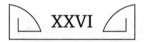

XXVI

1   Mencius said, 'Those who are fleeing from [the errors of] Mih naturally turn to Yang, and those who are fleeing from [the errors of] Yang naturally turn to orthodoxy. When they so turn, they should at once and simply be received.

2   'Those who now-a-days dispute with [those who had been] Yangists and Mihists, do so as if they had been pursuing a stray pig, the leg of which, after they have got it to enter the pen, they proceed to tie.'

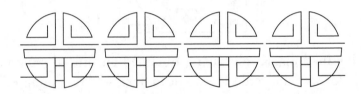

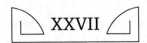

XXVII

1 Mencius said, 'There are the exactions of hempen cloth and silken thread, of grain, and of personal service. The wise ruler requires but one of these {at once], deferring the other two. If he require two of them [at once], then the people die of hunger. If he require the three [at once], then fathers and sons are separated.'

XXVIII

1 Mencius said, 'The precious things of the prince of a State are three; – the territory, the people, and the business of the government. If a prince value as most precious pearls and gems, calamity is sure to befall him.'

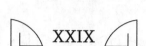

THE WORKS OF MENCIUS

XXIX

1 P'wan-shing Kwoh having obtained an official situation in Ts'e, Mencius said, 'He is a dead man, – P'wan-shing Kwoh!' P'wan-shing Kwoh having been put to death, the disciples asked, saying, 'How did you know, Master, that he would be put to death?' Mencius replied, 'He was a man who had a little ability, but he had not learned the great principles of the superior man. He was just qualified to bring death upon himself, but for nothing more.'

XXX

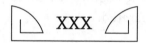

1 When Mencius went to Tăng, he was lodged in the upper palace. A sandal in the process of making had been placed there in a window, and when the keeper of the place [came to] look for it, he could not find it.

2 [On this], some one asked [Mencius] about the matter, saying, 'Is it thus that your followers pilfer?' 'Do you think, Sir,' was the reply, 'that they came here for the purpose of pilfering the sandal?' The man said, 'I apprehend not. But you, Master, having arranged to give lessons, do not go back to inquire into the past, and you do not reject those who come to you. If they come with the mind [to learn], you at once receive them without any more ado.'

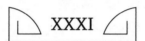

XXXI

1   Mencius said, 'All men have some things which they cannot bear [to see]; – extend that feeling to what they can bear, and the result will be benevolence. All men have some things which they will not do; – extend that feeling to the things which they do, and righteousness will be the result.

2   'If a man can give full development to the feeling which makes him shrink from injuring others, his benevolence will be more than can be put into practice. If he can give full development to the feeling which refuses to dig through or jump over [a wall, for a bad purpose], his righteousness will be more than can be put into practice.

3   'If a man can give full development to the real feeling [of dislike] with which he receives [the salutation of] "Thou," "Thou," he will act righteously in all places and circumstances.

4   'When a scholar peaks what he ought not to speak, by his speaking seeking to gain some end, and when he does not speak what he ought to speak, by his silence seeking to gain the same end; – both these cases are of a piece with digging through or jumping over a wall.'

XXXII

1   Mencius said, 'Words which are plain and simple, while their scope is far-reaching, are good words. Principles which, as held, are compendious, while their application is extensive, are good principles. The words of the superior man do not go below the girdle, but [great] principles are contained in them.

2   'The principle which the superior man holds is that of personal cultivation, but all under heaven is thereby tranquillized.

3   'The disease of men is this: – that they neglect their own fields and go to weed the fields of others, and that what they require from others is great, while what they lay upon themselves is light.'

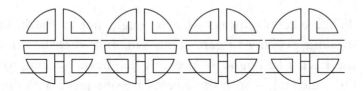

XXXIII

1   Mencius said, 'Yaou and Shun were what they were by nature; T'ang and Woo were so by returning to [their natural virtues].

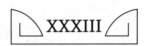

2 'When all the movements in the countenance and every turn [of the body], are exactly according to propriety, that shows the greatest degree of complete virtue. Weeping for the dead [should be] the expression of [real] sorrow, and not as the [proper affection] of the living. The regular path of virtue [is to be pursued] without any bend, from no view to emolument. Words should be in themselves sincere, not with a desire to make one's conduct [appear to be] correct.

3 'The superior man obeys the law [of right], and waits simply for what is appointed.'

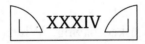

XXXIV

1 Mencius said, 'Those who give counsel to great men should despise them, and not look at their pomp and display.

2 'Halls several times eight cubits high, with beams projecting at the eaves several cubits; – these, if I could realize my wishes, I would not have. Food spread before me over ten cubits square, and attendant girls to the number of several hundred; – these, if I could realize my wishes, I would not have. Pleasure and drinking, and the dash of hunting, with a thousand chariots following after me; – these, if I could realize my wishes, I would not have. What they esteem are what I would have nothing to do with; what I esteem are the rules of the ancients. – Why should I stand in awe of them?'

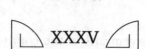

1 Mencius said, 'For nourishing the mind there is nothing better than to make the desires few. Here is a man whose desires are few: – there may be some [right qualities] not kept in his heart, but they will be few.'

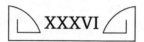

1 Mencius said, 'Tsăng Seih was fond of sheep-dates, and [his son] Tsăng-tsze could not bear to eat them.'

2 Kung-sun Ch'ow asked, saying, 'Which is better, minced meat and roasted meat, or sheep-dates?' Mencius said, 'Mince and roast-meat to be sure!' Kung-Sun Ch'ow went on, 'Then why did Tsăng-tsze eat mince and roast-meat, while he would not eat sheep-dates?' 'For mince and roast-meat,' was the reply, 'there is a common liking, while that for sheep-dates was peculiar. We avoid the name, but do not avoid the surname. The surname is common, but the name is peculiar.'

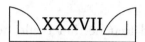

1 Wan Chang asked, saying, 'Confucius, when he was in Ch'in, said, "Why not return? The scholars of my school are ardent and hasty. They advance and seize [their object], but do not forget their early ways." When Confucius was in Ch'in, why did he think of the ambitious scholars of Loo?'

2 Mencius replied, 'Confucius, not getting men who would pursue the due medium, felt that he must take the ardent and cautiously-decided. The ardent would advance and seize [their object]; the cautiously-decided would keep themselves from certain things. It is not to be thought that Confucius did not wish for men pursuing the due medium, but being unable to assure himself of finding such, he therefore thought of the next class.'

3 'I venture to ask,' [said Ch'ow,] 'what sort of men they were who could be called "the ardent?"'

4 'Such,' was the reply, 'as K'in Chang, Tsǎng Seih, and Muh P'ei were those whom Confucius styled "the ardent."'

5 'Why are they styled "the ardent?"'

6 [Mencius] said, 'Their aim led them to talk magniloquently, saying, "The ancients! The ancients!" But their actions, compared with [their words], did not come up to them.

7   'When he found that neither could he get those who were
[thus] ardent, he wished to get scholars who would consider
anything impure as beneath them, and to communicate his
instructions to them. These were the cautiously-decided,
– a class next to the other.'

8   [Chang pursued his questioning], 'Confucius said, "They
are only the good careful people of the villages at whom I
feel no indignation when they pass my door without entering
my house. Your good careful people of the villages are the
thieves of virtue." What sort of people were they who could
be styled "the good careful people of the villages?"'

9   [Mencius replied], 'They say [of the ardent], "Why are they
so magniloquent? Their words have not respect to their
actions, nor their actions to their words, and then they say,
'The ancients! The ancients!' [And] why do these – [the
cautiously-decided] – act so peculiarly, and carry themselves
so cold and distant? Born in this age, we should be of this
age; – to be [deemed] good is all that is needed." Eunuch-
like flattering their generation, – such are your good careful
men of the villages.'

10   Wan Chang said, 'Their whole village styles those men good
and careful. In all their conduct they are so. Why was it
that Confucius considered them to be the thieves of virtue?'

11 [Mencius] replied, 'If you would blame them, you find nothing to allege. If you would criticize them, you have nothing to criticize. They agree with the current customs; they are at one with an impure age. Their principles have a semblance of right-heartedness and truth; their conduct has a semblance of disinterestedness and purity. All men are pleased with them, and they think themselves right, so that it is impossible to proceed with them to the principles of Yaou and Shun. On this account they are called "the thieves of virtue."

12 'Confucius said, "I hate a semblance which is not the reality, I hate the *yëw*-weed, lest it be confounded with the growing com. I hate glib-tonguedness, lest it be confounded with righteousness, I hate sharpness of tongue, lest it be confounded with sincerity. I hate the notes of Ch'ing, lest they be confounded with [true] music. I hate the reddish-blue, lest it be confounded with vermilion. I hate your good careful men of the villages, lest they be confounded with the [truly] virtuous."

13 'The superior man would simply bring back the unchanging standard [of truth and duty]. That being rectified, the masses of the people are roused [to virtue]. When they are so aroused, forthwith perversities and glossed wickedness disappear.'

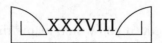

XXXVIII

1 Mencius said, 'From Yaou and Shun down to T'ang were five hundred years and more. As to Yu and Kaon Yaou, they saw [those earliest sages], and [so] knew [their doctrines], while T'ang heard those doctrines [as transmitted], and [so] knew them.

2 'From T'ang to king Wăn were five hundred years and more. As to E Yin and Lae Choo, they saw [T'ang], and [so] knew [his doctrines], while king Wăn heard them [as transmitted], and so knew them.

3 'From king Wăn to Confucius were five hundred years and more. As to T'ae-kung Wang and San E-sang, they saw [Wan], and [so] knew his doctrines, while Confucius heard them [as transmitted], and [so] knew them.

4 'From Confucius to now there are [only] a hundred years and [somewhat] more; – so far from being remote is the distance from the sage in point of time, and so very near at hand was the sage's residence. In these circumstances, is there no one [to transmit his doctrines]? Yea, is there no one [to do so]?'